ALSO BY ANTHONY EVERITT

*Cicero: The Life and Times of Rome's Greatest Politician*

# AUGUSTUS

AVGV

RANDOM HOUSE

NEW YORK

STVS

*The Life of Rome's First Emperor*

ANTHONY EVERITT

Published in the United States by Random House,
an imprint of The Random House Publishing Group,
a division of Random House, Inc., New York.

RANDOM HOUSE and colophon are registered trademarks of
Random House, Inc.

Published in the United Kingdom by John Murray
Publishers, Ltd. as *The First Emperor: Caesar Augustus and
the Triumph of Rome* in slightly different form.

Photo credits can be found in the Acknowledgments
section on page 329.

ISBN 978-1-4000-6128-0

Printed in the United States of America

*Book design by Simon M. Sullivan*

FOR RODDY ASHWORTH

# PREFACE

IMPERATOR CAESAR AUGUSTUS, TO GIVE HIM HIS PROPER
title, was one of the most influential men in history. As Rome's first emperor, he transformed the chaotic Roman Republic into an orderly imperial autocracy. His consolidation of the Roman empire two thousand
years ago laid the foundations on which Europe both as a region and as a
culture was subsequently built. If anyone qualifies as the founding father
of western civilization, it is Augustus.

His career was a masterly study in the wielding of power. He learned
how to obtain it and, more important, how to keep it. As the history of
the last hundred years has shown, empires are hard won and easily lost. In
the first century B.C., Rome governed one of the largest empires the world
had seen, but through foolish policies and bad governance risked its collapse. Augustus devised a political system that enabled the empire's survival for half a millennium. History never repeats itself exactly, but
today's leaders and students of politics will find his policies and methods
to be of interest.

Yet Augustus himself is a shadowy figure. Many books have been written about his achievements, but they have tended to focus on the Augustan age, rather than on the man as he was. My hope is to make Augustus
come alive.

As well as narrating his own doings, I place his story in his times and
describe the events and personalities that affected him. Shipwrecks, human sacrifice, hairbreadth escapes, unbridled sex, battles on land and at
sea, ambushes, family scandals, and above all the unforgiving pursuit of
absolute power—Augustus lived out an extraordinary and often terrifying drama.

The stage is crowded with larger-than-life personalities: the brilliant
and charming Julius Caesar; the ruthless Cleopatra, who is often said to

have used sex as an instrument of policy; the idealistic assassin Brutus; the intelligent drunkard Mark Antony; the dour Tiberius; the great but promiscuous lady Julia, and many more.

The incidents and actions that make up a life cannot be fully realized without also conveying a sense of place. So I have sought to evoke the main locations of Augustus' career, as they were at the time and as they appear today—among them, his house on the Palatine, the secret palace on the island of Pandateria, the low, sandy headland of Actium, and the spectacular city of Alexandria.

The Roman world is still recognizable to us who live two millennia later. The day-to-day practice of politics, the realities of urban living, the seaside resorts, the cultivation of the arts, the rising divorce rate, the misdemeanors of the younger generation: past and present have many things in common. However, certain forms of degradation—slavery, the low status of women, and the gladiatorial carnage of the arena—shock and astonish us. So, too, does the moral approval accorded to military violence and imperial expansion. Julius Caesar's largely unprovoked conquest of Gaul was hailed at Rome as a wonderful achievement, but it is estimated that one million Gauls lost their lives in the fighting.

Augustus was a very great man, but he grew gradually into greatness. He did not possess Julius Caesar's bravura and political genius (it was that genius, of course, which killed Caesar, for it made him incapable of compromise). He was a physical coward who taught himself to be brave. He was intelligent, painstaking, and patient, but could also be cruel and ruthless. He worked extraordinarily hard. He thought in the long term, achieving his aims slowly and by trial and error.

Augustus is one of the few historical figures who improved with the passage of time. He began as a bloodthirsty adventurer, but once he had achieved power, he made a respectable man of himself. He repealed his illegal acts and took trouble to govern fairly and efficiently.

One curious aspect of Augustus' life is that many of the leading players were very young men. The adults who started Rome's civil wars fell victim to long years of fighting, leaving the baton to be picked up by the next generation. Augustus and his schoolmates Maecenas and Agrippa were in their late teens when they took charge of the state. Pompey the Great's son Sextus was probably much the same age when he set himself up as a guerrilla leader in Spain.

Augustus died old, but throughout his long reign he never hesitated to entrust great responsibility to the young men of his family: his stepsons Tiberius and Drusus, and his grandsons Gaius and Lucius. The excitement of making one's way in an adult world must have been intoxicating.

We are right to call Augustus Rome's first emperor, yet the title is anachronistic. At the time he was simply regarded as the chief man in the state. The Roman Republic had, apparently, been restored, not abolished. Augustus developed a personality cult, but he did not hold permanent authority and had to have his powers regularly renewed. Only with the accession of Tiberius did people finally realize that they were no longer citizens of a free commonwealth, but subjects living under a permanent monarchy. So nowhere in this book do I call Augustus emperor.

The task of writing a life of Augustus is complicated by the fact that many contemporary sources are lost, casualties of the Dark Ages: the autobiography down to 25 B.C. that Augustus wrote in Spain; his correspondence with Cicero; Agrippa's memoirs; the history of his times by Pollio and Messala's commentaries on the civil wars after Julius Caesar's assassination; thirty books of Livy's great history of Rome, covering the period from 44 to 9 B.C. Only fragments of the life of Augustus written by a friend of Herod the Great, Nicolaus of Damascus, have survived, and Appian's detailed study of Rome's civil wars in the first century B.C. closes with the death of Sextus Pompeius in 35 B.C.

Dio Cassius gives a reasonably complete account in his Roman History, but his style is pedestrian and he wrote three hundred years after the event. The findings of the modern archaeologist (especially inscriptions and coins) add valuable information. Neither Suetonius nor Plutarch is a historian, properly speaking, but both inject some welcome anecdotes and personality assessments.

Much more is recorded about Augustus' first thirty years than about his later life and a thorough and coherent narrative of his youth can be constructed. However, important events of his maturity and old age call for the skills of the detective rather than the historian. Mysterious and incomplete narratives conceal as much they reveal, and sometimes only speculative explanations can be offered. For certain years nothing definite is known at all; between 16 and 13 B.C., we are told, Augustus was in Gaul and Germany, but we have no idea where he went or where he was at any particular time. For the second half of this book I have been obliged to switch from straightforward narrative to a more thematic approach to my subject.

This disjunction is not only due to the loss of texts, but also to a lack of governmental transparency. Once the imperial system had been established, Dio claims,

> *most events began to be kept secret and were denied to common knowledge. . . . Much that never materializes becomes common talk, while much that undoubtedly came to pass remains unknown, and in pretty well every instance the report which is spread abroad does not correspond to what actually happened.*

That is going a little too far: intentions are often revealed through actions, and the broad thrust of history cannot easily be concealed. However, Dio has a point.

Hindsight is not open to biographers, who have a duty to tell a life as closely as possible to how it was lived. I have tried not to forget that the past was once present and the future unknown, and have done my best to hide my guilty knowledge of what fate had in store for the actors in the drama.

The plural of a family name that ends in "-us" or "-ius" I give as "-i." Thus one Balbus becomes some Balbi, rather than the clumsy Balbuses. However, I am contentedly inconsistent; I allow "Caesar" to mutate into "Caesars" on the grounds that it is not inelegant and that the correct Latin would be the pedantic-sounding Caesarēs. I say "Pompey" and "Livy" rather than "Pompeius" and "Livius," because that is how the English-speaking world has termed them for many centuries. Place-names are usually given in their Latin form, except for well-known Anglicisms such as Rome and Athens. To convey the otherness of not-Rome, I have used Parthian and Armenian personal names in place of their Romanized or Hellenized versions. So Artavasdes becomes Artavâzd, Artaxes Ardashes, Orodes Urûd, Pacorus Pakûr, Phraates Frahâta, Phrataces Frahâtak, and Tigranes Dikran.

The modern-day interpretation of the ancient literary sources has reached a high level of sophistication and a skeptical eye is turned, usually wisely, on any claim made by a Latin or Greek historian. I incline to a minimalist view, often accepting what I am told unless there is an obvious or rational objection (for example, when two sources disagree). It is important to hesitate before ironing out inconsistent or surprising behavior;

human beings are capable of harboring contradictory emotions, of acting against their interests, or stupidly.

So, for example, Augustus' reported visit to see his grandson Agrippa Postumus on his island of exile may have been an odd and foolish thing for a sick old man to do, but it does not follow that the visit never took place. Even implausibility is a criterion of judgment to be applied with caution. Most of the contradictions in this story fall comfortably inside the usual bounds of human irrationality.

It is difficult to be categorical about the value of money, because the costs of providing different products and services are not the same as those of today. The basic Roman unit of account was the sesterce, very roughly worth between one and two pounds sterling.

The Romans dated their years from the supposed foundation of the city in 753 B.C., but it would confuse the reader if I placed Caesar's assassination in 709 A.U.C. (*ab urbe condita,* or "from the city's foundation"), rather than the familiar 44 B.C. I use modern dating, and in so doing allude on almost every page to the one great event of Augustus' life about which he and practically everyone else in the Roman empire knew nothing: the birth of Christ.

# CONTENTS

# CHRONOLOGY

45         Caesar defeats republican army in Spain
*autumn*   Octavius at Apollonia

44         Caesar Dictator for Life
*March 15*  Caesar assassinated
*April*     Octavius in Italy
           Octavius accepts adoption by Caesar; becomes Gaius Julius
               Caesar Octavianus, or Octavian

43         War at Mutina; Mark Antony defeated
           Octavian consul
           Mark Antony, Octavian, and Marcus Aemilius Lepidus
               form Second Triumvirate; Proscription launched;
               Cicero put to death

42         Campaign at Philippi; Brutus and Cassius commit suicide
           Sextus Pompeius in control of Sicily
           Julius Caesar deified
           Octavia's son, Marcus Claudius Marcellus (Marcellus),
               born
           Tiberius Claudius Nero, son of Livia Drusilla and Tiberius
               Claudius Nero, (Tiberius) born

41         Lucius Antonius besieged at Perusia
           Antony meets Cleopatra, winters at Alexandria

40         Perusia falls
           Marcellus, Octavia's husband, dies
           Octavian marries Scribonia
           Parthians invade Syria
           Calenus dies in Gaul
           Treaty of Brundisium; Antony marries Octavia

39         Treaty of Misenum
           Ventidius defeats the Parthians
           Agrippa campaigns in Gaul
           Octavian's daughter, Julia, born

38         Triumvirate renewed
           Nero Claudius Drusus (Drusus) born
*January 17*  Octavian marries Livia Drusilla
           Antony dismisses Ventidius

Sextus Pompeius defeats Octavian off Cumae and
    in straits of Messana

37    Virgil's *Eclogues* published
    Treaty of Tarentum

36    After initial defeat (August), Octavian defeats Sextus
        Pompeius at Naulochus (September 3)
    Lepidus dropped from Triumvirate
    Antony's Parthian expedition
    Octavian granted *tribunicia sacrosanctitas*

35    Sextus Pompeius killed
    Octavian campaigns in the Balkans

34    Antony annexes Armenia
    Donations of Alexandria

33    Octavian consul (2), Triumvirate lapses at end of year
    Agrippa aedile
    Tiberius Claudius Nero (father) dies

32    Antony divorces Octavia
    Octavian publishes Antony's will
    Consuls leave Rome for Antony
    Oath of loyalty to Octavian

31    Octavian consul (3)
    Battle of Actium

30    Octavian consul (4)
    Octavian captures Alexandria; Antony and Cleopatra
        commit suicide

29    Octavian consul (5)
    Octavian's triple triumph
    Temple of Julius Caesar and the Curia Julia dedicated
    Marcus Licinius Crassus pacifies Thrace

28    Octavian consul (6)
    Review of Senate
    Temple of Apollo on the Palatine dedicated
    Mausoleum of Augustus begun

27  Octavian consul (7)

January  First constitutional settlement; Octavian named Augustus; granted a large *provincia* for ten years

Agrippa builds Pantheon

27–24  Augustus in Gaul and Spain

26  Augustus consul (8)

Dismissal and death of Gaius Cornelius Gallus

Expedition to Arabia Felix

25  Augustus consul (9)

Julia marries Marcellus

Augustus falls ill in Spain, convalesces

? 24–23  Trial of Marcus Primus and conspiracy of Fannius Caepio and Aulus Terentius Varro Murena

24  Augustus consul (10)

23  Augustus consul (11)

Augustus at Rome, falls ill

Second constitutional settlement: Augustus resigns consulship, receives *imperium proconsulare maius* and *tribunicia potestas*

Death of Marcellus

Horace's *Odes* (three books) published

23–21  Agrippa with enhanced *imperium* in the east

22–19  Augustus in the east

21  Agrippa marries Julia, goes to Gaul

20  Augustus negotiates entente with Parthia; Tiberius in Armenia

Gaius born to Julia

Rufus Egnatius praetor

c. 19  Agrippa's daughter, Julia, born

19  Egnatius bids for the consulship

Virgil dies

Augustus, back at Rome, receives consular powers

Agrippa subdues Spanish tribes

18   Renewal of Augustus' *imperium maius* for five years
     Renewal of Agrippa's *imperium* for five years, plus grant of
       *tribunicia potestas*
     Review of Senate

18–17   Social and moral reforms (*leges Juliae*)

17   Lucius born to Julia, Augustus adopts Gaius and Lucius
     Celebration of the Ludi Saeculares

16–13   Augustus in Gaul; Agrippa in the east

15   Tiberius and Drusus campaign in the Alps
     Drusus' son, Nero Claudius Drusus Germanicus
       (Germanicus), born

13   Tiberius consul (1)
     Agrippa granted *imperium maius,* and *tribunicia potestas* renewed
     Theater of Marcellus and Ara Pacis dedicated

13–12 *winter*   Agrippa in Pannonia to suppress threatened rebellion

12   Lepidus dies, Augustus succeeds him as *pontifex maximus*
March   Agrippa dies
     Agrippa Postumus born

12–9   Tiberius campaigns in Pannonia; Drusus in Germany

11   Tiberius divorces Vipsania and marries Julia

10   Drusus' son, Tiberius Claudius Drusus Nero Germanicus
       (Claudius), born

9   Death of Drusus

9–7   Tiberius campaigns in Germany

8   Augustus' *imperium maius* renewed
     Deaths of Maecenas and Horace

7   Tiberius consul (2), celebrates triumph

6   Armenian revolt
     Tiberius granted *tribunicia potestas* for five years
     Tiberius retires to Rhodes

5   Augustus consul (12)

Gaius Caesar comes of age, appointed *princeps iuventutis,*
designated consul for A.D. 1

2    Augustus consul (13)
Lucius Caesar comes of age
Disgrace of Julia
Forum of Augustus and Temple of Mars Ultor dedicated
King Frahâta of Parthia murdered, succeeded by Frahâtak
Ovid publishes *Ars Amatoria*

1    Gaius Caesar sent to the east with *imperium*

A.D.

2    Agreement between Gaius Caesar and King Frahâtak
Tiberius returns from Rhodes
Lucius Caesar dies at Massilia

2–3    Gaius Caesar wounded

4    Gaius Caesar resigns his duties and dies
Augustus adopts Agrippa Postumus and Tiberius, who
    adopts Germanicus
Tiberius granted *tribunicia potestas* for ten years
Tiberius campaigns in Germany
*lex Aelia Sentia*
Review of Senate

5    Tiberius reaches the Elbe

6    Establishment of *aerarium militare*
Revolt in Pannonia and Dalmatia

7    Agrippa Postumus banished to Planasia

8    Julia, Augustus' granddaughter, and Ovid banished
Pannonians surrender

9    Dalmatia subdued
Varus defeated in Germany; three legions lost
*lex Papia Poppaea*

10–11    Tiberius campaigns in Germany

12    Germanicus consul
Tiberius' triumph

13    Germanicus takes command in Gaul and Germany
      Tiberius' *tribunicia potestas* renewed for ten years; he receives
          *imperium proconsulare maius* equal to that of Augustus
      Germanicus receives proconsular *imperium*

14 *August 19*   Augustus dies
      Agrippa Postumus put to death
      Tiberius becomes *princeps*
      Julia, Augustus' daughter, dies in exile

15    Germanicus visits the scene of the *Variana clades*

17    Ovid dies in exile

19    Germanicus dies, perhaps poisoned

23    Tiberius' son, Drusus, dies, perhaps killed by Sejanus

28    Julia, Augustus' granddaughter, dies in exile

29    Julia Augusta (Livia) dies

37    Tiberius dies; Gaius (Caligula) succeeds

41    Gaius assassinated; Claudius succeeds

43    Claudius invades Britannia

54    Claudius dies, perhaps poisoned; Nero succeeds

68    Nero commits suicide, last member of Augustus' family to
          be *princeps*

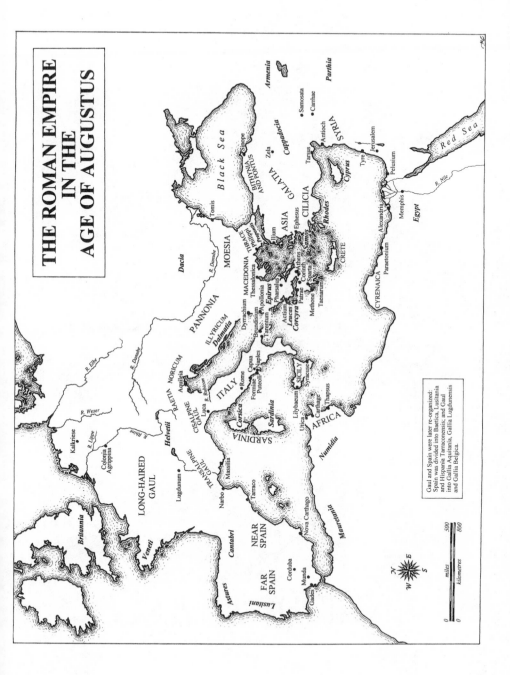

# THE ROMAN EMPIRE IN THE AGE OF AUGUSTUS

Gaul and Spain were later re-organized:
Spain was divided into Baetica, Lusitania
and Hispania Tarraconensis; and Gaul
into Gallia Aquitania, Gallia Lugdunensis
and Gallia Belgica.

miles 0    500
kilometres 0    800

*Britannia*

*Veneti*

LONG-HAIRED
GAUL

Kalkriese

Colonia
Agrippina

R. Weser
R. Lippe
R. Rhine

Lugdunum

*Helvetii*

TRANSALPINE
GAUL

CISALPINE
GAUL

Narbo

Massilia

Tarraco

*Cantabri*

NEAR
SPAIN

*Astures*

FAR
SPAIN

*Lusitani*

Corduba

Munda

Gades

Nova Carthago

*Mauretania*

*Corsica*

*Sardinia*

SARDINIA

RAETIA    NORICUM

Aquileia

ITALY

Rome

Capua

Naples

Formiae    Puteoli

Luca    R. Rubicon

PANNONIA

R. Danube

R. Danube

R. Elbe

*Dacia*

ILLYRICUM
*Dalmatia*

Dyrrachium

Brundisium

Tarentum

Apollonia

*Epirus*

Actium

*Leucas*

*Corcyra*

Methone

Taenarum

MACEDONIA

Thessalonica

Pharsalus

THRACE

Philippi

Byzantium

MOESIA

Tomis

Sinope

*Black Sea*

BITHYNIA
AND PONTUS

Zela

*Cappadocia*

GALATIA

ASIA

Ephesus

*Samos*

Athens

Corinth

Patrae

Sparta

CRETE

*Rhodes*

CILICIA

Tarsus

Antioch

SYRIA

*Cyprus*

Tyre

Jerusalem

Pelusium

Alexandria

Memphis

*Egypt*

R. Nile

*Red Sea*

Samosata

Carrhae

*Armenia*

*Parthia*

*Numidia*

Lilybaeum

SICILY

Syracuse

Utica

Carthage

Thapsus

AFRICA

CYRENAICA

Paraetonium

N
W    E
S

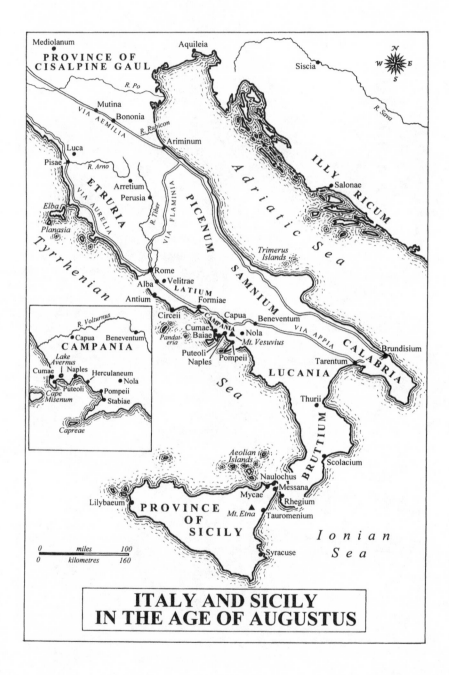

Mediolanum

**PROVINCE OF
CISALPINE GAUL**

Aquileia

Siscia

*R. Po*

Mutina

VIA AEMILIA

Bononia

*R. Rubicon*

Ariminum

*R. Sava*

Luca

Pisae

*R. Arno*

**ETRURIA**

VIA AURELIA

Arretium

Perusia

*Elba*

*Planasia*

*R. Tiber*

VIA FLAMINIA

**PICENUM**

*A d r i a t i c   S e a*

**ILLY
RICUM**

Salonae

*Trimerus
Islands*

*T y r r h e n i a n*

Rome

Alba • Velitrae

Antium

**LATIUM**

Formiae

Circeii

Capua

**SAMNIUM**

Beneventum

VIA APPIA

**CALABRIA**

Brundisium

*Pandat-
eria*

Cumae
Baiae

**CAMPANIA**

Nola

*Mt. Vesuvius*

Puteoli
Naples

Pompeii

Tarentum

**LUCANIA**

*R. Volturnus*

Capua    Beneventum

**CAMPANIA**

*Lake
Avernus*

Cumae     Naples

Herculaneum

Puteoli

• Nola

*Cape
Misenum*

Pompeii

Stabiae

*Capreae*

*Sea*

Thurii

**BRUTTIUM**

Scolacium

*Aeolian
Islands*

Naulochus

Messana

Mycae

Rhegium

Lilybaeum

**PROVINCE
OF
SICILY**

*Mt. Etna*

Tauromenium

*I o n i a n
S e a*

Syracuse

| 0 | miles | 100 |
| 0 | kilometres | 160 |

## **ITALY AND SICILY
IN THE AGE OF AUGUSTUS**

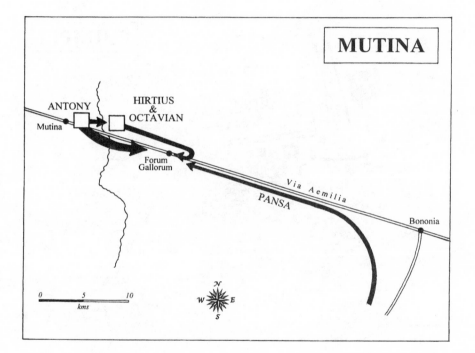

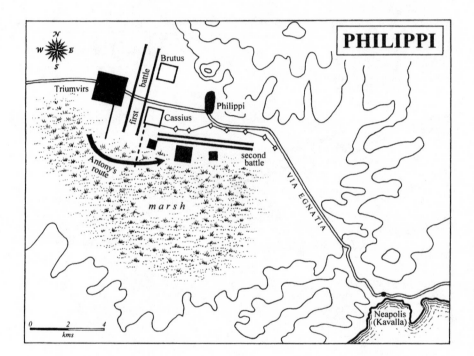

**PHILIPPI**

N W E S

Triumvirs

Brutus

first battle

Philippi

Cassius

Antony's route

second battle

*marsh*

VIA EGNATIA

0    2    4
*kms*

Neapolis
(Kavalla)

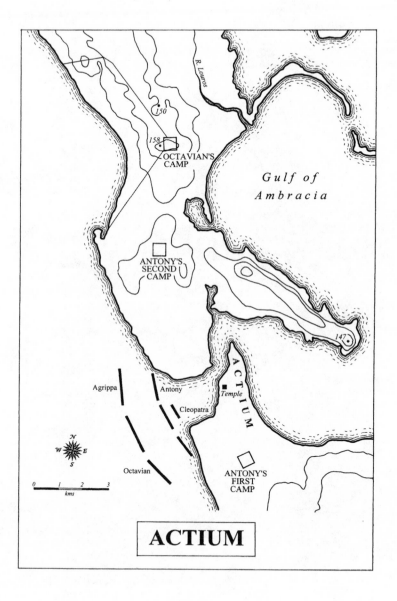

R. Louros

*150*

*158* OCTAVIAN'S CAMP

Gulf of
Ambracia

ANTONY'S
SECOND
CAMP

*147*

Agrippa

Antony

A C T I U M

■ *Temple*

Cleopatra

N
W  E
S

Octavian

ANTONY'S
FIRST
CAMP

0   1   2   3
*kms*

**ACTIUM**

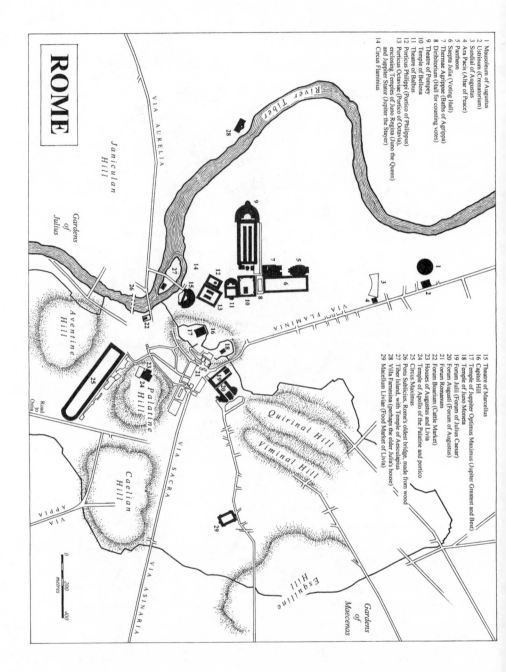

# ROME

1 Mausoleum of Augustus
2 Ustrinum (Crematorium)
3 Sundial of Augustus
4 Ara Pacis (Altar of Peace)
5 Pantheon
6 Saepta Julia (Voting Hall)
7 Thermae Agrippae (Baths of Agrippa)
8 Diribitorium (Hall for counting votes)
9 Theatre of Pompey
10 Temple of Bellona
11 Theatre of Balbus
12 Porticus Philippi (Portico of Philippus)
13 Porticus Octaviae (Portico of Octavia),
   enclosing Temples of Juno Regina (Juno the Queen)
   and Juppiter Stator (Jupiter the Stayer)
14 Circus Flaminius

15 Theatre of Marcellus
16 Capitol Hill
17 Temple of Jupiter Optimus Maximus (Jupiter Greatest and Best)
18 Temple of Juno Moneta
19 Forum Julii (Forum of Julius Caesar)
20 Forum Augusti (Forum of Augustus)
21 Forum Romanum
22 Forum Boarium (Cattle Market)
23 Houses of Augustus and Livia
24 Temple of Apollo of the Palatine and portico
25 Circus Maximus
26 Pons Sublicius, Rome's oldest bridge, made from wood
27 Tiber Island, with Temple of Aesculapius
28 Villa Farnesina (perhaps the elder Julia's house)
29 Macellum Liviae (Food Market of Livia)

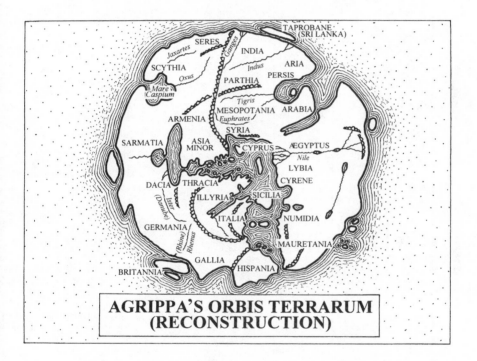

**AGRIPPA'S ORBIS TERRARUM (RECONSTRUCTION)**

# THE JULIO-CLAUDIAN DYNASTY

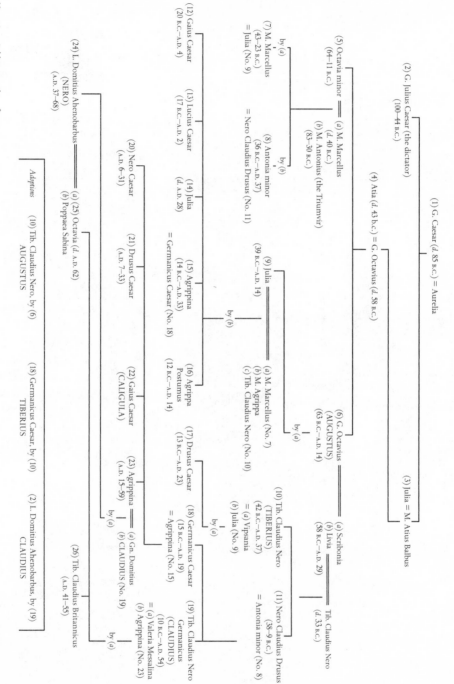

Names in capital letters are those of emperors.

# INTRODUCTION

## A.D. 14

THE OLD MAN LOVED CAPRI. IT WAS A PLEASURE TO BE BACK, if only for a few days. The visit would be not much longer than that, for he was about to manage his own death. Every detail had been decided.

The island was mountainous and almost completely inaccessible, with precipitous cliffs, sea grottoes, and strangely shaped rocks. Endless sunshine, abundant, almost tropical flora, and clear air made it a lovely place, as did its delightful inhabitants, who were originally colonists from mainland Greece. Here he could forget business of state and relax in complete privacy and safety.

Security was an important issue, for the old man was ruler of the known world and had many enemies. He had overthrown the partly and messily democratic Republic, and for more than forty years had governed the Roman empire alone. He was known as Augustus, or "Revered One," a name that separated him from ordinary mortals. However, he never paraded his authority; he did not like to be called *dominus,* "My Lord," but *princeps,* "top person" or "first citizen."

Capri was not just beautiful, it was easy to defend. Years ago Augustus had built a palatial villa here. Perched on a high promontory, it was like a ship's prow made from stone. The building contained every luxury— extensive gardens, a bath complex with hot rooms and splash pools, and spectacular views of the sea. There were no springs in this arid, rocky spot, so cisterns gathered a supply of rainwater. Four-story apartment blocks housed the many servants, slaves, and guards needed to look after the *princeps* and his guests.

Augustus was not the only lotus-eater. He wanted his staff to have a good time, too. Some of them lived on an islet off Capri, which he nicknamed the Land of Do-Nothings because they were so lazy.

. . .

Augustus was seventy-seven and in poor health. He had noticed the first signs of terminal decline the previous spring; the end was fast approaching. So, too, was his greatest challenge. For the good of Rome (he told himself) one-man rule had to continue, so he gave careful thought to the preparations that would ensure a smooth handover of power to his chosen successor. He knew that trouble lay ahead. As soon as he died, many Romans would want to go back to the days of the free Republic. People were already talking idly of the blessings of liberty. There was irresponsible chatter of civil war.

The *princeps* set up a small succession committee, comprising a handful of trusted advisers, and gave it the task of planning the transition. The trick would be to set everything in place before anyone noticed or had time to object. He chaired the meetings himself, and he took Livia, his seventy-one-year-old wife, into his confidence, as he always had done throughout his career; she attended some of the group's meetings.

Augustus intended his successor to be Livia's fifty-five-year-old son, an able military commander, Tiberius Claudius Nero. Ten years ago he had formally adopted Tiberius and shared his power with him.

If only, the old man thought to himself, he did not have to leave Rome to a man he did not really care for. Competent, hardworking, experienced—yes, Tiberius was all these things, but he was also gloomy and resentful. "Poor Rome," he muttered to himself, "doomed to be masticated by those slow-moving jaws!"

There was another possible pretender. Augustus had a grandson, Agrippa Postumus, now in his mid-twenties. He had always had a soft spot for Agrippa, but the child grew up into an angry and violent young man, unsuitable for public office. Nevertheless, Augustus adopted him as his son simultaneously with Tiberius, hoping that the lad would become more mature and responsible.

He did not, and his saddened grandfather had had to disown him. A few years ago, he had sent Agrippa to cool his heels at the seaside resort of Surrentum. But the boy still managed to get into trouble, and was now languishing under military guard on Planasia, a tiny island south of Elba: out of sight but, unhappily, not out of mind.

This was because Agrippa had influential friends at Rome, people who were tired of his grandfather's cautious, patient style of governing. Augustus had received reliable reports that a plot was afoot to spring the boy from his place of exile, take him to one of the frontier armies, and march on Rome.

Any resistance during the handover of power after Augustus' death would center on Agrippa. So the succession committee's first job was to deal with the threat he posed. In May of A.D. 14 Augustus let it be known that he was in need of some peace and quiet and intended to spend a couple of weeks at a villa in the countryside south of Rome. From there, he departed, under conditions of strictest secrecy, on the long sea journey north to Planasia.

Agrippa was astonished by the sudden arrival of his grandfather, and there were tears and hugs all round. But a little conversation showed that the boy was as moody and dangerous as ever. Augustus was moved, but pitiless. Right from his entry into public life at the age of eighteen, no one who threatened his power received any quarter. The greater the threat, even if it came from his nearest and dearest, the icier the punishment.

The *princeps* put his arm around Agrippa's shoulders and reassured him that he loved him and would soon bring him home to Rome. He calculated that this would dampen any enthusiasm for plotting escape and revenge. Then Augustus boarded his ship, upset but glumly reconciled to arranging his grandson's execution.

Everything would be much more manageable if all the main players in the succession game were out of Rome. The agreed plan was that when the time came, the *princeps* would dispatch Tiberius, his established deputy and heir, to settle affairs in the troublesome province of Illyricum (today's Croatia). He would be giving a clear sign to political observers that all was well, and (more to the point) that *he* was well. His own final destination would be his father's old villa at Nola, near the volcanic mountain of Vesuvius. If matters could be so arranged, he would die in the same room as Gaius Octavius had more than seventy years previously. This would be a dignified reminder of what the régime stood for: honoring the past and the old plain-living values of rural Italy.

At last, in the summer of A.D. 14, the moment of truth arrived. The *princeps* looked and felt more ill than ever. Neither he nor his doctors knew what was the matter with him; he seemed to be suffering from no particular illness, but felt feverish and very weak. It was clear to him as well as to

Livia and Tiberius that he had, at best, only weeks to live. It was time to put the succession plan into operation.

To make sure rumor and malice did not reach the legions on the frontiers before official news came of a change of leadership in the capital, top-secret dispatches were sent by rapid courier to the commanders of the German and Danube armies and to the governors of the eastern provinces. These warned of Augustus' failing condition, and Tiberius' succession. They advised strict discipline to reduce the risk of mutinies.

Augustus gave Tiberius his commission for Illyricum. As a very public sign of his confidence in him, he decided to accompany Tiberius for part of his journey south down the Via Appia, the great road that led to the port of Brundisium on Italy's heel. He was held up at Rome for some days by a long list of court cases that he was judging. Losing patience, he cried: "I will stay here no longer, whoever tries to detain me!" It occurred to him that when he was gone, people would remember that remark as prophetic.

Eventually the two men were able to leave Rome, accompanied by a large bodyguard of soldiers and an entourage of slaves, servants, and officials. Augustus noticed that a brisk sea breeze was rising and decided on the spur of the moment that the party would take ship that evening, although he disliked night voyages. This had the advantage of avoiding the malarial Pomptine Marshes, through which they would have had to pass if traveling by road.

It was a bad idea, for the old man caught a chill, the first symptom of which was diarrhea. So, after coasting past Campania, he decided to spend a few last sunlit days at Capri. He was determined to enjoy himself. The *princeps* sat for a long time watching local youths at the open-air gymnasium, and invited them back to a banquet. He encouraged them to play practical jokes, and they scrambled about for tokens that he threw at them, entitling the holders to small prizes such as fruit and sweetmeats.

The *princeps* and his party crossed over from Capri to Neapolis (today's Naples), where, although his stomach was still weak and his diarrhea returning intermittently, he attended the athletic competition that the city staged every five years in his honor. He then set off with Tiberius and said goodbye to him at Beneventum, retracing his steps as arranged to the villa at Nola. Privately, Tiberius was warned not to hurry, and to expect an early recall.

•  •  •

Augustus looked at Livia. The last thing either of them expected had happened: he was feeling and looking in excellent form. She stared back at him. There seemed to be a third person in the bedroom—an almost touchable awareness of the huge, difficult thing that needed to be done.

The problem was obvious. All the arrangements were in place for the *princeps'* death, but the *princeps* was recovering from his final illness. The timetable was at risk. The recently sent dispatches would soon be received. The longer Augustus lived, the more opportunity there would be for rumors to fly around Rome and the empire, fomenting disunity and trouble, imperiling the smooth transfer of power.

That afternoon, while Augustus was taking a siesta and the house was quiet in the summer heat, Livia went to the peristyle, a large cloister around an open-air garden. In the middle stood a fig tree, heavy with ripe fruit, which Livia had planted years ago. Augustus liked to pick a fig or two in the evening. Livia coated some of them with a poisonous ointment, leaving a few untouched.

Later, the aged couple walked out into the garden and Augustus picked two of the poisoned fruit and ate them. He noticed nothing. Livia ate a fig she had left alone. There was no reason for her husband to know exactly how he was going to die, she thought; indeed, if she was lucky, he might not guess that she had had to carry out what they had unspokenly agreed. Much more pleasant for him.

Augustus slept badly. He suffered from stomach cramps and renewed diarrhea, and developed a high fever. Guessing what had happened, he silently thanked his wife. In the morning, he called for a mirror. He looked terrible. He had his hair combed and his lower jaw, which had fallen from weakness, was propped up. He gave some orders to a military officer, who immediately set sail for the island of Planasia with a troop of soldiers. Hail and farewell, Agrippa!

A small group of notables, including Livia and Tiberius, recalled as prearranged, gathered round the bedside. The *princeps* uttered some suitable, obviously unspontaneous last words.

"I found Rome built of clay: I leave it to you in marble."

He was referring not simply to his redevelopment of the city, but also to the strength of the empire.

Augustus could not resist adding a bleak joke. He had always seen life as a pretense, something not to be taken too seriously, and at his house on the Palatine Hill at Rome, he had had his bedroom walls painted with frescoes of the tragic and comic masks that actors wore. Their image came into his mind, and he asked:

"Have I played my part in the farce of life well enough?"

After a short pause, he quoted a well-known theatrical tag.

*"If I have pleased you, kindly signify*
*Appreciation with a warm goodbye."*

# AUGUSTUS

# I

# SCENES FROM A
# PROVINCIAL CHILDHOOD

## 63–48 B.C.

VELLETRI IS A COMPACT HILL TOWN ABOUT TWENTY-FIVE miles southeast of Rome. It lies at the southern edge of the Alban Hills, overlooking a wide plain and distant mountains. The walk from the railway station to the center is a steep, hot climb.

Little remains of ancient Velitrae, but signs of the Renaissance are to be found everywhere. In the main square stands an old fountain with battered lions spouting water. The streets leading off the piazza are roughly parallel and are gridded, echoing the original pattern of the old Roman *vici.* At the town's highest point, where the citadel must have been, a sixteenth-century *palazzo communale,* which combines the functions of town hall and museum, was built on the foundations of a Roman building.

Here, on a stone platform, the modern life-size statue in bronze of a man in his late teens gazes blankly from empty eye sockets into the far distance, contemplating the life that has yet to unfold. This is Gaius Octavius, Rome's future ruler Augustus: for Velitrae was his hometown and Velletri is proud to celebrate his memory.

Gaius would recognize the lay of the land, the rise and fall of streets and alleys, perhaps the layout, certainly the views. Now as then, this is a provincial place, which seems farther from the capital city than it really is. Change has always come slowly. The community leaves a powerful impression of being self-contained and a little isolated. Even today, elderly locals squint blackly at strangers.

A certain dour feeling for tradition, a suspicion of newfangled ways, a belief in propriety, have always been typical of provincial life in towns such as Velitrae, and it would be hard to imagine a more conventional family than that into which Gaius Octavius was born in 63 B.C.

Every Roman boy received a *praenomen,* or forename, such as Marcus, Lucius, Sextus—or Gaius. Then came his clan name, or *nomen,* such as

Octavius. Some but not all Romans also had a *cognomen,* which signified a family subset of a clan. Successful generals were sometimes awarded a hereditary *agnomen;* for example, Publius Cornelius Scipio added Africanus to his existing names, in honor of his victory over Hannibal in north Africa. By contrast, girls were only known, inconveniently, by the feminine version of their nomen; so Gaius' two sisters were both known as Octavia.

An important feature of the infant Gaius' inheritance was that, although like most Italians the Octavii held Roman citizenship, they were not of "Roman" stock. Velitrae was an outpost on the borders of Latium, home of the Latin tribes that, centuries before, had been among the first conquests of the aggressive little settlement beside a ford on the river Tiber.

Two hundred years before Gaius' birth, Rome finally united the tribes and communities of central and southern Italy through a network of imposed treaties. The men of these lands provided the backbone of the legions and were eventually, as late as the eighties B.C., incorporated into the Republic as full citizens. The little boy grew up with a clear impression of the contribution that Rome's onetime opponents were making to its imperial greatness, a contribution not always fully recognized by the chauvinists in the capital. In a real sense, the Roman empire would be better called the Italian empire.

The Octavii were a well-respected local family of considerable means. A Vicus Octavius, or Octavius Street, ran through Velitrae's center (just as a Via Ottavia does today), past an altar consecrated by a long-ago ancestor.

The family seems to have been in trade, a sure sign that it was not of aristocratic status. Gaius' paternal great-grandfather fought in Sicily as a military tribune (a senior officer in a legion, or regiment) during the second war against the great merchant state of Carthage in northern Africa (218 to 201 B.C.). Carthage's comprehensive defeat was the first indication to the Mediterranean world that a new military power had arrived on the scene. Gaius' grandfather, who lived to an advanced age, was well-off, but had no ambitions for a career in national politics, being apparently content to hold local political office.

Later hostile gossip claimed that the great-grandfather was an ex-slave who, having won his freedom, made a living as a rope maker in the neighborhood of Thurii, a town in Italy's deep south. It was also rumored that the grandfather was a money changer, with "coin-stained hands." Friendly propagandists took a different tack and invented a fictitious link with a blue-blooded Roman clan of the same name.

When he came to write his memoirs many years afterward, Gaius merely noted that he "came from a rich old equestrian family." The *equites,* or knights, were the affluent middle class, occupying a political level below that of the nobility and members of the ruling Senate, but often overlapping with them socially. To qualify for equestrian status, they needed to own property worth more than 400,000 sesterces, and were not actively engaged in government. They were usually wealthy businessmen or landed gentry who preferred to avoid the expense and dangers of a political career. Many were contracted by the state to collect taxes on its behalf from the provinces. By the time of the boy's father, also named Gaius Octavius, the family had become seriously rich, and probably far exceeded the equestrian minimum.

The father Octavius, an ambitious man, decided to pursue a career in politics at Rome with a view to making his way, if he could, to the top. This was an extremely difficult project. The Roman constitution was a complicated contraption of checks and balances, and the odds were stacked against an outsider—a *novus homo,* or "new man"—from winning a position of authority.

Rome became a republic in 509 B.C., after driving out its king and abolishing the monarchy. The next two centuries saw a long struggle for power between a group of noble families, patricians, and ordinary citizens, plebeians, who were excluded from public office.

The outcome was an apparent victory for the people, but the old aristocracy, supplemented by rich plebeian nobles, still controlled the state. What looked in many ways like a democracy was, in fact, an oligarchy modified by elections.

The Roman constitution was the fruit of many compromises and developed into a complicated mix of laws and unwritten understandings. Power was widely distributed and there were multiple sources of decision-making.

Roman citizens (only men, for women did not have the vote) attended public meetings called assemblies, where they passed laws and elected politicians to govern the Republic. These leaders doubled as generals in time of war. Although in theory any citizen could stand for public office, candidates usually came from a small group of very rich, noble families.

If successful, politicians passed through a set sequence of different jobs, a process called the *cursus honorum* or honors race. The first step on the ladder, taken at the age of thirty or above (in practice, younger men were often elected), was to become one of a number of quaestors; this post entailed supervising the collection of taxes and making payments, either for the consuls in Rome or for provincial governors. Then, if he wished, a man could be elected one of four aediles, who were responsible for the administration of the city of Rome. During festivals they staged public entertainments at their own expense, so deep pockets were needed. The next position, that of praetor, was compulsory. Praetors were senior officers of state, responsible for presiding as judges in the law courts and, when required, to lead an army in the field.

At the top of the pyramid were two consuls, who were heads of government with supreme authority; they were primarily army commanders and conveners of the Senate and assemblies.

Consuls and praetors held *imperium,* officially sanctioned absolute power, although they were constrained in three important ways. First, they held office only for one year. Second, there were always two or more officeholders at the same level. Those of equal rank were allowed to veto anything that their colleagues or junior officeholders decided. Finally, if they broke the law, officeholders could face criminal charges once they were out of office.

On top of that, ten tribunes of the people were elected, whose task was to make sure that officeholders did nothing to harm ordinary Romans (patricians were not allowed to be tribunes). They could propose laws to the Senate and the people and were empowered to convene citizens' assemblies. The tribunes held power only within the city limits, where they could veto *any* officeholder's decisions, including another tribune's.

The power of the assemblies was limited. They approved laws—but only those that were laid before them. Speakers supported or opposed a proposed measure, but open debate was forbidden; all that citizens were allowed to do was vote. There were different kinds of assembly, each with its own rules: in the assembly that elected praetors and consuls, for example, the voting system was weighted in favor of property owners in the belief that they would act with care because they had the most to lose if any mistakes were made.

The Roman constitution made it so easy to stop decisions from being made that it is rather surprising that anything at all got done. The Romans realized that sometimes it might be necessary to override the constitution. In a grave emergency, for a maximum of six months, a dictator was appointed who held sole power and could act as he saw fit.

The Roman Senate was mainly recruited from officeholders. By Octavius' day, a quaestor automatically became a lifelong member, and he and his family joined Rome's nobility (if he was not already a member of it). Senators were prohibited by law from engaging in business, although many used agents or front men to circumvent the ban.

In theory, the Senate held little official power and its role was merely to advise the consuls. However, because the Senate was a permanent feature of the government, whereas consuls and other officeholders had fixed terms, its authority and influence were very great. It was responsible for managing foreign affairs, and it discussed laws before they were presented to the assemblies. Its decrees, although not legally binding, were usually obeyed.

The Senate appointed former consuls and praetors, called proconsuls and propraetors (Octavius was one), to rule Rome's provinces, usually for between one and three years.

The *equites,* who as has been mentioned were not members of the Senate, formed a second social class, mainly comprising businessmen and country gentry. Beneath them came ordinary citizens, listed in different categories according to their wealth. The poorest citizens were *capite censi,* the "head count."

Modern governments employ many thousands of administrators who carry out their decisions. This was not the case during the Roman Republic. There were no bureaucrats, apart from a few clerks who looked after the public treasury. There was no police force, no public postal system, and no fire service, and there were no banks. There was no public criminal prosecution or judicial service, and cases were brought by private citizens. Elected politicians acted as judges in the law courts. The consuls brought in servants and slaves from their households, as well as personal friends, to help run the government.

Gaius Octavius won a quaestorship, probably in 70 B.C., and joined the Senate. This was no mean achievement for a country gentleman outside the magic circle of Roman politics. The promise of political success brought with it an important benefit: a wife from one of Rome's great patrician clans.

Octavius was already married to a woman of whom history has recorded nothing except for her name, Ancharia. The couple had a daughter, and perhaps Ancharia died in childbirth, for families with only one child were rare, especially if the child was a girl. Her family was of obscure origin; she may have come from Velitrae or thereabouts. She would have been no help to an ambitious young man's career and, if alive, must have been divorced. Her removal from the scene enabled Octavius to achieve a splendid alliance, when he married Atia, a member of the Julian family.

The Julii traced their ancestry to before the city's foundation, traditionally set at 753 B.C. The legend went that when, after a ten-year siege, the Greeks sacked the city of Troy on what is now the Turkish coast near the Dardanelles, they killed or enslaved most of the leading Trojans. One exception was Aeneas, the son of the love goddess Venus and a handsome young warrior. He escaped the city's destruction with some followers and after many adventures made landfall in Latium. His son Iulus (sometimes also called Ascanius) founded the Julian dynasty.

By the first century B.C., high birth was not sufficient to guarantee political success. Money was also required, and in large quantities. The Julii were impoverished; for long generations few of them had won important posts in the honors race. Like aristocratic families before and since that fall on hard times, they used marriage as a means of income generation.

The current head of the family, Gaius Julius Caesar, was a rising politician in his late thirties, about the same age as Octavius. Talented, amusing, and fashionable, he had a voracious appetite for cash and had built up enormous debts to feed both his lifestyle and his career. One of his sisters married Marcus Atius Balbus, a local worthy from Aricia, a town not far from Velitrae. Balbus was not prominent in public life and his greatest attraction must have lain in the fact that he was a man of substance.

As a new man, Octavius knew that his dubious ancestry would damage his career. A commodious dowry would be of value in a wife, but what he really needed was entrée into the Roman nobility. As a niece of Julius Caesar, Balbus' daughter Atia was well placed to make that possible. Because the Balbi lived not far from Octavius' home base of Velitrae, they may well have traveled in the same social circles. In that case, Atia formed an ambitious man's bridge from provincial life to Rome.

Sometime before 70 B.C., the couple married and, in due course, Atia became pregnant. Disappointingly, the outcome was a second daughter.

Five or six years passed before another child arrived: a son, this time, Gaius. He was born just before sunrise on September 23, 63 B.C., at Ox Heads, a small property on the slopes of the fashionable Palatine Hill, a few minutes' walk from Rome's main square, the Forum, and the Senate House.

By tradition, the *paterfamilias* held the power of life and death over his household, both his relatives and his slaves. When a child was born, the midwife took the infant and placed it on the floor in front of the father. Should the father wish to acknowledge his paternity, he would lift the baby into his arms if it was a boy; if a girl, he would simply instruct that she be fed. Only after this ritual had taken place did the child receive his or her first nourishment.

Apparently, Gaius was lucky to survive this procedure, for an astrologer had given him a bad prognosis and he narrowly escaped infanticide. If Gaius had been rejected, he would have been abandoned in the open air and left to die; this was a fate to which illegitimate children and girls were especially liable, as were (one may surmise) sickly or disabled babies. Rejected infants were left on dunghills, or near cisterns. They were often picked up there by slave traders (although the family might reclaim the child later, if it so wished) or, more rarely, rescued by a kindly passerby. Otherwise, they would starve, unless eaten by stray dogs.

Rome, with about a million inhabitants, was an unhygienic, noisy, crowded megalopolis, no place for rearing a child, and there is evidence that Gaius spent much of his infancy at his grandfather's country house near Velitrae. More than a century later, Suetonius reported that the house still existed and was open to the public: "a small room, not unlike a butler's pantry, is still shown and described as [his] nursery."

Helped by the link, through Atia, to Julius Caesar, Octavius' political career was advancing rapidly. After serving as quaestor, he could move up to the next rung, as one of the four aediles. The aedileship being optional, it is not known whether Octavius held this office, but he could probably have afforded it.

At the age of thirty-nine, Octavius was eligible to run for praetor. According to Velleius Paterculus, he was regarded as "a dignified person, of upright and blameless life, and [was] extremely rich." In the praetorian election for 61 B.C., he came in first even though he was running against a number of aristocratic competitors.

The two-year-old Gaius would have seen little of his father, who spent a year in Rome discharging his judicial duties as praetor. Then, as was usual for senior government officials after their period of office, at the end of 61 B.C. Octavius went overseas for a twelve-month stint as governor, or propraetor, of the province of Macedonia.

Octavius was due to sail from Brundisium, a major port on the heel of Italy, but before he did so, the Senate asked him to make a detour to the town of Thurii on the toe and disperse a group of outlawed slaves.

More than ten years previously, these men had joined the great slave revolt of Spartacus, following him during the years when he won one victory after another over incompetently led Roman legions. They managed to avoid the terrible penalty exacted on the survivors of Spartacus' final defeat: thousands were crucified along the length of the road from Rome to Capua, where the rebellion had started at a school for slave gladiators.

Somehow the escapees managed to keep going as a group, reemerging briefly to join the forces of Lucius Sergius Catilina. In the year of Gaius' birth, this dissident aristocrat had plotted the violent overthrow of the Republic and its replacement by a regime of radicals which he would lead. The alert consul, Marcus Tullius Cicero, was a new man like Octavius; a fine public speaker and an able and honest administrator, he outwitted the conspirator and finessed him into a botched military insurrection.

The Romans depended on, but also feared, the hundreds of thousands of slaves who in large part ran their economy, providing labor for agricultural estates and manufacturing businesses. Slaves could also be found in every reasonably well-off home, cooking, cleaning, acting as secretaries and managers. If they were young and good-looking, slaves of either sex could well find themselves providing sexual services.

A slave was something one could own, like a horse or a table. In the Roman view, he or she was "a talking instrument." Slaves could not marry, although they could make and save money and could receive legacies. If a master was murdered by a slave, all the slaves in his ownership were killed. It was believed that a slave could give true evidence only under torture. Perhaps a third of the population of Italy were slaves in the late Republic—as many as three million people.

For Octavius, dealing with the surviving Spartacans was an important task. They did not pose a great threat in themselves; it was the principle that counted. No rebellious runaway should be allowed to enjoy the fruits of his illicit freedom.

As a victorious general, Octavius could acquire an honorific and hereditary title and it seems that he added Thurinus to his name to mark his defeat of the slaves, passing it on to his infant son. Suetonius, writing in the first century B.C., asserted:

> *I can prove pretty conclusively that as a child [Gaius] was called Thurinus, perhaps . . . because his father had defeated the slaves in that neighborhood soon after he was born; my evidence is a bronze statuette which I once owned. It shows him as a boy, and a rusty, almost illegible inscription in iron letters gives him this name.*

The truth is that Octavius was making himself slightly ridiculous, for the defeat of slaves conferred no great honor on the victor. In adult life his son was often insultingly referred to as the Thurian.

The new governor of Macedonia administered his province "justly and courageously" and won a high reputation in leading circles in Rome. It was clear to all that, despite his provincial origins, Octavius was well qualified for the top job in Roman politics, the consulship. But in 58 B.C., when he must have been only in his mid-forties, he died unexpectedly en route from Brundisium to Rome, before he had a chance to launch his candidacy.

It is not known what killed Octavius. An accident of some kind is a possibility, although one would suppose that the ancient sources would have mentioned that. He died in his bedroom at a country villa belonging to the family that stood on the slopes of Mount Vesuvius—a fact that suggests illness.

Most probably, he fell victim to one of the many health hazards in the Roman world. One of these was food poisoning; stomach upset was among the most common recorded complaints, and analysis of Roman sewage deposits suggests that certain intestinal parasites were often endemic, borne by bad fish and meat, among other sources. Despite the growing availability of fresh water brought in through aqueducts, standards of sanitation for most people were low, although the rich were able to afford separate kitchens, underfloor heating, domestic bathhouses, and private latrines. Few understood that human waste matter could spread disease. Oil lamps and open hearths or braziers generated irritant smoke, which caused and spread respiratory infections. Epidemics of all kinds regularly swept through Rome as a result of overcrowding and the fact that the capital of a great empire witnessed a continual influx of visitors, traders, and returning government officials and soldiers.

Gaius was only four years old when his father died. In addition to the sadness of his loss, his premature death will have caused a family crisis. Domestic life was rigorously patriarchal. A widow, especially one of independent means, was often expected to marry again at the earliest opportunity, although if she remained true to the memory of her dead husband she would deserve praise for being a *univira,* a one-man woman.

This may not always have been easy for a woman of a certain age with a growing family; but Atia was still young, and her connections made her highly eligible. A year or two after Octavius' death, she landed another apparently rising politician, Lucius Marcius Philippus, an aristocrat who proudly claimed descent from the royal line of Macedon. He had just returned from Syria, where he had been provincial governor, and he stood successfully for one of the two consulships of 56 B.C.

He backed his brother-in-law Julius Caesar as Caesar climbed the political ladder—but only cautiously so. Unlike his dashing ancestors, the Macedonian king Philip and Philip's son Alexander the Great, who conquered the Persian empire in the fourth century B.C., Philippus was temperamentally risk-averse—a neutral who preferred diplomacy to commitment.

After his father's death, little Gaius seems to have been brought up by his maternal grandmother, Julius Caesar's sister, in whose house Atia may well have passed her brief widowhood. That he stayed with her after his mother's remarriage is a little odd; it could be explained by mutual affection or by Philippus' lack of interest in a small stepson. It may have been in this house that he first met his famous great-uncle, Julius Caesar.

Romans of high social status took very seriously the education of children, and especially of boys. During his early years, a boy was looked after by the women of a household, but once he reached the age of seven he usually passed into the control of his father, whose duty was to instill in his offspring the qualities of a good man, a *vir bonus.* High among these were *pietas,* loyalty and a due respect for authority and traditional values; *gravitas,* a serious (sometimes oversolemn) approach to the challenges of life; and *fortitudo,* manliness and courage. A son was expected to learn by observation; he helped his father on the land and, wearing his smart little *toga praetexta,* an all-enveloping cloaklike garment with a red stripe indicating the wearer's childhood status, trotted around after him as he went about on public business or conducted religious ceremonies. In this way the boy would learn how the political system worked and how grown-ups were expected to behave.

It is not clear who, if anyone, played this paternal role for the orphaned Gaius. For a time a friend of Octavius, one Gaius Toranius, was the boy's guardian, but he left little mark (we know that the adult Gaius did not value him highly). However, Atia won a reputation as a strict and caring mother, even if she was not always directly involved in her son's day-to-day supervision. One positive masculine influence is recorded: a slave called Sphaerus was Gaius' "attendant" during his childhood. He seems to have been much loved; he was given his freedom and, when he died many years later, his charge, now adult and famous, gave him a public funeral.

Boys from affluent families were sometimes taught at home, but many went to private elementary schools, *ludi litterarii,* which inculcated reading, writing, and arithmetic. Girls might also attend, but their schooling ended with puberty, although they were trained in the domestic arts by their mothers and some received private tuition in their teens. It is probable that Gaius attended classes in Velitrae or Rome, accompanied by Sphaerus.

Teaching methods were painstaking, but hardly inspired, a matter of imitation and repetition. The school day opened with a breakfastless dawn and ran on into the afternoon. No attention was paid to games or gymnastics (fathers looked after boys' physical exercise), but the long hours of instruction ended with a bath. Pupils had to learn the names of the letters of the alphabet before being shown what they looked like; they chanted the letters all in order forward and backward. They then graduated to groups of two or three letters, and finally to syllables and words.

In about 51 B.C., when Gaius was twelve, his grandmother Julia died. It must have been a sign of their closeness that the boy was given the signal honor of delivering a eulogy at her funeral. The invitation is also evidence that he was growing into a self-possessed and clever teenager, who was likely to acquit himself well. He addressed a large crowd and was warmly applauded.

Gaius at last moved into his stepfather's household, where both Atia and Philippus took his secondary education into hand. He attended a school run by a *grammaticus,* a teacher of literature and language, the staples of the curriculum. Both Greek and Latin were taught, but literary studies centered on the Hellenic inheritance: the epic poems of Homer, the Athenian dramatists, and the great orators. (There was a Latin literature, but it was rough-hewn and heavily dependent on Greek paradigms.) As Cicero drily put it: "We must apply to our fellow-countrymen for virtue, but for our culture to the Greeks."

The teacher specialized in textual analysis, examining syntax and the rules of poetic scansion and explaining obscure or idiomatic phrases. The student learned to read texts aloud with conviction and persuasiveness, to master the art of parsing (that is, breaking a sentence down into its constituent grammatical parts), and to scan verse. This form of schooling had a long life: it survived into the Dark Ages and was reinvigorated in the Renaissance. As one modern commentator has observed, "There was not a great difference in the teaching of Latin and Greek between early nineteenth-century Eton and the schools of imperial Rome."

The *grammaticus* also introduced the student to rhetoric, the art of public speaking. Most upper-class Roman men were destined for a career in politics, so the ability to persuade people to adopt a course of action or entertain an opinion was an essential skill. But oratory was held to be more than a talent; it conduced to the leading of a good life. The statesman and moralist Cato the Censor defined an orator as "a good man skilled in speech."

Apparently Gaius showed great promise: if this is not a later invention, boys ambitious for a political career used to go around with him when he went out riding or visited the houses of relatives and friends. Like the adult senators, who used to walk through the city accompanied by crowds of dependents, Gaius was attracting young adherents whose support would be returned, they hoped, by help whether now or in the future. This will have had less to do with his charm or intelligence than with the fact that he was related to Rome's most powerful politician, Julius Caesar.

Gaius made two special school friends, very different from each other in personality. The first was Marcus Vipsanius Agrippa, a year younger than Gaius. The origins of his family are unknown, but Suetonius says that he was of "humble origin"; the name "Vipsanius" is highly unusual and Agrippa himself preferred not to use it. He may have come from Venetia or Istria in northern Italy. Like the Octavii, the family was probably of affluent provincial stock.

According to Aulus Gellius, a collector of curious anecdotes and other unconsidered trifles, the word "Agrippa" denoted an infant "at whose birth the feet appeared first, instead of the head." Breech births were difficult to manage and could endanger the mother's life. It is said that Marcus was born in this perilous manner, and was so named in memory of the event.

Gaius' second friend, Gaius Cilnius Maecenas, boasted a distinguished ancestry. He traced his lineage to the splendid, mysterious Etruscan civilization, based in today's Tuscany, which dominated central Italy before the rise of Rome. The Etruscans were believed by some to be immigrants from Lydia in Asia Minor. Maecenas was of regal stock, descending on his mother's side from the Cilnii, who many centuries before ruled the Etruscan town of Arretium (today's Arezzo). By the first century B.C., though, the family had come down somewhat in the world: they were now *equites*.

If one may judge by their later careers, Agrippa was likely a tough, down-to-earth boy who enjoyed physical exercise and warlike pursuits, while Maecenas had a more pacific, even feminine temperament and was especially interested in literature and the arts. They grew into adulthood alongside Gaius, learning to accord him total trust and forming a lasting, loving bond with him.

As his teens proceeded, an able upper-class adolescent moved from his secondary school to the ancient equivalent of a higher education. Leading politicians would often house writers and thinkers in their capacious homes. Young men were able to spend time there, learning from the conversation and watching the political career of their host. As a form of military service, they would also join the staff of a leading general.

For most of his life, Gaius had seen little or nothing of his astonishing great-uncle, Julius Caesar, who had spent ten years conquering Gaul. Soon the triumphant general would be back in Rome and able to provide the eager teenager with the most remarkable introduction to the twin arts of politics and war in the history of western civilization. That finishing school finished off the Roman Republic for good.

# II

# THE GREAT-UNCLE

## 48–47 B.C.

THE YEAR 49 B.C. SAW THE WORLD TURNED UPSIDE DOWN. The Roman Republic was facing catastrophe, thanks to a civil war in which one of the protagonists was Gaius' great-uncle.

What were the causes of the crisis? It was partly the product of stubborn political, military, and economic facts, and partly of colorful but obstinate personalities.

It was also the inadvertent outcome of astonishing success. As the patricians and the plebs fought for constitutional mastery, Rome's legions slowly fought their way through Italy in war after war until they controlled the peninsula. After a titanic struggle with Carthage in northern Africa, the Republic emerged as a Mediterranean power by the beginning of the second century B.C.

From then on, Rome increasingly acted as an international "policeman," sending its legions to right wrongs in foreign countries—especially the Hellenistic kingdoms of the Middle East. Invited to intervene by some Greek cities, it vanquished Macedonia and eventually annexed it as a Roman province. It went on to defeat Antiochus, king of Syria, who unwisely challenged Rome to a fight. In 133 B.C., the king of Pergamum (in today's western Turkey) died, leaving his kingdom to Rome, which renamed it the province of Asia.

The Republic was now the leading power not only in the western Mediterranean but also in the Middle East. It commanded an empire stretching from Spain (which it had inherited from the Carthaginians nearly a century before) to western Turkey. A band of client kingdoms marked the boundary with the Parthian empire (today's Iraq and Iran).

The triumph of Rome has puzzled historians down the centuries. Of the many factors that accounted for the city's emergence on the world stage, the most important was that from their earliest beginnings Romans lived in a permanent state of struggle—with their enemies abroad and with one another at home. Tempered in that fire, they became formidable soldiers as well as learning the political arts of negotiation, compromise, and anger resolution. Flexible and skilled at improvisation, they developed a practical imagination. They usually tried to settle a dispute, if they could, without violence, but when military force became necessary they applied it with a ruthless vigor.

Three important consequences followed Rome's emergence as a superpower. The first was a huge influx of wealth and slaves. Direct taxation for Roman citizens living in Italy was abolished. The lives of the ruling class became more and more opulent, the frequent festivals and gladiatorial games increasingly elaborate. With the opening up of foreign markets, cheap grain flooded into Italy, driving the native smallholder out of business and replacing him with large livestock ranches often run with slave labor.

The rural unemployed fled to the big city, which became yet bigger. Unfortunately, the job market could not expand to soak up the refugees from the countryside. The authorities began to provide free grain to quiet a febrile and uncontrollable urban population.

Second, to manage such extensive dominions demanded substantial military forces. In the old days, country smallholders were called up to fight short campaigns as and when necessary. Now standing armies were required, with soldiers serving for long periods. These soldiers depended on their generals to persuade the Senate to allocate farms to them when they retired, either in Italy or further afield. These farms would be their "pensions."

Largely as a result of conquest, the state owned a good deal of land. However, rich landowners, among whom were many senators, had quietly appropriated much of it without payment. These noble squatters were, to put it mildly, disinclined to disgorge their ill-gotten gains. So the legionaries depended on their generals to bully, finesse, or persuade the Senate to free up land for their retirement farms. They developed a loyalty to their generals rather than to Rome.

The third consequence of empire was the strain that its administration placed on the ruling class, and indeed on the Republic's constitution. So large was the throughput of elected officials that it is hardly surprising that their caliber was variable. A good number were corrupt and incompetent.

Many Romans believed that their traditional virtues of austere duty and healthy poverty were being eroded, and that this decadence explained the growing violence and selfishness of political life. The picture was not quite so bleak as it was depicted, for some *nobiles* worked hard to maintain standards. However, others did live in extravagant, irresponsible, and self-indulgent ways, and it was they who set the tone.

A tribune of the people, Tiberius Sempronius Gracchus (from one of Rome's oldest families), wanted to reform Italian agriculture by providing small plots of land for would-be peasant farmers. The Senate turned down the idea, but it was approved by the people and became law. In 133 B.C., Gracchus was murdered in the street by a group of angry senators, who claimed that he wanted to set up a tyranny. Ten years later, Gracchus' younger brother, Gaius, was elected tribune and proposed further reforms. He was either killed or took his life after being cornered in a street riot.

These acts of violence were a turning point in the fortunes of the Republic. A historian writing in the following century said: "From now onward, political disputes that had been resolved by agreement were decided by the sword."

The ruling class's long habit of cooperation was breaking down. Many leading Romans forgot that public office was meant to be held for the public good. Also, and more seriously, everyone could see that the Roman system of government was too unwieldy to manage an empire and needed drastic streamlining.

Crises came crashing in one after another, like waves against a storm-battered ship. For the first time in three centuries, hordes of invading Celts poured into Italy; they were destroyed only with great difficulty.

Italy was governed through a network of alliances, but its communities and tribes did not have full civic rights and had long pressed for Roman citizenship. In 91 B.C. they lost patience and revolted in what became known as the War of the Allies. Rome wisely gave them what they wanted, but too late to avoid much bitterness and bloodshed.

The eastern provinces, led by the wily Mithridates, king of Pontus, twice rebelled, and it was many years before Rome regained full control.

However, the real threat to the Republic lay in domestic dissension at home. While Rome had no political parties in the modern sense and, apart from the occasional new man like Octavius, almost all elected officials were drawn from a small number of noble families, two distinct trends of opinion marked the political scene.

The optimates, the "best people," represented conservative opinion, traditional values, and a collegiate approach to politics. They resented any challenge to the ruling oligarchy and, because they controlled the Senate, were able to block reform. The optimates' opponents, the *populares,* claimed to stand, as their nickname suggests, for the interests of the Roman people, of the citizenry at large. Although some of the *populares* were genuine reformers, others were simply ambitious individualists.

In the eighties B.C., two outsize political personalities collided. One was a respected *popularis,* Gaius Marius, victor over the Celts. The second was an optimate, Lucius Cornelius Sulla. In 88 B.C., despite the fact that it was illegal for armed soldiers to enter Rome, Sulla marched his army, loyal to him personally and to no one else, into the city to fight against Marius and his friends. Such an attack had never happened before in the history of the Republic. Sulla's action set a black precedent for ambitious Romans to follow in later years, as violence among politicians became more common.

One after another, Marius and Sulla staged massacres of their political opponents. In Sulla's case, the bloodletting was legalized. He was elected dictator and, using the supreme emergency powers this gave him, he posted in the Forum a list of his political enemies who were to be killed without trial. Sulla even offered rewards for their execution. Modern scholars estimate that about five hundred died, senators and a larger number of *equites.* This summary procedure was called a proscription.

Sulla introduced measures to strengthen the power of the Senate and weaken that of the people, and then retired into private life. When he died in 78 B.C., most of his reforms were quickly overturned.

Both of these bitter rivals won power but failed to make good use of it, and to its ruin, Rome grew ever more accustomed to the use of force to settle political disputes.

Julius Caesar never troubled to conceal the fact that he was a *popularis* both by conviction and by family tradition. As quaestor, aedile, and praetor, he had gone out of his way to infuriate respectable opinion. In 60 B.C., when Gaius was three years old, Caesar was in his fortieth year and planning his campaign to win the consulship for 59. He knew that his opponents in the Senate would do everything they could to stop him.

Caesar combined charm and determination in equal quantities. According to Suetonius, he was tall, fair, and well-built, with a rather broad face, keen, dark-brown eyes, and soft, white skin. He wore fashionable clothes. "His dress was, it seems, unusual: he had added wrist-length sleeves with fringes to his purple-striped senatorial tunic, and the belt which he wore over it was never tightly fastened." He was very attentive to his appearance, always keeping his head carefully trimmed and shaved (his growing baldness upset and irritated him), and depilating his body.

He was prone to headaches and suffered from epileptic seizures (which grew in frequency as he became older). Despite his luxurious tastes, he cultivated a healthy and energetic life. He kept to a simple diet and was an expert horseman from boyhood. He had trained himself to put his hands behind his back and then, keeping them tightly clasped, to put his horse to a full gallop; as the stirrup had not yet been invented, this was no mean feat. When on military campaigns he inured himself to long, hard journeys, sleeping night after night in the open.

Caesar spent much of his leisure time chasing after the wives of his political colleagues; it was widely rumored that he slept with men as well. He had extravagant tastes and once gave the favorite of his numerous mistresses—Servilia, the mother of Marcus Brutus—a pearl worth an astonishing 240,000 sesterces. He was a keen collector of gems, carvings, statues, and "old masters" (sculptures and paintings of the Greek artistic heyday in the fifth and fourth centuries B.C.). He liked to have clever and attractive people around him, and paid such high prices for good-looking and talented slaves that he was too ashamed to have them recorded in his account books.

A politician still on the way up, Caesar knew he would not win the consulship without help. He took the momentous decision to form an alliance with two leading *populares*. One was Gnaeus Pompeius Magnus (in English, Pompey the Great), who was, by common consent, the greatest man of his age. As a young man he had raised a private army to support Sulla, and behaved cruelly enough to win the nickname *adulescens carnifex,* the "butcher boy." He was a competent general but a manager of genius, who accomplished a series of special commissions with speed and efficiency—in particular, clearing the Mediterranean of pirates and finally putting paid to Mithridates. The second leading Roman in Caesar's sights was Marcus Licinius Crassus; he had defeated Spartacus and was a multimillionaire property developer who once quipped that a man could only count himself rich if he could afford to pay an army. In 60 B.C., they joined forces with Caesar, who sealed the deal by marrying Julia, his daughter and only legitimate child, to Pompey.

Modern historians call the pact the First Triumvirate; at the time it was nicknamed "the three-headed monster," because the three men made themselves the unofficial rulers of Rome. They pooled their financial resources and supporters to control the voting at assemblies. In this way they won consulships for one another and for their friends, and passed whatever laws they wished (including allocations of land for demobilized veterans) over the head of the Senate. They also gave themselves unusually long five-year governorships in the provinces (proconsuls traditionally served for only one to three years).

When Caesar was consul in 59 B.C., he ignored the vetoes of his optimate colleagues and pushed controversial legislation through the assembly. This was a breach of the constitution, and his enemies neither forgot nor forgave the high-handedness. However, officeholders were immune from prosecution and for the time being he could not be taken to court.

The Senate was furious but powerless. Sooner or later, it hoped, the trio would quarrel. Then the time would come when the optimates could take their revenge. The Senate's leading personality at this time was Marcus Porcius Cato—a dour man. Plutarch reports: "It was really very difficult to make him laugh, although once in a while, he allowed himself to relax his features into a smile." He refused to use perfume and his personal habits were severe. He always walked, and trained himself to endure extremes of heat and cold. He was a hard worker and prided himself on never telling a lie; his reputation inspired a proverb—"That cannot be true, even if Cato says it is." His way of life was a reproach to the decadence of the times, so much so that he could infuriate his friends as well as his enemies.

Whereas Caesar appears to have been an abstemious drinker, Cato was puritanical in everything except for an enormous capacity for alcohol and a surprising weakness for gambling. He remarked that "Caesar was the only sober man who tried to wreck the constitution."

After his consulship, Caesar went to rule Cisalpine Gaul and Transalpine Gaul (northern Italy and southern France). Wanting to prove himself as a general, he invaded the rest of Gaul (central and northern France and Belgium). When he needed more time to complete the conquest, he arranged a second five-year term as governor. By 49 B.C., he had added a huge new province to the empire—and in so doing created an experienced army that would follow wherever he led.

In 53 B.C., Crassus commanded an expedition against the Parthian empire. The Parthians were fierce former nomads who became the dominating force on the Iranian plateau during the third century B.C. From about 190 B.C., they intermittently governed Mesopotamia, the heartland of the old Assyrian and Babylonian empires. They were highly skilled horsemen, famous for the "Parthian shot": they rode up to the enemy, then suddenly galloped away, turning round in their seat to loose an arrow. The Romans, who depended on infantry, found these highly mobile fighters hard to defeat.

This was problematic, for the Parthian monarchs were aggressive, with a tendency to meddle in Rome's eastern provinces and in the client kingdoms that acted as a buffer between the two empires and that Rome saw as within its sphere of influence. Both sides aimed to control the strategically important, semi-independent kingdom of Armenia (it looked both eastward and westward, being attached to the plateau of Asia Minor and the Iranian plateau, and it had long been a bone of contention). Luckily, murderous dynastic disputes often distracted the Parthians from foreign adventures.

Rome was itself frequently guilty of interference. A few years previously, the proconsul of Syria had supported a claimant to the Parthian crown, a move which, although unsuccessful, naturally infuriated the sitting monarch.

As a result, relations between the two powers were icy, and each side felt it had good reason to launch a preventive war against the other. Hostilities were hastened by Crassus' personal ambitions, for he was intent on winning military glory that would rival the achievements of Pompey and Caesar.

Crassus marched an army of about thirty-five thousand men into Mesopotamia. Near a place called Carrhae he came up against a force of about ten thousand mounted archers. The terrain was open downland, ideal for cavalry maneuvers, and the Parthians steadily shot down the helpless legionaries. The Romans sought terms and Crassus was killed during the negotiations. Only ten thousand of his men survived the debacle. Humiliatingly, many legionary standards were captured.

This was a massive blow to Rome's pride that would demand revenge as soon as the political situation at home permitted it.

Gaius was too young to understand these events when they took place. But he lived in a family that had been engaged in high politics for at least two generations, and the issues of the day must have been regularly discussed at home. Close relatives found themselves on different sides of the fence, and at least one of them, Gaius' stepfather, Philippus, preferred to sit on it. His full sister Octavia, not his half sister of the same name by their father's first marriage, was wedded at the age of fifteen or sixteen to Gaius Claudius Marcellus, a middle-aged optimate twenty years or so her senior, who strongly disapproved of Caesar's constitutional recklessness.

In 56 B.C., when the boy was seven, Philippus became consul. Gaius did not need to master the complexities of his great-uncle's alliance with Pompey and Crassus to enjoy the glamour and excitement of the consulship. It was the peak of achievement for a Roman and, although the boy mostly lived in the country, we may imagine that he was brought to Rome to witness Philippus in all the splendor of his office.

Roman consuls inherited the ceremonial grandeur of the Etruscan kings whom they replaced when the Republic was founded in 509 B.C. A consul wore a distinctive toga with a broad purple hem, and the high scarlet shoes of royalty. He sat on a special chair of state, the *sella curulis,* inlaid with ivory, and was always accompanied by an official bodyguard of twelve lictors. Each member of this escort carried the emblem of state authority, an ax bound with rods; this was the fasces, which symbolized the consul's absolute power, or *imperium.* When a consul visited a house, the lictors stood guard at the front door and would instantly arrest anyone whom he pointed out.

As Gaius approached his teens, the political situation in Rome deteriorated. Caesar and the Senate hired gangs that fought pitched battles in the Forum. Public life was badly disrupted; elections were postponed and officeholders attacked in the street. No doubt the careful Atia insisted that Gaius stay safely in the country. As an emergency measure, the Senate arranged for Pompey to be appointed sole consul in 52 B.C. and entrusted him with the task of restoring order, which he did with his customary efficiency.

The First Triumvirate proved that men with the support of the people and soldiers of Rome, lots of money, and a fair amount of nerve could disregard the ruling class and, in effect, hijack the Republic.

However, as expected and despite Caesar's best efforts, the alliance at last broke up. Crassus was gone and, as the fifties drew to a close, Pompey, jealous of Caesar's military achievements in Gaul, became increasingly friendly with the optimates.

Once his governorship was over, Caesar intended to return to Rome, a conquering hero, and stand for consul for 48 B.C. His term in Gaul was due to end in late 50 or early 49 B.C.; he arranged for an extension, so that there would be no interval before the beginning of his second consulship, and permission to stand in absentia. This was important because, as a private citizen, he would be liable for prosecution for his illegal acts when consul ten years before. Cato and his friends in the Senate wanted a showdown with Caesar: they were set on having their day in court and pressed for Caesar's early recall.

Naturally, Caesar tried to prevent this from happening, for he would certainly be found guilty of constitutional crimes and his political career would be prematurely aborted. Fruitless maneuvers and debates took place as people began to realize that Caesar would never hand himself over to his enemies. However, the senatorial extremists, increasingly sure of Pompey's support, refused to compromise. Civil war seemed inevitable.

Gaius was now thirteen years old and well able to understand the seriousness of the situation. He will have been aware that opinion in his family, as in many others, was sharply divided. His brother-in-law, Gaius Claudius Marcellus, was consul for 50 B.C. and, despite his family connection with Caesar, was anxious to bring him to justice. Closer to home, Philippus, never known for strength of conviction, had astutely married his daughter Marcia to his uncle-in-law's sworn enemy Cato, thus keeping a careful foot in both camps. Philippus was not the only noble Roman to hedge his bets by ensuring that relatives could be found on each side. After all, it was not clear who would emerge the victor.

Caesar bought the services of indigent young tribunes of the people, who vetoed any hostile senatorial decrees on his behalf. One of these was Philippus' son (yet another insurance policy), but the most important was the thirty-three-year-old Marcus Antonius, or Mark Antony as he is known to us, a distant relative of Caesar through Antony's mother, a member of the Julian clan.

Mark Antony came from a good but impecunious family. He showed little interest in politics in his youth, sowing wild oats in spectacular manner and running up large debts. At one stage, he was rumored to have become the kept boy of a wealthy young aristocrat.

Sometime in his early twenties, Mark Antony realized that it was time to settle down. Following in the footsteps of many ambitious young Romans, he went on a "grand tour" to finish his education by studying public speaking in Athens or one of the great cities of Asia Minor. He took to what was called the Asiatic style of oratory, florid and boastful and swashbuckling—"in common with Antony's own mode of life," as Plutarch sharply remarked.

He also underwent military training and quickly showed his aptitude for soldiering, being tough and brave and possessing a gift for leadership. In 55 B.C., when he was twenty-five or twenty-six, he played a junior role in a Roman invasion of Egypt to restore an unpopular monarch, Ptolemy XII Auletes, to his throne. While in Alexandria he met for the first time one of the Auletes' daughters, a fourteen-year-old princess called Cleopatra. According to Appian, he was "provoked by the sight of her."

Antony then caught Caesar's eye and fought bravely with him in Gaul, becoming one of the victorious general's most trusted followers. His features were bold and masculine. He had a broad forehead and an aquiline nose, and wore a well-grown beard. He reminded people of traditional sculptures of Hercules, an association he cultivated in his choice of dress: at public events, he would wear his tunic low over his hips, with a large sword by his side and a heavy cloak. It was observed that his behavior was as Herculean as his appearance; he liked talking dirty and getting drunk in public. He used to sit down beside his soldiers as they ate, or he took his food standing up at the common mess table; they loved him for it.

He much enjoyed having sex with women, a weakness that won him considerable sympathy, writes Plutarch, "for he often helped others in their love affairs and always accepted with good humour the jokes they made about his own." When he was in funds, he showered money on his friends and was usually generous to soldiers under his command.

•   •   •

Few senators had any appetite for civil war; in December 50 B.C. the Senate voted by a huge majority that Pompey and Caesar, both of whom had armies, should demobilize. It looked as if peace would break out, a prospect that the die-hard consul Marcellus, Octavia's husband, was determined to avoid. He believed that Caesar would be easily defeated on the battlefield, and wanted to see him eliminated. He decided to act decisively. Without senatorial approval or the other consul's consent, he put a sword in Pompey's hand and gave him authority to defend the state.

On January 7, the Senate acknowledged that matters were now past recall and declared a state of emergency. Fearing for their lives, Antony and other supporters of Caesar fled to their commander, who was waiting at the little river Rubicon in northern Italy, which separated his province of Cisalpine Gaul from Roman territory proper.

While these high events unfolded, Philippus will have felt obliged to be at the heart of affairs in Rome, as would Atia as a close relative of Caesar's. There was much at stake, and a threat to Caesar could be equally a threat to them. However, they quietly sent Gaius to one of his father's country places, near Velitrae, where he would be out of harm's way.

During the night of January 10, in the full knowledge that he was launching a civil war, Caesar ordered his soldiers, all passionately loyal to him, to invade Italy.

"Let the dice fly high!" he said, as if he were playing a game of chance.

There was panic in Rome. The consuls fled southward. Pompey, whom the Senate appointed commander in chief, gave up Italy as a lost cause and sailed to Greece. His idea was to recruit a large army from the eastern provinces. He would invade Italy when he was ready and, with the help of some legions in Spain, crush Caesar as if in a pincer.

Caesar had hoped to catch Pompey, but just missed him. So, after a whirlwind stay at Rome, he rushed off to Spain. A praetor, Marcus Aemilius Lepidus, was instructed to look after his interests in the city, and Mark Antony was put in command of the troops remaining in Italy and given the responsibility for its administration.

Caesar was a master of the art of persuasion. When senior opponents fell into his hands, he did not take revenge, as expected, and execute them. Instead, he freed them all. Clemency was to be "the new style of conquest." Some middle-of-the-road senators gratefully took the hint and returned without fanfare to the capital.

Philippus was on tenterhooks, knowing that he would soon have to choose sides. He had left Rome with everyone else, but not for Pompey's camp. We hear of him a few weeks later in Naples, then a charming city founded by Greek colonists and called variously Parthenope or Neapolis. But, uncommitted as ever, he did not cross over to join Pompey, and eventually Caesar gave him leave to travel abroad if he wished (there is no evidence that, in the event, he took up this permission). Interestingly, the bellicose Marcellus, who as consul had precipitated the fighting, belatedly remembered into which family he had married, began to regret his bold stand, and unobtrusively slid into neutrality.

What Gaius made of these fine judgments and cautious calculations is unknown. His health was delicate and he did not have the full-blooded Roman delight in soldiering. So it may be that he was less impressed than others by Caesar's extraordinary military adventures in Gaul. It should be borne in mind that, unless in infancy, he had never met his great-uncle, who had left Rome for his governorship when Gaius was only four years old. If their paths did cross in his earliest years, Gaius would have had at most a dim memory of his celebrated relative.

At the very least, though, the boy would have known all about the sensational doings of the head of the Julian clan: they must have been a frequent, sometimes anxious topic of conversation among his relatives.

Letters arrived in Rome from Spain. After some early setbacks when he had been cornered by flash floods, Caesar had won a brilliant campaign of maneuver with minimum bloodshed. With the western arm of Pompey's pincers put out of action, he returned to Rome, where he was voted dictator. He made sure that at last he won the much-disputed consulship of 48 B.C., the prize for which he had set off the conflagration.

We may guess that Philippus visited Rome with Atia and Gaius and was present at Senate meetings as one of the few ex-consuls in Italy. So at some time during these eleven action-crammed days during the late autumn of 49 B.C., a momentous but inevitably brief encounter may have taken place between a busy fifty-one-year-old man at the height of his fame and his powers and an unknown teenager in his fifteenth year. Caesar would have had no time to make a considered judgment of Gaius, except perhaps for noting that he seemed a bright boy who had promise.

Then Caesar was off again—down to Brundisium and overseas to seek out his great rival Pompey.

Rome reverted to its default setting of worried waiting. Once again, the news seesawed. Letters traveled unpredictably back to Italy through messengers dispatched by participants, whether by the northern land route or, once spring had set in, over the dangerous seas.

In mid-August of 48 B.C., astonishing reports reached the city. Pompey's army had been utterly defeated in a great battle near the town of Pharsalus in central Greece. Fifteen thousand of his legionaries were dead, against only two hundred of Caesar's. The Republic's commander in chief had survived, but promptly disappeared, presumably making his way eastward. Caesar followed. For the moment, no one knew where either man was.

In Rome, the immediate reaction was to accept that Caesar had become the first man in the state. He was awarded unprecedented honors and powers. In the middle of September, within a few weeks of the battle, Caesar was nominated dictator for a year (the usual limit was six months), and Mark Antony was proclaimed his deputy as *magister equitum,* master of the horse.

It emerged that Pompey had fled to Egypt, where he hoped that the boy pharaoh, Ptolemy XIII, would give him refuge and a base from which he might be able to recruit a new army in Asia Minor and raise the resources to pay for it. The king's advisers, feeling that it was far too dangerous to become implicated in someone else's civil war on what looked like the losing side, and wishing to ingratiate themselves with the winner, had the defeated general killed even before he landed on Egyptian soil.

Caesar arrived in Alexandria on October 2 in hot pursuit. To his public disgust, but also his private relief, he was presented with Pompey's head. He refused to look at it and shed a well-judged tear; but he accepted the dead man's signet ring as evidence to send to Italy. Roman public opinion was saddened, but not surprised, when it learned a month later of the death. As Caesar remarked of Pompey during the campaign in Greece, "He does not know how to win wars."

It was at this high point of his great-uncle's career that Gaius stepped out from the shadows of childhood and joined the adult community.

# III
# A POLITICAL MASTER CLASS

## 48–46 B.C.

OCTOBER 18 IN THE YEAR 48 B.C. WAS A RED-LETTER DAY FOR Gaius. He was now fifteen, and his family had decided that the time had arrived to mark his entry into adult life.

The ceremony was a crucial rite of passage. Before leaving his house, Gaius dedicated a key symbol of his childhood to the *lares,* the divine spirits that protected a home. This symbol was the *bulla,* an amulet, usually made of gold, that hung around his neck. After the dedication, he offered the *lares* a sacrifice at the small altar and shrine in their honor in the main hall, or atrium.

Surrounded by his family, friends, and supporters, the young man stepped out of doors and walked to the Forum, Rome's main square in the city center, where he exchanged his boy's toga with the red stripe for the pure white gown of manhood, the *toga virilis.* (Only if he was elected to the Senate or to a priesthood would a man again be entitled to sport the red stripe.)

While Gaius was putting on the toga, he tore his undertunic on both sides, so that it fell to his feet, leaving him naked except for a loincloth. On the face of it this was a bad omen, but with some presence of mind, he quipped: "I shall have the whole Senatorial Order at my feet." This boyish comeback is almost certainly an invention, although it has a certain astuteness characteristic of the man into whom he grew.

Gaius had been taught to understand the importance of religious ritual; he would grow up to become a devout and superstitious traditionalist. For the Romans, religion had little to do with individual spirituality or with theological doctrine; rather, its task was to ensure that the gods were not offended and that their intentions were identified and publicized. The chief mechanism for these purposes was a complex web of rituals, including animal sacrifice.

It is hard to exaggerate the centrality of the ceremonial killing of animals to Roman religion. Animal sacrifice was a common feature of daily life, the means by which anyone could give thanks to the gods, ask them for a favor, or find out what their wishes were. Domestic animals—lambs, or young steers, or chickens—were killed in large numbers, their throats slit with a special knife and their blood gathered in a shallow dish for pouring on the altar. The meat was cooked, formally offered to the relevant god, and then eaten. Altars swam in the detritus of death.

Religious ceremonies had to be conducted with absolute accuracy; if a mistake was made or if there was some interruption—for example, if a rat squeaked or a priest's hat fell off—the entire procedure had to be repeated.

In the earliest times, the Romans were animists; that is, they believed that *numina,* spirits, lived inside all natural objects—trees, rivers, dwellings. As time passed, they settled on a list of named deities, who looked and behaved like humans. Most of them were taken to have counterparts in the gods and goddesses of ancient Greece. Rome's Jupiter was the same as Zeus; Juno, Hera; Minerva, Athena; Mercury, Hermes; Venus, Aphrodite; Mars, Ares; and so on. Apollo was the same in both languages. As the Republic's horizons expanded, equivalences were found with the deities of other, non–Greco-Roman cultures.

There were few corners of a Roman's life—whether public or private—that were not governed by ritual. Every home had a shrine to its *lares* and to its *penates,* the deities of the household stores.

In public life, a priest-king, the *rex sacrorum* (literally, "king of holy things"), performed sacrifices that had once been the king's duty. Beneath him there were two colleges of priests—the *pontifices,* or pontiffs, and, in second place, the augurs. There was no separate class of "religious" specialists, like vicars or bishops; all the priests (except for the *rex sacrorum*) were practicing politicians.

The *pontifices* decided the dates of annual festivals and kept a record of the major events of every year, the Annals. Some days were believed to be lucky (*fasti*) and some accursed (*nefasti*). Public business could be conducted only on a lucky day, and the *pontifices* decided which days fell into which category.

On major public occasions, the augurs took the "auspices," a word that originally meant "signs from birds." The augur searched for signs in the song or flight of birds, in thunder and lightning, or in the movement of animals, which he would then interpret. Portents could also be detected by consulting the Etruscan priests called *haruspices,* who examined the intestines of sacrificed animals for anything irregular or unusual. Finally, public records were kept of prodigies, extraordinary natural or supposedly supernatural events, which could range from a temple being struck by lightning to "blood" raining from the sky.

At one end of the Forum stood the circular temple of Vesta, goddess of the fire on the domestic hearth. In the temple, a sacred flame burned; in the large building behind it lived the Vestal Virgins, noble-born women sworn to chastity, who tended the flame. And adjacent the Domus Publica, Public House, was the official residence of the chief priest, or *pontifex maximus* (a title to be assumed centuries later by the Roman Catholic pope). He was the Vestals' guardian and the chairman of the college of pontiffs.

The current *pontifex maximus* was Julius Caesar. There was a vacancy in the college, and it was surely at his instance that his great-nephew was appointed to fill it on the day of his coming of age, a high honor. Immediately putting aside his brand-new *toga virilis,* Gaius assumed the garments of priestly office—a conical hat made of undressed leather, and a red-striped toga—and then conducted a public sacrifice for the first time in his life. Although the procedure was familiar, the strain on him will have been intense. Animals do not always behave predictably and, of course, every detail of the ceremony had to be correctly observed.

Gaius then made his way up the winding road that led from the Forum to the Capitol, Rome's citadel, where a great temple of Jupiter stood. Chief of the Olympian divinities, Jupiter was, above all, the god of the civic community, into which he welcomed the new citizen.

As an adult, Gaius was referred to as Octavius, the first of a number of name changes during his life, and that is what he will now be called.

Octavius had matured into a most attractive youth. He was not very tall, perhaps only five feet, six inches, but, writes Suetonius, "with body and limbs so beautifully proportioned, one did not realize how small a man he was, unless someone tall stood close to him." He had near-blond, curly hair, small teeth, and clear, bright eyes. His eyebrows met above a Roman nose, and his ears were of average size. Birthmarks on his chest and stomach resembled the Big Dipper. His health was delicate and he was prone to illness, although the ancient sources do not reveal what sort.

Nicolaus writes: "He attracted many women because of his good looks and, as a member of the Julian clan, good birth." Atia was well aware of her son's charms and, alarmed at what uninvited attentions he might attract, from men as well as from women, continued to keep Octavius firmly under her thumb. Also, thanks to the fact that his great-uncle now held the Republic in his sole control, Octavius was a personality of some importance, who might be able to exert influence on Caesar. He could easily fall victim to every kind of blandishment from those eager to court his favor, and through him that of the all-powerful dictator.

So although Octavius was now officially an adult, his mother would not allow him to leave the house any more freely than he had as a child. She kept him under strict supervision and made him sleep in the same nursery apartment as before. A Roman's life was circumscribed by numerous rituals, and Octavius attended the temples of the gods on the appropriate days, but he did so after dark to escape attention. According to Nicolaus, who knew him personally in later years, "he was of age only by law, and in other respects was taken care of as a child." Atia's fears were rational enough, but it is hard to escape the impression of a woman reluctant to see her son grow up.

Octavian was obedient, but he may have agreed with a friend of later years, the poet Horace, who observed in one of his Epistles:

> *The year*
> *Drags for orphan boys in the strict care of their mothers.*

Caesar had been mysteriously silent for more than six months until at long last, in the summer of 47 B.C., letters from him were delivered from Alexandria. He was safe and sound, but had a most curious story to tell, which had its roots in the past relationship between Egypt and Rome.

The once proud and still fabulously rich Ptolemaic kingdom had become one of the Republic's client states, theoretically independent but subject to political interference by the Senate and leading politicians. Egypt was of special importance to Rome because it was a major exporter of grain.

The ruling dynasty was not of native stock, but descended from one of

Alexander the Great's Macedonian commanders, Ptolemy. When Alexander unexpectedly died at the early age of thirty-three, he had completed the conquest of the Persian empire but had made no effective arrangements for the succession. So a huge territory, stretching from Egypt to the gates of India, was divided up among his generals. Ptolemy grabbed Egypt; he also hijacked the dead king's embalmed body on its long journey back to Macedon and installed it in a gold and glass coffin in the center of Alexandria, which the new pharaoh made his capital city. He and his successors saw themselves as Greek and showed little interest in their indigenous subjects, except as a source of wealth.

When Caesar arrived at Alexandria with a handful of troops in 48 B.C., a boy king, Ptolemy XIII, had succeeded to the throne. One of the conventions that the Macedonian Ptolemies picked up from their Egyptian predecessors was for pharaohs to marry their sisters. A habit of incest could in the long run be genetically damaging, but it had the great advantage of keeping power strictly within the family.

Ptolemy XIII was only eleven years old and not in a position to exercise power. He wedded his sister Cleopatra, who was twenty-one or twenty-two, clever, ambitious, and eager to take the reins. The court hierarchy in the palace at Alexandria was not so keen. They preferred to run the country themselves; the queen was driven out, and the pharaoh married another of his sisters, Arsinoe. Civil strife beckoned.

Caesar offered his impartial adjudication, and Cleopatra realized she needed to make her way into his presence through a ring of troops loyal to her brother if she was to influence his verdict. Together with a friend from Sicily, a merchant called Apollodorus, she embarked on a small boat and landed at the royal harbor when it was getting dark. She stretched herself out full-length inside a bed-linen sack; Apollodorus tied up the bag and carried it indoors to Caesar (in another version of the story she wrapped herself inside a carpet). According to Plutarch, "this little trick of Cleopatra's, which first showed her provocative impudence, is said to have been the first thing about her which captivated Caesar."

Caesar soon announced his judgment. Cleopatra and her brother were to reign jointly, with equal rights; while appearing equitable, in practice this shifted the balance of power from the latter to the former. Her opponents called in the royal army—an experienced force of twenty thousand soldiers—which laid siege to Caesar in the royal palace at Alexandria.

Eventually, long-expected reinforcements arrived, and on March 27

Caesar destroyed the royal army in a set-piece battle at the delta of the river Nile. The pharaoh boarded a boat to make his getaway, but the vessel was overturned by panicking soldiers trying to clamber aboard from the water. The hapless boy drowned.

It might have been supposed that, having extricated himself from a very difficult situation brought on by arrogance and carelessness, the dictator of Rome would immediately leave Egypt to conclude the civil war at home and establish his rule on a permanent basis. Nothing of the kind occurred.

Caesar, the fifty-two-year-old womanizer, had fallen for Cleopatra and they began an affair. The queen was attractive, although perhaps not conventionally beautiful. Plutarch reports:

> *As far as they say, her beauty was not in and for itself incomparable, nor such as to strike the person who was just looking at her; but her conversation had an irresistible charm; and from the one side her appearance, together with the seduction of her speech, from the other her character, which pervaded her actions in an inexplicable way when meeting people, was utterly spell-binding. The sound of her voice was sweet when she talked.*

Her appearance on coins of the period ranges from the witchlike to the radiant but does little to confirm this account of a woman whose charm was at its most powerful when she was moving or talking. However, the eyes and lips of a fine marble bust in the Berlin State Museum, which has been identified as being a portrait of her, reveal a fresh, sensuous willfulness.

The queen was very much more than a pretty face. She was highly intelligent and must have received a good education, for she was fluent in many languages, among them Ethiopian, Hebrew, Arabic, Syrian, the languages of the Medes (who lived in Babylonia, or today's Iraq) and Parthians, and (above all) Egyptian. In an interesting aside, which reveals how seriously Cleopatra took her role as queen, Plutarch notes: "Many rulers of Egypt before her had never even troubled to learn the Egyptian language, and some of them had even given up their native Macedonian dialect [in favor of regular Greek]."

Traveling with a flotilla of four hundred ships, Caesar went for a long cruise up the Nile in Cleopatra's company to look at the country, and, writes Appian, he "enjoyed himself with her in other ways as well."

Caesar left Egypt in June 47 B.C. to deal with a revolt in Asia Minor a few weeks before Cleopatra gave birth to a son, Ptolemy Caesar, derisively nicknamed by the Alexandrian mob Caesarion, or Little Caesar.

By October he was back in Rome, having been away for nine months. Largely thanks to Mark Antony's incompetence as an administrator, Italy was in disarray and the legions were in a mutinous frame of mind. Cato with fellow optimates had assembled a powerful force in Africa.

Caesar acted fast. First, he dismissed Antony and, with cold brilliance, faced down his troops. Caesar's relationship with his men was almost that of a love affair. Although from time to time they had lovers' tiffs, the soldiers adored him and he in turn was utterly loyal to them. Few deserted from his legions. This link of trust and affection to many thousands of soldiers was a political fact of the highest importance and a crucial guarantee of his power.

What is more, many of Caesar's men came not from Roman Italy but from the provinces of Cisalpine Gaul and Transalpine Gaul. Mostly they were not Roman citizens (as in principle they should have been). They had no compunctions about invading Italy and fighting Romans. They might complain about their length of service, but never about where or against whom their commander was leading them.

It was during this visit to Rome that Octavius definitely met Caesar, if he had not already done so. Caesar made up his mind quickly about people. He was impressed by Octavius, who was growing into a thoughtful and prudent young man, and detected great promise in him. He arranged for the boy to be enrolled as a patrician. The patricians were Rome's original aristocracy and were distinguished from the plebeians, who made up the rest of the population. They may originally have been the city's founding citizens; or possibly an "aristocracy of invaders" who lorded it over the native population; or a grouping of royal appointees when Rome was a kingdom. Whatever the truth of the matter, patrician status became a nobility of birth.

The symbolism of Octavius' promotion was significant. Caesar, as a Julius, was a patrician, but an Octavius, albeit connected through his mother to the Julii, was not. Without going so far as to adopt him, Octavius' great-uncle was hinting that he regarded Octavius as an honorary member of the Julian clan.

Another signal honor was conferred on the teenager: appointment as *praefectus urbi* (city prefect) during the Feriae Latinae, the Latin Festival. This important ceremony was conducted at a shrine on the Alban Mount (today's Monte Cavi) some twenty miles south of Rome. The Feriae was originally a celebration of the unity of the Latin League, an alliance of the Latin communities in Latium (Lazio); the Romans took it over for themselves when the league was incorporated into the Republic.

The festival was accompanied by a sacred truce: no battle could be fought while it was taking place. Both the consuls headed a procession from the city to the Alban Mount, on the top of which stood a very ancient shrine to Jupiter. An ox was sacrificed to the god and the victim's flesh distributed among the towns and cities that made up the community of Latins. Individual towns also offered lambs, cheeses, milk, or cakes. A symbolic game, called *oscillatio,* or swinging, was played and, back in Rome, a four-horse chariot race took place on the Capitoline Hill, the winner of which received as his prize a drink called *absynthium,* or essence of wormwood (perhaps like the absinthe of modern times mixed with wine).

In theory, the *praefectus* was in charge of the city during the consuls' absence, but the role was temporary and purely symbolic. Octavius presided over a ceremony in the Forum, where he sat on a speaker's tribunal. According to Nicolaus, many people turned up "for a sight of the boy, for he was well worth looking at."

Early in December, Caesar was to sail across to the province of Africa, where Cato and ten Pompeian legions were at large. The dictator hoped it would be his final campaign. Now in his seventeenth year, Octavius asked permission to accompany his great-uncle so that he could gain military experience. Atia opposed the idea. He said nothing by way of argument and dutifully agreed to remain at home. Caesar, too, was unwilling for him to take the field. He was worried about his great-nephew's physical fitness and feared that "he might bring on illness to a weak body through such a sharp change of life-style and so permanently injure his health."

The African campaign was by no means a walkover. Caesar quickly got into trouble, but fought his way out of it, decisively defeating the enemy near the port of Thapsus. Cato, standard-bearer of the Republic but no military man, had played little direct part in the campaign. Realizing the hopelessness of the situation, he now decided to take his own life. In this way he would avoid the humiliation of falling into Caesar's hands and, worse, having to endure a pardon. After spending the night reading the *Phaedo,* Plato's great dialogue about the last days of Socrates, he stabbed himself.

For all his intransigence and incompetence when alive, Cato's death had an enormous impact on public opinion. People remembered his principled incorruptibility, not his blunders. His shining example unforgivingly illuminated Caesar's selfishness and ambition, which threatened to destroy the centuries-old Republic.

The modern reader may be intrigued by the elite Roman's propensity to kill himself in adverse circumstances, and indeed, despite undercurrents of popular and religious disapproval, the classical world's attitude toward suicide was very different from today's.

People killed themselves in many different ways and for many different reasons, as they have done throughout history. But there was, at least among the upper classes and in military circles, what could be called a culture of suicide. In certain circumstances it was the honorable thing to do, and had about it a certain gloomy glamour.

The two main justifications for a "noble" suicide were *desperata salus* (no hope of rescue or deliverance) and *pudor* (shame). Julius Caesar in his account of his wars in Gaul gives a spectacular example of the former. Roman survivors of an ambush "had hard work to withstand the enemy's onslaught till nightfall; in the night, seeing that all hope was gone, every single man committed suicide."

In feeling *pudor,* a Roman meditating self-destruction did not so much suffer from guilt at some bad thing he had done (although this could be the case) as recognize a catastrophic collapse in his social or political standing. Such reversals of fortune happened from time to time, and for a senior politician suicide was a recognized professional hazard. It was *pudor* that did for Cato.

In July of 46 B.C., Caesar returned to Rome. Most people—including critics such as Cicero—were relieved that peace and, above all, certainty had returned. There was a widespread expectation that, if they had won, the republicans would have massacred their opponents, and even those who had been neutral in the civil war. Caesar's famous clemency, although regarded with some suspicion, contributed to an atmosphere of calm.

The Senate offered the victor new, extravagant, and unprecedented honors, which he accepted. In return Caesar followed a policy of reconciliation. According to Dio, he promised not to "take any cruel action simply because I have conquered, and am able to say exactly what I like without being called to account, and have complete freedom to do whatever I choose." He needed the cooperation of the surviving optimates to help him run the empire. He could not undertake this task single-handed, but many of his leading followers were inexperienced and unreliable. That Antony was the best of them indicates the abilities of the rest.

In fact, Caesar felt impatient and thwarted. Behind adulation, he detected dumb insolence, a reluctance to award him true loyalty. When talking to his associates, he was less than discreet. "The Republic is nothing," he said crossly, "a mere name without form or substance."

IV

# UNFINISHED BUSINESS

## 46–44 B.C.

WHAT NOW TOOK PLACE FLOWED FROM A MISMATCH OF EX-
pectations between the dictator and the political nation. The seventeen-
year-old Octavius spent a good deal of time with his great-uncle and was
able to witness the sharp contrast between public politeness and private
frustration.

He kept up with his old school friends, and, now that he had regular
and free access to Caesar, he was able to do one of them a signal favor.
Agrippa's brother had been made a prisoner of war during the African
campaign. Evidently he had fought on the republican side before and
been pardoned, for Caesar tended to punish repeat offenders. Fearing for
his brother's life, Agrippa asked Octavius to put in a good word for the
man. Octavius hesitated, for he had never yet used his special position in
this way and knew Caesar's anger with those who abused his clemency.
Taking his courage in both hands, he made the request, which Caesar
granted. This not only bound Agrippa to his friend, but won Octavius a
reputation for loyalty.

Toward the end of September there were eleven days of victory celebrations, during which Caesar held an unprecedented four triumphs on
four days. The Roman "triumph" was a military procession held by a general to mark outstanding success in a campaign against a foreign enemy.
The dictator planned to mark the conquest of Gaul, the brief Egyptian
war, the even briefer Asian war, and the defeat of Juba, the king of the
northern African kingdom of Numidia. Juba was a stand-in for Cato and
the republican army, Caesar's real opponents: a fact that could not be
openly admitted because they had been Roman citizens, with whom it
was forbidden to go to war.

It so happened that Octavius' seventeenth birthday fell during this
festival of triumphs, on September 23; to honor his great-nephew, Caesar

invited Octavius to accompany him in the parade for the African war and awarded him service medals as if he had actually served on his staff during the campaign. The day of the triumph will have been one of the most exciting in Octavius' life so far. Here were fame and glory manifest, the ultimate prize to which a Roman could aspire.

The ceremony opened in the Campus Martius, the field of the war god, Mars, an open space northwest of the city (stretching roughly from today's Piazza Venezia to Vatican City). This was originally the exercise ground of the army, but a number of important public buildings now dotted the area. One of these was the temple of Bellona, goddess of war and sister of Mars. The Senate met there to receive the victorious commander before following his triumphal procession into the city.

On the day of the triumph, Caesar arrayed himself in some of the attributes of Jupiter, king of the gods and protector of Rome. His face was smeared with the same red paint that covered the great statue of Jupiter on the Capitoline Hill. Underneath an embroidered toga, he wore a purple tunic interwoven with gold and embroidered with palm leaves, a symbol of victory.

After making a speech and presenting military awards and decorations, Caesar reviewed the troops. These were then marshaled in column of route, and Caesar mounted a gilded chariot. A slave stood on the chariot with him, to hold a golden crown above his head and say in his ear that he was mortal. Octavius rode proudly behind on a horse.

The procession moved off in the direction of the city. The Senate led the way, after which came trumpeters and garlanded white oxen with gilded horns; the oxen would be sacrificed later. Then followed the spoils of war and floats with tableaux and paintings illustrating highlights of the African campaign. These caused outrage, Octavius noticed. One of the paintings carried on the floats depicted the republican general Quintus Caecilius Metellus Pius Scipio stabbing himself in the chest and then throwing himself into the sea; in another, worse still, Cato was shown tearing himself apart like a wild animal. It would have been far wiser to avoid any mention of battles fought by Romans against Romans, but Caesar had still not forgiven his old opponent Cato for evading his forgiveness. As the floats were driven along the narrow city streets the crowd, too intimidated by the soldiery to do more, groaned.

Finally, Caesar and his legions arrived. The soldiers, carrying sprays of laurel, exercised their traditional privilege of singing satirical and sometimes ribald songs about their commander. They had a good deal to say about his reputation for philandering.

On the Capitoline, the ceremonies drew to a close with a mass sacrifice of the oxen, followed by a banquet in the Temple of Jupiter. To the sound of flutes, Caesar was escorted home to the Domus Publica, the official residence of the *pontifex maximus*.

The triumphs were interspersed with a varied diet of extremely costly spectacles, including theater and dance performances and chariot races in a stadium called the Circus Maximus beneath the Palatine Hill. The most popular attraction in a crowded program of events was a gladiatorial contest. Such contests were usually held in the Forum, where a temporary wooden arena was erected above a network of tunnels beneath the pavement. In these tunnels the gladiators would wait for their turn in the arena.

It is very hard to understand the appeal of killing human beings as entertainment. In the developed world, few people regularly encounter physical violence, but in premodern societies, as in the developing world today, pain, disease, and the frequency of sudden or premature death were routine and expected. Against this background, Rome's imperial success rested on a culture of military prowess. War was glorious. Young men were trained to inflict and to endure violent death, and to value personal heroism above most other virtues. Indeed, *virtus,* from which the English word derives, not only encompassed manliness and moral excellence but conjoined these to the concept of physical courage.

The gladiatorial shows had originated centuries before, as human sacrifices, conducted in the community's most sacred space, the Forum. Before it became a public square, the Forum was a marshy area where the villagers who lived on the surrounding hills buried their dead; perhaps a faint memory of this primary function survived in people's minds. The victims' blood sank between the flagstones to slake the thirst of the *manes,* the spirits of the dear departed who lived a sad, otherwise bloodless life in the underworld.

Most gladiators (the name comes from the Latin for sword, *gladius*) were slaves, but some citizens joined a gladiatorial troupe of their own free will. The profession gave asylum to social outcasts, the dispossessed, the bankrupt, and men on the run. Free fighters were much sought after, presumably because they performed with more zest than those who did so under compulsion. A volunteer won a bonus if he survived to the end of his contract. The contract was a fearsome document, threatening any who broke it with burning, shackling, whipping with rods, and killing with steel. In effect, it made a temporary slave of the signatory.

Successful gladiators became household names. On the one hand, they were the lowest of the low, ranking alongside male prostitutes and the worst categories of criminal, such as the parricide, and had lost all their *dignitas* as human beings. On the other hand, they were sexy pinups, as the graffiti at Pompeii show: Celadus the Thracian was "a girl's heart throb and shining delight," and Crescens the *retiarius* (net fighter) "every virgin's doctor in the night."

Some promoters were proud of allowing no losers to escape death, although this would make the games much more expensive; these contests were called *munera sine missione,* games without quarter. The death rate in the gladiatorial profession is unknown, but it was probably lower than bloodthirsty descriptions would imply. There is evidence of fighters surviving many bouts, eventually receiving their freedom (symbolized by a wooden sword) and retiring into provincial respectability. In this sanguinary form of live theater, an imaginative impresario could stage-manage suspense and copious blood without excessive mortality.

Another spectacle that drew the crowds was the wild-beast hunt, or *venatio.* All kinds of animal were captured in different corners of the empire and brought back to Rome to end their lives in the arena. Thousands could be killed in a day. Men armed with spears, bows, daggers, and even firebrands, and sometimes accompanied by packs of hounds, battled with terrified and enraged panthers and lions, leopards and tigers. Red cloths were waved in front of bulls, in a precursor of the modern Spanish bullfight. Other creatures that were hunted, if more rarely, included hippopotami, ostriches, and crocodiles. Caesar staged five *venationes* during the festivities, in one of which he pitted elephants against each other. In addition, he imported six hundred lions and four hundred other large cats.

It was widely noticed that at the theatrical events and public banquets, Octavius was invariably in attendance on his great-uncle, who treated him as affectionately as if he were his own son. At sacrifices and when entering temples for religious rituals, he kept the young man by his side and he arranged for others taking part in these public occasions to give him precedence.

Increasingly, suppliants approached Octavius and asked him to intercede for them with Caesar in one way or another. His success with Agrippa's brother and his growing familiarity with the dictator gave him the courage to put forward requests, which seem to have been invariably granted. This was, in large part, because of the tactful approach he adopted. Nicolaus observes: "He took care never to ask a favour at an inopportune moment, nor when it was annoying to Caesar."

Caesar decided it was time to give the young man some administrative experience. He turned over to him the responsibility for managing the theatrical program of the triumphal celebrations. Keen to show his commitment, Octavius stayed to the end of all the performances, even on the hottest and longest days. This strained his already delicate health and he fell seriously ill.

Caesar was beside himself with anxiety and, to cheer him up, visited the sufferer every day or sent friends in his place. Doctors were in permanent attendance. On one occasion a message came while he was dining that Octavius had suffered a serious relapse and was in danger of dying. The dictator leaped up at once and ran barefooted to the house where Octavius lay. Frantic and deeply upset, he cross-examined the doctors about their patient's prognosis and then sat down by the boy's bedside. Gradually Octavius recovered, but he remained weak for some time.

The nature of Octavius' illness on this occasion is not known; it may have been a severe bout of sunstroke.

The triumphs were quickly followed by Cleopatra's arrival in Rome as Caesar's houseguest. Her journey from Egypt was delayed until after the Egyptian triumph. One of the captives in the procession had been her sister Arsinoe, who had been briefly recognized as queen by the Alexandrians before falling into Caesar's hands, but, although she loathed her, Cleopatra had not wished to witness her sibling led in chains and her kingdom presented as a vanquished power.

The queen was accompanied by the youngest of her brothers, and new husband, the fifteen-year-old Ptolemy XIV, and, it may be assumed, a substantial retinue. Doubtless she was accompanied by her baby son, Caesarion. Caesar lodged them all in his mansion set in lovely gardens (his *hortus*) on the other side of the Tiber near the southeastern corner of the Janiculum Hill. Here Cleopatra held court and received Rome's senior politicians. Her airs and graces of royalty did not go down well among Rome's determinedly republican elite, even when accompanied by lavish presents and cultivated entertainments. Men like the orator Cicero cordially disliked her, for all the queen's efforts to ingratiate herself.

It may be surmised that Cleopatra returned the compliment, with equal cordiality. Her mind-set was irredeemably autocratic. Nothing in her life had prepared her for the noisy bear pit of Roman politics and for competing aristocrats who refused to acknowledge that anyone was superior to them. Back in Alexandria her response to dissent was to use force and she must have been bewildered by Caesar's policy of clemency.

Neither Caesar's wife, Calpurnia, nor the convalescent Octavius has left a recorded opinion of the Egyptian interloper, but neither can have been pleased by the presence of a rival for both his affections and his limited time.

It turned out, maddeningly, that the fighting was not over after all. The two sons of Pompey the Great, Gnaeus and Sextus, aged about thirty and sixteen respectively, had extricated themselves from the African debacle and made their way to Spain, where their father had had a large and faithful *clientela*.

The client system was a crucial feature of Roman life and politics. A powerful Roman was a patron, or protector, for many hundreds or even thousands of clients, not just in Rome and Italy, but also across the Mediterranean. These networks of mutual aid cut across social classes and linked Romans to people in the provinces.

Clientship was not legally binding, but its rules were almost always obeyed. A patron's client list lasted from generation to generation and was handed down from father to son.

A patron looked after his clients' interests. He would help them out by giving them food, money, or small parcels of land, or by standing up for them if they got into trouble with the law. In return, clients were expected to support their patron in any way they could—voting as he wished at assemblies and campaigning on his behalf when he stood for office. In Rome, clients would pay their respects at their patron's house every morning and walk with him to the Forum.

Gradually Gnaeus raised an army of thirteen legions, although many of these were inexperienced Spaniards. The dictator's legates in Spain were unable to make headway against the rebels; by the beginning of November 46 B.C., it became clear that Caesar's personal intervention was required to put out a fire that had reignited and was blazing out of control.

At short notice, Caesar set off for yet another campaign. Rome, once again, was left waiting for news.

Caesar had hoped to have Octavius accompany him to Spain; this time, there seems to have been no parental objection. Now in his eighteenth year, he was no longer a child, and for those of his social class the next step in one's education was a spell of service on a general's staff. Evasion would have been seen as evidence of cowardice.

Unfortunately, the young man had not yet fully recovered from his illness; his great-uncle told him to follow as soon as he was well enough. Anxious to leave Rome as soon as possible, Octavius gave his full attention to restoring his health. Even before he was perfectly well, he made arrangements for his journey—in his words, "according to my uncle's instructions," for that was how he referred to Caesar when he sought prompt compliance with his demands.

Many volunteers wanted to join his expedition, including (to his intense embarrassment, we may guess) his mother. Like many parents of children with a weak constitution, Atia was finding it difficult to let go of her grown-up son. In the event, Octavius selected a very small escort from among his strongest and speediest servants. He was also accompanied by three of his closest companions, among them, it can be assumed, his dear friend Agrippa.

He had a dangerous journey. It is not known exactly when he set out or which route he took. During the winter months, sailing was unsafe, and it is plausible that he left Rome in February or March and followed the land route via southern France. Once Octavius had reached Spain, though, he would have encountered signs of the enemy, who dominated the north, and of brigands, too. He may then have taken his courage in both hands and boarded a ship at Tarraco (today's Tarragona).

Despite the risky weather it would be safer to sail down the coast to Nova Carthago (Cartageña), which, all being well, would still be in Caesar's hands and where he would be fairly sure either to find him or at least to establish his whereabouts. This was a sensible decision, but sailing anywhere in the winter months could be dangerous. Boats seldom drew more than three hundred tons and were often struck by sudden Mediterranean squalls; the compass not having been invented, sailors tended to hug the coasts. Presumably a storm did overtake Octavius, for he apparently suffered a shipwreck before reaching his destination.

He and his small party arrived to find the war over and Caesar victorious. Once again he had missed the chance to blood himself in a real battle. He soon briefed himself on the lightning campaign:

After some maneuvering, the two armies had met at Munda (near Osuna in southern Spain) on March 5, 45 B.C. Caesar was a commander of genius; he was decisive, brave, and, even in the heat of battle capable of creative thinking. He understood the importance of luck in war, and he worked hard to earn it. In particular, he prided himself on his *celeritas*, moving his forces with great speed and turning up where and when the enemy least expected him. His weakness was an occasional overconfidence, but he always managed to extricate himself from problems of his own making. For once, though, there had been no refinements of strategy, no brilliant insights on the battlefield by the commander. Munda had been a blood-soaked slog.

Most of the Pompeian leaders died fighting and their heads were brought to Caesar for his inspection. There was no revulsion now, one notes, as had been the case when Pompey the Great's head had been presented to him in Egypt. Gnaeus escaped the battle, but was quickly caught and killed. His head, too, found its way to the victor, who had it displayed to the crowd to prove the death, and then buried.

Nobody was greatly bothered when it was noticed that Gnaeus' little brother, Sextus, had slipped away and disappeared from view. He was surely too young and inexperienced to cause trouble. Sooner or later the boy would turn up and there would be plenty of time to deal with him then.

About the battle, Caesar remarked wryly: "I have often fought for victory, but on this occasion I fought for my life as well."

Octavius eventually caught up with Caesar near a town called Caepia, where he was presumably still conducting mopping-up operations. The busy general was delighted and surprised to see his great-nephew and enfolded him in a warm embrace. In fact, he would not let Octavius out of his sight, but made him live in his own quarters and share his mess. He complimented the young man on his enthusiasm and loyalty—and also will have remarked on his astuteness, for he was among the first of what would become a flood of dignitaries making their way from Rome to greet, and sometimes make their peace with, the all-conquering dictator.

Octavius had not waited, as others had, for the outcome of the war before setting out on a long and dangerous expedition.

During the month or so before leaving Spain, Caesar went out of his way to get to know his great-nephew better. According to Nicolaus, "He made a point of engaging him in conversation, for he was anxious to make a trial of his understanding, and finding that he was sagacious, intelligent, and concise in his replies, and that he always answered to the point, his esteem and affection for him increased." As the weeks passed, Caesar gradually came to a final, firm, and highly positive view of his young relative.

Years later, Octavius' enemies claimed that he slept with his great-uncle in return for his favor and affection. It is true that Octavius was a pretty boy, that Caesar may have been sexually omnivorous, and that Roman laws against incest prohibited only sexual relations between paternal kin. However, military campaigns are not an ideal setting for romance, and sex between soldiers was an offense: a wise commander would not break the rules he expected the rank and file to obey. Had there been anything much in the story, it would surely have been common gossip at the time and received wider and earlier currency in contemporary accounts.

Caesar's next destination was Nova Carthago; he arranged for Octavius to board the same boat as his, together with five of his personal slaves. Without seeking permission, Octavius could not resist slipping his three closest companions aboard as well. Doubtless the journey was to be in a naval galley, where most of the limited space below decks was taken up by rows of oarsmen and space was at a premium. Not unnaturally, Octavius feared that his great-uncle would be cross, but there was no trouble. Caesar approved of Octavius' friends, whom he found to be observant, enthusiastic, and competitive. It was good that Octavius liked to have them around him—partly for protection, but also to enhance his own reputation as someone supported by men of good sense.

Caesar had to decide everything and, like rulers in all ancient, prebureaucratic societies, he was obliged to spend much time receiving petitions, agreeing on and bestowing awards and rewards, and adjudicating quarrels. Octavius was able to help. He had already learned the art of mediating between his great-uncle and the rest of the world, every member of which seemed to have an urgent demand.

A long queue of petitioners sought Octavius' good offices, as they had done a few months previously in Rome. This role of benevolent broker had surely been agreed in advance between him and the dictator, partly to smooth the conduct of business but also as on-the-job training in public administration.

At last it was time to go home—to Calpurnia and Cleopatra, to Atia and Philippus. The civil war *was* definitely over. No enemy was left standing. What now? This was a hard question to answer. At the pinnacle of his success, Caesar should have had little on his mind to trouble him. But like so many conquerors before and after, he had learned the hard lesson that military victory does not necessarily win consent from the vanquished.

The army soon encountered streams of noble Romans approaching from the opposite direction. Everyone of importance had felt it necessary to take to the road and greet the Republic's new master. At Narbo (today's Narbonne), Mark Antony arrived, to find that his misgovernment of Italy in 49 B.C. had been forgiven. So far as Caesar was concerned, their quarrel was over. He invited Antony to ride with him, displacing Octavius, who traveled in the following carriage with another Caesarian supporter, Decimus Junius Brutus Albinus.

Under the pressure of the dictator's displeasure, the reprobate appeared to have turned over a new leaf, toned down his public extravagances, and directed his thoughts to marriage. His eye lighted on Fulvia, the widow first of a murdered gang leader, and then of a Caesarian tribune. The alliance was as much political as personal. According to one ancient commentator, she had "nothing womanly about her except for her body." Intelligent and intemperate, she was able, and more than willing, to give her new husband some sensible career guidance.

The dictator and his entourage arrived in northern Italy in July. He planned to hold a triumph in October, but the legal fiction that it marked a victory over a foreign enemy was embarrassingly unconvincing. Nevertheless, he observed the convention that a conquering general had to remain outside Rome until the date of his processional entry into the city.

He made for an estate of his southeast of Rome at Labici (today's Monte Compatri), where he spent a few weeks. Here he was able to find some peace and quiet, and time for thought. For years, he had been extraordinarily busy, fighting or legislating, and he needed a holiday. He was aware, too, that his health was deteriorating; his proneness to what may have been a form of epilepsy, or spells of dizziness, was getting worse. He was reported to have had a fit in Africa and another on the day of the battle of Munda.

It is probable that Octavius stayed with him for a while. Their relationship was becoming closer and closer, and Octavius, who had tested his physical stamina to the limit, would have profited from a rest as well. At some point he asked leave to go home to see his mother, who had doubtless pressed him to do so in a letter, and Caesar gave his permission.

Although he was approaching his eighteenth birthday, Octavius retreated into domesticity. After the excitements of his Spanish adventure, his life became quiet and uneventful. He spent much of his time with his mother and stepfather, seldom leaving them. Occasionally he invited some of his young friends to dinner, Agrippa and Maecenas presumably among them. He lived soberly and moderately. Nicolaus reports that, unlike many upper-class young Romans, especially those with access to money, he abstained from "sexual gratification."

Octavius' good behavior is as likely to reflect a concern for his health as a virtuous disposition. This was an age when the principles of hygiene were little understood, surgery was life-threatening, medicines and medical advice were of uncertain value, and few illnesses were easily cured. Unsurprisingly, many Romans concentrated their attention on prevention. According to Celsus, a medical expert who wrote in the first century A.D., a healthy man "should sail, hunt, rest sometimes, but more often take exercise." He should spend time in the countryside and on the farm as well as in town. Doctors advised that people whose health was delicate should take care to avoid any kind of physical excess. We may take it that Octavius and his ever-anxious mother did exactly that.

Caesar set in motion a flurry of important social and economic measures, but he was wearying of Rome with its tiresome and self-destructive politics. He had received reports of a conspiracy against his life. If he had ever intended to reform and restore the constitution, he now gave up the attempt. He would leave Rome to its own devices, for power lay wherever he happened to be, not in the Senate House or Forum. He was worried by the growth of a Dacian empire in the untamed region of the southern Danube. The barbarians there needed to be taught a sharp military lesson.

Also, the Parthian empire had been restive since Crassus' failed invasion of 53 B.C. Once the Dacians were dealt with, Caesar decided to lead a great punitive expedition against it. He began to assemble an army of sixteen legions and ten thousand cavalry; six thousand troops had already crossed over to Greece and, encamped near the city of Apollonia, awaited the launch of the campaign the following March. He expected to be away for three years.

Since the victory in Spain, the Senate had awarded him ever more extravagant honors. Caesar was allowed to add the word *imperator,* "commander in chief," to his name as a hereditary addition (until then it had been awarded by soldiers in the field after an important victory); likewise, his son or adopted son was to be designated *pontifex maximus* on his death. These two heavy hints pointed to the possible establishment of a dynasty, even if no obvious successor existed, or was even on the horizon.

The dictator loved women but begot few children; the only known offspring had been a beloved daughter, Julia, and (one assumes) Caesarion. If he had no legitimate son himself, he would have to find somebody else's. Adoption was common in Roman life, a strategy for binding clans to one another, as well as for making good genetic deficits. Kinship and loyalty to the *familia* and *gens* were valued very highly, but little attention was paid to strict blood ties. Men often adopted the grown sons of others.

Octavius will have pondered these matters. Where, if at all, did he fit into this glorious future? Might he, at some stage, be designated his great-uncle's heir? These were daydreams. The dictator showed no sign of leaving the stage, and even if he were to do so, Octavius was far too young and inexperienced to step into his giant shoes. If Caesar lived another ten years, and if Octavius proved himself worthy of responsibility, then, just possibly, he might be seen as a potential ruler with all the *gravitas* and *auctoritas* such a figure would have to command. . . . For now, though, Octavius had more immediate matters to engage his attention.

The dictator was burdened with business, but he did not forget his great-nephew. He decided that the boy would accompany him on the great Parthian campaign planned for the next spring. Toward the end of 45 B.C., he sent him to Apollonia. There the young man would spend four months completing his education in literature and public speaking.

He would also undertake training with the army, as it awaited its general and the long march to the east. At last Octavius would acquire some military experience.

# V

# A BOY WITH A NAME

## 44 B.C.

THE RUINS OF APOLLONIA LIE NOT FAR FROM THE COAST OF southern Albania, about a hundred miles north of the island of Corcyra (today's Corfu) and fifty or so south of the port of Dyrrachium (formerly the Epidamnus familiar to readers of Thucydides).

The city stood on an extended hill overlooking the river Aous, where the remains of its ancient perimeter walls can still be seen. Today the marble columns of the council chamber, and a street with a central stone pavement on an extended hill overlooking the Aous, are evidence that the place thrived in antiquity. In spring, this part of the site is smothered in wildflowers. Not far away are the foundations of a public bath and a large *stoa,* or roofed colonnade. A small theater, or odeon, with seats for six hundred, has had its steps restored and is used for modern concerts. A larger theater, seating 7,500, is in a poor state of repair.

The small acropolis at the far end of the city, where a few olive trees grow, gives a spectacular view of the surrounding landscape; originally it housed a temple, probably dedicated to Apollo or his sister, Artemis.

Apollonia, although little remembered today, was what Cicero called a "great and important city." Founded in the seventh century B.C., for many years it was a place of no very great significance, because it gave access only to the turbulent tribes of Illyria and Macedonia. Italians traveling to Greece or the Middle East found it easier and safer to make their way by sea from Brundisium.

However, Rome needed a fast and reliable connection between Italy and its new provinces, especially for the safe and speedy movement of armies. So in 130 B.C. the Via Egnatia was built. This highway, linked by a loop road to Dyrrachium and Apollonia, transformed the strategic importance of the two ports. It ran along a river into high uplands, skirted two mountain lakes, and descended to a plain near Thessalonica on the seacoast. It then followed the littoral to the small town of Philippi and on to the Hellespont (the Dardanelles).

In late 45 B.C., the eighteen-year-old Gaius Octavius settled into lodgings at Apollonia. He was accompanied by Agrippa and another early friend, Quintus Salvidienus Rufus, who was older than Agrippa and, like him, not of noble blood; also, perhaps, by Maecenas. Little is known of Salvidienus' origins, but he may have been an officer of Caesar's. Perhaps Octavius got to know and like him in Spain; in any event, he was one of the small group of intimates on whom he depended.

The young men exercised with squadrons of cavalry. By virtue of his kinship with the dictator, Octavius was of high status, and senior officers used to call on him. He gave everyone a warm welcome and was popular both in the city and in army circles. He was given good reports by his instructors.

Apollonia housed a well-known school for public speaking (or rhetoric), comparable with those at Athens and Rhodes. Octavius studied there, and read Greek and Roman literature. He wanted to become proficient in Greek as well as Latin, and he was an assiduous student. As well as literature, he studied elocution. He brought with him a tutor from Rome, Apollodorus of Pergamum, one of the most celebrated teachers of the day, although a very old man.

The month of March, 44 B.C., would soon be over. The legions were in a high state of readiness. Julius Caesar was expected any day now, and would soon lead them against Parthia.

Then, one afternoon, a messenger arrived with an urgent letter for Octavius, just as he and his companions were going into dinner. A freedman of Octavius' mother, the man was in a state of high excitement and dismay. No wonder, for Atia had terrible news to tell. Writing on March 15, 44 B.C., she reported that Julius Caesar had been assassinated at Rome before midday by Marcus Brutus, Gaius Cassius Longinus, and others. She asked Octavius to return to her as she had no idea what would happen next. According to Nicolaus, she wrote: "You must show yourself a man now and consider what you ought to do, and implement your plans as fortune and opportunity allow."

The freedman confirmed the contents of the letter, saying that a large number of people had taken part in the murder, and they intended to hunt down and massacre all Caesar's relatives.

In no time, rumors spread through Apollonia that some catastrophe had taken place, although no one was entirely sure what. After sunset, a delegation of distinguished Apollonians, carrying torches and followed by numerous curious bystanders, presented themselves at Octavius' front door. They asked, as his well-wishers, what news had come. To avoid setting off a panic, Octavius decided to answer only the leaders of the group, who with some difficulty persuaded the rest to disperse and then, having learned what had happened, eventually departed as well.

Sitting in lamplight, he and his small circle of inexperienced friends spent the rest of the night talking and talking. What was to be done? One line of thought was that they ought to join the army outside the city. Octavius should persuade its commander, Marcus Acilius Glabrio, to let him lead the troops to Rome, where they would take revenge on his great-uncle's murderers. The soldiers had loved Caesar and would loathe his killers. Their sympathy would increase when they met his young, now defenseless relative.

But the cautious Octavius felt that he was too inexperienced to carry off a bold action of this kind. Too much was uncertain, too little known. He would wait for further news.

Soon another letter from Atia and Octavius' stepfather arrived. They advised him not to get overexcited or overconfident yet, but to bear in mind what Caesar, who had eliminated all his enemies, suffered at the hands of his closest friends. He should, at least temporarily, take the less dangerous course of acting like a private citizen. The letter repeated Atia's earlier advice to return to Rome quickly and quietly.

This must have struck Octavius as rather odd. Why should Atia and Philippus suppose that their mild-mannered and totally inexperienced son should be considering bold measures? It was too soon for them to have heard back from Octavius about any proposal to invade Italy, even if he had decided to discuss it with them. There is only one plausible answer to the puzzle: his family were aware that Caesar's closest supporters—his personal friends and his kitchen cabinet of aides and advisers—were talking about Octavius at Rome, and were planning a political role for him of some sort. One or more of them must have written to him, telling him of the bitter gloom into which the dictator's inner circle of professionals had been plunged, and of their determination somehow or another to fight back. They knew or guessed that the now leaderless army was enraged, but impotent; and that the city mob, after a day or two of stunned silence, bitterly missed the one politician on whom they could depend to protect their interests. What had happened was not a revolution, but a coup from above.

Since Octavius' departure from Rome a few months previously, letters and correspondents must have made him aware that the atmosphere had steadily deteriorated even before the assassination. Now dispatches gave him the details of how his great-uncle had died.

The dictator's position was simultaneously impermeably strong and invisibly very weak. Romans were enormously proud of the Republic formed after the expulsion of the kings in the sixth century B.C. The *bien-pensant* ruling class expected Caesar, having won his civil war and being in complete control of Rome and its empire, to reinstall Rome's traditional constitution.

But many were beginning to suspect that Caesar had no intention of doing this. His critics believed that, with an insatiable desire for total power, he was set on establishing a monarchy; they decided that the time for talking had passed. A conspiracy was formed, led by former enemies in the civil war, leading members of the regime, and even close friends.

Caesar himself almost certainly did not aim at kingship. However, he realized that his reconciliation policy had failed. The gap between him and Romans of the old school was unbridgeable and, seeing no point in disguising his power, in February of 44 B.C. he had himself declared dictator for life. For the plotters, this was the clinching proof of their worst fears. The tyrant had to be struck down before he left for the east.

The dictator was due to quit Rome on March 18 to join his legions in Greece. He was to meet the Senate for a final time before his departure three days earlier, on the Ides of March. (The Roman month lasted either twenty-nine or thirty-one days; "Ides" was the name for the thirteenth or the fifteenth, depending on the month's length.) The meeting with the Senate took place in Pompey's theater on the Campus Martius. Caesar did not arrive until about eleven o'clock in the morning. He was not in the best of form; there had been a storm the night before, and both he and his wife, Calpurnia, had slept badly. She said she had had a dream portending disaster.

Caesar entered the meeting hall and took his seat at one end, on his special chair between the seats of the two consuls. One of these was Antony, but he was delayed in the anteroom by a conspirator. In spite of his closeness to Caesar, he knew that the assassination was being planned; he had treacherously kept the information to himself. Before the session opened, a large number of senators pressed around the dictator presenting various pleas. They were all members of the plot.

One of them grabbed the dictator's purple toga to stop him from getting up or using his hands. "Why, this is violence!" he shouted. Someone stabbed him from behind, but he managed to struggle to his feet and turn round to grab his assailant's hand. Men pressed around Caesar in a tight scrum as each tried to stab him; in the process, a number of the assassins accidentally cut one another.

The wounded victim twisted from side to side, bellowing like a wild animal. He was amazed to see in the throng Marcus Junius Brutus, the son of his favorite mistress, Servilia, and a man of whom he had grown very fond. After Brutus had delivered his blow, Caesar saw that further struggle was pointless. He wound himself in his toga so that he would be decently covered, and fell neatly at the base of the statue of Pompey the Great. He was later found to have received twenty-three wounds, of which only one had been fatal.

Within a day or so, Octavius decided to follow his parents' advice that he should set sail for Italy. He had become a well-lived figure in Apollonia and many of its citizens came to his house begging him to stay. He would be safe with them in a dangerous world. When he insisted on leaving, a large crowd escorted him to the quay.

Octavius had discovered that the legions he had met in Greece were on his side; on his way to Rome he intended to test opinion among the troops who had been waiting at Brundisium to accompany Caesar across the Adriatic. Having no idea what their reception would be, the small band of friends made landfall a little way from Brundisium, near a small town off the main road called Lupiae (today's Lecce, in Puglia), to which they walked. There they met people who had been in Rome when Caesar had been buried. This had been a sensational occasion.

The dead dictator had lain in state in the Forum, where Mark Antony, who had briefly gone into hiding, gave a eulogy. The mob, infuriated by the assassination, went berserk. They burned down the Senate House and looted the shopping arcades on either side of the Forum, dragging out anything combustible and building an enormous makeshift pyre. Caesar was cremated on the spot.

The conspirators, or *liberatores* (freedom fighters) as they liked to call themselves, had had no other agenda apart from their act of violence. They supposed that once Caesar had been eliminated, the Republic would automatically come back into being. Peace, order, and constitutional government would resume without any further intervention on their part. This was a disastrous error in judgment, as Brutus and his friends now realized. They hurriedly left the city, where they were no longer safe, and dispersed to their country estates.

Hearing what had happened at the funeral and remembering his great-uncle and his affection for him, Octavius burst into tears.

The young man now received an even more extraordinary piece of news. Unbeknownst to him, Caesar had written a new will during the brief Italian holiday on his return from Spain in 45 B.C., and had lodged it with the Vestal Virgins (who ran a safe deposit service for important confidential documents). Three days after Caesar's death, his father-in-law, Lucius Calpurnius Piso Caesoninus, read out the testament at the house of the consul Mark Antony, on the Palatine Hill.

Caesar named as his chief heirs his sisters' two male grandchildren, one of whom was Octavius, and a nephew, Quintus Pedius. After certain legacies had been deducted, including an expensive commitment to give three hundred sesterces to every Roman citizen (there could be as many as 300,000 beneficiaries), two of the inheritors each received an eighth of the residue—and Octavius received the remaining three quarters. Added to the personal fortune we must presume he inherited from his father, this would make him a very rich man.

The Roman people received another gift: Caesar's garden estate across the Tiber, presently occupied by Cleopatra, who was busy packing her bags for a rapid exit to Egypt.

At the end of the document came the greatest surprise. Caesar adopted Octavius as his son (although it was unusual to make such an arrangement from beyond the grave, it was possible, requiring only that a special law be passed, a *lex curiata*). The adoption was a personal, not a political, act. However, Caesar was handing Octavius a priceless weapon: his name and his *clientela,* all those hundreds of thousands of soldiers and citizens who were in his debt. As he must have known, he was giving the boy an opportunity to enter politics at the top if he wished to do so—and if he had sufficient talent.

The troops at Brundisium came out to meet Octavius on the news of his approach. They greeted him enthusiastically as Caesar's son. Much relieved, he conducted a sacrifice and made the crucial decision to accept his inheritance. More letters from Atia and Philippus awaited him. His mother repeated her request that he come home as soon as possible; his designation as Caesar's son had placed him in grave danger. Meanwhile, the fence-sitting Philippus strongly advised him to take no steps to secure Caesar's bequest, and to keep his own name. If he wanted to live safely, he should steer clear of politics. Philippus could foresee the political strife in which his family would be implicated if the boy was to assume his dangerous inheritance.

All his life, Octavius had been risk-averse; now he acted without hesitation. He rejected his stepfather's advice, and wrote to him saying so. According to Nicolaus, he insisted that he "already had his eyes on great things and was full of confidence." He would accept the legacy, avenge his "father"'s death, and succeed to Caesar's power. This was an uncompromising statement of his political aims.

Although it would be some months before the legal formalities of adoption could be put into effect, Gaius Octavius styled himself from now on as Gaius Julius Caesar Octavianus. The change from Octavius to Octavianus signaled a transfer from one family to another, but contained a reminder of his original kin; he soon dropped it and insisted on being addressed as Caesar. This was a message to his enemies that if one Caesar was destroyed another would immediately arise to fill his place. (To avoid confusion, I follow the convention of calling him Octavian, an anglicized version of the name he himself rejected.)

Here was the first great challenge of Octavian's life, a once-and-for-all turning point, and he met it with calm decisiveness. We do not have enough information about his childhood and adolescence to speak definitively, but certain early experiences may have contributed to the formation of his firm and careful character and equipped him for a dangerous future.

Octavian was in effect an only child (his sisters were much older than he). This, when combined with poor health and a very protective mother, will have given him a sense of being set apart. He was "different" or special in two other, contradictory respects. On the one hand, he was a boy from the provinces, not a member of the handful of great and ancient clans that governed Rome. It is telling that his best friends were not young *nobiles;* Agrippa's background was Italian and obscure, and, while Maecenas boasted an exotic Etruscan origin, his family remained aloof from public life and was content with equestrian status.

On the other hand, Octavian trumped his aristocratic contemporaries by having privileged access to the patrician conqueror of the Republic. He was, in real life, the outsider-insider of fairy tale and childish fantasy—a shepherd's son who turns out to be of royal blood; like Rome's founders, Romulus and Remus.

Nicolaus, who gives the fullest account of Octavian's early years, portrays an adolescent still treated as a child, then pitchforked into adult life under the tutelage of his remarkable great-uncle. Suddenly he found himself at the gorgeous, exhilarating power center of the Roman world. The relationship with Caesar became the most important one in his life.

When confronted with such opportunity, many boys would have lost their heads. Not Octavian. As an intermediary between Caesar and multitudes of suppliants, he took care not to irritate his great-uncle with untimely requests, he was discreet and totally loyal, and he behaved in a modest and friendly manner with petitioners.

Octavian may have had an innately cautious cast of mind; but if environmental factors helped to shape him, this was the kind of behavior one would expect to find in an intelligent boy whose circumstances and upbringing fostered self-containment.

Octavian now proceeded to Capua and Rome along the Via Appia. He attracted large crowds, especially of demobilized veterans who were grief-stricken by the Ides of March and wanted the killers brought to justice.

Before entering Rome, Octavian called in at his parents' seaside villa at Puteoli (now Pozzuoli), which happened to be next to a house belonging to Cicero. He needed to come to an understanding with his family, who were worried by the direction he was taking. The suspicious old orator noted that the young man's "followers call him Caesar, but Philippus does not, and neither do I."

This was the first chance for Octavian to meet Caesar's disconsolate aides and advisers. Mostly *equites* or freedmen, who could not aspire to political careers of their own, they had no political constituency and with their employer's death had lost their purchase on power. Octavian had a long conversation with Lucius Cornelius Balbus, a multimillionaire from Spain, who had run Caesar's secretariat and been his leading fixer. There are no records of their discussions, but we can surmise that Balbus and his colleagues wanted to make a cool assessment of the teenage heir, and then to lay a plan of campaign. We can be sure that, from the outset, these Caesarians had every intention of demolishing the restored Republic and taking revenge on the conspirators. However, they would have to wait and see whether the young man was capable of heading a new autocracy.

For the present, they were in a weak position; it would be wise to conceal their intentions. Octavian held no official position and was simply a private citizen. Many senators, even though they had been appointed by the dictator, were inclined to accept his removal as a fait accompli. Once the emotion of the assassination and its aftermath had died down, even moderate Caesarians, like the next year's consuls, Aulus Hirtius and Gaius Vibius Pansa Caetronianus, believed that almost anything was better than a renewed civil war.

Mark Antony took the same line. As consul he controlled the levers of power, was popular with the troops, and saw himself as the dead dictator's *political* heir. He might have been expected to pursue the assassins and their republican supporters. In fact, his silent foreknowledge of the conspiracy suggests that he was not without sympathy with them, and he preferred to negotiate a compromise in which he agreed to an amnesty for Brutus and the other *liberatores* in return for the Senate's agreement not to overturn any of the dead dictator's legislation and executive decisions.

A long-term strategy for the Caesarians was not feasible; what was needed was a series of improvised tactics that made the most of any opportunity that presented itself. Consistency was irrelevant. The first tasks were to detach Antony from the Senate, discredit him in any way possible, and then replace him with Octavian as the leader of the Caesarian faction.

•  •  •

The weather had been terrible since the Ides of March. For much of 44, there was continuous gloom and a persistent rusty dry fog, and the sun was often invisible. This was probably the consequence of a major eruption of Mount Etna in Sicily; today's scientists have identified acid snow from the period in the ice cores of Greenland. Years later, the poet Virgil recalled this time as one of "wars that grow in the dark like cancer."

On the day in early May when Octavian entered Rome, stars could be seen in the daytime around a dim sun, looking like wreaths made from ears of wheat and rings of changing color. This was widely seen as a favorable omen, a prophecy of royalty.

Octavian's most urgent task was to make his position official. The adoption had to be legally authorized by a *lex curiata* and he wanted to collect his legacy. He went straight to Antony to ask for the money. He found him in his garden house (*hortus*) on the edge of the Campus Martius.

After going to ground for some hours on the Ides of March, Antony in his capacity as Caesar's fellow consul had persuaded Calpurnia to hand over to him all Caesar's papers. He had also won control of Caesar's financial resources. It was very likely that he had improperly salted away substantial sums of cash; the word was that, having been forty million sesterces in debt, he had suddenly become solvent.

From Antony's point of view, the arrival of Caesar's heir was an annoying distraction. He was an inexperienced teenager, "a boy," Antony gibed, "who owes everything to his name." Octavian was kept waiting in an anteroom and was admitted only after a long delay. Pleasantries were exchanged, and then he asked for Caesar's money so that he could pay his legacies to the people.

Octavian's request was awkward, and Antony angrily refused it. He said that he had found the state treasury empty and needed funds for the conduct of public business. He also made the technical point that the adoption was not yet official (later, he did his best to delay confirmation).

Octavian was furious, but there was little he could do to change the consul's mind. However, even without access to Caesar's estate, Octavian had large sums of money at his disposal. He is reported to have expropriated Caesar's war chest for the Parthian expedition; while at Brundisium he may also have received, or seized, tax receipts from Asia on their way to the Roman treasury. Octavian decided to trump the consul. He announced that he would pay his adoptive father's legacies out of his own pocket, even if Antony held back the moneys due. He also put up for sale all Caesar's properties and estates.

A highly effective campaign of words was launched to discredit the consul further in the public mind. The aim was clever and twofold—first, to smear Antony before the people and the legions and, second, to break Antony's concordat with the Senate by forcing him into a popularity contest for Caesarian support.

In accordance with a senatorial decree, Octavian planned to display at some games held in mid-May Caesar's golden chair and a diadem (a white cloth strip worn around the head to denote royalty), which he had been offered and refused a few weeks before his death. The consul lost his temper and forbade it.

Octavian wandered around the city center, with a crowd of followers like a bodyguard, making speeches about the disgraceful treatment he was enduring. "Heap as many insults on me as you like, Antony, but stop plundering Caesar's property until the citizens have received their legacy. *Then* you can take all the rest." Antony was furious and responded with threats.

At this point the consul's officers intervened and forced a reconciliation. They loved Caesar's memory and, equally loyal to his trusted friend and his adopted son, refused to fight for either against the other.

Antony was compelled to reassess his situation; although he still saw the "boy" as little more than a nuisance, Octavian *had* destabilized the situation. In order to stay on terms with his soldiers, Antony abandoned his statesmanlike compromise with the Senate, with which his relations had deteriorated sadly. Cicero, who thought him an unreliable drunkard and a political gambler (*aleator,* "dice thrower"), suspected his good faith and was stirring up opinion against him among republicans. Antony needed to secure his personal safety and to continue to dominate the political scene in Rome.

When his consulship came to an end in December, he was due to become governor of Macedonia—a little far away if trouble were to threaten him in the capital. So he exchanged the post for a five-year term in Cisalpine Gaul. From that vantage point he could overawe the capital, and if need be intervene directly, as Caesar had done in 49. It did not matter that a governor had been selected who was already in possession of the province. This was Decimus Junius Brutus Albinus, a distant relative of Marcus Brutus. A onetime follower of Julius Caesar, he had lost confidence in the dictator and taken part in the assassination on the Ides of March. Antony planned to transfer the army in Macedonia to Italy and lead it northward. He would make short work of the interloper.

In an attempt to weaken the republican cause, Antony initiated measures to persuade Brutus and Cassius to get out of Italy. To begin with, they were offered insulting proconsular posts: responsibility for the collection of grain in Sicily and Asia. "Could anything be more humiliating?" complained Cicero. The appointments were later upgraded, to the governorships of the politically and militarily harmless provinces of Crete and Cyrenaica. Brutus settled in Athens to wait on events, and in the meantime he pursued philosophical studies. Cassius eventually went to the east, whence little was heard of him for a while.

Now that Antony's position was secure, Octavian was the odd man out in the great political game. He held no official post and controlled no army. If he was not careful he would be finessed into insignificance. In the first place, he had to keep open his lines of communication with the Senate. He spent a lot of energy flattering Cicero, whose suspicions of him were partially alleviated. The elder statesman wrote to a friend on June 10:

> Octavian . . . does not lack intelligence or spirit, and he gave the impression that his attitude towards our heroes [the freedom fighters] were such as we would wish. But how much faith to put in one of his years and heredity and education—that's a great question . . . still he is to be encouraged and, if nothing else, kept apart from Antony.

Octavian staged Caesar's annual Victory Games in July, the month that had been renamed in the dictator's honor. Determined to make his presence felt at Rome, he spared no expense, and the festival was a splendid affair.

The skies produced another auspicious omen to match that on Octavian's arrival in Rome. He recalled the occasion in his autobiography:

> On the very day of my games a comet was visible for seven days in the northern part of the sky. . . . The common people believed that this star signified the soul of Caesar received among the spirits of the immortal gods, and for this reason the emblem of a star was fixed to the bust of Caesar that we shortly afterwards dedicated in the Forum.

The records of Chinese astronomers show that this comet was not a later invention but almost certainly a contemporary phenomenon—further evidence of the improvisatory skill of Octavian and his advisers.

After more squabbling between Octavian and Antony, another unconvincing reconciliation ensued. The ceremony was staged on the Capitol under the watchful gaze of Caesar's veterans, who, in a pointed signal to the consul, accompanied the dictator's heir to his front door.

Octavian did not restrict his efforts to winning the hearts of Rome's citizens. He sent agents disguised as tradesmen to mingle with the troops that Antony was bringing over from Macedonia and the veterans' settlements in Italy. They distributed leaflets and sounded out opinion. While Antony was a well-liked and competent leader, the soldiers were put out that he had come to terms with the Senate, even if he was now changing his stance. They had known Octavian in Apollonia and very much liked what they had seen. Dangerously for Antony, they were inclined to regard the young man as Caesar's political as well as personal heir.

Antony was soon told about the subversion of his soldiers; he unexpectedly announced that Octavian's aim was not simply to weaken their loyalty, but to arrange his assassination. He claimed to have uncovered a conspiracy among his bodyguard, some of whom he sent away.

Many people believed the story, and for once the young man lost his habitual self-possession. "Mad with anger," he ran to Antony's house and shouted at the front door that Antony was the plotter, who wanted to ruin Octavian's popularity with the people. He swore all kinds of oaths and challenged Antony to bring him to court. When no one appeared, he said in desperation: "I agree to be judged by your friends." With this he tried to go inside, but was stopped. He hurled abuse at the men at the door and, before going away, claimed that if anything happened to him, his death would be due to Antony's treachery.

The assassination plot was almost certainly an invention, Antony's attempt at a publicity coup. As Appian noted:

*A few people, who had the ability to think a problem out, were aware that it was in Octavian's interest for Antony to survive, even if he did Octavian some harm, because Caesar's assassins were afraid of him; while if he died the assassins, enjoying strong support from the Senate, would embark with less apprehension on every venture.*

Octavian's panic-stricken reaction won around public opinion, although a few skeptics suspected that the two men were colluding in some kind of contrivance against their mutual enemies.

As summer gave way to autumn 44 B.C., matters were coming to a head. It would only be three months before new consuls were in place: Hirtius and Pansa, moderate Caesarians who were profoundly irritated by Antony's clumsy maneuvering to secure his personal position and were aligning themselves cautiously with republicans. They would be entitled to raise troops; once they had done so, the Senate would be able to defend itself militarily, as it had not been able to do so far.

Out of sight but not out of mind, Brutus and Cassius were playing a waiting game. If possible, they wanted to avoid a new civil war, but, should the Republic be at risk, they, too, would recruit an army, with which to save it from its Caesarian enemies, such as Antony and Octavian.

Since his arrival on the scene, Caesar's teenaged heir had played his hand with cool skill. Young and inexperienced, he had that most essential of political talents, the ability to take good advice. Ruthless and patient, he would do whatever was necessary to the achievement of his goals. However, he was still without an army and without a role. As Julius Caesar's adopted son, he was hugely popular with the masses, but had not found a way of translating this into tangible power.

# VI

# FROM VICTORY, DEFEAT

ON OCTOBER 9, 44 B.C., THE CONSUL MARK ANTONY, ACCOM-
panied by his hot-tempered wife, Fulvia, left Rome for Brundisium,
where the four Macedonian legions, having crossed the Adriatic Sea from
Greece, were awaiting him. The soldiers met Antony in the city center.
They were in a bad mood. They criticized him for not avenging Caesar's
murder and made him mount the general's platform, without the usual
applause, to explain himself.

Beneath Antony's easygoing, affable manner lay a harsh and unforgiving nature. Furious at the men's attitude, in his speech he blamed them
for not bringing Octavian's secret agitators to him; if they would not help
him, he would find them himself. He ended, nonetheless, by offering each
soldier present a small donative, or bonus, of four hundred sesterces.

The soldiers laughed at this cheapskating, and when he lost his temper
they became rowdy and began to disperse. This was looking like mutiny, so
Antony obtained from his officers the names of those soldiers who were
known for being disruptive, and had some of them (chosen by lot) beaten
to death in his and Fulvia's presence. It was said that blood was spattered on
his wife's face. "You will learn to obey orders," he told the rest.

Meanwhile, in the consul's absence, Octavian set off to Campania to visit
new colonies of Julius Caesar's veterans (a colony was a settlement spe-
cially founded to house demobilized soldiers), as well as two legions, the
VII and the VIII. Ostensibly he was going to sell some of his father's property, but his real purpose (which he kept even from his mother, lest she
try to stop him) was to raise a private army from the dead dictator's loyal
legionaries.

The attempt met with success. The legionaries and veterans at colonies
near the city of Capua were faced with an offer they could not refuse: an

immediate grant of two thousand sesterces to every soldier (more than twice his annual pay), with a promise of additional largesse later. This generosity compared well with Antony's parsimony. Soon an army of more than three thousand men had been mustered.

But what now to do with it? One senses a mood of unusual overexcitement. Octavian wanted to confront Antony, although his soldiers were much keener on catching and killing Caesar's assassins. He decided to risk all and march on Rome, hoping for the backing of the Senate and leading personages. He pestered Cicero with a stream of letters asking for advice and practical support. For his part Cicero suspected that the political class would be uncooperative. He said of Octavian: "He is very much a boy."

He was right to be skeptical. The Senate was conspicuous by its absence when Octavian arrived with his troops and illegally occupied the Forum. Meanwhile, Antony was making his way toward the capital with the Macedonian legions. Octavian's men had not joined up to fight their comrades, much less a lawfully elected consul, and many of them melted away. The bold throw of the dice had failed; the inexperienced leader led his remaining forces to the comparative safety of the hill town of Arretium. He must have been thoroughly depressed, and anxious for the future.

Fortunately for Octavian, matters went no better for Antony. Back in Rome he called a meeting of the Senate on November 24. His intention was to denounce Octavian, but the session never took place. According to Cicero, not an impartial witness, he attended "a blowout in a public house" and was too drunk to address the Senate. If this is so, Antony may have been drowning his sorrows, for he had just received the appalling news that one of the Macedonian legions, the Martian, had declared for Octavian. He rushed off to talk with them; they not only refused him admittance to the town near Rome where they had billeted themselves, but also shot at him from the walls.

A few days later news came of another defection, this time of the IVth Legion. Despite the failed march on Rome, Octavian was winning the battle for the soldiers' hearts and minds. He held the great advantage of being Caesar's heir and carrying his name. His generous bonuses reinforced his legitimacy. Hoping that activity would stanch the hemorrhage of loyalty, Antony immediately marched north to expel the assassin Decimus Brutus from his province of Cisalpine Gaul.

It would be wrong to overinterpret these events. Antony had certainly been humiliated, but he was down, not out. By contrast, Octavian lacked both military experience and *imperium,* constitutional authority; he could see that he was in a corner, and had to devise a way out of it.

The career of Marcus Tullius Cicero had been a brilliant failure. A new man, he had risen to the consulship in 63 solely by virtue of his abilities as an administrator and (above all) as a public speaker. Following his exposure of Catilina's conspiracy, he had been hailed as "father of the country" (*pater patriae*).

Justifiably proud of his achievement, Cicero could not stop telling everyone about it, even writing a bombastic epic about the rebirth of Rome during his year as consul.

This was not merely vanity. In the aristocratic cockpit that was Roman politics, Cicero could not boast a long line of noble ancestors, as his colleagues and competitors constantly did, and so had little choice but to bore on about his own astonishing career.

Although he could be tedious and long-winded, the orator was also famous as a wit; Julius Caesar made a point of collecting his bons mots. On one occasion, an ambassador from Laodicea in Cilicia (the southeastern coast of modern Turkey) told him that he would be asking Caesar for freedom for his city. Cicero replied: "If you are successful, put in a word for us at Rome too."

His politics were moderate and conservative. A resolute civilian in a militaristic society where politicians doubled as generals, he promoted the rule of law. In his eyes, the Roman constitution was unimprovable, and he opposed risky radicals like Julius Caesar, though admiring his prose style and enjoying his company. He was dismayed by Caesar's rise to power. The republican values for which he had campaigned all his life had been overthrown, and he was obliged to retire from active politics.

Cicero was too much of a gossip for the freedom fighters to trust him to hold his tongue, and so he was not let into the conspiracy against Caesar. However, he applauded the event. His only regret was that Mark Antony, whom he had long distrusted and disliked, had not been put to death as well as his master. "The Ides of March was a fine deed, but half done," he commented ruefully.

Now in his sixty-third year, Cicero watched with dismay the unspooling of events during the spring and summer of 44. When he saw Antony shift position and come out against the Senate, he returned to frontline politics and delivered the first of a series of great oratorical attacks on Antony, which were soon nicknamed the Philippics after the speeches the Athenian orator Demosthenes made against Philip, king of Macedon in the fourth century B.C. Cicero soon dominated the Senate and became so influential that he was, in effect, the unofficial ruler of Rome.

At a meeting of the Senate on December 20, Cicero delivered his third Philippic, in which, to universal surprise, he went out of his way to shower Octavian with praise. He told the house:

> *Gaius Caesar is a young man, or almost a boy, but one of incredible and, so to speak, godlike intelligence and courage. . . . He recruited a very powerful force of invincible veterans and lavished his inheritance—no, lavished is not the right word, he invested it in the survival of the Republic.*

There was no hesitation now to address Octavian as Caesar; even more remarkably, the great constitutionalist was complimenting a private citizen on his creation of a completely unauthorized army.

Addressing the Senate on January 1, 43 B.C., he returned to the theme of Octavian, "this heaven-sent youth." Cicero put forward and carried a motion that Octavian be made a propraetor (a post usually held by a man who had already served as a praetor) and a member of the Senate.

The orator went on to claim that he had a unique insight into Octavian's motives. "I promise, I undertake, I solemnly engage, that Gaius Caesar will always be such a citizen as he is today, and as we should especially wish and pray he should be." In a word, he guaranteed the young man's good behavior as a sincere supporter of the restored Republic.

What was going on? The dictator's heir, who had sworn vengeance on his adoptive father's murderers, is revealed as entering into an alliance with a man who rejoiced at the Ides of March.

It must have cost Octavian and his advisers, the financiers and political agents who had once worked for Julius Caesar and were now devoted to his adopted son's cause, a great deal emotionally to discard their deepest ideals and join forces with republicans. But the discarding was only apparent; they were acting from necessity, not conviction.

Octavian's position, after his failed coup in November, was perilously weak. How long, he must have asked himself, would his demoralized veterans stay with him? Mark Antony had already briskly outmaneuvered Decimus Brutus and bottled him up in the old Roman colony of Mutina (today's Modena) in northern Italy. The new consuls, backed by the Senate, were raising legions with a view to relieving Decimus and putting an end to Antony's ambitions.

From Cicero's point of view, Octavian would reinforce the Senate's new military strength by placing himself and his army at the Senate's disposal, and thus would hasten the day when Antony could be challenged and eliminated. This was important, for dispatches from Decimus Brutus suggested that he was hanging on at Mutina only with difficulty. In the longer run, Cicero and his followers feared that at some stage Octavian would reconcile with Antony. The new entente made that a less likely prospect.

As for Octavian, he was no longer outside the law, for at one leap he had acquired a senior constitutional position. Above all, he had bought time. His soldiers will have been mystified, even perturbed, by the volte-face, but could see the advantage of their army being legitimized.

Neither side had any illusions about its sincerity; there was a good deal of playacting. Octavian used to call Cicero father, and was much too discreet to betray his real motives. The gossipy Cicero, on the other hand, could not keep his mouth shut. He joked about Octavian: *"Laudandum adolescentem, ornandum, tollendum."* That is, the boy must be "praised, honoured—and raised up." But *tollendum* was a pun, with the second meaning of "must be removed." Someone was kind enough to pass the witticism to Octavian, who was unamused and almost certainly unsurprised.

In February, Octavian marched off to join forces with the new consul Hirtius, while the other consul, Pansa, stayed behind to recruit four new legions. The young propraetor probably commanded about two legions. In the last few months, he had had to learn fast the duties of a military commander. He had never witnessed a battle and had had little time for the military training that upper-class Romans were expected to undertake in their teens.

The legion, the standard army unit, was usually led by the commanding general's deputy, a *legatus,* or legate. The legate also had at his disposal a number of military tribunes, staff officers recruited from upper-class families (unlike the civilian tribunes of the people).

Officially, a legion had a strength of between four thousand and six thousand men, although in practice it could be smaller (this was almost certainly the case with Octavian at Arretium). It was divided into ten cohorts, which were in turn subdivided into six centuries commanded by centurions; these junior officers were a legion's backbone. The first cohort always stood in the front row at the right end of the line (the most honorable position) and was sometimes larger than the others.

Men signed up for at least six years' service. Each legionary carried on his back a large quantity of equipment, weighing at least sixty-five pounds. This included sixteen days' worth of rations, a cooking pot, tools for digging, two stakes for the camp palisade, two javelins to throw in battle, clothes, and any personal possessions. On the march, Roman soldiers resembled not the smart upright legionaries of Hollywood movies, but beasts of burden.

A soldier's armor consisted of a bronze helmet, a cuirass of leather or metal, an oblong or oval shield made of sheets of wood covered by oxhide, a *pilum* or javelin (the head was designed to break off, so that it could not be thrown back), and a short, two-edged thrusting sword, the *gladius*. In Julius Caesar's day, a legionary was paid nine hundred sesterces a year—not a princely wage, but frequently supplemented by a share of the booty won in victorious campaigns.

Discipline was severe, ranging from food rationing and pay deductions to public floggings and execution for desertion. The worst penalty, for mutiny or collective cowardice before the enemy by a group of troops (usually a cohort), was decimation. One in ten men was chosen at random and the remainder clubbed them to death. This brutal punishment could be effective, but, as when Antony had applied it at Brundisium, was more likely to impose sullen and temporary obedience than to restore morale.

More constructively, much attention was paid to fostering an esprit de corps. Every century carried its standard (a pole with insignia or emblems at its top), and a legion was represented by a silver eagle, carried by the *aquilifer,* a special standard-bearer in a lionskin headdress. These standards embodied a collective pride and honor, and the loss of a legionary eagle was an irretrievable disgrace. In the confusion of battle the standard helped to orient soldiers by showing them where their military unit was.

Today hand-to-hand fighting is relatively rare, but, after a preliminary phase of javelin throwing and sometimes archery, it was how battles were won and lost in the ancient world. It is hard to imagine the noise, crush, smells, blood, and terror of an ancient battle. Even then, it was recognized as being a particularly demanding experience. A line of soldiers at close quarters to the enemy would fight for only about fifteen minutes; the line would then retire and have its place taken by soldiers in the rear. The dead and wounded were dragged back and replaced by fresh men.

Octavian reached Hirtius north of Arretium, and their legions moved on in the direction of Mutina. Their aim was to break the siege and relieve the proconsul, Decimus Brutus, now dangerously short of provisions.

Despite this progress on the military front, Octavian was in a gloomy frame of mind. First and foremost, a propraetor was junior to a consul, and when he and Hirtius met he was clearly the subordinate officer: Hirtius divided command of the army between them, but insisted on having control of the two Macedonian legions. Octavian bit his lip and complied.

He was also irritated by the continuing efforts on the part of certain senators and the consuls to negotiate a settlement with Antony. He needed a war with a victorious outcome, for if Antony and the republican faction were reconciled, he would once again be isolated. That said, he did not want Antony destroyed: he could envision a time when the two men might need to combine against the Senate and Brutus and Cassius. The Senate had recently awarded the province of Syria to the tyrannicide Cassius. It was looking very much as though there was a conscious plan to build up the republican party and ruin the Caesarians. Appian summed up Octavian's feelings: "He reflected on the way they [the Senate] had treated him like a boy, offering a statue [equestrian, in the Forum] and a front row at the theatre and calling him Propraetor, but in fact taking his army away from him."

Octavian's blood baptism was approaching. Mark Antony was encamped just outside Mutina, around which he had constructed a rampart. In the first week or so of April, news filtered north that the consul Pansa would soon (and at last) be arriving with four newly recruited legions, marching up from Bononia (today's Bologna) to Mutina. It occurred to Antony that it would be a good idea to attack these raw, barely trained soldiers on the road, before they joined Hirtius and Octavian.

It simultaneously occurred to Hirtius that that was exactly what Antony might do. So, under cover of night, the consul sent the Martian legion (one of those that had defected from Antony) and Octavian's Praetorian Guard, an elite body of about five hundred men, to reinforce Pansa.

The next day, Antony laid an ambush for Pansa's army, sending in some cavalry and hiding two legions in a roadside village, Forum Gallorum, and nearby marshland. The Martian legion and the Praetorians could not be held in check and rushed at the horsemen. They noticed some movement in the rushes and here and there the glinting of a helmet; suddenly they were confronted by Antony's main force.

A grim, speechless, waterlogged combat ensued, lasting for some hours. Pansa was wounded by a javelin in his side and taken back to Bononia, and Antony pushed the consul's forces back to their camp. Meanwhile, Hirtius again engaged in some quick thinking, and came up with two more legions on the double to intercept the victors.

It was already late in the evening. Antony's men, expecting no trouble, were singing songs of triumph and marching in no sort of order. To their horror, a fresh and disciplined army emerged from the twilight. They were cut to pieces, although Hirtius steered clear of the marshes and had to call off the fighting at nightfall. Those who had escaped death or serious injury made their way back to Antony's camp. Out of victory had come catastrophe.

Wide areas of bog were clogged with dead or dying men who had tried to find safety there from the enemy. It is evidence of the care Antony took for his soldiers that he sent his cavalry during the night to hunt around and rescue as many of them as possible. According to Appian, "they put the survivors on their horses, changing places with some and lifting others up beside them, or they made them hold the tail and encouraged them to run along with them."

Meanwhile, what of Octavian? He did not accompany his Praetorians, who were wiped out, nor the Martian legion, bloody but unbowed. According to Dio, he stayed behind to defend the camp, a useful if inglorious duty. Years later, Antony accused Octavian of running away from the battle of Forum Gallorum: "He did not reappear until the next day, having lost both his horse and his purple general's cloak."

The truth cannot be recovered, but it is clear that, at the very least, the inexperienced commander failed to distinguish himself. The fault would have to be quickly rectified: a noble Roman was expected to be as busy on the battlefield as in the Forum. The legions had loved his adoptive father at least in part for his intrepid generalship.

Decimus Brutus, beleaguered in Mutina, was in urgent need of rescue, and on April 21 Hirtius led his troops to the back of the town to make an entry. Antony felt obliged to respond, by sending out first his cavalry and then legions from other, more distant camps, which took some time to arrive.

On this occasion Octavian steeled himself to fight in the thick of the fray. Hirtius rode into Antony's camp and was struck down and killed fighting around the commander's tent. Octavian burst in and took up the body, like a Homeric hero dragging his friend out of the mêlée. He held the camp for a short while, but was then forced out. No matter, for the day was his. According to Suetonius: "Though bleeding and wounded, he took an eagle from the hands of a dying *aquilifer* and bore it back upon his shoulder to the camp."

Antony had been comprehensively defeated, and the seize raised. After a pause for thought, he withdrew with the remnants of his army across the Alps to Gallia Comata ("Long-haired Gaul"). His men endured terrible hardship on the journey. In a fine display of leadership, Antony shared their sufferings, drinking foul water and eating wild fruit and roots.

Octavian visited Pansa, who was seriously ill and died some days later. Pansa's Greek doctor, Glyco, was suspected of poisoning his wound, presumably in Octavian's interest. Another story had it that Octavian had personally struck Hirtius down in the fighting in Antony's camp. The accusation concerning Hirtius is almost certainly malicious gossip: a battlefield is not a private place and one would have expected eyewitness accounts of a consul being murdered.

Doubtless, Pansa's injury was a flesh wound from which he would have been expected to recover; that he did not suggests an insuperable infection, a common enough occurrence in the days before antibiotics. In May, having heard the rumor, Marcus Brutus spoke up for Glyco, who was being kept in custody: "It is quite incredible. Pansa's death hit nobody harder. Besides, he is a well-conducted, decent fellow, who would not be likely to be driven to crime even by self-interest."

What was certain, though, is that sheer good luck—the untimely elimination of both Hirtius and Pansa—had placed Octavian in an extraordinarily powerful position. For the time being, though, he decided to take no precipitate action. When the Senate ordered that the dead consuls' armies should be handed over to Decimus Brutus, he refused and took command of them himself, with the result that he now controlled eight legions, loyal to him rather than the Republic. He explained, with some plausibility, that the established legions would refuse to fight under the command of one of Julius Caesar's assassins.

He would not cooperate with Decimus Brutus, either, and told a delegation from the proconsul, "Nature forbids me either to set eyes on or talk to Decimus. Let him seek his own safety." Decimus strongly, and rightly, suspected that Caesar's heir was looking for an opportunity to take revenge on him.

Octavian also refused to chase Antony. When an officer of the former consul was captured at Mutina, Octavian treated him respectfully before setting him free and sending him on to join his general in Gaul. The officer asked what his policy was toward Antony. Octavian replied dryly: "I have given plenty of hints to people who have their wits about them. Any more would still not be enough for the stupid."

When Rome learned of the relief of Mutina, there was unalloyed delight. It seemed that what Cicero called "this abominable war" was over. The Senate was so excited by Antony's defeat that they completely misread the consequences of the consuls' deaths. Decimus was awarded a triumph. A promised bounty for the soldiers was reduced from the (extremely generous) twenty thousand sesterces to ten thousand, and a commission was appointed to distribute the money directly to the soldiers (rather than routing it, as was the custom, through their general). Both Octavian, who was not even offered a place on the commission, and his men were infuriated, and their discontent was communicated to Rome.

Meanwhile reports began to filter south of an astonishing transformation in Antony's fortunes. After his crossing of the Alps and arrival in Gaul, he made contact with three provincial governors. They were Marcus Aemilius Lepidus of Narbonese Gaul (today's southern France) and Hither (northern) Spain, who commanded seven legions; Lucius Munatius Plancus of Long-haired Gaul (central and northern France); and Gaius Asinius Pollio of Farther (southern) Spain. Antony won them over to his cause and found himself the commander once more of a large army. The misery of Mutina could be forgotten.

Decimus Brutus had struggled after Antony with his bedraggled legions, but was now trapped. Antony renewed was too strong for him, and if he retraced his steps to Italy, he would find Octavian waiting to destroy him. His men saw the position was hopeless; they deserted. With a handful of supporters, Decimus tried to escape to Macedonia and Marcus Brutus, but fell into the hands of a Gallic chieftain, who killed him on Antony's orders.

Caesar's heir was now ready to pounce. Both consulships were vacant, and the disorganized and increasingly uneasy senators had no obvious and willing candidates. Octavian knew that the time for caution was past and he was more than ready to submit a claim. Obviously he was far too young, for according to the constitutional rules a consul had to be at least forty-two years old. However, it could be countered that in times of emergency men in their twenties had occasionally been elected—Publius Cornelius Scipio Africanus, for example, had been about twenty-nine when he won the command to defeat Hannibal in the third century B.C. Closer to the present day, Pompey the Great became a leading figure in Roman politics at the age of twenty-three and won proconsular authority when he was thirty.

In July a deputation of four hundred centurions arrived in Rome to lay proposals before the Senate. They wanted the soldiers' promised bounty paid in full, and for their commander they required, rather than requested, the consulship. With extraordinary short-sightedness, the Senate refused.

As soon as this news reached him, Octavian, who was waiting in Cisalpine Gaul, called a soldiers' assembly. They told him to lead them at once to Rome and they would elect him consul themselves. Octavian marched them off the parade ground—eight legions, cavalry, and auxiliaries—and took the road south.

As he neared the city, he became worried about the safety of his mother, Atia, and sister, Octavia. They clearly had great value as hostages, and with help from Caesarians in the city they went into hiding. There being no consuls, the praetors were in charge of Rome's defense, but their men would not fight.

Determined to put on a show of constitutional propriety, the young candidate for the consulship waited twenty-four hours before entering Rome. On October 19, ostensibly without the slightest evidence of external threat, the people elected Octavian and the dim and unambitious Quintus Pedius, a nephew of Julius Caesar and one of his heirs, to the supreme governance of the Republic. Pedius had the advantage of being a safe pair of hands and could be guaranteed not to oppose his young colleague's wishes. On the next day, Octavian made his way through the city to the Forum, surrounded by a precautionary bodyguard. His political opponents came out to meet him along the route, with what Appian called "spineless readiness to serve."

Much to his relief, the new consul saw Atia and Octavia at the Temple of Vesta, waiting to greet him. They had survived the last few difficult days unscathed. Although she had advised against his accepting Caesar's will only a short year previously, his mother must have been proud to see him at the pinnacle of power when he was not yet twenty years old. She was lucky to have witnessed this day, for within a few weeks or months she was dead. We do not know what killed her, nor has any account survived of her son's reaction.

One of Octavian's first official tasks was to preside over a sacrifice to the immortal gods in the Campus Martius. As he did so, he looked up and saw six vultures. This was a good omen, but an even better one followed: later, while he was haranguing his troops, twelve vultures appeared, as had happened to Romulus at Rome's foundation in 753 B.C. The livers of the animal victims Octavian slaughtered were found to be doubled up at the lower end—an omen the *haruspices* unanimously declared to foretell a prosperous and happy future. The supporters of the new regime made the most of this lucky propaganda opportunity.

The message the vultures gave to the world was that Rome was being founded for a second time.

By the summer of 43 B.C., Octavian had made good progress toward fulfilling the three-point program he set out in the letter he wrote Philippus on reaching Italy after the catastrophe of the Ides of March. One, he had accepted the legacy, and the *lex curiata* confirming his adoption, which Antony had obstructed, was now finally passed. Two, with the consulship, he had "succeeded to [Caesar's] power," at least in part, although there was more to do as and when opportunity offered. Three, now at last, he was in a position to "avenge his 'father''s death."

The consul calmed the public by completing the payments that Julius Caesar had bequeathed to citizens, and by settling the bounties promised to the legions. He behaved with pretended gratitude to the Senate, but dared not attend its meetings without a bodyguard.

Then his colleague Pedius won approval for a bill that made Caesar's killing a crime and outlawed the conspirators. A special court was set up, which sat for one day and found all the accused guilty. Different prosecutors were appointed, at least of the leading conspirators; Agrippa took on the case against Cassius. None of those charged were present and able to defend themselves; indeed, many were governors of provinces. Those who happened to be in Rome quietly disappeared abroad.

This business done, Octavian left the city with his eleven legions, ostensibly to do battle with Antony but in fact to come to terms with him. He proceeded at a leisurely pace up the Adriatic coast. Meanwhile Pedius urged a reluctant Senate to reconcile itself with Antony and Lepidus. The reason for this policy switch was obvious; both they and Octavian were, in their different ways, Caesarian leaders and would soon need to defend themselves against the mighty host that the *liberatores* were reportedly assembling in the eastern empire. Victory over a legionless Senate had been an easy piece of work. Brutus and Cassius backed by the manpower and wealth of the east were a very different matter.

# VII

# KILLING FIELDS

## 43—42 B.C.

A SMALL LOW ISLAND LAY IN THE RIVER LAVINIUS, BETWEEN the colony of Mutina and the town of Bononia. It was to this spot that in November 43 the Caesarian leaders, Antony and Octavian, led their armies. For a year they had been bitter enemies, and now they meant to be friends. They marched slowly, one from Rome and the other from the far side of the Alps, to avoid any risk of receiving or delivering surprises, and to allow time to negotiate the delicate details of the encounter.

Octavian was in the weaker position, for Antony's forces, which brought together those of three provincial governors, including the former consul Lepidus, could easily have wiped him out. However, he calculated that his onetime enemy recognized that a united front among Caesarians was essential to maximize the chances of defeating Brutus and Cassius. They needed to come to an understanding. Also, the last twelve months had taught all military commanders that Julius Caesar's veterans would fight against anybody except his heir.

Antony and Octavian brought five thousand men each to positions on opposite sides of the river. Then three hundred soldiers approached the bridges at either bank. Lepidus crossed over to the island; he inspected it for weapons or hidden assassins, then waved an all-clear with his cloak. Octavian and Antony now left their bodyguards and advisers at the bridgeheads and walked to the island, where they sat down with Lepidus in full view of everybody. They met for two days, from dawn to dusk.

There were three items on the agenda: how to legalize their power; how to raise the funds needed to finance the war against Brutus and Cassius; and how to keep the opposition from regaining its strength.

During the weeks following the Ides of March, when Antony was on good terms with the Senate, he had enacted a law abolishing the post of dictator. Now it was reinvented in tripartite form. A Commission of

Three for the Ordering of the State was to be established for five years (modern historians call it the Second Triumvirate), with Antony, Octavian, and Lepidus as the commissioners, or triumvirs. They were empowered to make and repeal laws and to nominate officeholders. There was no appeal from their decisions. Octavian would resign the consulship in favor of one of Antony's generals.

It is a little hard to see what the undistinguished Lepidus, who had given Antony his army a few months previously in Gaul, contributed to the Triumvirate. Of the three men, Antony was by far the most powerful and experienced figure; he was probably responsible for promoting Lepidus, who in the event of any disagreements could be counted on to take his side.

The commissioners immediately nominated the consuls and other officeholders for the coming five years, and they also decided the provincial governorships. Antony was to take Gaul (except for Transalpine Gaul); Lepidus, his old province of Transalpine Gaul and the two Spains; and Octavian, Africa, Sardinia, and Sicily. (Sensibly, the empire east of the Adriatic, now in the hands of Brutus and Cassius, was left undecided.) This distribution showed with embarrassing clarity that Octavian was the junior partner of the three. In due course, all these constitutional arrangements were approved by a people's assembly in Rome.

A single solution was found for the second and third agenda items: a proscription. Proscription was an official mechanism for liquidating political opponents and amassing large sums of money from their confiscated estates; as already mentioned, it had first been used by Lucius Cornelius Sulla, in 81 B.C.

The negotiators found it easier to agree on the principle of having a proscription than on the actual names of those to die. The choice of victims took a good deal of private haggling. To begin with, Octavian was of two minds about the project; but, Suetonius writes, once the proscription had been decided on, "he carried it out more ruthlessly than either of the others."

The triumvirs marked down not only their political opponents whom they saw as public enemies (*hostes*), but also personal foes (*inimici*). They exchanged relatives and friends with one another. Lepidus abandoned his brother Paullus. Octavian allowed onto the list his onetime guardian, Gaius Toranius, who had been aedile in the year of his blood father's praetorship.

He also deserted Cicero—but only, if we can believe the sources, after resisting Antony, who so much wanted revenge for the Philippics that he let his own uncle be proscribed as payment for the superannuated orator.

Having concluded their island discussions, Antony, Lepidus, and Octavian arrived in Rome and posted the proscription decree on white boards in the Forum. Everyone named in the decree automatically forfeited his citizenship and protection from the law. The list was not final and new victims were added later, as the triumvirs decided. Informers who betrayed a proscribed man to the authorities were rewarded, and any person who killed one was also entitled to keep a share of his wealth. (The remainder went to the state.)

From a modern viewpoint, a proscription is a strange device. With the examples of the French and Russian revolutions before us, we expect the state to undertake mass liquidations if it deems them necessary; but, as has already been pointed out, the Roman state was remarkably nonbureaucratic; with no police force, no tradition of incarcerating offenders, and no professional judiciary, it was simply not equipped to execute large numbers of its citizens. The task had to be privatized.

The triumvirs betrayed signs of unease, of the need not to alienate public opinion. According to Appian, the proscription decree stated: "No one should consider this action unjust, or savage, or excessive, in the light of what happened to Gaius [Caesar] and ourselves." The triumvirs promised not to punish "any member of the masses," a guarantee they wisely honored. The decree closed with an assurance that "the names of none of those who receive rewards will be noted in our records." What was to be done was shameful and it called for concealment.

The proscription brought out the best and worst in human nature. Appian records many terrible stories of those times:

> *Many people were murdered in all kinds of ways, and decapitated to furnish*
> *evidence for the reward. They fled in undignified fashion, and abandoned their former*
> *conspicuous dress for strange disguises. Some went down wells, some descended into*
> *the filth of the sewers, and others climbed up into smoky rafters or sat in total silence*
> *under close-packed roofs. To some, just as terrifying as the executioners were wives or*
> *children with whom they were not on good terms, or ex-slaves and slaves, or creditors,*
> *or neighbouring landowners who coveted their estates.*

One tragic tale may evoke the selfishness and despair of the time. It concerns a teenager, whom we only know as Atilius; he probably belonged to an old noble plebeian family that originated in Campania. His father was dead, and he had inherited a rich estate. He had just celebrated his coming of age at Rome and was proceeding with his friends, as the custom was, to sacrifice in various temples in or around the Forum. Adulthood rendered him liable to legal penalty. Suddenly his name was added to the proscription list displayed on the speakers' platform, presumably because of his wealth, and when this was noticed all his friends and slaves ran off. The boy went, deserted and alone, to his mother, but she was too frightened to shelter him. After this betrayal, Atilius saw no point in asking anyone else for help; he ran away to the mountains.

Forced by hunger to come down into the plains, he was kidnapped by a bandit who made a living by preying on passing travelers, putting them in chains and forcing them to work for him. Atilius, brought up in luxury, could not endure the hard labor. Still wearing his fetters, he made off to a main road, where he incautiously identified himself to some passing centurions. They killed him there and then, doubtless taking his head back to Rome for their reward.

A funerary inscription dating from the late first century B.C. tells a very different story. It records the speech a grieving husband made at the funeral of his wife after forty years of marriage. We know neither his name nor hers, but she is usually called Turia, the name of a woman who led a similar life and who was once thought, wrongly, to be the same person.

Turia's husband, an unrepentant republican, was proscribed and went into hiding. He recalled: "You provided abundantly for my needs during my flight and gave me the means for a dignified life-style, when you took all the gold and jewellery you wore and sent it to me."

A year later, when the need for the proscription had ended, Octavian pardoned Turia's husband, but Lepidus, then in charge of the city of Rome, refused to acknowledge his colleague's decision. He seems to have enjoyed the proscription and did not wish it to be over.

Turia presented herself before Lepidus to ask him to recognize the pardon, and prostrated herself before his feet. He did not raise her up (as, according to convention, he should have done), but had her dragged away and beaten. This characteristically unpleasant behavior apparently angered Octavian and, according to Turia's husband, contributed to his downfall.

"That matter was soon to prove harmful to him," the widower remarked with dry satisfaction.

The cruelty and confusion that the proscription brought about was widespread. As many as three hundred senators were butchered—among them Cicero—and perhaps two thousand *equites*. The republican opposition in Italy was largely liquidated.

Antony had a streak of savagery in his character and entered fully into the spirit of things (unless the record has been distorted by subsequent propaganda against him). He always inspected the heads of victims, even at table when eating a meal. His wife was equally ferocious.

As for Octavian, while the proscription was in progress some observers found him a good deal too fond of victims' expensive furniture and their Corinthian bronze figures, objets d'art that were highly prized. According to Suetonius, someone scrawled on the base of a statue of him an insulting poem recalling the old story that his family's fortune derived from the shameful business of moneylending.

> *I did not take my father's line;*
> *His trade was silver coin, but mine*
> *Corinthian bronzes . . .*

The proscription was not as effective as its designers had intended. Much less money was made than had been expected, for too much land and built property came on the market at the same time and prices collapsed. Also, the more respectable felt some qualms about buying the estates of innocent victims.

The triumvirs were at their wits' end, for they had to find the resources to finance forty-three legions. They produced a new proscription list that merely confiscated property. They even stole the personal savings that people had placed in the sacred care of the Vestal Virgins. Ingenious new taxes were devised to swell their war chest.

All this came as a great shock to the citizens of Rome in Italy, who, thanks to the wealth of empire, had been exempt from personal tax for the last century. With the western provinces exhausted and the east off limits, they found themselves, for the first time, paying for their civil war.

• • •

Meanwhile, the republican cause was prospering. A new maritime leader in the west had emerged to complement the land power of Brutus and Cassius in the east. He was Sextus Pompeius, Pompey the Great's youngest son. Although still a very young man, he had already lived an extraordinary life.

In 48 B.C., with the civil war in full swing, Pompey the Great sent Sextus, then a child of thirteen or so, with his third wife, the young and beautiful Cornelia, to Mytilene on the island of Lesbos in the north of the Aegean Sea, where they would be safe from the fighting. He joined them there after Pharsalus, and they sailed with him on his final journey.

Sextus witnessed his father's murder off the coast of Egypt. A small fishing boat set out from the beach, with a Roman soldier in it and a few court officials. The passengers looked too unimpressively workaday for the reception of a great Roman commander, even one fallen on hard times. Pompey's entourage grew increasingly suspicious and advised him to have their ship rowed back out of range of the shore.

It was too late, for soon the boat had come alongside and the Roman soldier, a certain Lucius Septimius, whom Pompey recognized, saluted him with the title of *imperator,* commander in chief. Turning to Cornelia and Sextus before leaving the ship, Pompey kissed them and quoted a couple of lines from Sophocles:

> *Whoever makes his journey to a tyrant's court*
> *Becomes his slave, although he went there a free man.*

Cornelia and Sextus were in a frenzy of anxiety, but they relaxed when the little boat neared the beach where what they took to be a welcome party was waiting. However, as Pompey got to his feet before stepping down onto the sand, Septimius struck him with his sword, followed by others in the boat. Pompey pulled his toga over his head and sank down with a groan.

The people on the trireme gave out a great wailing sound when they saw what was happening, a cry so loud that it was heard on the shore. But Cornelia and Sextus knew there was nothing that could be done. Their ship weighed anchor and, with a strong following wind in its sail, ran out to sea.

. . .

The shock of what he had seen marked Sextus forever. The greatest personality not simply in the boy's own life, but in the Roman world (as he will have been told), was dead, not falling honorably on the battlefield but butchered in a squalid ambush. Although the records of Sextus' doings are scant, enough evidence survives to suggest that he modeled himself on his father. He gave himself an unusual *agnomen,* Pius, to convey the meaning that he was "loyal to his father's memory."

Cornelia went back to Rome, but Sextus made his way to Africa, where he joined his elder brother, Gnaeus. After the defeat at Thapsus and Cato's suicide, he and his brother fled to Spain, where the Pompeius clan were popular. Gnaeus had little difficulty in raising an army of thirteen legions, in the main recruited from Spanish tribesmen and slaves. As we have seen, that force was largely destroyed at Munda, and Gnaeus was hunted down and killed. Sextus, however, made a getaway and disappeared into Spain's tribal hinterland. Caesar published a pardon for Sextus and did not pursue him, believing he was too young to be a serious threat.

This was a mistake, for the young man soon gathered new forces. Although only a teenager, he ran a highly effective guerrilla war against the provincial governors whom Caesar appointed. Appian makes it clear that he understood the principles of irregular fighting, a long tradition among Spanish tribesmen: "With his greater mobility [Sextus] made unexpected appearances, disappeared again, harassed his enemies, and ended up taking a number of towns, small and large."

The Ides of March changed everything. From being an enemy of the state, Sextus, now about eighteen years old, was suddenly in a position to support the republican cause. The Senate appointed him prefect of the fleet and the seacoasts in 43 B.C., whereupon he gathered together all the ships he could find and set sail for Massilia (today's Marseille).

Sextus' fortunes soon went into reverse. After the establishment of the Triumvirate, the consul Pedius canceled his appointment as admiral. However, Sextus hung on to his ships and, in a bold stroke, decided not to return to Spain, instead settling in Sicily, where he persuaded the governor to hand over the island. The triumvirs, seeing their danger, added his name to the proscription list (despite the fact that he had nothing whatever to do with Caesar's assassination).

Sextus was now in an extraordinarily strong position; from his maritime vantage point in Sicily he controlled the grain supply to Rome from Egypt, Africa, and Sicily itself. Many proscribed men flocked to him, as did refugees and escaped slaves from all over Italy. Sextus encouraged this development, as Appian reports: "His small boats and merchant vessels met any who came by sea; his warships patrolled the shores, made signals to help the lost, and picked up anyone they encountered. He came in person to meet the new arrivals."

A new strategy began to take shape in republican minds: Brutus and Cassius were in charge of the east, and Sextus of the west. Italy and Gaul were isolated. It would only be a matter of time before the dead dictator's poisonous faction was isolated and crushed.

Octavian had the same idea, but from the opposite standpoint. He sent a squadron to put paid to Sextus, but it was defeated, and Cassius then sent ships and reinforcements to Sextus. For the time being, Octavian did not press the issue.

The mood in Rome was bleak and panicky. On January 1, 42, a religious ceremony of great political importance was conducted. The triumvirs took an oath that Julius Caesar had become a god, all of whose acts were sacred and binding, and made the Senate swear to the same effect. They laid the foundations of a small temple dedicated to Caesar in the Forum, on the spot where his corpse had been cremated by the grieving mob. His birthday was made a public holiday; celebrations were compulsory and senators or senators' sons who did not take part were liable to a severe fine of one million sesterces.

Julius Caesar's deification calls for some explanation. In the classical world, the boundary between gods and men was not clear-cut. Heroes in Greek legends, such as Heracles, were thought to be half human and half divine. From the third century B.C., kings in the Middle East regularly arranged for themselves to be "deified" in their lifetimes. Nobody really believed that they were of a different nature from the rest of humanity, but divine status added majesty to their office and created a respectful distance between them and their grateful subjects.

Roman governors were also sometimes awarded divine honors, although these were held to be valid only in the east. The novelty of Caesar's deification is that it took place in Rome and under the auspices of the state.

As for Octavian, his standing was considerably enhanced, for he could style himself *divi filius,* the son of a god. His supporters lost no opportunity to publicize his adoptive father's elevation to the stars.

. . .

Since leaving Italy in the summer of 44 B.C., Brutus and Cassius had been doing extremely well. In theory, they should have made their way to their insultingly unimportant provinces: the island of Crete, and Cyrene, on the north coast of Africa next to Egypt. They chose other and more interesting destinations.

Cassius, a competent soldier, traveled at top speed to Syria, where he was well known and liked. Seven legions based there flocked to his standard. Another four in Egypt also joined him.

For a time Brutus played the student at Athens, the nearest thing the ancient world had to a modern university town. He attended lectures given by leading philosophers of the day. However, behind the calm appearance of academic withdrawal, Brutus and his agents were busy making friends and winning over opinion in Macedonia. By the end of 44 he was in control of most of the province; the legions of neighboring Illyricum came over to him as well, and he captured and eventually executed the official incoming governor, Mark Antony's brother Gaius.

Brutus and the freedom fighters were extremely reluctant to commence hostilities; they issued manifestos in which they declared that, "for the sake of ensuring harmony in the Republic, they were even willing to live in permanent exile, they would furnish no grounds for civil war." But Octavian's second march on Rome, the Triumvirate, and, finally, the proscription persuaded them that peace was no longer an option.

At present, the joint power of Antony and Octavian was too great for Brutus. So he turned away and marched eastward to join forces with Cassius, to recruit more men, and to raise money for the legions' wages. Cassius also wanted to secure their rear by eliminating potential enemies, such as the island of Rhodes with its powerful fleet.

After draining the east of its human and financial resources, the freedom fighters finally felt ready to march against the triumvirs.

Thrace, a largely ungoverned territory to the east of Greece and Macedonia, stretched up to the river Danube and along to the town of Byzantium and the Hellespont. In today's topography it covered northeastern Greece, southern Bulgaria, and European Turkey. It was hot, mountainous, and heavily forested.

The territory's inhabitants were fierce and warlike tribes who formed separate little kingdoms. Greek colonists founded city-states on the coastline, exploited the area's deposits of gold and silver, and recruited Thracian soldiers, but, by and large, they left the Thracians to themselves in their uncultivated hinterland.

These were the lands over which the Romans established a shaky and uneven dominance from the second century onward and made into a province in 46 B.C. Through it they drove the Via Egnatia, the great highway that led from the Adriatic Sea to Byzantium and the provinces of Asia Minor. At the road's eastern end stood the town of Philippi, named after Philip of Macedon, who had rebuilt it as a strongpoint against the Thracian tribes. Well supplied with springs, it occupied a precipitous ridge, which Philip ringed with walls. Not far west of Philippi was the Hill of Dionysus, with a gold mine called the Refuges. Just over a mile beyond this, and a couple of miles from the town, two hills flanked the road on either side.

Wooded high ground fell away down to the northern edge of the town, while to the south a marsh stretched eight miles or so to the coast. The Via Egnatia skirted the marsh and continued across a mountain pass called the Symbolon, or Junction, to the small port of Neapolis, a rocky headland with a spacious harbor. A few miles out to sea lay the island of Thasos.

Here was the place where the two largest Roman armies that had ever faced each other in battle were to meet. The triumvirs controlled forty-three legions (more than two hundred thousand men if they were up to strength). However, strong forces had to be stationed in the west, especially in northern Italy and Gaul, to prevent unrest. Octavian and Antony deployed twenty-one or twenty-two legions (perhaps a hundred thousand men) and thirteen thousand cavalry for their encounter with Brutus and Cassius. In principle, the two sides were fairly evenly matched, for the freedom fighters led an army of nineteen legions (say, about seventy thousand men) and twenty thousand foreign cavalry including some Parthian mounted archers; but the opposing generals were all aware of the potentially significant fact that many of these men had served under Julius Caesar and probably remembered him with affection.

Militarily, Antony, who had served with Caesar during the Gallic Wars, was by far the ablest soldier of the Triumvirate and, we may assume, was in charge of planning the campaign. His first task was to prevent Brutus and Cassius from taking over Greece and bringing their fleet into the Adriatic before he had had a chance to transport his forces there and establish himself. So he sent across the Adriatic Sea an advance guard, which marched down the Via Egnatia past Philippi and through the Symbolon, until it reached two further passes that provided the only known routes to Asia. But this force was quickly outflanked and compelled to retire.

Brutus and Cassius moved on to Philippi and were delighted by what they found there. The two hills in front of the town on either side of the road, flanked by woods on their right and the marsh on their left, made a very strong defensive position. Here they would stand and wait for the triumvirs.

The two generals built a fortified camp on each hill, connected by a palisade. Their strategy was to deny Antony a set-piece battle. He would have to maintain long supply lines across Greece, and transport from Italy would be halted, or at least harried, by the republican navy, which would blockade the seaways. It would not be long before he and Octavian were short of food. Eventually they would simply have to retreat—but where to, if the escape route by sea to Italy was barred?

A happy portent conveyed a general sense of optimism. Two eagles flew down onto two silver eagles, pecked at them, and then perched on the standards. As they stayed there the decision was taken to feed them regularly. Fortune was smiling on the republican cause.

The triumvirs and their legions slipped through the republican blockade and disembarked at Dyrrachium, where Octavian fell sick and had to be left behind, his army staying with him. According to Agrippa and Maecenas, his boyhood friends, he was suffering from dropsy (a morbid accumulation of fluid in the body) on this occasion. What may be significant is that he tended to be indisposed at times of great personal crisis. An inexperienced military leader, Octavian was approaching a fearsome challenge and it is possible that his illness was psychosomatic in origin.

Antony rushed on toward Philippi and encamped on the plain a mile or so from Brutus and Cassius. Ditches, earthworks, and palisades were built, and wells sunk for drinking water. Antony was in a most unfavorable position, on low-lying land prone to flooding. He judged that by setting up residence contemptuously close to the freedom fighters, he would communicate a powerful impression of self-confidence that might dampen his opponents' morale; but when an ambush he set for some enemy foragers failed, he and his men began to lose hope of victory.

Octavian's health did not improve, but when he learned that things were not going well, he immediately set off for Philippi. He was as suspicious of his colleague as of the freedom fighters. As Dio commented:

*[Octavian] heard of the situation and feared the outcome in either case—whether Antony, acting alone, should be defeated or should conquer; for in the first case, he felt that Brutus and Cassius would be in a stronger position to oppose him, or in the latter case, Antony certainly would be.*

When Octavian arrived, he shared the same camp as Antony and his forces.

For a while, nothing much happened, except for a few sallies and skirmishes. On or about September 30, the two eagles on the freedom fighters' standards unexpectedly flew off, a discouraging sign for them. On the following day, Antony decided that something had to be done to break the deadlock and force a battle. With typical Caesarian dash, he ordered a detachment of men to cut a way secretly through the marsh, building a causeway by means of which a substantial number of men could outflank the left of Cassius' position, cutting the freedom fighters' supply line down the Via Egnatia to Neapolis. Tall reeds prevented the enemy from seeing what was going on over the ten days needed to complete the work. Then, one night Antony sent a force along the causeway to the dry land on the far side, where the party quickly established fortified outposts.

Cassius was astonished when he realized what had happened. Not to be outdone, he had a fortification wall built through the marsh, which bisected Antony's causeway and cut off the legionaries in the outposts. Antony responded by leading his army to attack and demolish a palisade that ran between Cassius' camp and the marsh, for which purpose they carried with them crowbars and ladders. Their mission then was to attack and destroy the camp.

Cassius' men could hardly believe their eyes, for the maneuver seemed extraordinarily foolhardy. Brutus' men were ready and armed; they were unable to resist turning to their left and charging Antony's men as they marched past. Brutus' army would have endangered itself if it had pressed this attack for too long, because it would have exposed its own side and rear to a possible counterattack by Octavian's forces. Before this could happen, they changed course and attacked the camp of Antony and Octavian. Sweeping all before them, they captured it.

Antony at last had his battle. Although he understood the difficulties the triumvirs' soldiers were facing in the plain, it was too risky to lead his troops back down the hill. So he pressed on. The best account of the engagement is written by Appian, but at this point his description goes out of focus. Antony easily and quickly broke through the palisade and stormed Cassius' camp, which was lightly defended. He led the attack in person, but presumably did so with only a part of his army, the rest of which must have been fighting Cassius' main force, drawn up (we may suppose) along the line of the palisade to the marsh. The republican legionaries were gradually pushed back, and then lost further heart when they saw their camp being taken and scattered in disorder. The cavalry galloped off in the direction of the sea.

It had been a bizarre day. Both sides had won—and both had lost. Brutus' men were plundering Octavian's camp, and Antony's that of Cassius. As a further complicating factor, there had been little rain and tramping feet had raised great clouds of dust over the battlefield—the "fog of war" *avant la lettre*. The various victors and vanquished had no idea what had happened to their friends and colleagues. Having looted the camps, soldiers began to go back to find their units. In the gloom they did not know to which army other legionaries belonged. Appian writes that they "returned looking more like porters than soldiers, and even then they did not notice or see each other distinctly."

This confusion had an unexpected and disastrous consequence. When Cassius had been driven back from his palisade, he retreated quickly with a few followers to the hill on which Philippi stood and from there looked down on the battle. Being nearsighted, he could hardly see the looting of his camp, while the dust prevented any of his entourage from determining how Brutus was doing at the far end of the battlefield.

A large body of cavalry was seen riding toward his position, and Cassius feared that it was the enemy. However, to make sure, he sent one of his staff, a certain Titinius, to reconnoitre. In fact, the horsemen had been sent by Brutus and when they recognized Titinius approaching, they shouted for joy. Some of them leaped off their horses, hugged Titinius, shook him by the hand, sang, and clashed their weapons as a sign of victory.

Cassius jumped to the wrong conclusion, thinking that Titinius had been taken prisoner and that Brutus had been defeated. He withdrew into an empty tent and made his armor-bearer, a freedman called Pindarus, accompany him. While Pindarus, guessing what would be asked of him, hesitated, a messenger ran up to say that Brutus was victorious and was sacking the enemy camp.

"Tell him I wish him total victory," Cassius replied, according to Appian.

Then turning to Pindarus, he said:

"Hurry up. Why won't you release me from my disgrace?"

He pulled his cloak over his head and bared his neck for the sword. Later Cassius' head was found severed from his body. Pindarus, knowing better than to wait around for consequences, had vanished.

Cassius' death is usually presented as the tragic result of a mistake. But if Appian is correct, he committed suicide *after* learning that the day had not been entirely lost. It seems that he died of shame. An experienced commander should have parried Antony's eccentric and foolhardy onslaught. Cassius had not been able to do so; that Brutus, a lesser general, had succeeded when he had failed simply added to the disgrace.

The one commander of whom nothing had been seen or heard was Octavian. How did he pass the day of battle? This is rather hard to say. Still convalescent, he appears to have remained at the camp when the troops were marshaled. After it had been captured, a rumor went around that he had been killed, for the enemy riddled his empty litter with their spears. But he was very much alive; he must have left the camp shortly before it was attacked.

The question arises as to where Octavian went. According to one ancient commentator, he "gave orders that he should be carried into the fray on a litter." When we recall that his troops were rapidly routed with serious loss, it seems implausible that Octavian would have risked himself in this way. How could he have survived, and why did no one mention such a brave exploit? In fact, at the time, word soon spread that the *divi filius* had spent three days skulking in the marshes, and even his friends Agrippa and Maecenas did not deny it.

The likeliest scenario is that when it became clear that there was to be a battle, Octavian was advised by his doctor that he was too ill to play an active part, and would be wise to withdraw to a place of safety. Not very admirable behavior, but understandable in a sick young man with little experience of battle. The damaging consequence, though, was that Octavian acquired a reputation for cowardice.

. . .

Both sides' armies were in a bad way. Octavian and Antony's camp had been thoroughly looted. The weather broke. The autumn rains fell in torrents, flooding everyone's tents with mud and water, and the temperature dropped below freezing. Antony gradually outflanked Brutus by pressing forward past his southern wing; to avoid encirclement, Brutus extended his own lines with fortifications along the Via Egnatia. However, the triumvirs, short not only of food but of money, could not afford to recompense their men for property lost or destroyed.

Then some terrible news arrived. On the same day as the battle, a great sea fight had taken place in the Adriatic. A republican fleet had encountered a convoy conveying two legions to join the triumviral forces. A few transport ships escaped, but then the wind fell and the remainder drifted about in the calm to be rammed or set on fire with ease. The soldiers were helpless in the face of their destruction. Appian writes:

> Some committed suicide when the flames reached them, some jumped aboard the enemy warships, to do or die. Half-burnt ships sailed about for a long time with men on board who were incapacitated by burns or by hunger and thirst. Some men even clung to spars or planks and were washed up on deserted cliffs and beaches.

The disaster was a grim reminder that the republicans controlled the seas. If the triumvirs failed to defeat them by land, they would find it difficult if not impossible to withdraw to Italy; they would be cornered in Greece and would soon run out of supplies. Unsurprisingly, morale among the troops was badly shaken, and Antony and Octavian determined to try to keep the news of the naval catastrophe from Brutus and his men, whom it would excite and reinvigorate.

Although living conditions were not so bad as down in the plain, the situation in Brutus' camp left much to be desired. The mood among the republicans darkened. Some eastern princes and levies slipped away homeward and a local Thracian leader, who had been a firm ally, changed sides. The soldiers resented being cooped up "like women, inactive and afraid." Against his better judgment, Brutus decided to take his officers' advice and give battle.

Late in the afternoon of October 23, he led out his troops and combat commenced. There seems to have been little in the way of maneuver; the two sides simply slugged it out like tired boxers. Octavian's troops fought bravely, and silence about his whereabouts suggests that their general was sufficiently recovered to lead them. Eventually they began to push the enemy back "as though they were tipping over a very heavy piece of machinery." Retreat turned to rout. Antony led the pursuit until night fell. Octavian, still weak and doubtless now exhausted, was meant to guard the camp, but he delegated the duty to a deputy.

Brutus retreated into the wooded hills above Philippi with a sizable force, four understrength legions. His plan was to make his way back to his camp when night came, or perhaps escape to the sea, for through his navy he still ruled the waves. However, Antony had ringed his hideaway with guardposts and spent the night under arms on watch opposite him.

Hope was dying and Brutus began to consider suicide. It is hard to escape the impression that the defeated freedom fighter was consciously giving a public performance for the benefit of posterity. He quoted apt tags from the *Medea* of Euripides, and from another play about Heracles, who when dying said:

> *O wretched valour, you were but a name,*
> *And yet I worshipped you as real indeed;*
> *But now it seems you were but Fortune's slave.*

During the night it became clear that the four legions were no longer willing to obey orders and were planning surrender. For Brutus, this disloyalty was conclusive. At first light, someone said it was time for everyone to go and make their escape. Brutus jumped up and answered: "Yes, that's right, but with our hands, not our feet!" He went round them all to bid them goodbye, saying that it was a great joy that not a single friend of his had failed him. He then walked a little distance with two or three companions. Grabbing one of their swords, he held the point to his left nipple and threw himself on it.

Marcus Junius Brutus was a man of contradictory qualities. In his arrogance and ruthlessness, he represented the worst of the old republican elite. Breaking the rule that senators should not engage in trade or moneylending, he practiced usury in the Middle East on a breathtaking scale. He turned coat after Pharsalus, and revealed to Julius Caesar that the fleeing Pompey's likely destination was Egypt—a betrayal of trust, if ever there was one.

At the same time, Brutus was high-minded, an intellectual who took ideas seriously. He saw the assassination of Caesar as a sacrifice rather than a political act. He was a man with "a singularly gentle nature," who feared civil war almost (although not quite) as much as tyranny.

Brutus lived long enough to see the dead Cato transcend history and enter legend, and the story of his own end suggests that he understood that the final contribution he could make to his cause was to be a martyr. Here his judgment was perfect. The image of Brutus as a defender of liberty has survived the ages.

After the battle, Octavian behaved extremely badly. This can be attributed in part to the fact that he was still ill. The previous four weeks had been the most testing of his short life and he must have been emotionally as well as physically prostrated. He may also have thought that retribution would be good policy. One way or the other, though, he was in the mood for blood. His conduct betrayed ice-cold anger.

The remaining units of the republican army surrendered. About fourteen thousand regular soldiers negotiated their surrender with the triumvirs in return for a pardon. Although many senior figures had died on the battlefield (among them Cato's son), there were distinguished prisoners of war to deal with—the last defenders of the demolished Republic. Octavian decided that they should be put to death. He insulted the more distinguished of the captives who came before him for judgment. When one man humbly asked to be given a proper burial, Octavian merely replied: "That's a matter for the carrion birds to decide." It was reported that a father and son pleaded for mercy. Octavian determined that one of them would be spared. The decision would be made by casting lots or playing *morra* (a game in which one contestant thrust out some of his fingers, while his opponent simultaneously shouted the number of fingers thrust out; a correct guess won the round). They refused to play. The father offered his life for his son's, and was executed. The son then committed suicide. Octavian watched them both die.

The remaining captives were so disgusted by his behavior that while they were being led off in chains they courteously saluted Antony and shouted obscene insults at Octavian.

Antony knew how to win graciously, treating Brutus' body with respect and laying over it his own general's scarlet cloak. Octavian was less generous with the remains: he had the head chopped off and sent to Rome to be thrown at the feet of a statue of Julius Caesar.

Philippi, following hard on the heels of the proscription, marked the end of the Republic. Rome's ancient ruling class was decimated, and surviving *nobiles* were scattered to all corners of the empire. In theory, the triumvirs' task was to restore the old order of things, but this was evidently not their intention.

Many ordinary people will have heaved a sigh of relief, for the uncertainties, confusion, bloodshed, and, above all, ruinously high taxes brought about by eight years of civil war appeared to be over.

However, it was unwise to be too optimistic. How Rome was to be governed in the future was altogether unclear; government by three men did not promise stability. Two of them had been enemies and, although allies for now, were still rivals for Julius Caesar's inheritance, and the love of the people and the legions.

As for Octavian, the coming months and years promised to be difficult. Since the Ides of March he had played his cards with great skill (no doubt advised by the clever men his adoptive father had gathered around him). He had acted unscrupulously, but his lies and killings were always for a carefully planned purpose. He had learned his politics from Caesar, and from the outset he aimed to reestablish an autocracy, not only out of personal ambition but also from a conviction that the Republic was incompetent and needed to be replaced.

But although Octavian had much for which he could congratulate himself, his position was subordinate and insecure. The real victor of Philippi was Mark Antony, whose generalship contrasted shamingly with his own performance on the battlefield. For the time being, Octavian had no choice but to accept his colleague's predominance; he must seize each opportunity to advance his authority as and when it presented itself.

Antony and Octavian held a magnificent sacrifice for their victory. Then the living left the two hills, the plain, and the marshes of Philippi as soon as possible. The scarred landscape fell silent and the evidence of slaughter slowly disappeared, although to ensure a memory of what had taken place the town was renamed Julia Victrix Philippi (Victorious Philippi of the Julian Clan) and some soldiers settled there.

The unloving triumvirs parted company. Antony stayed in Greece for a while, where he attended games and religious ceremonies, and listened to the discussions of scholars. He soon had enough of that and moved on to Asia Minor, intent on having a good time.

Octavian was carried back to Italy, where his arrival was awaited with fear and loathing. His illness flared up again dangerously on the journey, and he stayed for a while at Brundisium. He was thought unlikely to survive and at one point a rumor circulated that he was actually dead. Some thought his sickness was a charade, that he was delaying his return because he was planning some devilish new scheme for fleecing the citizenry. Despite his reassurances to the contrary, people hid their property or left town.

Followers of Brutus and Cassius, such as Cicero's son, who were, even now, unwilling to accept defeat, made their way to join Sextus Pompeius in Sicily, or to the two republican admirals, Lucius Staius Murcus and the high-and-mighty nobleman Gnaeus Domitius Ahenobarbus. But many survivors shared the view of one of Brutus' military tribunes, a plump young man called Quintus Horatius Flaccus, whose experience at Philippi gave him a loathing for warfare that lasted his lifetime. Known to us as Horace, he became one of the greatest poets of the age.

Years later he wrote a poem welcoming a friend back to the pleasures of civilian life after long military postings. They had fought together at Philippi, as the poet ruefully recalls. He is amused by his own cowardice and not a little scornful of the valor that kills.

> We two once beat a swift retreat together,
>     Upon Philippi's field
>     When I dumped my poor shield,
>
> And courage cracked, and the strong men who frowned
> Fiercest were felled, chins to the miry ground. . . .
>
> . . . In my laurel's shade
> Stretch out the bones that long campaigns have made
>     Weary. Your wine's been waiting
>     For years: no hesitating.

# VIII

# DIVIDED WORLD

## 42–40 B.C.

AFTER PHILIPPI, NEARLY ALL THE MEN WHO HAD ASSASSI-
nated Julius Caesar were dead, and so was the Republic.

The great families that had controlled the Senate and the consulship
had been bloodily culled and many now disappear from the historical
record. Most of the senior politicians active before the civil wars had
joined their ancestors. New men from the provinces with unfamiliar
names entered the Senate and commanded armies. Aristocracy gave way
to meritocracy, and Rome became a city of opportunity for men with energy and talent.

Before going their separate ways after Philippi, Antony and Octavian
signed an agreement and reconfirmed the division they had made of
Rome's provinces, with a few changes. The loser was Lepidus, who had
commanded the triumviral forces in Italy during the Philippi campaign.
He was not only idle but was suspected of treasonable communication
with the republican leader, Sextus Pompeius, master of Sicily. He was
made to disgorge Spain to Octavian and Narbonese Gaul to Antony. If
Lepidus could clear his name, Octavian might be persuaded to give him a
province or two from his allocation. Antony retained Long-haired Gaul,
but gave up Cisalpine Gaul, which the triumvirs decided should be incorporated into Italy instead of continuing as a province. Originally an idea of
Julius Caesar, this had the great advantage that it removed the risk of an
overmighty provincial governor in command of an army only a few days'
march from Rome—in short, the risk of another Julius Caesar.

Octavian and Antony liked each other no more than they had in the
past, but they were now bound together as permanent partners. They
agreed that each should automatically approve the political decisions of
the other. However, the two men were not on an equal footing. The victor of Philippi was a world-bestriding colossus. Little wonder then that, as

before, when it came to a division of tasks, the junior colleague came off worse.

Antony was to reorganize the east, raise money there, and restore the state's solvency; in due course, he would pick up the baton let drop by the murdered dictator and launch the much delayed expedition against the Parthian empire. By contrast, Octavian's thankless duty was to demobilize a large number of troops and settle them on smallholdings in Italy.

About fourteen thousand survivors from the legions of Brutus and Cassius were incorporated into the victorious army. Old Caesarian veterans and soldiers who had been recruited in 49 and 48 B.C., some forty thousand in all, were sent to Italy and civilian life. That left enough men to make up eleven legions, eight of which Antony took to the east; the remaining three came home with Octavian.

Unfortunately, there was insufficient state-owned land to accommodate the veterans. The exchequer was empty, so compulsory purchase was out of the question. Eighteen cities in Italy were marked down for land confiscation and freeholders were summarily dispossessed. Public opinion was outraged. Those threatened flooded into Rome. Appian writes: "People came in groups . . . young men, old men, women with their children, and gathered in the Forum and the temples, lamenting and declaring that they had done no wrong."

Octavian explained to the towns that he had no choice. "From what other source, then, are we to pay the veterans their prize money?" he asked complainants. This was nothing less than the truth. There was no countervailing force with which to gainsay the soldiers. Worse, the allocated land was still not enough and some men used violence to expropriate farms they had not been granted, often with more fertile fields. In many parts of Italy, law and order were breaking down. Relations between the soldiers and their commander also deteriorated, as an unnerving incident demonstrated only too clearly.

Veterans were summoned to the Campus Martius to hear announcements on the allocations. They were so eager for news that they arrived early, before first light. Octavian was late; they became angry, and when a centurion gave them a severe dressing-down they first jeered at him and then killed him.

Octavian made a calculated and very brave decision. What had suddenly become a crisis would, he judged, end in catastrophe if he stayed away from the assembly. So he walked there as planned, turning aside when he saw the centurion's body and politely asking the legionaries to behave with greater restraint in future.

He then announced the expected land grants, handed out some bounties, and invited further applications for reward. This disarmed the angry soldiers, who became ashamed of what had been done and asked Octavian to punish the centurion's murderers. He agreed to do so, but carefully (and wisely) imposed two conditions: that the culprits admit their guilt and that the army as a whole condemn them. The men's mood cleared.

For much of 41 B.C. Octavian was caught between two fires. At the same time that he sought to pacify the veterans, he made conciliatory gestures toward the civilian population. As Dio put it, "He learned from actual experience that weapons had no power to make the injured feel friendly towards him." So he no longer confiscated senatorial estates and kept his hands off other kinds of private property.

However, the veterans were annoyed by this; Dio reports that they killed a number of centurions and others whom they saw as taking his side: "They came very near to killing [Octavian] himself, making any excuse justify their anger." Relations between them and the dispossessed citizens went from bad to worse. Riots took place, in which the two sides fought against each other in the streets. The capital and even Italy were slipping out of official control. At one point there seems to have been something approaching a general strike at Rome. Appian writes: "The civilian population shut the workshops and made the elected office-holders leave, saying that they had no need of either office-holders or crafts in a starving and plundered city."

For years the landless poor had gravitated to Rome, and many thousands depended on the supply of subsidized grain to keep body and soul together.

Every year the city consumed between 140,000 and 190,000 tons of wheat. More than 300,000 citizens were on the dole and received free supplies of grain. Some of this was homegrown, but much came from overseas, from Sicily, Africa, and Sardinia. The fact that Italy was not agriculturally self-sufficient made Rome heavily dependent on the vagaries of international politics, just as today's industrial societies rely on imports of gas and oil.

Pompey the Great had understood this well; in 67 B.C. (as already noted) he had cleared the seas of pirates, who had become so widespread and powerful as to blight the free passage of goods, including wheat. He began by "entirely clearing pirates from the seas adjoining Etruria, Libya, Sardinia, Corsica and Sicily." A quarter of a century later, his son Sextus controlled these waters himself; one wonders if, as a boy, he had heard his father reminisce about his past exploits and learned of the pirates' strategic stranglehold.

Sextus set out systematically to starve the city. The republican admirals Ahenobarbus and Murcus strengthened the blockade by standing off Brundisium in the Ionian Gulf. Exploiting the confusion pirates raided southern Italy.

The ancient sources usually dismiss Sextus as a pirate himself. He was much more than that. By applying pressure on the triumviral regime, he meant to pave the way for his return to Rome and the restitution of his family's confiscated property. Not without reason, Sextus may have supposed that he could then easily come to terms with Antony, who would be grateful to see the last of his infuriating young colleague and competitor.

It is argued that he should have invaded Italy, but that was hardly necessary. If he had done so, Caesarian veterans would have put up a die-hard resistance. Far better to let starving dogs lie.

Octavian's tribulations were all the more painful and humiliating in the light of news from the east, where his colleague was at the height of his powers and prestige. Trumping the *divi filius,* Antony decided to claim divine status on his own account.

He presented himself to the people of Asia as the New Dionysus. Dionysus, also widely known as Bacchus, was a god with two interrelated dimensions: on the one hand, he was the patron of wine, agriculture, and the abundance of nature; on the other, he presided over mystical cults whose secret rituals induced ecstatic or out-of-body experiences and delivery from the daily world through physical or spiritual intoxication. Dionysus stood for a euphoric eastern irrationalism that could be set against the western clarity of Apollo, god of reason and light.

The triumvir–cum–Greek god had more on his mind than establishing an iconic image for himself and having a good time. His most urgent task was to raise funds to refill the bankrupt Roman exchequer, and he set about his work with ruthless enthusiasm.

The trouble was that the eastern provinces had already been called on to finance much of Rome's civil wars. Now Antony used any method that came to hand to squeeze out all remaining wealth. Recalling that the god had his dark side, Plutarch notes acidly:

> To most people, [Antony] came as Dionysus the Cruel and Eater of Flesh, for he stripped many noble families of their property and gave it away to rogues and flatterers. In other cases, men were allowed to steal fortunes from owners who were still living by making out that they were dead.

Antony saw he was going too far, and reduced his demand for nine years' worth of taxes to two. He had to look elsewhere for additional cash; and at this point the New Dionysus, equivalent to the Egyptian god Osiris, thought of his divine sister, the New Isis, alias Cleopatra, queen of Egypt, who saw herself as an incarnation of the kingdom's celebrated goddess of fertility. Antony had last met her in Rome when she was Caesar's mistress. Aware of Egypt's untold riches, he decided to invite her politely but firmly to make a substantial contribution to his running costs. From Tarsus in Cilicia (in today's southern Turkey), where he was then based, he sent one of his aides to fetch the queen.

He chose for the task Quintus Dellius, a versatile character who was said to have been his sexual pet when a boy, and who built a reputation in these dangerous times for switching sides at precisely the right moment. A memorable putdown described Dellius as a "circus-rider of the civil wars," adept at jumping effortlessly from horse to horse.

When Dellius arrived at Alexandria he was struck by Cleopatra's charm, and suspected that Antony would be too. Knowing that the triumvir routinely fell for pretty women, he advised the queen to wear her most alluring attire when presenting herself to him. Antony was a gentleman, he added, and she had nothing to fear from him.

Impressed by Dellius, Cleopatra took his advice. She came to meet the triumvir at Tarsus, sailing up the river Cydnus to the city in a splendid barge. Plutarch evoked the scene brilliantly (perhaps adding some color):

> [She] was in a barge with a poop of gold, its purple sails billowing in the wind, while her rowers caressed the water with oars of silver which dipped in time to the music of the flute, accompanied by pipes and lutes. Cleopatra herself reclined beneath a canopy of cloth of gold, dressed in the character of Aphrodite.

Antony was waiting in state on a dais in the central square of Tarsus to give the queen a formal welcome. Rumors spread through the crowds of bystanders of the floating spectacle that was sailing up the river into port and mooring at the quayside. Gradually they drifted away to have a look, leaving Antony and his entourage alone in the marketplace.

Word spread that Aphrodite (whom many worshippers identified with Isis) had come to revel with Dionysus "for the happiness of Asia." This notion doubtless originated with Cleopatra, but it shows that Antony's religious propaganda featuring himself as the New Dionysus was evidently working its way into the public mind. She herself well understood the role of religion in royal self-promotion. If she was consciously presenting herself as Aphrodite, she was at one level making a direct sexual offer; but, more profoundly, she was also putting in a claim to be Antony's divine partner.

The triumvir sent the queen a message inviting her to dinner, but she had already determined what the next step in their relationship should be. Well-informed about Rome's leading personalities, she will have known that Antony's character was essentially simple and easy to read. He greatly enjoyed the display of wealth. He was easygoing and had a broad sense of humor that belonged to "the soldier rather than the courtier," as Plutarch put it. He loved practical jokes. These were not exactly the tastes to which Cleopatra, educated in the sophisticated court of the Ptolemies, was accustomed, but in his company she made every appearance of sharing them.

The queen countered the triumvir's invitation to dinner with one of her own; always complaisant with the ladies, he gracefully gave way and attended a banquet on board ship. On the following day, the queen dined with Antony. The gustatory exchanges were repeated for four days.

At a certain point, business supplanted pleasure. Antony required practical support from Cleopatra for the invasion of Parthia. She agreed to provide it, but on certain conditions. She required the execution of a few inconvenient personages, and in particular of her hated half sister, Arsinoe, who had briefly seized her throne and had been given sanctuary at the temple of Artemis at Ephesus. Antony obliged.

The queen now invited him to spend the winter with her at Alexandria. The couple sailed off to Egypt, where Antony laid aside the garb of a Roman official and wore an informal tunic in the Greek manner. The couple formed a dining club called the Inimitable Livers and spent much of their time enjoying themselves.

In February or March of 40 B.C., bad news reached Egypt. Having decided not to await Antony's planned attack on them, the Parthians had launched an invasion of Syria. The triumvir quickly set off for Asia Minor.

Mark Antony's critics have made much of his oriental debauchery, as though he were acting in an original and shocking way. In fact, he did nothing out of the ordinary but rather behaved very much as he had always done. There are no reports that, at this stage of life, he was sexually promiscuous. He had sex with the queen, but with no one else. (She gave birth to twins, Alexander and Cleopatra, later in the year.) However, he was not in love with her and left Egypt without qualms. The couple were not to meet again for three and a half years. He had spent a most enjoyable holiday, and that was all.

Something more serious, though, was taking place in his personality: a gradual and growing loss of focus. The Greek word for this process was *eklusis,* the term for the unstringing of a bow. Dio remarks that Antony "had earnestly devoted himself to his duties so long as he had been in a subordinate situation and had been aiming at the highest prizes; but now that he had got into power, he no longer paid strict attention to these things."

When things are as bad as they can be, fate finds a way to deliver another blow. One of the consuls in 41 B.C. was Lucius Antonius, Mark Antony's brother, who decided to launch a military challenge against Octavian. He was in collusion with Mark Antony's wife, the virago Fulvia. At this time she played an active and influential political role, to the point where she seemed to be as much of a consul as those elected to that office.

The two played a double game, simultaneously sympathizing with dispossessed Italian farmers and telling the legionaries that Octavian was acting disloyally to the absent Mark Antony, for whom they claimed to speak. All would be well, they argued, once Mark Antony returned to Italy. Lucius backed a protest against Octavian in Rome, managed to raise eight legions, and occupied the capital. He then marched north, hoping to link with two Antonian generals and their armies. However, the generals were unsure of Antony's wishes and held aloof.

Fulvia raised troops and, most unusually for a Roman woman, issued orders directly herself. Dio writes: "And why should anyone be surprised at this, when she would wear a sword at her side, give out the watchword to the soldiers, and on many occasions give speeches directly to them?"

Octavian kept his nerve. He was not at ease on the battlefield, and was helped, or more likely masterminded by, his boyhood friend Agrippa, who had a gift for generalship. He and Salvidienus outmaneuvered Lucius, who took refuge in the strongly fortified hill town of Perusia (today's Perugia, in Umbria), where he waited for the Antonian generals to come to his relief. Fulvia, infuriated, pressed them to do so, but Agrippa confronted them before they had succeeded in joining forces. Still without instructions from Antony, the generals were unenthusiastic about pressing on to Perusia in the first place and pulled back. Lucius was on his own.

Meanwhile, Octavian sealed the town with a ditch and rampart seven miles long. At one point in the siege he was surprised by a sudden sortie by the enemy while holding a sacrifice outside the town walls, and was lucky to escape with his life.

Both sides hurled stone and lead slingshot at each other. About eighty of these lead balls have been discovered by archaeologists and many have brief, extremely rude messages scratched on them. Examples include "I seek Fulvia's clitoris"; "I seek Octavian's arse"; "Octavian has a limp cock"; "Hi, Octavius, you suck dick"; "Loose Octavius, sit on this"; and, rather more feebly, "Lucius is bald."

Lucius' men launched numerous attacks on the enemy, including one by night, but they all failed. The formal act of surrender was carefully stage-managed. The defeated legions laid down their weapons and were pardoned. Octavian placed their commander and some of his senior followers under discreet arrest. They were later freed, and Lucius was sent to be governor of Spain (there was no point needlessly annoying his brother).

Despite the appearance of clemency, the triumvir appears to have been coldly and bitterly angry for what he had been obliged to endure. Perusia was given over to the troops to plunder, and accidentally burned to the ground. Other prisoners of war were less fortunate than Lucius and his intimates. According to Suetonius,

> [Octavian] took vengeance on crowds of prisoners and returned the same answer to all who sued for pardon or tried to explain their presence among the rebels. It was simply: "You must die!" According to some historians, he chose 300 prisoners of equestrian or senatorial rank, and offered them on the Ides of March at the altar of the god Julius, as human sacrifices.

This story is repeated by Dio, and is very possibly true. Although human sacrifice was forbidden by senatorial decree in 97 B.C., it runs through Roman history as a recurrent ritual idea. Roman religious ceremonies contain traces of the practice, with dolls replacing human victims. On three occasions, during times of great crisis during the third and second centuries, two pairs of Gauls and Greeks, each a man and a woman, were buried alive in the cattle market (*forum boarium*) as a human sacrifice. In the sixties B.C., Catilina was reported to have sacrificed a boy and eaten his entrails. The most recent recorded instance took place during Julius Caesar's triumph at Rome in 46 B.C., when, in a fury, he had had two rioting soldiers sacrificed to Mars.

Lucius surrendered in January or February 40 B.C., only a few weeks before the anniversary of the assassination. A commemorative altar had been erected on the site of Caesar's cremation in the Forum, and this was where Octavian conducted the mass sacrifice. It shocked Roman opinion to the core, both for its scale and for the status of the victims. So far as the *divi filius* was concerned, it was the end of a story; four years had passed and now he had finally slaked the blood thirst of his deified adoptive father. The drama of murder and revenge had run its course.

The butchery came at a price, for the public long and bitterly recalled

> . . . *our fatherland's Perusian graves,*
> *The Italian massacre in a callous time.*

What did Lucius and Fulvia mean by this disastrous enterprise? Did Antony know and approve of what his wife and brother were doing? These are hard questions to answer. Although Lucius does not give the impression of being particularly able, Fulvia was evidently energetic and experienced.

She may have been irritated by, even jealous of, Antony's infidelity with Cleopatra. However, such behavior was commonplace and wives were expected to take it in stride. A political motive is much more plausible. Octavian was a nuisance, and here was a chance to eliminate him— a chance that Lucius and Fulvia seized, to give Antony the supreme power he scarcely seemed to covet.

Antony claimed that he was completely ignorant of much that was done in his name, and that he learned of what was happening in Italy too late to influence the course of events. However, Octavian and others wrote him many letters about the situation. It would have been amateurishly odd for Fulvia to act without her husband's knowledge. We must conclude that Antony knew perfectly well what Lucius and Fulvia were up to, although it may not have been his idea. He was anxious to be regarded as a man who kept his word, and wanted to exploit the outcome whatever it happened to be. So he turned a blind eye.

The Perusian war proved that Antony and his supporters were poorly organized and prone to miscalculation. By contrast, it greatly strengthened Octavian's political position and provided evidence of his staying power. Now twenty-three years old, he was no longer a virginal boy overprotected by his mother, but a fully grown adult and one of Rome's two most powerful citizens. The year and a half since Philippi had been miserable, unglamorous, and testing, but it had brought out the best in him. He had succeeded in every endeavor.

His reputation for physical cowardice in the field was probably not unjustified; he was never at ease as a soldier. But Octavian had demonstrated something better—a dogged moral courage that saw him impose an unpopular but necessary policy of land confiscation and nearly cost him his life when confronting angry soldiers in the Campus Martius.

He would not shirk what needed to be done and moved patiently from task to task. This methodical approach to politics had two important dimensions: Octavian was naturally cautious and avoided impulsive gestures; and he showed an unforgiving fury to anyone who crossed him.

So far as contemporaries were concerned, the inexperienced triumvir was no nine days' wonder, as some had predicted or hoped he would be. He had earned himself a permanent place at the head of affairs. Barring accident or ill health, he was there to stay.

We have relatively little information about Octavian's personal life; what we do have falls broadly into two categories—dynastic marriages and stories put about by his enemies.

Julius Caesar's heir was the finest match in Rome. Since he was only of middling provincial stock (despite his connection with the patrician Julii), it was in his interest to ally himself to blue blood. This would not only increase his personal social status but also be a signal that he wanted a political reconciliation with the aristocracy, thinned by the civil wars but still powerful, if only as an obstacle.

Probably in the spring or early summer of 43 B.C., Octavian married the daughter of Publius Servilius Vatia Isauricus, a member of Rome's most ancient nobility. However, the union lasted only a few months, for Mark Antony and Octavian, uncomfortable colleagues, agreed that it would be wise to cement their political deal, enshrined in the Second Triumvirate, with a family bond. Antony's wife, Fulvia, had a daughter, Claudia, by her first husband, a lordly rabble-rouser, Publius Clodius Pulcher. She was only just of marriageable age and too young to have sex, but a match was arranged.

A girl was considered ready for wedlock at about twelve, a boy at fourteen. Husband and wife must both have reached puberty. Children could be betrothed provided that they were old enough to understand what was being put to them—say, from seven upward.

We are told rather more about Octavian's sex life away from the marriage bed, by his opponents. Politicians often publicized the sexual peccadilloes of those with whom they disagreed, and were expected to be capable of producing scabrous lampoons. Octavian was no laggard in this regard; and a scabrous verse attributed to him survives, which is very probably authentic. It broadcasts a cheerfully indecent explanation of the motives that underlay Fulvia's political activity. One can imagine the guffaws in the Forum and among the soldiery.

*Because Antony fucks Glaphyra [a current mistress], Fulvia is determined to punish me by making me fuck her in turn. I fuck Fulvia? What if Manius [a freedman of Fulvia] begged me to sodomize him, would I do it? I think not, if I were in my right mind. "Either fuck me or let us fight," says she. Ah, but my cock is dearer to me than life itself. Let the trumpets sound.*

Octavian was accused of loose living. His girlishly attractive appearance doubtless inspired Sextus Pompeius to accuse him of effeminate homosexuality, of being a "queen."

Lucius Antonius asserted that Octavian had sold his favors to Aulus Hirtius, the consul who lost his life at Mutina in 43 B.C., for the princely sum of 300,000 sesterces. The incident supposedly took place in Spain in 45 B.C., during the last campaign of the civil war, which culminated in Caesar's victory at Munda. This was not long before Caesar returned to Italy and wrote his will. Lucius added, perhaps to lend verisimilitude to his claims, that Octavian used to soften the hair on his legs by singeing it with red-hot walnut shells.

With their circumstantial detail, these allegations just might be true, though that is unlikely. It does appear that the young triumvir won a reputation with the Roman mob for sleeping with men, whether or not it was deserved. One day at the theater an actor came onstage representing a eunuch priest of Cybele, the Great Mother. As he played a tambourine, another performer exclaimed, "Look how the queen's finger beats the drum!" Since the Latin phrase can also mean "Look how this queen's finger sways the world!" the audience delightedly applied the line to Octavian, who was watching the show, and burst into enthusiastic applause.

Most evidence suggests that Octavian, in fact, preferred sleeping with women, and he was widely credited with multiple adultery. It was probably during his early years of power that a private banquet he gave caused a public scandal. The event became known as the Feast of the Divine Twelve. It was a costume party with a difference; guests were invited to dress up as one or other of the gods and goddesses of Olympus. Octavian came as Apollo (always his favorite deity), god of the sun and of healing, and patron of musicians and poets. Suetonius notes that Antony mentioned the affair in a "spiteful letter," but adds that an anonymous popular ballad confirmed it.

> *Apollo's part was lewdly played*
> *By impious Caesar; he*
> *Made merry at a table laid*
> *For gross debauchery.*

What made the scandal worse was that the feast allegedly took place at a time of food shortage (caused, presumably, by Sextus Pompeius' blockade). On the next day people were shouting "The gods have gobbled all the grain!" and "Caesar is Apollo, true, but he's Apollo of the Torments" —this being the god's aspect in one city district at Rome.

In the spring of 40 B.C., Antony was on his way to arrange his Parthian expedition when he learned that Perusia had fallen and that Fulvia had been forced to flee Italy. Antony met her at Athens and spoke very sharply to her, blaming her for the debacle. What she replied is unknown, but she was deeply shaken; an able woman, she had done everything in her power to advance her husband's interests, and this was her recompense. The couple traveled to Sicyon, a port on the Gulf of Corinth, where Fulvia fell ill.

We do not know what her sickness was, but it was exacerbated by a bout of depression. According to Appian, she "aggravated her illness deliberately," which suggests self-harm.

Another lady paid Antony a visit: his mother, Julia, who had left Italy for her safety and taken refuge with Sextus Pompeius in Sicily. She conveyed a message from Sextus, offering an alliance against Octavian. Antony replied cautiously; if he went to war with Octavian he would regard Sextus as an ally; if not, he would try to reconcile them.

Meanwhile, the political situation was darkening. Antony's ally Quintus Fufius Calenus, the governor of all Gaul beyond the Alps, unexpectedly died. As soon as he heard the news, Octavian rushed off to take control of Calenus' eleven legions, which the dead man's terrified son handed over to him without offering any resistance.

This was a clear breach of the agreement among the triumvirs and, so far as Antony was concerned, tantamount to a declaration of war. He laid plans for the invasion of Italy. Civil strife was set to resume, and everyone knew who would win. After Philippi, Antony was regarded as the greatest general of the day; he would make short work of his junior partner in power.

Somehow or other Octavian had to prevent Sextus and Antony from entering into an alliance against him. The depth of his anxiety can be gauged by his next step. He put aside his untouched wife, Fulvia's daughter Claudia, sent Sextus' mother, Mucia, to Sicily to convey a friendly message from him to her son; and wed Scribonia, Sextus' aunt-in-law. Married twice before, she was considerably older than her new husband, perhaps in her early to mid-thirties. Scribonia was not a life partner of personal choice, but this did not prevent him from quickly consummating the union and making Scribonia pregnant.

Antony set off for Italy from Sicyon hurriedly, giving Fulvia the further grievance that he was leaving her on her sickbed. He did not even say goodbye before his departure. Estrangement from her husband seems to have been the final blow for this Lady Macbeth of the ancient world, for she soon died. It would appear that her steely determination to advance her husband's cause concealed a fragile psyche. Antony was greatly upset by her death, and blamed himself for it.

The triumvir set a course for Brundisium with only a small number of troops, but with two hundred ships. En route he joined forces with

Ahenobarbus' powerful republican fleet. The two men had come to a secret agreement that they would work together as partners.

This was an important moment, for it marked a change of opinion among republicans about the victor of Philippi. A number of leading personalities had escaped the proscription by fleeing to Sextus Pompeius in Sicily, but he was a young and untried leader. Now surviving optimates, recalling his readiness to come to terms with the Senate and freedom fighters in 44 B.C., increasingly placed their hopes in Antony and joined his following.

The understandings with Ahenobarbus and Sextus strongly suggest that Antony was ready to succeed where his brother Lucius had failed, and bring about the destruction of his tiresome young colleague. He had had his fill of him, not merely from personal irritation but because the triumvirs' dysfunctional relationship was destabilizing Roman politics and needlessly delaying the invasion of Parthia. The ancient sources are studiously vague about Antony's exact intentions; it may be that a renewed civil war was meant to be a last resort if Octavian proved uncooperative and undependable. More probably, Antony actively sought a showdown.

Supported by Ahenobarbus, he made his way to Brundisium. The port, garrisoned by five of Octavian's cohorts, closed its gates to them, and Antony immediately laid siege to it. He sent to Macedonia for immediate reinforcements. It was a sign of the depth of his anger that he also asked Sextus, with whom he had no formal alliance, to launch naval attacks against Italy; the young commander enthusiastically complied. He sent a large fleet and four legions to Sardinia, then in Octavian's possession, capturing it and its two legions.

Octavian, with a leaden heart, took the road to Brundisium. Although he had many more troops at his disposal than did his fellow triumvir, he did nothing but watch and wait outside Antony's fortifications. As often happened at times of crisis, he fell ill for several days, we are not told with what ailment.

The Roman world was about to be convulsed once more, were it not for one familiar obstacle. Not for the first time, the soldiers took a hand in events. Octavian's veterans came to a secret decision that they would reconcile the triumvirs if they could; they would fight for Octavian only if Antony refused to come to terms (in fact, some turned back from the march to Brundisium). Fraternization between the armies grew and compelled a reconsideration. There was to be no war, because there was no one willing to fight it. This was a blow to the generals' authority, but there was nothing they could do about it, no punishment they could order, that would not make matters worse. Their only realistic option was to come to terms.

Peace negotiators were appointed to resolve the dispute, among them Maecenas, Octavian's trusted school friend, for Octavian. The two sides agreed that there should be an amnesty for the past acts of both triumvirs. Each side had bitter claims to put forward about the other's behavior, but it was time, as political realists have said throughout history, to move on.

The arrangement they came to distinctly favored Octavian, for it left him with Gaul and Calenus' legions. However, this seems not to have troubled Antony; he came to a strategic decision that he could not go on treating Octavian as a temporary annoyance who would either disappear through illness (quite likely) or mistakes (unlikely), or whom he would swat like a fly at some convenient moment. He wanted a full, final, and permanent settlement. To achieve it, he was willing to make substantial compromises.

The Triumvirate was renewed for another five years. The empire was cut neatly in half, with Octavian taking all of the west, including Gaul, and Antony the east from Macedonia onward. Italy was to be common ground, where both men would be allowed to recruit soldiers. The increasingly insignificant Lepidus retained Africa, a courtesy granted by Octavian. Antony had received help from the anomalous and threatening Sextus Pompeius, who still held Sicily and the western Mediterranean; he now had to abandon him. It would be Octavian's duty to dispose of Sextus, just as Antony would punish Parthia.

Divisions on a map were insufficient to guarantee a permanent peace, however. Octavian and Antony had never got on with each other and were unlikely to do so in the future. Unless something decisive was done to bind them personally as well as politically, the Treaty of Brundisium, as the accord is called, would not be worth the marble on which it was inscribed. A solution to the conundrum was made possible by two recent deaths. That of Fulvia not only enabled Antony to blame her for his past misdeeds, but also made of him a merry widower (Roman opinion regarded the queen of Egypt as an innocuous diversion). In the same year, 40 B.C., Octavia, Octavian's sister, lost her elderly husband, Gaius Claudius Marcellus, and, perhaps five years older than her brother, became a highly eligible widow (albeit with two daughters and an infant son).

The proposition that the treaty should be sealed by their marriage was irresistible. Although Octavian's brief betrothal to Fulvia's daughter Claudia had failed to reconcile the two triumvirs, there was a benign precedent for such a union in the long-ago and extremely happy marriage between Pompey the Great and Julius Caesar's daughter, Julia. As long as she lived the two warlords had stayed friends; history would now be given an opportunity to repeat itself.

Octavian's short but dazzling political career had exposed a ruthlessness that overrode ordinary affection, but on this occasion we may guess that he sincerely wanted reconcilation with Antony. Plutarch records that he was "deeply attached to his sister, who was, as the saying is, a wonder of a woman." He is unlikely to have handed her over into the hands of his unpredictable and womanizing colleague if he did not have his adoptive father's example in mind.

Great celebrations took place to honor the historic accord. At Brundisium, the triumvirs entertained each other at banquets in their respective camps, Octavian "in military and Roman fashion and Antony in Asiatic and Egyptian style." They then moved on to Rome, where the wedding of Antony and Octavia was held; Antony struck a coin showing their heads (the first time a woman's likeness is known to have appeared on a Roman coin). They marched into the city on horses as if celebrating a military triumph.

Only one shadow was cast across the new landscape of peace and harmony. Octavian's friend and supporter, the talented Quintus Salvidienus Rufus, was in command of the legions in Gaul. Sometime before the triumvirs became reconciled, he had opened a secret correspondence with Antony, hinting that he might be ready to switch sides. His motives are obscure; perhaps there were hidden jealousies in Octavian's circle of intimates, or Salvidienus may simply have judged that his leader's prospects were poor.

Astonishingly, if we are to believe the ancient sources, Antony told Octavian that Salvidienus had been plotting to defect to him and had sent a message to that effect while he was besieging Brundisium. Octavian was loyal to a fault, but if a friend betrayed him he was merciless. He immediately sent the proconsul a summons to come to Rome for urgent consultations, after which he would return to his command in Gaul. Salvidienus unwisely obeyed. Octavian arraigned him before the Senate and had him condemned both an *inimicus* (a personal enemy) and a *hostis* (a public enemy), and put to death. It was the end of a spectacular career. Salvidienus came from a humble background and had started out as a shepherd boy. He had been designated a consul for the following year, 39 B.C., without ever having held civilian office or sat in the Senate.

Whatever the background to this mysterious affair, Appian remarks drily that "Antony did not win general approval for making this admission" about Salvidienus. In these murky and shifting times, few were without guilty secrets and Antony might have been expected to turn the same blind eye to Salvidienus as others were to his own maneuverings. It is hard to see what he expected to gain from his treachery. Perhaps he simply wanted to demonstrate, at someone else's expense, that he was sincerely committed to his new friendship with Octavian.

Salvidienus' death is a reminder of an alienation deep inside Antony's personality. It was easy to be misled by his celebrated bonhomie, his fondness for fun and games, for binge drinking and easy women; but below the affability lay a casual brutality and an inability to imagine the feelings of others.

# IX

# GOLDEN AGE

## 40–38 B.C.

THE RELIEF FELT THROUGHOUT THE MEDITERRANEAN WORLD
after the Treaty of Brundisium could almost be touched. The nightmare
of the proscriptions, the soldiers killed and wounded, the ruination of
Italy, the theft of the provinces' wealth—in sum, the empire falling apart
through self-cannibalism—was over, and rosy-fingered dawn heralded
the day.

The rising poets of the age celebrated the arrival of peace with works
that still speak vividly of their relief and joy. One of these, Publius Vergi-
lius Maro (Englished as Virgil), came from the middle or lower middle
ranks of Italian society, but his father ensured he received a good education. Virgil migrated to Rome, where, like any ambitious young man, he
studied rhetoric. Painfully shy, though, he apparently lost the first law
case at which he spoke.

Suetonius gives a portrait sketch of the man: "He was tall and bulky,
with a dark complexion and the appearance of a countryman. He had
changeable health [and] ate and drank little. He was always falling in love
with boys."

Virgil was thirty, approaching the height of his powers. Having abandoned Rome and a public career, he lived in Neapolis. His first major publication was the *Eclogues* (from the Greek for "selection"), a series of ten
poems that describe an ideal countryside. But in Virgil's neverland of
lovely young shepherds and shepherdesses, real emotions and real events
(such as the loss of the author's farm because of Octavian's veteran settlements, and its return thanks to the triumvir's intervention) lie close to
the surface.

The young poet could recognize reality when he saw it. Whatever emotional scars his brush with triumviral power left him with, he made his

peace with the regime. In these days before print, a professional writer without a personal fortune had no large middle-class market to provide him with an income from book sales. He needed rich patrons to supply his means—in the form of money or gifts of property and slaves—and to pay for the laborious copying out of his books. In the first instance, then, Virgil probably attached himself to Octavian's cause for the sake of financial security. However, he also acted from political conviction, for the triumviral regime promised stability and prosperity. The two men became fast friends.

Virgil wrote that the Golden Age had returned to Italy, and with a curious infantine addition. This was the messianic theme of his fourth eclogue:

> *The Firstborn of the New Ages is already on his way from high heaven down to earth.*
>
> *With him, the Iron Age shall end and Golden Man inherit all the world. Smile on the Baby's birth, immaculate Lucina [goddess of childbirth]; your own Apollo is enthroned at last.*

What exactly is Virgil getting at? Who is this baby? Is he a metaphor for something, or is a real person being denoted? Some detective work is needed to unravel the mystery.

The poem is addressed to Gaius Asinius Pollio; he was a friend of Antony and had assisted him in the recent negotiations with Octavian. A man of principle in an age of turncoats, he was about to leave politics and write his *History of the Civil Wars* describing the period from the First Triumvirate to Philippi (sadly lost).

Pollio had a dry sense of humor and a reputation for straight talking. When Octavian once wrote some lampoons about him, Pollio only observed: "For my part I am saying nothing in reply; for it is asking for trouble to write against a man who can write you off."

Some commentators have wondered whether the child could be Pollio's son, but it is hard to see why Virgil should have imagined such a boy as savior of the world. A more likely candidate would be the predicted offspring of Antony and Octavia, whose union presaged peace after long years of war. Indeed, she was soon pregnant. Some scholars even believe that the poem was written as a wedding hymn.

However, we should not forget that Octavian, too, was a newlywed, albeit somewhat unsuitably. It was known that Scribonia was carrying a child. A detail from the eclogue suggests that the answer to the conundrum may lie here. This is the reference to Apollo "enthroned at last"; just as orientalizing Antony favored the dionysiac Dionysus, so throughout his life Octavian appropriated the logical, severe god of light, Apollo. It is rather more likely that Virgil had Octavian's unborn child in mind than Antony's.

In the event, the issue turned out to be academic. In 39 B.C. both women bore daughters, Julia and Antonia.

For all the poet's fine words, optimism was fading. Before the Treaty of Brundisium, Sextus Pompeius had attempted to help Antony against Octavian, only to be called off at the last moment. He was angry and threatening.

Sextus employed two admirals, ex-slaves and former pirates called Menodorus (or Menas) and Menecrates. Perhaps they had been taken prisoner and enslaved by Pompey the Great during his highly successful campaign in 67 B.C. against the pirate fleets that used to dominate the Mediterranean. Having secured control of Sardinia and Corsica, they maintained the blockade of Italy.

At Rome, the price of goods soared. For once Octavian lost touch with public opinion, which wanted him to restore peace by coming to an understanding with Sextus. He obstinately refused to do this, and to pay his soldiers he levied a new tax on property owners (fifty sesterces per slave, plus a death duty).

For many, this was the final straw. Forced settlements, war, proscription, and famine—these things had all been endured, but now the people lost patience. There were demonstrations and riots. As he had done with the mutinous soldiers, Octavian decided to brave the mob in person and explain why it was wrong to blame him for the situation. He came to the Forum, attended only by some associates and a handful of bodyguards.

As soon as the crowd caught sight of him, they started bombarding him with missiles. They did not stop even when they saw they had injured him. Octavian stood his ground, although this meant that he was, in effect, placing himself in their hands. When Antony was told what was happening, he rushed to the rescue. As he came down the Via Sacra into the Forum, the crowd did not at first throw anything at him, for he was known to favor peace with Sextus, but they warned him to go back. When he refused they began to stone him.

Antony summoned reinforcements. His soldiers quickly surrounded the Forum, broke into small groups, and marched down alleyways into the square. The crowd could not escape and a number of people were killed. Pushing his way through the press, Antony reached Octavian only with the greatest difficulty and escorted him home. There was no doubt that he had saved his colleague's life, and in spectacular fashion.

This was a most instructive episode. It illustrates the continuing growth of a bloody-minded courage in Octavian. Through the exercise of will, Octavian, now twenty-four years old, was tempering himself in fire.

What kept Antony and Octavian in power was the active support of the people and the legions: this was a lesson they had already learned many bitter times. Octavian eventually realized that he would have to give way on the matter of Sextus. Discreet feelers were put out and soon an entente was in prospect. Menodorus in Sardinia wrote to Sextus, counseling against peace; either he should make war wholeheartedly, he recommended, or he should wait and see if the famine at Rome would enable him to drive a harder bargain.

Sextus rejected this advice and met the opposing leaders at a peace conference in the summer of 39 B.C. Accompanied by many of his Roman supporters, he sailed from Sicily in a huge flagship, with six banks of oars, leading a fine fleet. He anchored off Misenum, a headland at the northern end of the Bay of Naples dotted with the holiday villas of the rich, where the meeting was to be held. Wooden planks had been laid on piles in the sea, to create two platforms. Antony and Octavian went to the one nearer the coast and Sextus to the seaward platform. Enough water lay between them to allow the members of each party to talk among themselves without being overheard; exchanges between them had to be shouted, in a primitive and literal form of megaphone diplomacy.

These cautious arrangements were presumably made at the initiative of Sextus. Perhaps recalling the nightmare scene when he had watched his father go to his death on the Egyptian coast, he was determined not to risk his life by abandoning his ship for the terra firma of his enemies.

Sextus opened the discussions by demanding on behalf of the proscribed the return of all their confiscated property. Antony and Octavian agreed to buy back a quarter of the properties from their new owners. The news was published and immediately welcomed by victims of the proscription.

The final agreement did little more than confirm what everyone knew to be the unstable status quo. Sextus was officially installed as governor of what he had already captured—Sardinia, Corsica, and Sicily. To these was added the Peloponnese (southern Greece). He was honored by membership of the College of Augurs, the committee of senior statesmen who were charged with taking the auspices at Rome, and he was nominated for the consulship in the following year, 38 B.C. Sextus' followers in Sicily had their personal positions secured: all the exiles from Italy in his army (excepting, always, Julius Caesar's assassins) were to have their civil rights restored; the buyback offer to proscribed senators and *equites* was confirmed; the runaway slaves in Sextus' force were to be freed; and Sextus' soldiers were to receive the same demobilization awards as those serving the triumvirs.

Sextus could claim that this was a reasonably good deal for him, in that he was no longer an outlaw. The Treaty of Misenum brought him inside the political fold. Privately, though, he already regretted rejecting Menodorus' advice to avoid coming to terms with the triumvirs.

By contrast, Antony and Octavian had every right to be pleased with themselves. They had given Sextus nothing essential to their interests, but had won something beyond price. Although they may not have realized it at the time, they had initiated the process of detaching opposition politicians from Sextus. Once it became clear that the triumvirs were not planning a new bloodbath, many began trickling back either to Italy or to join Antony when he returned to the east. To Sextus' alarm, the Pompeian constituency was set to decline.

The principals celebrated the peace with a series of banquets. They drew lots to decide the order. Sextus acted as host first, on his flagship ("My only ancestral home left to me"). The two sides did not trust each other; the triumvirs had their ships moored nearby, guards were posted and the dinner guests carried daggers underneath their clothes. On the surface all was smiles and friendship. Sextus gave a warm welcome to Antony and Octavian. The atmosphere softened and the conversation became coarse and convivial. Jokes were made about Antony's passion for the queen of Egypt, a topic that Octavia's brother and husband would ordinarily have found embarrassing.

As at Brundisium, the bond between the parties was incarnated in a marriage union. At the dinner table, Sextus' infant daughter was formally engaged to the three-year-old Marcellus, Antony's stepson and Octavian's nephew.

According to Plutarch, Menodorus came to Sextus and spoke to him out of the hearing of his guests. "Shall I cut the cables and make you master not just of Sicily and Sardinia, but of the whole Roman empire?"

Sextus thought for a moment, and then burst out: "Menodorus, you should have acted, not spoken to me beforehand. Now we must be content with things as they are. I do not break my word."

This famous anecdote has a suspiciously glib quality, yet it may be true, for it illustrates two facets of Sextus' character. When he called himself Pius, "Dutiful" or "Honest," the reference was primarily to his father's memory, but it also indicated that he saw himself as a Roman of the old school, honorable and straightforward. In addition, the story points to a certain passivity that can be detected throughout his career, an absence of the killer instinct that marked out, in their different ways, Antony and Octavian.

On the following two days, Antony and then Octavian entertained Sextus, erecting dining tents on their sea platform. After this they left for their respective destinations—Octavian to Gaul, where there were disturbances; Antony to the east and the Parthians; Sextus back to Sicily. Most of the refugees in Sextus' entourage said goodbye to him and left for Rome.

With the onset of autumn Octavian did something that, on the face of it, was out of character: for once letting his heart sway him, he fell passionately in love. The object of his affection was Livia Drusilla; about nineteen years old, she was intelligent and beautiful, although with a small mouth and chin. However, she suffered from one signal disadvantage: she was already married, to an aristocrat and cousin of hers, Tiberius Claudius Nero. Not only that, but she was heavily pregnant.

To add to the complications, Octavian's wife, Scribonia, gave birth to her daughter, Julia, sometime in 39 B.C. Despite the happy event, the marriage—a political union if ever there was one—was not going well. As was pointed out earlier, Scribonia was substantially older than her husband; too, she was reputed to be a *gravis femina,* a dignified or serious woman. This did not much suit a young man with a reputation for copious adultery.

On the very day that Julia arrived in the world, her father divorced her mother. "I couldn't bear the way she nagged at me," he explained.

In September—perhaps on his birthday, the twenty-third—Octavian conducted a rite of passage. He did not have a hairy body, and at twenty-four had still not found it necessary to shave: now the moment had come. Being prone to devise a ritual for almost every aspect of daily life, the Romans made a ceremony of their first shave—the *depositio barbae,* which in most cases took place about the time a boy came of age, usually at sixteen or seventeen.

Octavian made a great to-do over the ceremony, throwing a magnificent party and paying for a public festival. The event could be seen as a statement that, with the arrival of peace, the "boy who owed everything to his name" had attained his political as well as physical maturity. But it was whispered that his true motive was to please Livia.

Livia had an impeccable family background. While Octavian was unquestionably smitten, it is also true that marriage with her would give him a valuable connection to the Claudii, one of Rome's most aristocratic clans. The triumvir's father had reached the praetorship and so qualified as a *nobilis.* He himself had been enrolled as a patrician; however, he was still regarded as something of a provincial upstart. The union afforded Livia's family access to her lover's political power, in return for which she contributed her ancestry.

Livia Drusilla's life, although short, had been full of incident. She was born on January 30, 59 or 58 B.C., probably at Rome. Not long after the Ides of March in 44 B.C., a husband was found for her. At fourteen or fifteen years old, Livia was approaching the upper limit of a girl's customary marriageable age. Most marriages were arranged by the parents and love ("friendship gone mad") was not expected to enter anybody's calculations. A daughter was often a pawn in the alliances—social, economic, or political—that a great family struck to maintain its position in Roman public life. Husbands could be much older than their wives, and for the physically immature the wedding night must have been a savage introduction to sex.

Despite the potentially inauspicious opening to her married life, the Roman wife was a powerful figure in the household, being its *domina,* or mistress. Old forms of marriage in the early Republic, according to which she lived in complete subjection to her husband, the all-powerful *pater-*

*familias,* had given way by the third century B.C. to a new and freer arrangement by which the woman remained under her father's authority and from the age of twenty-five held possession of her own property.

The man Livia married was Tiberius Claudius Nero, from another branch of the Claudian clan, the Claudii Nerones; he was probably in his mid- to late thirties. Of impeccable birth, he had great promise, but (as it turned out) poor judgment.

Tiberius took a stand against the First Triumvirate during the fifties B.C., but then, with the onset of the civil war in 49, turned his back on his optimate friends and sided with Julius Caesar. His services were recognized generously and Tiberius must have felt that fortune was smiling on him, but then on the Ides of March 44 B.C. the Caesarian regime came crashing down. Tiberius immediately returned to his old optimate allegiance. When the Senate voted for an amnesty for the assassins, he went an obsequious step further and supported a proposal to reward them.

In 42 B.C., Livia became pregnant. She was very anxious to have a boy, and to find out in advance what the sex of her child would be she took an egg from under a broody hen and kept it warm against her breast; also, she and her attendants held it in turn in their hands. In due course, she hatched a fine cock chick already with a comb. The prophecy was exact. On November 16, Livia gave birth to a son at the family home on the Palatine Hill at Rome. As was the Roman custom with first-born males, he was given his father's *praenomen,* Tiberius.

After the defeat of the republican cause at Philippi, Tiberius agilely changed course again. He now became a supporter of Mark Antony; in that capacity, he was elected praetor for 41 B.C., the same year in which Antony's brother, Lucius, was consul.

Although we have no idea what opinion Livia held of her husband, she demonstrated a personal quality he certainly did not share: a steady loyalty, even, or perhaps especially, when under pressure. When Tiberius, with his usual poor judgment, decided to follow Lucius Antonius' star, Livia and the infant Tiberius went along with him to Perusia. The family endured the terrible privations of the siege, and after Perusia fell Tiberius was the only Roman officeholder in the city to refuse to capitulate.

He somehow managed to escape with mother and child; the family went on to Neapolis, where Tiberius tried to foment a slave revolt by promising them freedom. Octavian's forces soon broke into the city and the family had to flee again. Following bypaths to avoid the soldiery and accompanied by only one or two attendants, including a nurse to carry Tiberius, they secretly made their way to the coast. The baby twice started crying and nearly gave them away. The family found a ship—it must have been arranged for in advance—and sailed to Sicily, where the elder Tiberius expected a welcome from Sextus Pompeius.

In fact, Sextus received him coolly and was slow to grant him an audience; doubtless he was considered something of an embarrassment. Soon he and Livia set off again, this time to Greece. But what to do now? Antony was no more interested than Sextus in having anything to do with this undependable nobleman. He sent Tiberius to Sparta, which had long been in the Claudian *clientela*. Here the family at last received a warm welcome. However, some unrecorded danger arose, and a hurried departure once more became necessary. According to Suetonius, Livia and the baby nearly lost their lives when, fleeing by night, they ran into a sudden forest fire and were encircled by it. In this mysterious incident, Livia's hair caught fire and her dress was scorched.

At the Treaty of Misenum, Sextus eventually placed Tiberius' name on the list of exiles to be restored, and so, at long last, he, Livia, and little Tiberius were allowed to abandon their nomadic life. At some point in the late summer of 39 B.C., they returned to Rome. They found themselves in comparatively reduced circumstances. As an exile and opponent of the Triumvirate, Tiberius had forfeited his property, including the grand house on the Palatine. The deal struck at Misenum promised only to return one quarter of it.

It was at or about this moment of bittersweet celebration that Livia learned that she was pregnant again. It would be unwise to conclude from this that she was content with her lot. Livia must have felt that she had done her best for her husband under extremely trying, even harrowing, circumstances. It was time she looked out for herself.

It is easy in the light of hindsight to criticize Tiberius' behavior. Many of his contemporaries in the ruling class faced the same dilemmas and were equally uncertain and inconsistent in their responses. Where, they wondered desperately, were the old, fixed points of guidance in a political landscape made unrecognizable by successive earthquakes?

Where Livia was concerned, Octavian was determined to let nothing stand in his way. He met her very soon after her return to Rome; indeed, she may have been introduced to him by Scribonia. He quickly made up his mind to marry her, and she decided equally quickly to say yes. Tiberius complaisantly agreed to a divorce.

It is likely that, soon after the *depositio barbae,* in late September or early October, Octavian and Livia became engaged. It was a slightly scandalous event, but a grand betrothal banquet was held. Like other fashionable people of the time, Livia owned little slave boys called *deliciae,* or darlings (often Syrians or Africans), who ran around naked and amused people with their chatter. Like court jesters, they had license to say the unsayable. On this occasion, one of these boys saw Livia and Octavian sharing a dining couch and Tiberius lying on another alongside a male guest. He went up to Livia and said: "What are you doing here, mistress? For your husband [pointing to Tiberius] is over *there.*"

The couple paused before translating their engagement into marriage. The problem was Livia's unborn child by Tiberius. Octavian went to consult the appropriate religious authority, the *pontifices:* could he marry Livia while she was pregnant?

The *pontifices* offered their seal of approval and it seems that Livia now moved in with Octavian in his house on the Palatine. However, the wedding did not take place until after the birth of her second child, who was born on January 14 and given the *praenomen* Drusus.

People suspected that he was the product of adultery with his stepfather. This was obviously wrong, for Octavian had not met Livia when she conceived in the spring of 39. Nevertheless, the story was too good to disbelieve, and Suetonius records that the following epigram went the rounds:

> *How fortunate those parents are for whom*
> *Their child is only three months in the womb.*

The birth of Drusus cannot have been a very difficult one, for three days later the couple wed. The Roman marriage ceremony, a changeless ritual, dramatized the bride's removal from her father's house to the groom's. Livia's father was dead; apparently, Tiberius gave her away. She must have spent the night before the wedding at his home.

On the day itself, Livia gathered her hair in a crimson net and put on an unhemmed tunic, secured at the waist by a woolen girdle tied with a double knot. Over this she wore a saffron-colored cloak; she was shod in saffron-colored sandals and fastened a metal collar around her throat.

Her hair was protected by six pads of artificial hair separated by narrow bands; a veil of flaming orange covered the top half of her face. It was crowned by a wreath of verbena and sweet marjoram.

In this spectacular outfit, Livia stood surrounded by family and friends and greeted the groom when he arrived with his people. An animal sacrifice to the gods was then offered (probably a pig, although it could have been a ewe or even an ox).

Livia then said to Octavian, in an age-old formula, *"Ubi tu es Gaius, ego Gaia"*—"Where you are Gaius, I am Gaia."

This was the heart of the ritual, and everyone present shouted *"Feliciter,"* "Congratulations."

Octavian now led Livia in a street procession from Tiberius' house to his own, not a long journey as they both lived on the Palatine Hill. Flute players led the way, followed by five torchbearers. As they walked along, people sang cheerfully obscene songs. Three boys whose parents were still alive accompanied the bride; one held a torch of hawthorn twigs and the other two took Livia by the hand.

On reaching her new home, garlanded with flowers for the occasion, Livia was obliged to conduct an inconvenient and messy ritual: she wound wool around the doorposts and coated them with lard or (harder to find, one would imagine) wolf's fat. Then, men who had been married only once lifted her through the front door; this was to avoid the risk of her tripping on the threshold, a very bad omen. They were followed by three bridesmaids, two of whom carried the symbols of domestic virtue, a distaff and spindle for home weaving.

After a wedding breakfast and some more rude songs, Livia was led to the bridal bed. Octavian took off her cloak and untied the girdle, after which the wedding guests made their excuses and left.

The law gave the *paterfamilias* absolute authority over his children, so the little Tiberius, a toddler of three, stayed behind with his father. Octavian also handed over the newborn Drusus. Livia's feelings about this are unknown, but a story told about her suggests that her attention was fixed, rather, on the future splendor of her position.

Apparently, when she was returning shortly after the wedding to a house she owned at Veii a few miles from Rome, an eagle flew by and dropped into Livia's lap a white pullet it had just pounced on. Noticing that it held in its beak a laurel twig with berries on it (the laurel was a sign of victory, and generals wore a laurel wreath at their triumphs), she decided to keep the bird for breeding and to plant the twig. Soon the pullet raised such a brood of chickens that the house became known as Ad Gallinas Albas, White Poultry, and the twig grew so luxuriantly that Octavian plucked laurels from it for his official wreaths.

Five years later, in 33 B.C., if she had not negotiated their earlier return, Livia was able to reclaim her sons, for her former husband died, from what cause is unknown—his last stroke of bad luck.

Octavian's political situation was by no means secure, but he had managed to hold on to the gains of the Treaty of Brundisium. Through cold-blooded courage he had survived the anger of the mob and of the soldiers, his two fundamental bulwarks. The agreement at Misenum had settled nothing, but had at least won him a breathing space and measurably weakened Sextus' position. His willingness to risk his life was a sign of a growing self-confidence, of a conviction that he was owed respect for his achievements as much as for his inheritance.

Octavian's marriage is the first occasion for which we have evidence when he gave priority to his feelings. The union had its political importance, too. Livia was one of many exiles who had gathered around the last forlorn hope of the defeated Republic, Sextus Pompeius, given up on him, and returned home to Rome. That she was willing to wed the Republic's archenemy is interesting evidence that the ruling class was beginning to reconcile itself to an altered world.

## X

# FIGHTING NEPTUNE

### 38–36 B.C.

SEXTUS' POPULARITY WITH THE ROMAN MOB WAS RISING and squabbles between the signatories of the Treaty of Misenum were already breaking out. Octavian was increasingly convinced that the agreement had been a mistake.

However, the most important development by far was the defection of Sextus' admiral Menodorus, who was in Sardinia. The former pirate was losing confidence in his master's strategic ability and long-term chances of survival. Menodorus delivered to Octavian Sardinia and Corsica, three legions, and some light-armed troops.

Treaty or no treaty, here was an opportunity to dispose of Sextus. But before he showed his hand, Octavian sought help from Antony, whom he asked to visit Italy for consultations. He sent for an army from Agrippa, who had succeeded Calenus as proconsul in Gaul, commissioned warships at Ravenna, and arranged for other necessities of war to be assembled on the eastern and western coasts of Italy at Brundisium and Puteoli.

Unfortunately, Antony opposed hostilities with Sextus. He turned up at Brundisium on a mutually appointed date in 38 B.C., but to his annoyance found no Octavian. After waiting for a short time, he left, but wrote to his fellow triumvir, strongly counseling against war.

It is not clear what Octavian meant by the snub. The most benign, and not implausible, explanation is that he was detained by his military preparations (perhaps, too, he was not unhappy to delay Antony's Parthian plans). However, it is rather more probable that Octavian was yielding to an unusual bout of overconfidence. With Menodorus at his side, he was privy to all Sextus' secrets. On reconsideration, he could do perfectly well without Antony's advice or assistance.

Octavian's plan was to defeat Sextus at sea and then ferry troops from

Italy to occupy Sicily. He would launch a two-pronged attack. One fleet would sail south from Puteoli; it would be led by Gaius Calvisius Sabinus, once an officer of Julius Caesar and one of a new breed of politicians from the provinces, who in the previous year had been the first-ever non-Latin consul. He was one of the two senators who had sought to protect Caesar on the Ides of March. Calvisius shared the command with Menodorus. The other fleet, for which Octavian appointed himself admiral, would set out from Tarentum and approach Sicily from the east.

In classical times, the sea was a frightening place. Ships were vulnerable to bad weather and sailing was avoided so far as possible during the winter months. Roman war fleets mainly consisted of rowing galleys, many of them triremes and quinqueremes. We do not know exactly how they worked. A trireme either had three banks of oars, or one bank with the oars grouped together in threes with one man per oar. It displaced about 230 tons and was nearly 150 feet long. Quinqueremes probably had one bank of oars with five men pulling each oar. There were up to 150 rowers; they were often non-Romans, though they were not, as in Hollywood films, slaves chained to their oars. Every ship had a captain, or trierarch; a helmsman; and a *hortator,* or encourager, who set the rowing rate. Under oar, a trireme was capable of bursts of speed—between seven and ten knots.

Warships had brass battering rams on their prows, and the usual tactic was to ram the side of an enemy ship. The Romans tended to fight sea battles as if they were on land. A grappling device was invented, the *corvus* or crow, which enabled soldiers to board the enemy ship and take it over. If boarding was impractical, it was possible to destroy galleys by using flaming projectiles to set them afire.

Triremes and quinqueremes found it hard to cope with storms. Their high bows made them difficult to hold into the wind. A large rectangular sail midships and one or more small ones were used during ordinary voyages, but square-rigging made it extremely difficult to gain headway against a wind. When waves hit such vessels beam-on (that is, from the side), they became hard to maneuver and were prone to being swamped or capsizing, although, being of fairly light wooden construction, they seldom sank completely.

•    •    •

Sextus learned of the desertion of Menodorus when the enemy fleets were under way. He immediately dispatched the old pirate Menecrates to confront Menodorus with most of his ships, and decided to await Octavian, whom he judged to be the lesser threat, off Messana (today's Messina) in the narrow straits between Sicily and mainland Italy.

Menecrates found Menodorus and the Roman admiral Calvisius off Cumae on the Campanian coast and had the better of the engagement, although he himself was wounded and died. When dusk fell the two fleets separated, and Sextus' ships returned to port at Messana without following up their victory.

When news came on the following day of what had taken place at Cumae, Octavian decided to brave the strait and make his way to Calvisius. This was a bad mistake. Sextus dashed out of Messana in large numbers and attacked Octavian's fleet, which fled toward the Italian shore. Many were driven onto the rocks and set on fire. As night fell Sextus caught sight of Calvisius' fleet sailing south to the rescue and withdrew to Messana.

Octavian, in danger of his life and not yet aware that Calvisius was close by, scrambled ashore with his attendants, pulled men out of the water, and took refuge with them in the mountains. They lit bonfires to alert those still afloat to their existence and whereabouts. However, the warship crews were too busy putting their boats to rights and trying to make good the waterlogged wrecks to come to their aid. The survivors spent the night without food or any other necessities. Octavian did not sleep, but went about the various groups and did his best to keep their spirits up.

By great good fortune, the XIIIth Legion happened to be marching through the mountains by night (presumably making all speed to Rhegium, a port opposite Messana, in anticipation of the planned invasion of Sicily). Its commander learned of the disaster at sea and, guessing that the fires in the hills denoted survivors, led his force in their direction.

Octavian and his men were in a poor way. They were given food, and a makeshift tent was pitched for the exhausted triumvir. With typical self-discipline, he sent messengers in all directions to announce that he was alive and still in charge. Having learned, too, of Calvisius' arrival with his fleet, he now allowed himself to snatch some sleep. It had been a terrible twenty-four hours, as he was reminded all too graphically when he awoke. Appian describes the scene: "At daybreak, as he looked out over the sea, his gaze was met by ships that had been set on fire, ships that were still half-ablaze or half-burned, and ships that had been smashed."

As if that were not enough, a gale came up in the afternoon, one of the fiercest in living memory, whipping a vicious swell with a strong current in the narrow seas. Sextus was safely inside the harbor of Messana; Menodorus, with an experienced eye for the unpredictable Mediterranean weather, sailed out to sea, where he rode out the storm; but Octavian's surviving ships were blown against the craggy coast and pounded against the rocks and one another. Night fell, but there was no letup in the wind until morning. More than half of the fleet was sunk, and most of the rest was badly damaged.

Another dark night of traveling through mountains ensued—and, surely, a dark night of the soul, too; for this was the worst crisis of Octavian's career. His humiliating double defeat at sea not only signaled the ruin of his hopes to eliminate Sextus Pompeius but might well set off conspiracies against him in Rome.

Methodically, Octavian took the necessary steps to reduce this risk. Orders were sent to all his supporters and military commanders to watch out for trouble. Detachments of infantry were posted along the coastline to deter an invasion by Sextus. Men were left behind to salvage and repair his galleys.

Meanwhile, the son of Pompey the Great celebrated his great victory. Since his arrival in Sicily, he had identified the god of the sea, Neptune, with his father on coins that he had issued. Now he proclaimed himself the son of Neptune, took to wearing a dark blue cloak (instead of a commander's regulation purple), and sacrificed some horses (and, it was rumored, men) to the god by driving them into the sea.

With a heavy heart, Octavian journeyed north to Campania, brooding on what he should do next. He needed many new ships, but had neither money nor time to build them.

Embarrassing though it was, he realized that he would have to humble himself and ask again for assistance from his fellow triumvirs—Lepidus, half forgotten in Africa; Mark Antony, whom he had snubbed only months before. Without their support, he could make no progress; also, left to their own devices, his colleagues might well open discussions with Sextus. He sent them an urgent appeal.

Almost at once, though, Octavian wished he had not done so, for he was given new heart by the return from Gaul of his friend Agrippa. The twenty-four-year-old commander had great achievements to his credit, having secured the frontier on the Rhine and founded a new city, Colonia Agrippinensis (or, as it became, Cologne). He was offered a triumph, but, sensitive to his friend's distress, declined.

Now the victorious young general turned his attention to a style of warfare with which he was almost completely unfamiliar: fighting at sea. He decided exactly what he needed—a sufficient stretch of water, with large supplies of wood in the vicinity, where he could build a new fleet, then train both it and himself, safe from the maraudings of Sextus Pompeius, safe even from Sextus' knowledge.

Agrippa knew the very place. According to Homer, the lake of Avernus was the gateway into Hades, where the dead led shadowy and enfeebled existences. Not far from Cumae, Avernus was a huge water-filled crater, with a diameter of nearly five miles and a depth of thirty-seven yards. Except for one narrow entrance, it was completely surrounded by densely wooded hills, giving it a somber, oppressive atmosphere. Here and there on the slopes, volcanic springs spewed a mixture of water and flames, steam and smoke.

A short way south was the Lucrine lake, separated from the sea by a low thin strip of land ("as broad as a wagon road," wrote the contemporary geographer Strabo).

No sentimentalist, Agrippa was undaunted by the gloomy spirit of the place. He had the brilliantly simple, highly ambitious idea of cutting a canal south from Avernus to the Lucrine lake and thence to the sea. This was quickly done, while a tunnel was also driven northward to the seaside town of Cumae, so creating a second means of access. In this way, a huge, new, completely secure, secret harbor was created, which was named Portus Julius.

The trees on the slopes of Avernus were cut down; keels were laid and galleys built. Twenty thousand freed slaves were recruited as oarsmen, and learned their craft in safety and secrecy. Among other things, they were able to practice using a lethal refinement of the *corvus* that Agrippa had invented: this was the *harpax*, a grapnel fired from a ship-borne catapult.

This vast enterprise called for substantial resources. Wealthy supporters of Octavian financed ships, and a message came from Antony offering military help. It is likely that Agrippa brought funds with him from Gaul, and money was raised from the empire's provinces.

* * *

In response to Octavian's plea, transmitted by the emollient Maecenas, Antony, who had spent the winter at Athens, agreed to return to Italy in the spring or early summer of 37 B.C.; it was in his interest to ensure that the west was quiet before he set off against Parthia and also he needed (as was allowed by the Treaty of Brundisium) to recruit troops in Italy.

He sailed with a large fleet to Brundisium, but once again found its port closed to him. Irritated by this evidence of Octavian's renewed fickleness, he sailed round to Tarentum, where he invited Octavian to join him. He was now not at all sure that he would support his fellow triumvir against Sextus. Octavia was accompanying Antony and was very upset at the prospect of another quarrel breaking out between her brother and her husband. "If the worst should happen," she wrote to her brother, according to Plutarch, "and war break out between you, no one can say which of you is fated to conquer the other, but what is quite certain is that my fate will be miserable."

Octavian took the point; indeed, he had probably done so even before his sister approached him. His refusal to meet his colleague had been as much of a blunder as his original cry for help. He was certainly not ready for war with Antony and had no excuse even for wishing it. There were matters that the triumvirs needed to discuss—for example, an extension of the Triumvirate, which was on the point of expiry. A meeting was evidently in order. The only eventuality Octavian wanted to avoid was Antony joining him in the war against Sextus. To ensure his future as co-ruler of the empire, he must win his own battles.

So it was agreed that a conference be held at Tarentum. Maecenas traveled down from Rome to make the arrangements and plan the agenda. He was also an unofficial minister of culture, who recognized the importance of the arts to the promotion of a political regime. He had a sharp eye for literary talent, and was always on the lookout for it. He gathered a group of poets around him, to whom he gave the freedom of his house at Rome. Chief of these was Virgil, now in his early thirties.

Another member of the inner circle was Horace, twenty-seven years old and Maecenas' favorite. A lover of the peaceful life, Horace agreed with the Greek philosopher Epicurus that pleasure was the only good. Completely without vanity, he has left thumbnail descriptions of his rotund appearance:

*Come and see me when you want a laugh. I'm fat and sleek,*
*In prime condition, a porker from Epicurus' herd.*

And

*Of small build, prematurely grey, and fond of the sun,*
*He was quick to lose his temper, but not hard to appease.*

His eminent patron was portly too, and wrote him an epigram in verse: "If I don't love you, Horace, more than my life, may your friend look skinnier than a rag-doll."

It was typical of the man that Maecenas assembled some poets to accompany him on the journey, probably for the fun of it and for good conversation, though these literary personalities may have been dragooned into providing secretarial services.

Horace wrote a lighthearted poem describing the trip. After two days' leisurely travel from Rome he and a companion, a professor of rhetoric, arrived at a great malarial swamp, the Pomptine Marshes (before his death, Julius Caesar had planned to drain them, but this was not accomplished until Benito Mussolini did it in the 1930s). They left the road for a night and were hauled through wet wasteland in a barge.

Horace was then joined by Maecenas, and the following day by Virgil and two other poets. The company stopped at Capua (today's Santa Maria Capua Vetere), where they took an afternoon off from travel. Capua was one of the richest cities in Italy; Cicero had called it a "second Rome." A great center for gladiatorial combats, it boasted a fine amphitheater (the ruins that can be seen today are of a later building), where Spartacus once fought.

However, no one was interested in seeing the sights; Maecenas went off to take some exercise, while Horace, who had an eye infection, and the delicate Virgil took a siesta, "for ball-games are bad for inflamed eyes and dyspeptic stomachs."

Some days later, when the arid hills of Apulia (today's Puglia), Horace's homeland, came into view, the travelers took refuge from the heat in a villa at Trivicum (Trevico). Horace's sore eyes were irritated by a smoky stove, but his spirits were lifted by the prospect of an amorous encounter.

On this occasion, his hopes were frustrated:

*Here, like an utter fool, I stayed awake till midnight*
*Waiting for a girl who broke her promise. Sleep in the end*
*Overtook me, still keyed up for sex. Then scenes from a dirty*
*Dream spattered my nightshirt and stomach as I lay on my back.*

Three more days rolling along in wagons were made exceptionally un-comfortable and exhausting because the roads had been damaged by heavy rain, still bucketing down. The weather improved as Horace and his friends approached Brundisium, before making their way to the elegant Greek city of Tarentum and the world of great affairs.

The principals—Mark Antony and Octavian—eventually met at the little river Taras, which flowed into the sea at a point between Tarentum and Metapontum, another city founded by mainland Greeks. It was a splendid sight: an army peacefully encamped on land and a great fleet lying quietly offshore. The idea was that the stream should separate the two mutually distrustful parties. Without planning to do so, the triumvirs arrived at the same time. Antony, who was staying at Tarentum, leaped down impulsively from his carriage, jumped unaccompanied into one of the small boats moored at the riverbank, and started to cross over to Octavian.

Realizing that he would lose face if he did not immediately return this demonstration of trust, Octavian, too, boarded a boat himself. The triumvirs met in midstream, and immediately fell into an argument, because each politely wanted to disembark on the other's bank. Octavian won, on the grounds that Octavia was at Tarentum and he would not see her if Antony and he met on his side of the river. He sat beside Antony in his carriage and arrived unescorted at his colleague's quarters in the city. He slept there that night, without any of his guards.

This little incident is of no great importance in itself, but it does illustrate a difference between the two men. When they disagreed, it was always Octavian who got his way. When he wanted something, he tended to pursue it with single-minded intensity, whereas Antony, seeing himself as the senior partner in government, had the careless self-confidence to give way.

Antony was eventually persuaded to back Octavian and abandon any thought of going over to Sextus. It was agreed that the Triumvirate, the term of which had expired on December 31 of the previous year, 38 B.C., be renewed for a further five years. The triumvirs also rescinded all the concessions to Sextus and promised mutual assistance. Antony offered 120 ships from his fleet (which was expensive to keep up and not very useful for a general intent on conquering the Asian landmass), and in return was promised four legions.

Once more the colleagues parted. Everyone was becoming accustomed to treaties signed with great solemnity that almost instantly became obsolete, so there were no celebrations of the kind that had marked the accord at Brundisium. However, a coin of Antony's, issued at Tarentum, shows Antony's and Octavia's heads facing each other: unusual in Roman coinage, although common enough among Hellenistic kings who wished to emphasize harmony between husband and wife.

Octavian now prepared for a showdown with Sextus. He was pleased to receive his colleague's ships, but had no serious intention of finding him his legions. This raises the question of his good faith. It was clear that Antony took their entente seriously, but Octavian's behavior betrays a patient and undeviating pursuit of power. A sharp-eyed opportunist, he seized every gain that came his way, giving as little as possible in return.

During 37 B.C. and the spring of 36, Agrippa continued with his preparations in the lake of Avernus and the Lucrine lake. At last, the armada was ready. The plan of campaign was complex but potentially devastating. Three fleets were to set sail simultaneously for Sicily. Lepidus had been roused from his torpor in Africa; he would come with a thousand transport ships, seventy warships, sixteen legions, and a large force of Numidian cavalry, make landfall on the south of the island, and capture as much territory as he could. Another fleet, including Antony's donated ships, would sail from Tarentum, and Octavian himself from Puteoli.

To counter this formidable convergence of military and naval power, Sextus could muster no more than three hundred ships and ten legions. Unlike his opponents, he did not have an inexhaustible supply of manpower. Nevertheless, his successes to date gave him every reason to suppose he could maintain his mastery of the seas.

To begin with, fortune favored Octavian. Lepidus succeeded in landing twelve legions—a large part of his army—on Sicily and immediately invested the port of Lilybaeum on the island's western tip. If there was one way in which he could be depended on, though, it was that his loyalties were undependable. He seems immediately to have opened a line of friendly communication with Sextus, so that he would be ready to profit from any eventuality.

On July 3, disaster struck. The skies opened and the fleets were all overwhelmed by another terrible storm. The ships from Tarentum returned to port as soon as the wind began to rise. Octavian took refuge in a well-protected bay on the west coast of Italy, but then the wind veered to the southwest and blew straight onto the shore. It was now impossible to sail out of the bay, and neither oars nor anchors could hold the ships in position. They smashed against one another or the rocks. The tempest lasted into the night. Many ships were lost. It would take a month to rebuild the fleet.

It was probably now that, in a combination of defiance and despair, Octavian cried out, according to Suetonius, "I will win this war even if Neptune does not wish me to!"

Unfortunately, the end of summer was already in sight. A wise commander would call it a day until the following spring, especially after such a mauling. At Rome the popular mood was swinging against the triumviral regime and in favor of Sextus. A current lampoon demonstrated the scorn with which the people now regarded Octavian:

> *He took a beating twice at sea*
> *And threw two fleets away.*
> *So now to achieve one victory*
> *He tosses dice all day.*

The criticism was unfair; Octavian did indeed like to gamble in his leisure hours, but he was not idling now. He sent Maecenas to Rome to try to quiet his critics, while he himself rushed around Italy talking to settler veterans and reassuring them. Strenuous efforts were made to refurbish the damaged ships and lay new keels.

For Octavian *was* going to take a gamble, one of the riskiest of his life. He could not afford a long winter of discontent at Rome, so he would stake everything on one last throw of the dice. The war against Sextus was to resume.

Now that Lepidus was safely established on Sicily, Octavian and Agrippa saw that their best tactic was to find a way of landing more troops on the island so that they could bottle up Sextus in Messana. With massively superior land forces, it would then be a relatively simple matter to crush him or drive him into the sea. To attain this objective, they would have to draw most of Sextus' navy into an engagement in the seas off northern Sicily. While he was so distracted, the legions in the toe of Italy would have an opportunity to slip across to Tauromenium (Taormina), south of the straits of Messana, unchallenged, perhaps even unnoticed.

That was the idea. It did not work. Lepidus ferried his remaining four legions from Africa, but unfortunately one of Sextus' squadrons came upon them. In the misapprehension that the flotilla was friendly, the transports sailed up to it and many were destroyed. Two legions drowned.

While Octavian sailed down the western coast of Italy, the fleet at Tarentum set out for the port of Scolacium (today's Squillace), on the "sole" of the Italian boot. It was accompanied by an army marching along the coast beside the ships.

Seeing a large number of enemy sails in ports on the northern seaboard of Sicily, Octavian correctly judged that Sextus must be present, and that the moment was ripe for the army at Scolacium to embark for Tauromenium. He handed over command of the fleet to Agrippa and sailed to Italy to join his legions.

The following day, Agrippa engaged the enemy fleet off the northern port of Mylae and gained the upper hand. However, the Pompeians withdrew in good order and, with evening coming on, Agrippa decided it was too risky to give chase. Sextus cleverly guessed that Agrippa's activities were a blind. Immediately after supper, he set off for Messana with his main fleet, leaving a detachment of ships to deceive Agrippa into thinking he was staying where he was. Hiding in port, he would await the triumvir's arrival and catch him unawares.

Octavian, having climbed to a high point to survey the sea and finding no sign of the enemy, loaded as many legionaries as he could onto troopships and sailed from Scolacium to Italy's toe, the cape of Leucopatra. Vulnerable to attack because of the troopships, he had thought of crossing the straits under cover of night, a dangerous stratagem in the days before radar, but safer than risking interception by Sextus. However, when he received news of Agrippa's success at Mylae, Octavian decided, in Appian's words, not "to steal over like a thief in the night but to cross in daylight with a confident army." The war was drawing to a triumphant close, Sicily would soon be in his hands, and Sextus' days as the last republican in arms were numbered.

Octavian made landfall on Sicily south of Tauromenium and disembarked his troops. Suddenly, before the army had even finished making camp, Pompeius appeared over the northern horizon with a large fleet. Riding in parallel on the shore was his cavalry. Then up from the south marched Sextus' infantry. The surprise was total. The cavalry harried the soldiers still at work on the fortifications, but both Sextus' fleet and infantry held back. This was a serious error, for they missed the opportunity not only to win a decisive victory but also to capture the triumvir.

Nightfall should have afforded some rest, but Octavian's soldiers had to complete their defenses; when dawn came they were sleepless, exhausted, and unfit for battle. It was a desperate situation. Octavian knew he had to save the fleet; if it was not to be picked off at will on the beaches or at anchor, it must sail away as soon as possible, even if doing so meant risking battle with Sextus. So he handed command of the legions to Lucius Cornificius, an early follower of his who had prosecuted Brutus in 43 B.C. for Julius Caesar's murder and was one of the new breed of politicians from outside the magic circle of great families.

Octavian himself put out to sea with his fleet, making the rounds of the ships in a fast, light trireme, called a liburnian, to encourage his sailors and raise their morale. Once he had done this, he stowed his admiral's standard, presumably because he believed himself to be in extreme danger and anonymity would increase his chance of survival. Evidently he did not expect to win any encounter.

Sextus sailed out of Messana on the attack. There were two fiercely fought engagements, in which the triumvir's ships came off worse. Numerous galleys were captured or set alight; some made off without orders to the Italian mainland. Other crew members swam to the Sicilian shore and were either caught and killed by Sextus' cavalry or scrambled up to Cornificius' camp and safety. Eventually darkness drew a veil over the catastrophe.

Octavian did not know what to do. He spent most of the night among his fleet's small auxiliary craft, wondering whether to risk sailing back to Sicily through all the wreckage to find Cornificius, or to seek out his troops on the mainland. He decided on the latter course. Setting off in a single ship, he was hotly chased; it was probably now that, believing he was about to be captured, he asked a loyal aide, the *eques* Gaius Proculeius, to be ready to kill him.

However, Octavian just managed to elude his pursuers and reach the shore, where he disembarked. He was out of immediate physical danger, but found himself completely alone except for his armor bearer. Apparently he hid for a time in a cave. When he thought of his army isolated and under siege on the Sicilian coast, he was, according to Dio, "terribly distressed." The war was about to be lost and his glittering career was in ruins.

His travails were not over. Octavian was walking on the coast road in the direction of Rhegium when he saw a flotilla of biremes heading for the shore. He went down onto the beach to greet them, only realizing in the nick of time that they were Pompeians. As he made his lucky escape by narrow, winding paths, he encountered a new and completely unexpected danger: an attack by the slave of an officer on his staff whose father he had proscribed. No more details of the attempt on his life are known, except that he survived.

Some people from the mountains came down to see what was going on and found Octavian nearing the limits of mental and physical endurance. They transferred him from one small boat to another to evade detection and at last brought him to his waiting legions.

Octavian gave another immediate and characteristic display of sangfroid. Food and sleep could wait; first, he dispatched a liburnian to Cornificius in Sicily to brief him on what had happened, and sent messengers around the mountains to let everyone know he was safe. Thoroughminded as always, he was not going to allow any administrative slipup or communication failure to nullify this new opportunity for a comeback.

The situation looked more difficult than it really was. Two immediate things had to be achieved if momentum was to be regained. First, somehow or other Octavian's legions had to get themselves to Sicily. This seems to have presented few difficulties now that Agrippa, profiting from his sea victory, had occupied some ports on the island's northern coast. A successful transfer was soon effected.

Second, Cornificius, pinned down by Pompeius' troops near Tauromenium, had to extricate himself and join Agrippa. This was accomplished too, although it entailed a painful march across an arid expanse of old, cooled lava near Mount Etna.

Only a few days had passed since Octavian's debacle, but the tables were turned. He was master in Sicily of twenty-three legions, twenty thousand cavalry, and more than five thousand light-armed troops. His forces were overrunning the island, and Sextus recalled his army in the west to the northeastern enclave, which was all that was safely left to him of his island realm.

Sextus realized that the only way he could retrieve a rapidly deteriorating situation was to provoke a confrontation at sea. On September 3, his fleet sailed north out of Messana, rounded the cape of Pelorum (today's Cape Faro), and met Agrippa's fleet in the sea between the ports of Mylae and Naulochus.

Octavian appears to have played little part in the battle. If we are to believe Suetonius, he was suffering some sort of psychological crisis—a relapse to his state of mind at Philippi.

*On the eve of the battle he fell so fast asleep that his staff had to wake him and ask for the signal to begin hostilities. This must have been the occasion of Antony's taunt: "He could not face his ships to review them when they were already at their fighting stations; but lay on his back in a stupor and gazed up at the sky, never rising to show that he was alive until his admiral Marcus Agrippa had routed the enemy."*

The surviving descriptions of the encounter say little about the opposing fleets' tactics; maybe this grand mêlée of about six hundred warships was little more than a multitude of individual encounters, trireme against trireme, while from the land the infantry of both sides looked on apprehensively.

As time passed it began to appear that Sextus was losing more ships than his adversary (thanks in good part to Agrippa's *harpax*). Some of his galleys began to surrender, and Agrippa's men raised the paean, or victory shout, which was picked up and echoed by the soldiers onshore. A setback became a rout. One of Sextus' admirals killed himself, the other surrendered to Agrippa. Only seventeen warships survived.

Sextus was so stunned by what had taken place that he omitted to give any orders to his infantry, with the result that they, too, immediately surrendered. He rushed to Messana and changed out of his commander in chief's uniform with its blue cloak into civilian clothes. He loaded everything of any use, including all the money he had, into the poor remainder of his fleet, embarked with his daughter and some of his entourage, and sailed eastward, intending to apply to Mark Antony for help. Yet again, unconsciously no doubt, he was following his father's example, who, when shocked by his defeat at Pharsalus, fled to seek safety in the east.

The battle of Naulochus, as it was named, was over, and with it the Sicilian war.

Lepidus was feeling extremely pleased with himself. Sidelined by Antony and Octavian, he had found the last few years less than satisfactory; but now he was having an excellent war. As commander of a great army, he was the master of Sicily. The chance of a lifetime presented itself. It was time for him to flex his muscles. He laid claim to the island on the grounds that he had landed there first and received the largest number of surrenders by cities.

Octavian, enraged, took action typical of him, at once careful and bold. He sent out some agents, who discovered that Lepidus' soldiers thought little of him, admired Octavian's courage, and were exasperated by the prospect of another civil war.

Once the ground had been prepared, the moment came for a bravura display of personal heroism. Octavian rode up to Lepidus' camp with some cavalry, which he left by the outer defenses. Then, unarmed and dressed in a traveling cloak, he walked with a handful of companions into the camp—as one contemporary commentator put it, "bringing with him nothing but his name." It was a striking piece of political theater, repeating his earlier forays into potentially hostile crowds. As he walked through the lines, the soldiers he met saluted him.

As Naulochus had shown, Octavian still found it hard to cope with the experience of battle, but when stung by opposition to him personally he did not hesitate to place his life at risk. For him, bravery was not an assertion of collective defiance and solidarity among colleagues but a solitary, obstinate act of will.

Lepidus, alerted by the uproar that something was amiss, rushed out of his tent and ordered that the intruder be repelled by force. Suddenly Octavian was in mortal danger. According to Appian, Octavian "was hit on the breastplate but the weapon failed to penetrate to the skin and he escaped by running to his cavalry. The men in one of Lepidus' outposts jeered at him as he ran."

It was a painful humiliation. Yet in the next few hours Lepidus' men began to desert him. He went out and pleaded with them to remain loyal. He caught hold of a standard, saying he would not release it. "You will when you're dead!" one of the standard-bearers said. Now it was Lepidus' turn to be humbled. Frightened, he let go: the game was up. Seeing that this was so, he changed out of uniform and made his way to Octavian at top speed, with spectators jogging along beside him as if at a public entertainment.

Octavian was well able to be ruthless and cruel when opponents fell into his hands; his performance to date had been an implicit criticism of his adoptive father's policy of clemency. But now he made a decision that presaged a change of approach.

At this very moment, for the first time since leaving Apollonia eight years previously, he faced no visible threat to his position. He knew that what everyone wanted was peace and a return to the rule of law. As a demonstration that this was his desire, too, he stood when Lepidus came up to him, and prevented the suppliant from falling to his knees as he intended. He administered no punishment and sent Lepidus to Rome dressed as he was, as a private individual.

Most significantly of all, Octavian did not strip him of his highly prestigious position as *pontifex maximus,* where his predecessor had been Julius Caesar. He was, however, deposed as triumvir; he left public life and spent his remaining twenty years in comfortable retirement at Circeii, a seaside resort about fifty miles south of Rome.

The town was built on the side of a steep crag, crowned by a temple of the sun and a lighthouse; it was originally an island, and the malarial Pomptine Marshes lay on its landward side. According to legend, in one of the numerous caves on its slopes the witch Circe had once lived, she who changed visitors into swine. It was not an inappropriate spot for one of Rome's least appealing politicians to end up in.

When he gathered together all the various armies, Octavian found that he had under his command a grand total of forty-five legions, twenty-five thousand cavalry, about thirty-seven thousand light-armed troops, and six hundred warships. It was impractical to demobilize them all at once, for to acquire land on which they could settle would take time and money. Instead he paid part of the promised donatives, distributed honors, and pardoned Sextus' officers.

The soldiers, especially his own, mutinied, demanding full payment of everything owed and immediate discharge. In response, Octavian announced a campaign against the Illyrians (in today's Albania), for which he would need legions, and increased the number of awards to officers and men. He also made some conciliatory gestures, discharging those who had fought at Mutina and Philippi and offering an additional donative of two thousand sesterces. Calm returned to the camp.

After Naulochus, Sextus Pompeius made good speed to the eastern Mediterranean and, in another uncanny echo of his father's flight in 48 B.C., put in at Mytilene. Only sketchy accounts survive of his next moves. He seems to have been well provided with cash, for he crossed over to the province of Asia, where he managed to raise large numbers of troops. Soon he was in command of three legions.

Antony showed little interest in Sextus, but was irritated to find that he had offered his services to the Parthian king. The governor of Asia, Gaius Furnius, offended by Sextus' incursion into his province, marched against him with a large force. A sensible man would have surrendered, and Sextus was promised honorable treatment if he did so. Unaccountably he dug his heels in, tried to escape, but was caught.

The son of Pompey the Great had wasted his last chance of survival. He no longer had the slightest political or military value and could not be trusted to behave intelligently. In 35 B.C., Sextus Pompeius was executed, presumably with Antony's approval. He was about twenty-six when he died—an age at which most men are launching, not concluding, their lives and careers.

Why did Sextus not win his war? For a long time he went from victory to victory. If he had taken Menodorus' advice and refused to discuss terms with the triumvirs he could have starved Italy into submission and this biography might well have had him instead of Octavian as its subject.

The later ancient literary sources depict Sextus as a pirate, but he and his contemporaries saw him as a great Roman nobleman in pursuit of his rights. Appian claims that Sextus had no discernible strategic purpose and a pronounced tendency to avoid following up successes. There is some merit in the charge that Sextus failed to prosecute a long-term aim with adequate vigor.

He also did not take into account the disproportion in the relatively limited resources over which he had control and those at the disposal of the triumvirs, even when taken singly. This meant that he could not afford to wait on events, for sooner or later he would be outnumbered.

The youthful challenger to the post-republican regime lost, not so much through lack of intelligence or military and naval ability, but because he failed to think things through.

# XI

# PARTHIAN SHOTS

36–35 B.C.

TO THE VICTOR, THE SPOILS. EVEN BEFORE OCTAVIAN REACHED
Rome in September 36, the Senate voted him many honors and allowed
him to choose whether to accept them all or only those he approved. He
celebrated his twenty-seventh birthday on the twenty-third and may
have timed his entry into the city to coincide with it.

Octavian accepted three honors from those that had been voted to
him. The first was an annual festival to mark the victory at Naulochus,
the second a gold-plated statue of himself in the Forum, dressed as he was
when he entered Rome and standing on top of a column decorated with
ships' rams.

The third honor was by far the most important: *tribunicia sacrosanctitas.*
This meant that his person was *sacer,* consecrated and inviolable on pain of
outlawry. This protection was given to tribunes of the plebs, but Octavian
did not have to hold the office of tribune, although he was additionally
awarded the right to sit on the tribunes' benches at meetings.

Of greater practical benefit to citizens, Octavian forgave unpaid install-
ments of special taxes as well as debts owed by tax collectors. It was announced that documents relating to the civil wars would be burned. The
administration of the state was returned to the regular magistrates, and
Octavian agreed to hand back all his extraordinary triumviral powers
when Antony returned from Parthia.

Octavian owed a great deal to his friends and supporters, and he made
sure they were well rewarded. Agrippa, who had masterminded the Sicilian victory, was given a probably unprecedented honor—a *corona rostrata,*
or golden crown decorated with ships' beaks, which he was entitled to
wear whenever a triumph was celebrated. Priesthoods were liberally distributed. Booty and land flowed into the hands of the triumvir's friends;

thus, Agrippa was granted large estates in Sicily and married one of Rome's greatest heiresses, Caecilia, daughter of Cicero's friend the multi-millionaire Titus Pomponius Atticus.

Some men did not know how to handle success with the expected decorum. Cornificius, awarded the consulship in 33, so prided himself on his Sicilian exploits that he had himself conveyed on the back of an elephant whenever he dined out.

It is hard to exaggerate the importance of the Sicilian victory. In his early years of struggle, Octavian had boasted of his connection to Julius Caesar; but from now on he no longer insisted on his rank as *divi filius*. He was who he was in his own right.

And what of Mark Antony? Octavian's victory over Pompeius and his acquisition of Sicily and Africa (taken from the dismissed Lepidus) marked an important shift in the triumvirs' respective positions. His two rivals for control of the west were now gone.

This simplification of the political scene had an important consequence. Despite the years of bloodshed, there was still a republican faction, an assorted group of diehards who were unwilling to accept what looked increasingly like the settled verdict of history.

With the end of Sextus Pompeius, the only remaining refuge was Mark Antony. In part, this was because, compared with Octavian, Antony was the lesser of two evils. But they could also detect in him a more relaxed approach to autocracy. In the last resort, he liked an easy life. He was no revolutionary and, provided that he could retain his *dignitas* and *auctoritas*, a preeminence of respect and influence, he had no difficulty in envisaging a return to the familiar rough-and-tumble of the Republic.

In the spring of 36, Antony launched his long-planned invasion of Parthia, leading an army of sixty thousand legionaries and other troops. His task was to settle an overdue piece of military business: to avenge the catastrophe of the battle of Carrhae in 53 B.C., the death of the Roman commander, Marcus Licinius Crassus, at the hands of the Parthians, and the loss of many Roman legionary standards. Few people doubted that Antony would score a great victory, which would set the seal on his predominance.

Information took time to filter back from the eastern deserts, and when the battle of Naulochus was fought nobody in Italy had any idea how the Parthian campaign was going. Then, sometime during the autumn, dispatches from Antony arrived announcing victory. Although it would have suited him very well if Antony had at least met with a setback, facts were facts and Octavian must needs rejoice.

It had taken Mark Antony years to prepare for his Parthian war. After the Treaty of Brundisium in October 40, he faced two challenges. The first was posed by the Parthini, an Illyrian tribe that occupied rough and mountainous country overlooking the port of Dyrrachium and the beginnings of the Via Egnatia, which, we remember, gave access to Greece and Rome's eastern provinces. The Parthini, who had sided with Brutus and served in his army, were in a state of revolt. They invaded Macedonia and by moving south were able to cut one of the empire's crucial communications links. They also captured the Illyrian port of Salonae in the north (Salon, near Split, in Croatia). Antony dispatched eleven legions, which efficiently suppressed the rebellion.

The second challenge concerned the Parthians, who posed a far more serious threat than an Illyrian hill tribe. They were well aware that once a senior Roman took time off from fighting other Romans, he would assemble all the forces of the empire to punish them for the Carrhae disaster. Would it not be sensible to launch a preemptive strike?

In the spring or summer of 40 B.C., Parthian horsemen, led by Pakûr, the brilliant son of King Urûd, swept across the province of Syria, killing the governor. The invasion was the greatest threat to Roman rule since the days of a rebel monarch, Mithridates of Pontus, half a century before.

Unfortunately, dealing with Octavian and the aftermath of the Perusian war distracted Antony for much of this year. He decided not to take the lead, perhaps wanting to hold himself in reserve for the full-scale Parthian invasion. Instead, he dispatched one of his best generals, Publius Ventidius, who had served under Julius Caesar and understood the need for celerity in war.

In a two-year campaign Ventidius won three great battles, the last of which was fought northeast of Antioch, the capital of Syria, on June 9, 38 B.C. Pakûr was killed. The Parthian prince had been well liked in the Syrian region; Ventidius sent his head around various cities to deter his sympathizers. Having smashed and dispersed the invaders, the general marched east and besieged the city of Samosata (now Samsat, in Turkey) on the Euphrates.

Time passed and rumors spread that Ventidius was accepting bribes to hold back from taking Samosata. Antony decided to come and conclude the campaign in person. He dismissed Ventidius and never employed him again. However, Samosata proved a tougher nut to crack than he had thought. Antony negotiated a settlement, and returned to Athens for the winter of 38–37 B.C. According to Plutarch, he received three hundred Greek talents, the equivalent of more than seven million sesterces, to pay for his departure. How did this price compare, one wonders, with what Ventidius received?

The thought of Antony assuming the moral high ground on account of a subordinate's financial impropriety seems out of character. It is rather more likely that the triumvir was "jealous of [Ventidius] because he had gained the reputation of having carried out a brave exploit independently." Whatever the truth of the matter, the jettisoning of a commander of Ventidius' caliber combined arrogance with carelessness.

Octavian had little difficulty in keeping up-to-date with Mark Antony's activities. Although communications were slow and could be difficult or even dangerous, individuals, whether businessmen or state officials, wrote home with news and gossip. The triumvir had plenipotentiary powers, but he was expected to send dispatches to the Senate and keep his colleague in the picture. Octavia, back in Rome while her husband was on campaign and looking after her large brood of six children and stepchildren, worked to promote his interests and to smooth relations between the two men in her life.

The first reports from Antioch, which Antony fixed as his headquarters, showed him at his best. The invasion by Pakûr was evidence that the client kingdoms, which acted as buffers between the Parthians and the Roman empire, needed strengthening. Antony redrew the map, carving out large territories for men he trusted, all of them Greek-speaking west Asians—Amyntas in Galatia, Polemo in Pontus, Archelaus-Sisinnes in Cappadocia, and Herod in the much smaller but strategically important kingdom of Judea. As the ruler of the Roman east, he needed monarchs stable enough to resist military shocks and strong enough to react effectively to them.

But the monarch on whom the triumvir placed the greatest reliance was the queen of Egypt. Nearly four years had passed since the pair had met. One would suppose that they kept in touch by letter, if only to discuss their twins, Alexander and Cleopatra, who had grown into sturdy toddlers. It would be wrong to think, though, that either party was in love; their relationship was essentially that of two professional politicians who needed to do business with each other.

Antony and Cleopatra renewed their friendship at the respective ages of forty-five and thirty-three. They quickly came to an understanding (and, equally quickly, the queen became pregnant again); Egypt's resources were placed at the triumvir's disposal, and in return Cleopatra received substantial territories. These included a string of coastal cities running from Mount Carmel in the south to today's Lebanon, part of Cilicia, and other regions north and south of Judea. The queen viewed this enlargement of her power as being of the first importance. She had largely reconstituted the Ptolemaic empire as it had been in its heyday, two centuries before.

Back at Rome nobody saw anything especially scandalous about these developments; Antony's reorganization of the east made very good sense, and it appeared that, a good judge of character, he had chosen able and intelligent people for his client kings. As a onetime appendage of Julius Caesar, Cleopatra was familiar to the Roman political class, even if they did not particularly like her. She was obviously a competent ruler; it mattered little that Antony had stepped into his predecessor's bedroom slippers.

Octavian, though, found the renewal of the liaison disagreeable and threatening. It was an insult to his sister, Octavia; also, he noted with interest that Antony's children were provided with additional names about this time, being now called Alexander Helios (Greek "Sun") and Cleopatra Selene ("Moon"). Being illegitimate, the children had no hereditary status either Roman or Egyptian, but the new cognomens gave them a quasi-divine prestige.

More serious, though, and more embarrassing for Octavian, was the fact that Cleopatra was almost part of the family. Her co-monarch, Ptolemy XV Caesar, was the son whom she claimed, almost certainly truthfully, to have had by Julius Caesar. In his eleventh year, Caesarion was the murdered god's real, not adoptive, offspring; it would not be so very long before he could create some trouble, if backed by Antony and his mother.

•  •  •

How did Mark Antony's contemporaries regard a man who was unfaithful to his wife? This question cannot be answered without an understanding of Roman sexual mores.

The Romans took an unsentimental view of sexual relations. Romantic love, as we know it, was rare. Public displays of affection were frowned on, as was excessive sexual activity. Marcus Porcius Cato the Censor, who lived in the second century B.C., set the standard for conventional good behavior when he expelled a man from the Senate for kissing his wife in the street.

A Roman man, almost invariably locked into a marriage of convenience (although second or later unions often permitted a freer choice), did not suffer feelings of moral guilt about sex, nor did he feel necessarily bound to any particular sexual object. He would not have understood modern terms such as "heterosexuality" and "homosexuality," which categorize people as sexual types. What he *did* was the issue, not what he *was*.

To judge by the literary sources, it did not greatly matter whether the randy husband fancied a young man or woman. The poet Horace was not untypical of his age:

> *When your organ is stiff, and a servant girl*
> *Or a young boy from the household is near at hand and you know*
> *You can make an immediate assault, would you sooner burst with tension?*
> *Not me. I like sex to be there and easy to get.*

According to Suetonius, Horace had his bedroom lined with mirrors; he brought hookers or rent boys there and enhanced his pleasure by turning his own sexual experience into pornographic imagery.

Two chief concerns governed sexual conduct. First, a free male citizen should be the one who performed the penetrative or insertive act, who was the "active" rather than the "passive" partner. For him to be sodomized was shameful, a betrayal of his masculinity. Anyone who was known to enjoy being buggered was scorned. This was why Julius Caesar deeply resented the story that in his youth he had been the catamite of the king of Bithynia, and the gibe of a political opponent that he was "every woman's man, and every man's woman."

Second, an adulterer or fornicator was meant to restrict his attentions to noncitizens and slaves, as in Horace's case; freeborn boys and women were out of bounds. Although there is plenty of evidence that this was a custom honored mostly in the breach, it was essential that there should be no doubt as to the identity of a Roman citizen's father. This was why Octavian ordered a favorite freedman of his to commit suicide after he had been convicted of adultery with Roman matrons. In addition, foreign genes should not be permitted to enter the Roman gene pool; only citizens could marry citizens, and to wed a foreigner was frowned on; if not illegal, such a union was unrecognized by the law, especially when it came acknowledging heirs in a will.

What all of this signified so far as Antony was concerned was straightforward: he could not marry Cleopatra, who was as non-Roman as they came, but if he wanted to conduct an affair with her it would be odd if anyone complained. Roman women, such as Octavia, well understood the conventions; her husband's extramarital dallying did not strain her loyalty to him. It was her loving brother who could not stand the idea of her betrayal by Antony's entanglement with an eastern temptress.

Surprising information started trickling out of the east during the autumn and winter of 36–35 B.C. Personal letters from officers and others to their families and friends indicated that Antony's laurel-wreathed communiqués did not tell the whole truth about the Parthian war. Indeed, Octavian and the political elite in Rome were intrigued to learn that Antony's campaign had come perilously close to defeat. A careful but confidential investigation was commissioned to establish the facts.

This was what had actually happened. Antony followed Julius Caesar's original plan of campaign, and to begin with things went well. Rather than struggle across the desert plains of Mesopotamia, harried by the Parthian cavalry, and slowly lose a war of attrition, he marched through the independent and (he expected) friendly kingdom of Armenia. He then turned south and invaded Media Atropatene (roughly speaking, today's Azerbaijan), with a view to besieging and capturing its capital, Phraata.

Unfortunately, Antony made four bad mistakes. Because he had launched his attack in June, he could not afford setbacks or he would find himself campaigning in winter. He placed confidence in a senior Parthian defector, who was in fact spying for his king. To compound this error, Antony failed to impose garrisons and to take hostages from the Armenian king, Artavâzd. It may be that he had neither the time nor enough troops to do this, but the consequence was unfortunate.

Antony's final mistake was to let his slow baggage train (with all the siege equipment for Phraata) travel at its own speed with a relatively light guard. The well-informed Parthians turned up out of the blue with a force of fifty thousand mounted archers, who set on fire all the siege equipment and destroyed it. The Armenian king and his forces defected.

This was a catastrophe, for it would no longer be possible to take Phraata, where Antony had intended to winter. He was forced to march back the way he had come, now through incessant snowstorms. More than twenty thousand men, one third of the army, were lost in the month it took to march to the comparative safety of Armenia, where the king saw no advantage in trying to impede the Roman retreat.

Antony was very upset and, rightly, blamed himself. He had all his silver plate cut up and distributed to the soldiers as an improvised bonus to keep them happy. Several times he prepared for suicide, asking his sword bearer to be his executioner. Like any good general, he went around the hospital tents to comfort the wounded; if Plutarch is right, his men realized that his need for comfort was as great as theirs. They "greeted him with cheerful faces and gripped his hand as he passed: they begged him not to let their sufferings weigh upon him, but to go and take care of himself."

At last the battered army reached Syria. Messengers had been sent ahead to ask Cleopatra to bring money and clothing for the soldiers. The legions waited by the sea for the queen to arrive. Antony's self-confidence was still at a low ebb and he started drinking heavily. Unable to bear the waiting, he kept jumping up and running to the shore to look for Egyptian sails.

Cleopatra took her time, but when she appeared she brought everything that was needed. Once the soldiers were fully supplied, their general returned to Alexandria, there to do some hard thinking about how to proceed.

At Rome, Octavian absorbed the news of his colleague's discomfiture. He could see that from a strictly military perspective Antony had suffered only a setback—serious, certainly, but by no means a total disaster.

No records exist of Octavian's secret intentions; it may be that like many politicians he was merely an intelligent opportunist, and did not cherish a long-term ambition to oust Antony and become sole master of the Roman world. However, the evidence of his behavior—his patience

and pertinacity, his persistent reluctance to do more than a bare minimum to help his fellow triumvir, his ruthlessness with other competitors—suggests a covert plan.

Always the realist, though, Octavian knew better than to strike too
soon. The correct approach, he decided, would be to accept his colleague's account of his campaign at face value, and in no way to question
it. So victory celebrations were staged, sacrifices conducted, and festivals
held. On the face of it this was convenient for Antony, who, it was said,
soon came to believe his own propaganda and convinced himself that in
escaping from Media and Armenia he had won the day.

Octavian was aware that Antony would need to replace the men he
had lost, but never allowed him to raise troops in Italy as he was entitled
to do. He was also determined not to fulfill his promise in the Treaty of
Tarentum to send Antony four legions in return for the ships he had received. He wrote to his colleague saying, with hidden but barbed sarcasm,
that in the light of his resounding victory Antony ought to have no trouble raising any additional soldiers he might need in his own half of the
empire.

To add injury to insult, Octavian sent his sister, who had been living
in Rome since last seeing Antony in Greece, to join her husband. She
brought with her large stores of clothing for his troops, money, presents
for Antony's staff, and two thousand picked men, splendidly equipped
with full armor, to serve as his Praetorian Guard (that is, the ex officio
bodyguard of a general). She was also accompanied by seventy warships,
the survivors of those Antony had lent to her brother. This apparently
kind and thoughtful gesture was, in fact, multiply wounding.

First of all, the provision of help for Antony's troops betrayed Octavian's knowledge of the real outcome of the Parthian campaign. Second,
the dispatch of two thousand soldiers rather than the twenty thousand
promised was an almost laughable insult. Third, it was widely known that
Antony was living with Cleopatra, and sending his wife to him was mis-
chievously tactless.

Charitable historians have conjectured that Octavian wanted to apply
pressure on his colleague with a view to detaching him from Cleopatra.
But Octavian knew his Antony by now. He probably guessed that Antony
would react intemperately, and show himself in a bad light.

When Octavia reached Athens, she received a curt message from her husband, instructing her to send on the legionaries and supplies and then return to Rome. Her brother advised her to move out of Antony's palatial residence and set up her own independent household. Octavia obeyed her husband's order but declined her brother's advice: she came back to the capital, but refused to move house.

Plutarch presents the rejection from a romantic perspective, giving a highly colored account of Cleopatra staging a nervous breakdown to persuade Antony to send Octavia away. No such explanation is necessary; the decision was political and intended as a firm response to Octavian's hostile, or at least unfriendly, actions.

The literary sources regard Octavia as a saintly figure, characterized by a "truly noble devotion and generosity of spirit." One may detect here the hand of her brother's propagandists. However, factual claims about matters familiar to contemporaries—and so not worth lying about—suggest that she did everything she could to save her marriage. She went on looking after the large brood of Antonian children, entertaining Antony's friends in Rome on business, and doing everything she could to obtain what those friends wanted from Octavian.

It was beginning to be clear to all but the most determined optimists that the triumvirs were approaching a parting of the ways. Their personalities had always been diametrically opposed. Octavian suffered from frequent bouts of ill health; Antony was strong and gloriously fit. Octavian was dutiful and self-disciplined; Antony was prone to binge drinking and worked hard only when he had to. Octavian planned and schemed; Antony reacted more spontaneously to events. Octavian was fiercely loyal to those who put their confidence in him; Antony easily betrayed them. Octavian often broke his agreements; Antony fulfilled his promises.

At issue was not only a dysfunctional personal relationship but also opposing political philosophies, or at least casts of mind. Antony was an old-fashioned kind of politician, who was happy with things as they were provided that he could maintain a leading role in public life. Octavian was a revolutionary, who meant to transform the Roman world.

For the time being, though, the triumvirs silently agreed to forget about each other and concentrate on their own projects. There was room enough in the empire not to trip over each other.

# XII

# EAST IS EAST
# AND WEST IS WEST

## 35–34 B.C.

ILLYRICUM WAS A WILD AND SAVAGE PLACE. IT LAY ALONG much of the length of the eastern shore of the Adriatic Sea, its northern boundary touching Italy and contiguous with the territory of the Pannonian tribes who lived below the river Danube. The Illyrians were a warlike people, divided into dozens of tribes and much given to piracy and brigandage. To the cultivated Roman, it was unnerving that a stronghold of barbarism should lie so dangerously close to civilized Italy.

Everywhere the land was covered by thick and tangled forests and there were few tilled fields. Occasional small clearings could be found where spelt and millet, the staple grains of the population, were grown. Here and there hills were crowned with fortress towns, to which people could retreat in time of war. The inhabitants were poor, but, according to Dio, were "considered to be the bravest of all men about whom we have knowledge."

Roman legions marched into Illyricum for the first time in 229 B.C. Rome declared the region a province but never completely bent the untamed tribes to its will. In 35 B.C., despite Antony's successes against the Parthini, Octavian in his new role as bringer of peace decided that the time had come to restore order. Italy would thank him for yet another contribution to its security.

His motives, however, were not straightforward. He needed a war for his own purposes. First, he wanted an excuse to retain most of his legions, in case he might require them in some future confrontation with Antony. The army in the east had to be matched by one in the west if the two triumvirs were to be seen as equal in authority.

More important, though, Octavian knew that he had a difficulty with his public image. While winning great respect for bravery during the Sicilian war, everyone knew that the man behind the victory was Agrippa. Public opinion had not quite forgotten Octavian's invisibility at Philippi. To match Antony, who was bruised by his failure in Parthia but still preeminent, he had to score an undoubted military success, for which he was seen to be wholly responsible.

Octavian had a liking for complicated offensives, using armies and fleets to attain simultaneous but different objectives. The plan in the final campaign against Sextus Pompeius had involved three fleets and two armies; for Illyricum, he again decided on a three-pronged approach. We say "Octavian," for the impression was studiously given that he was personally in charge and made all the key decisions. However, it is known that Agrippa was present during the Illyricum campaign and, just as he played a key role in Sicily, we can perhaps detect his guiding hand.

The fleet was brought around from southern Italy and given the task of eliminating the pirates who operated out of Illyrian harbors. At the same time, two armies congregated at the Italian frontier with Illyricum. One force, commanded by Octavian's legates (or deputies), was to strike in a northeasterly direction, toward the tribes of Pannonia. The remaining legions, led by their young commander in chief, would strike southeast down the valley of the river Colapis (today's Kupa).

The first aim was to reduce the Iapudes, a fierce tribe not far from the coast. The campaign started well and a few strongholds surrendered. Then the going grew harder. The terrain the legions marched through often consisted of precipitous hills and deep ravines along which torrents rushed. At the tribal capital, Metulum (perhaps the modern hill of Viničica near Munjava), the resistance of the Iapudes stiffened.

Octavian had a large mound built against the town wall, which would allow his soldiers to storm the place. The Iapudes used tunneling devices captured from the Romans in an earlier campaign to undermine it. They set fire to Roman siege engines, including the large catapults that bombarded Metulum with missiles and battered the wall.

Two more mounds were raised and four wooden gangways installed to enable the Romans to gain access from them to the wall and storm the town, but the Iapudes cut away the supports. Gangway after gangway collapsed, until only one was left. The legionaries hesitated and stood still.

At this crisis in the assault, Octavian ran down from a temporary wooden tower from which he had been directing operations and snatched the shield from a soldier who was hesitating to make the crossing. Accompanied by the inevitable Agrippa and his bodyguard, he strode over the gangway. The men followed. Unfortunately, too many soldiers clambered onto the gangway at the same time and it collapsed.

Octavian was wounded and one leg and both arms were badly crushed. However, he survived and was protected by troops on the wall who had already made the crossing. More gangways were quickly run out and soldiers poured across. The defenders' morale failed and the town fell.

This was a display of conspicuous bravery. In classical times generals were expected to risk their lives alongside their men, although they were closely surrounded by friends and followers and, being needed to control the battle, were seldom in the front line. Leading an assault on a besieged city was an exceptionally dangerous enterprise and only the most audacious commanders, such as Alexander the Great, took such risks.

Octavian was not a man for acting in hot blood or on the spur of the moment, and his action was out of character. One wonders whether he and his advisers were looking in advance for an appropriate opportunity to offer a bravura exhibition of valor. It is noteworthy that he was well guarded at all times during the incident. Also, the seriousness of his injuries may have been exaggerated, for there is no record of a pause in the army's onward march to allow time for them to heal.

In any event, the propaganda value of this event was substantial, and public opinion was impressed. The contemporary historian Livy remarked that Octavian's "beauty of person [was] enhanced by blood and his *dignitas* by the danger in which he found himself."

Throughout 35 B.C., Octavian kept as close an eye as practicable on Mark Antony's activities, or lack of them, in the east. His worst fear was that Antony, who had not been in the capital since 39 B.C. and had time on his hands, might take it into his head to visit Rome. There he would be able to overshadow Octavian, who was becoming used to regarding the city as his exclusive patch. Worse yet, once Antony came back to Italy it is hard to see how Octavian could in practice prevent him from raising troops.

But Antony did not come. It may be that his presence was needed to prepare for a renewal of the Parthian war, even if a new expedition was to be postponed to 34 B.C. The more likely cause, though, was his increasingly strong relationship with Cleopatra. The triumvir and the queen were now a settled couple. It has been suggested that they married in 36, at the time of Antony's territorial allocations; however, although a ceremony of some sort is reported, this seems unlikely, for both Romans and Greeks strongly disapproved of bigamy and (as we have seen) Romans did not recognize foreign marriages. Perhaps what was intended as a mystical partnership between the New Isis and the New Dionysus was maliciously misinterpreted in Rome as an earthly union. In 35, the queen gave birth to her fourth child, and her third by Antony, a boy called Ptolemy Philadelphus.

As he settled down to an indefinite reign as the de facto monarch of the east, amid the uncompetitive luxuries of Alexandria, Antony must have thought of Rome with annoyance and distaste. He could do without the scratchy tetchiness of triumviral politics. His supporters in the capital were perfectly capable of looking after his interests without him having to go there in person.

But was that all there was to be said about Antony's continuing absence? Perhaps something more sinister was at work than his characteristic idleness. Information was coming in that the eastern portion of Rome's empire was rearming. Antony commanded twenty-five legions, although after the Parthian disaster some were very weak in numbers. He had recently recruited five more, making a grand total of thirty legions.

All this could well have an obvious and innocent explanation—namely, that before he renewed the Parthian war Antony had to make good his losses, especially given that Octavian was continuing to withhold the Italian legions he had long promised. However, Antony was also investing heavily in warships. Tellingly, he issued a series of coins, each with the number of one of his legions and backed by a warship. What could he need a vast armada for, if not to invade the western empire?

However, if that was the idea, its execution would not be immediate, for the Parthian aftermath was attracting all Antony's attention. In the spring of 34 B.C., the Romans stormed into Armenia. The king, who had betrayed Antony during the failed invasion, quickly caved in. He and his two younger sons were taken prisoner, probably lured into a meeting and kidnapped. Here at last was a success—too easily won to make much of, one would have thought, but a success all the same. Armenia was turned into a Roman province and the country was opened up to trade and economic exploitation.

Dispatches were sent to Rome, but the mood there had altered since 36 B.C. and the insincere festivities that marked the Parthian "victory" of that year. Octavian (sensing that pretense was no longer appropriate or necessary), the Senate, and the people of Rome honored Antony's genuine achievement in Armenia with a studied and stony silence. After all, Crassus' standards were still in Parthian hands and, indeed, had been joined by some of Antony's.

Back in Alexandria, though, it was time to celebrate.

Having dealt with the Iapudes, Octavian marched east to fight the Pannonian tribes in the interior beyond Illyricum. It is not entirely clear what they had done to deserve his attention. Dio has his own bleak take on the triumvir's motives: "He had no complaint against them [the Pannonians], not having been wronged by them in any way, but he wanted to give his soldiers practice and to support them at the expense of an alien people."

There is something in that, but it may also have occurred to Octavian and his military planners that control of the coastal strip of Illyricum would not of itself secure Rome's dominance; permanent mastery demanded a defensible frontier. The obvious candidate was the river Danube, which bordered the far or northeastern end of Pannonia. Eventually, this meant that Pannonia would have to become a Roman province. However, that was a long-term aspiration; for now, Octavian probably wanted to spy out the land and estimate how difficult a permanent conquest might be.

The legions were making for the Pannonian fortress of Siscia, at the confluence of the Colapis and Savus (Save) rivers. Octavian hoped a display of force would suffice to elicit surrender. However, the infuriated tribesmen harassed the Romans mercilessly. In response, Octavian burned the villages and crops he came across and took all the booty that could be found.

On two sides, the Colapis and Savus made Siscia nearly impregnable, but on the third there was a gap between the rivers that was fortified with a palisade and a ditch. The Romans attacked simultaneously by water and on land. The defenders learned that the Romans had successfully brought over a number of tribes to their side; the news made them lose heart and they quickly negotiated a surrender. Meanwhile the Roman fleet had defeated the Adriatic pirates and killed or enslaved coastal tribes.

As the campaigning season of 35 drew to a close, Octavian was able to congratulate himself on a successful year. He left a garrison of more than two legions to hold Siscia, and returned to Rome to spend the winter on civilian business.

To have defeated some barbarian tribes was good, but hardly glamorous. He decided to stage an invasion of the island of Britannia (following up his adoptive father's brief forays ten years earlier). It lay on the edge of the known world and its remoteness exerted a great fascination on the Roman mind; the conquest would be a coup.

Then, before the winter of 35–34 was over, a rumor filtered back to Rome that the garrison at Siscia had come under attack, so Octavian abandoned his plans and dutifully returned to Illyricum. Discovering that the tribal forces had been fought off, he traveled down to the south of the province, where he joined Agrippa and devoted the campaigning season to a major onslaught on one of Illyricum's largest tribes, the Dalmatae. It was hard slogging in an inhospitable rocky landscape. Octavian was struck in the knee by a sling stone and laid up for several days.

Once recovered, he returned to Rome late in the autumn to ready himself for his second consulship, to begin on January 1, 33.

Shortly after his return to Egypt in 34 B.C., Antony staged an event that looked at first glance very like a triumphal procession. He rode into the city on a chariot, preceded by his Armenian prisoners of war, and made his way to a central square where the queen sat in splendor awaiting him. Banquets followed, accompanied by distributions of money and food.

When Octavian learned of this, he unscrupulously used it as a means of criticizing Antony. It was unheard-of and offensive for a Roman general to hold a triumph anywhere except in Rome. Evidence was building up that, in some way, Antony was going native—cutting loose from his *romanitas*, his Romanness, and behaving more and more like a grand Hellenistic monarch.

In fact, Antony seems to have been staging an exotic eastern spectacle, not mimicking a triumph. Rather than dressing as a Roman general, he presented himself as a human version of Dionysus. His head was bound with an ivy wreath, his body was enveloped in a robe of saffron and gold; he held the thyrsus (a fennel stalk topped with a pinecone or vine or ivy leaves, which Dionysus' followers carried) and wore buskins (the raised boots used by actors in plays staged at the festival of Dionysus in Athens). He was reported as riding in the "Bacchic chariot"; this was traditionally drawn by big cats, such as leopards or panthers. By identifying himself with an appropriate divinity, Antony was merely continuing his policy of establishing a public persona that would appeal to the inhabitants of the eastern provinces.

A few days later, he presided over an even more unusual ceremony, which came to be known as the Donations of Alexandria. It took place in the city's great Gymnasium, a splendid colonnaded building for athletic training and lectures on philosophy. A silver-gleaming dais with two golden thrones was erected, either in the open air in the *palaistra* (παλαίστρα, "exercise ground") or in the Gymnasium's largest covered space, reserved for ball games and called the *sphairisterion* (ϛφαιριστήριον). Antony and Cleopatra, who was dressed as the goddess Isis, seated themselves on the thrones. Caesarion, now aged thirteen, was officially Ptolemy XV Caesar and Cleopatra's co-ruler (for a woman was not allowed to reign alone). He and the queen's children by Antony sat on lower thrones.

When everyone had arrived and settled into their places, Antony stood up and delivered an address. Cleopatra, he said, had been married to Julius Caesar, and so Ptolemy Caesar was his legitimate son. This preposterous claim was aimed at undermining Octavian's position. It ignored the existence of Caesar's wife, Calpurnia, and of the Roman avoidance of marriage to foreigners. Perhaps what Antony had in mind was another symbolic or heavenly union between two gods.

He then proceeded to shower Cleopatra and the children with honors and territories. Alexander was to receive Armenia, Media, and all the land to the east as far as India—in other words, the as yet unconquered Parthian empire. Little Ptolemy Philadelphus was to become king of all the Syrian territories already awarded to Cleopatra, and overlord of the client kingdoms of Asia Minor. Cleopatra Selene, Alexander's twin sister, received Cyrenaica (the eastern half of today's Libya, abutting Egypt) and the island of Crete. Caesarion was declared king of kings, and Cleopatra (the mother) queen of kings.

At about this time, Antony issued a coin, a silver denarius, which graphically illustrated his partnership with Egypt's female pharaoh. One side showed Antony's bare head, and behind it the royal tiara of Armenia, with the message "Antony, after the conquest of Armenia." Scandalously for Roman currency, which never depicted foreigners, the head of Cleopatra, diademed and with jewels in her hair, was on the other side, accompanied by the prow of a ship. The inscription read: "To Cleopatra, queen of kings and of her sons who are kings."

What strategy underlay the Donations of Alexandria? Antony has not shared his ideas with posterity, and the literary sources mainly regurgitate the Octavian version. So we can only speculate.

It is important to be clear what Antony was *not* doing. He was not giving the eastern half of the Roman empire away for good to Cleopatra and her brood of little Ptolemies. This was no abdication. As triumvir and commander of the armies of Rome, Antony remained the ultimate authority, and behind him stood the Senate and people of Rome. What he gave, he could take back.

The Donations were in line with the thinking that underlay Antony's previous reorganization of the east. That is, it was far easier to allow locals to manage most of the eastern provinces on behalf of Rome, administering justice and raising taxes, than for the imperial authorities to do it. The Romans being unsupported by a permanent civil service, this would save them a world of trouble, as well as helping to solve the problem of rapacious public officials. The empire would be far more stable if its inhabitants did not feel that they were under foreign occupation.

However, unkind commentators, both at the time and later, saw something more alarming. A large part of the east, Antony's allocated territory as triumvir, was being gathered together into a single monarchy, with Antony as emperor and Cleopatra as empress. Their long-term aim, it was suggested, was to overthrow Rome. Rumor assiduously put it about that the queen's favorite oath was "so surely as I shall one day give judgement on the Capitol."

This is implausible. Antony had a conventional mind that could not imagine an end to Roman dominion, and Cleopatra was too much of a realist to wish for more than the reassertion of Egypt as the dominant power in the eastern Mediterranean, under Roman protection. Most probably, the Donations were a symbolic gesture, a way of settling public opinion in the east and marshaling it behind Antony as Dionysus/Osiris and Cleopatra as Isis/Aphrodite. In fact, few if any practical changes were noticeable on the ground in Syria, or Cappadocia, Pontus, or Galatia. Hordes of Egyptian administrators did not spread through the Middle East, replacing local authorities and Roman officials and tax farmers.

It is hard to disagree with the sentiments that the great twentieth-century Alexandrian poet Constantine Cavafy attributed to the audience at that glittering ceremony in the Gymnasium.

> *And the Alexandrians thronged to the festival*
> *Full of enthusiasm, and shouted acclamations,*
> *In Greek, and Egyptian, and some in Hebrew,*
> *Charmed by the lovely spectacle—*
> *Though they knew of course what all this was worth,*
> *What empty words they really were, these kingships.*

# XIII

# THE PHONY WAR

## 33–31 B.C.

DURING THE FIVE CENTURIES OF THE REPUBLIC, THE BUSINESS of government took place in and around the Forum. This rectangular piazza, which lay in a valley between the Capitoline and Palatine Hills, was lined with temples to gods and heroes.

Trials were conducted here in the open air, senators met and debated in the Senate House, citizens' assemblies were convened in an open space called the Comitia. Money could be borrowed in the Forum, and prostitutes bought. Statues of famous statesmen stood on columns, and large paintings illustrated Roman victories. Down the Forum's long sides stood two *basilicas,* which combined the functions of shopping mall and conference center.

With the Second Triumvirate and Octavian's growing domination of the political scene, a gradual change could be detected. Politics moved from the noisy open square up to a complex of houses on the fashionable Palatine Hill, where Octavian and Livia lived and worked. From "Palatine" derives the word "palace," meaning that enclosed space where autocrats make decisions in private.

Today the Palatine is a quiet, almost pastoral spot, overshadowed by tall maritime pines. A short but brisk climb from the Forum leads to the summit of the hill, a flat area pockmarked with ruins, some of them protected from the weather by modern roofs. The top of the Palatine is a maze of shaded lanes and hidden corners.

To the northwest stand the buildings where Octavian and Livia spent most of their lives. In 36 B.C., a grateful popular assembly voted that a house should be presented to him at public expense. Octavian had already bought an expensive property at the southwest end of the Palatine Hill, but it had been struck by lightning—an omen that persuaded him to demolish the unlucky building and replace it with a temple to Apollo. With his grant from the Senate, he arranged the purchase of a house, or more accurately a group of houses, next door.

The location was chosen with great care, for Octavian wanted his residence to signal and embody his role in the commonwealth. Near it stood a hut, built on the hill's natural tufa and with a sloping thatched roof, its reed walls daubed in clay. This was said to be the home of Romulus, Rome's founder, and was carefully preserved in his honor. By closely associating himself with Rome's beginnings, Octavian was telling the Roman world that he stood for traditional values, for *mos maiorum,* the customs of ancestors.

There was no question about it in anyone's mind: Rome did not look like the capital of a great empire. Over the centuries, the city had grown untidily and organically. There were no broad avenues and few open spaces, apart from the Forum and the *forum boarium.* Few streets were wide enough to allow vehicles to pass one another and most of them were unpaved. (In the daytime there was no wheeled transport, for, in an attempt to eliminate daytime traffic jams, Julius Caesar had restricted it to the hours after dark; the night clattered with the cacophony of wooden carts.) Projecting balconies and upper rooms sometimes nearly touched one another.

The rich lived in houses with no outside windows, so that it was possible (as in traditional Arab town houses) to escape the urban hubbub; rooms were grouped around one or more open-air courtyards. The poor rented single rooms or crowded into multistory apartment blocks, or *insulae.* These were often jerry-built and liable to fire or collapse.

Shops lined many of the main streets, but they were usually no more than a ground-floor room with a masonry or wooden counter for selling goods and a space at the back for stock. All kinds of goods were on display—jewelry, clothing and fabrics, pots and pans, and books. There were numerous bars and restaurants, catering mainly to people from the lower classes, whose houses did not have properly equipped kitchens.

Rome was a city of horrible smells. Rubbish and sewage, even, occasionally, human corpses, were tipped into the street. Passersby were so often hit by the contents of chamber pots emptied from the second floor or the roof that laws were passed regulating the damages that could be claimed.

City life was made bearable only by the ready availability of water. Four aqueducts (the first of them built in the fourth century B.C.), high arcades, strode across the land, bringing fresh, clean water from springs and lakes miles away. The water was piped to fountains, some of them no more than stone troughs, in the small public squares that dotted Rome. The rich and famous could obtain the Senate's permission to tap the pipes. Ordinary citizens collected water from the nearest fountain or had it delivered by a water seller.

This abundance of water made possible one of Rome's most popular pastimes, going to the public baths. These received their own supply and were much like modern Turkish baths or hammams. The price of entry was so small that everyone except the poorest could afford it. Many Romans would go to the baths every day, often in the early afternoon, after work and before the evening meal. Here they could meet friends and exchange gossip.

In 33, Octavian and Agrippa were back in Rome from Illyricum. How could they give the regime legitimacy, they asked themselves, how persuade public opinion that, after the long years of division, bloodshed, and power politics, Octavian meant to govern in the people's interest, not just his own?

They found an answer in their run-down megalopolis. Investment in public buildings and services would achieve three useful purposes. First, it would improve the city's grandeur, making its appearance worthy of its role as the capital of the known world. Second, the quality of life of Rome's volatile citizenry would be enhanced. Third, the refurbishment of the city's architectural heritage would be the first concrete illustration of Octavian's commitment to restoring Rome's antique values. An appeal to the old ways was a powerful means of sweetening the revolutionary nature of the Triumvirate.

Octavian called on his generals to signal their successes in the field by restoring one or another Roman landmark at their personal expense. They embellished temples and basilicas, and on the Campus Martius the extremely competent commander Titus Statilius Taurus built Rome's first stone amphitheater.

But a diet of visually splendid *grands projets* was not enough. The average inhabitant of Rome must feel some personal benefit from these public works.

. . .

In 33 B.C., Agrippa took up the post of aedile—an unusual step, even a self-demotion, for he had already served as consul, the state's highest post.

One of an aedile's duties was to look after the city's water supply, street cleaning, and drains; Agrippa reorganized and refurbished the aqueduct system. He also commissioned a new aqueduct, the Aqua Julia (some years later he added the Aqua Virgo, so called because a young girl pointed out springs to the soldiers who were hunting for water). He had five hundred fountains built as well as magnificent public baths, the Thermae Agrippae. The reservoirs and the fountains, or *nymphaea,* were elaborately decorated, with many bronze and marble statues and pillars. Agrippa also repaired and cleansed Rome's underground drainage system.

The regime's bid for popularity was unrelenting. During his aedileship, Agrippa distributed olive oil and salt and arranged for the city's 170 baths to open free of charge throughout the year. He presented many festivals, and because those attending were expected to look smart he subsidized barbers to offer their services gratis. At public entertainments, tickets good for money and clothes were thrown to the crowds. Also, massive displays of many kinds of goods were set up and made available free on a first come, first served basis. All these measures were paid for from the fortune Agrippa had amassed (from war booty, legacies, and grants of land and money) during his ten years of working and fighting for Octavian.

Agrippa's aedileship signaled in the most attractive and practical way that prosperous times were back. Agrippa's investments in Rome's infrastructure (to say nothing of the public buildings constructed or restored by other leading members of the regime) greatly enhanced its appearance. The construction work also provided welcome jobs in a city with a high rate of unemployment. While the other, long-absent triumvir was squandering time in the east, everyone could see the concrete advantages that Octavian's regime was bringing to the ordinary citizen.

Octavian was ready for a showdown with Antony. His career since his acceptance of his legacy from Julius Caesar makes complete sense only if it is understood as a careful and undeviating pursuit of absolute power. A typically competitive and ambitious Roman, he wanted that power for himself; he was the heir of Rome's greatest sole ruler since the expulsion of King Tarquin the Proud in the sixth century B.C., and it was only what he

deserved. But Octavian also despised the incompetent and unruly selfishness of the ruling class, epitomized by the destructive and pointless policies of Fulvia and Lucius Antonius, that had led to the Perusian war;
Sextus Pompeius' absence of policy; and Mark Antony's loss of discipline
and focus. With respect to the latter, one senses a dismissive scorn for an
older colleague who ought to have known better, and who had, in Octavian's view, "failed to conduct himself as befitted a Roman citizen."

Step by step, Octavian had built up his strength over the years, seizing
every chance that came his way. The Illyrian campaign was the last piece of
the puzzle: it gave him the military status he had so conspicuously lacked.
Agrippa's rebuilding of Rome was a sign that he and his supporters were
planning a long-term strategy for the empire's governance. However, if
matters were not brought to a head now, the initiative might well pass
back to Antony, especially if he finally scored a substantive victory over
the Parthians and covered himself in glory.

The Triumvirate's second term was due to end in December 33 B.C., and
it would be in Octavian's interest to avoid any risk of an amicable renewal,
for that would freeze a status quo he wanted to terminate. He was in as
strong a position as he would ever be.

In 33 B.C., Octavian was consul for the second time. Early in the year he
delivered a blistering speech against his fellow triumvir. He criticized Antony's activities in the east: Antony had had no right to kill Sextus Pompeius, whom *he* would willingly have spared, and Antony had been wrong
to trick the Armenian king into captivity. This behavior had damaged
Rome's good name.

Octavian also attacked Antony's cruel treatment of Octavia and his relationship with Cleopatra. The Donations of Alexandria were unacceptable.
Even more offensive, seeing that it was clearly aimed at undermining Octavian's position as Julius Caesar's heir, was Antony's promotion of young
Ptolemy Caesar, or Caesarion, as the great dictator's natural son.

Little of this was very convincing in itself. It strains credulity that Octavian had a soft spot for Sextus or cared a sesterce for the fate of a far-off
country of which most people knew nothing. And as for Antony's sexual
life, it had always been colorful.

Pamphlets and letters were published, and envoys traveled assiduously
between Rome and Alexandria making claim and counterclaim. Antony
huffily stood his ground. He complained that he had been prevented
from raising troops in Italy, as had been freely agreed; that his veterans

had not received their fair share of lands on demobilization; that, after defeating Sextus Pompeius, Octavian had taken over Sicily without consulting him; and that Lepidus had been arbitrarily deposed.

Antony's case was stronger than that of Octavian, who had consistently been an untrustworthy partner. Whenever compromise or concessions were needed, it was always the older and more reasonable triumvir who had given way. But some of the issues he raised were no more than debating points; for example, Sicily was in the western half of the empire, and once captured would naturally have fallen to Octavian.

The accusations grew more and more personal. Octavian castigated his colleague's drunkenness. He also made fun of Antony's high-flown and overelaborate use of Latin; he was "a madman, for writing to be admired rather than understood," who introduced into "our tongue the verbose and unmeaning fluency of the Asiatic orators."

Antony gave as good as he got. He ridiculed Octavian's provincial ancestry and accused him of lustfulness, cruelty, and cowardice (for instance, the scandalous fancy-dress party that Octavian had attended as the god Apollo, and his curious behavior when he hid in the marshes at Philippi, were unkindly exhumed). Antony also made an angry charge, very probably with good reason, of sexual hypocrisy:

> *What's come over you? Is it that I am screwing the Queen? But she isn't my wife, is she? It isn't as if it's something new, is it? Or has it actually been going on for nine years now? What about you then? Is Livia the only woman you shag? Good luck to you if, when you read this letter, you haven't also shagged Tertulla or Terentilla or Rufilla or Salvia Titisenia, or all of them. Does it really matter where and in whom you insert your stiff prick?*

What truths lie behind these quarrelsome exchanges? Personal insults were the stock-in-trade of debate. Distinguished Romans often expressed political disagreements in slanderously personal terms and seized on their opponents' sexual misdemeanors with lip-smacking enthusiasm. But while disputants' allegations may have been exaggerated, they needed to embody at least a poetic truth if anyone who knew the principals was to take them seriously.

Each triumvir claimed that he stood for a restoration of the Republic, and the other for tyranny by one man. Neither was telling the truth. Ten years after the murder of Cicero, the Republic was a thing of the past, irretrievable. The choice was simply between two kinds of autocracy—tidy and efficient, or laid-back and rowdy.

Octavian was approaching a very dangerous moment. He was trying to precipitate a war without receiving the blame for it. For the present, he set himself limited objectives. First of all, he had to make his public position crystal clear, announce the inevitability of a showdown, and force the political world to choose which triumvir to back in the coming struggle. At the same time, he had to mobilize maximum support throughout Italy, which Antony might very well invade.

Octavian's final letter in the war of words reached Antony in October 33, when he was at the Armenian border with Media, preparing to renew his Parthian war. When he read what his brother-in-law had to say, Antony realized that once again Parthia would have to wait. Having rejected every charge leveled against him, Octavian concluded, with biting derision: "Your soldiers have no claim upon any lands in Italy. Their rewards lie in Media and Parthia which they have added to the Roman empire by their gallant campaigns under their *imperator*."

Accepting that relations with Octavian had irretrievably broken down and that consequently war was inevitable, Antony set off with a small advance force on the long journey back to the Aegean, ordering one of his generals, Publius Canidius Crassus, a loyal and able supporter who had campaigned successfully in Armenia, to follow with an army of sixteen legions. He summoned Cleopatra, who joined him en route, bringing with her an ample war chest of twenty thousand talents (about 480 million sesterces), and the pair made the port of Ephesus (near the modern town of Selçuk in southern Turkey) their headquarters.

At the end of December, the Triumvirate came to an end. Octavian's purpose now was to maintain his new public image as a strict observer of the constitution. He had no governmental status of any kind and in theory was taking a very dangerous risk by politically disarming himself this way. However, after more than ten years at the head of affairs he had built up a formidable *auctoritas,* the power that came from his record and his proven ability. Furthermore, by now he was the master of a multitudinous *clientela;* many thousands of people had obligations to him. Perhaps most important of all, the legions in the west remained his to command. Tactfully, he withdrew from Rome to await events.

In January 32, two new consuls took office. In the days when the tri-umviral machine was still more or less in working order, consuls had been named for years ahead, drawn on a roughly equal basis from sup-porters of the two triumvirs. It so happened that those for the new year were partisans of Antony.

The senior consul was Gnaeus Domitius Ahenobarbus (the cognomen means "Bronze Beard"), the aristocrat who had proved to be a good admi-ral for Brutus and Cassius. His colleague was the able and determined Gaius Sosius, a new man. As was typical of the time, he was a provincial, perhaps from Picenum in northern Italy.

The consuls had an important commission from Antony to execute. Late in the previous autumn, the triumvir had sent them a letter which they were to read out to the Senate once they had taken office. His aim was to set out his case fully, authoritatively, and persuasively; he probably restated his eastern settlement, his various *acta,* and in particular his wel-come Armenian victory.

However, the consuls made a curious decision, as Dio writes: "Domi-tius and Sosius . . . being extremely devoted to [Antony], refused to pub-lish [the dispatch] to all the people, even though Caesar urged it on them." This can only mean that in the consuls' view its impact on public, or at least senatorial, opinion would be the opposite of that intended by its author. The problem must have lain with a proud, or at least a compla-cent, description of the Donations of Alexandria. Antony would have been unaware that Octavian's anti-Cleopatra propaganda had been all too effective and that his references to the Donations would merely add fuel to the flames.

On February 1, Sosius went on the attack. He strongly defended Antony and proposed a motion of censure of Octavian. His message will have been that, if there was a threat to peace, it did not come from Antony, who had shown no sign whatever of aggression toward his colleague.

Although a tribune friendly to Octavian entered a timely veto, Sosius' intervention flushed Octavian out. In mid-February he gathered around him supporters and Caesarian veterans, and returned at their head to Rome. This was, in effect, his Rubicon, for he was staging something very like a coup d'état. On his own initiative, he convened a meeting of the Senate. He had absolutely no right to do this, but the consuls and the sen-ators turned up at the session. He must have wondered whether he was riding events or they were riding him. Dio reports that he surrounded "himself with a bodyguard of soldiers and friends who carried concealed daggers. Sitting between the Consuls in his chair of state, he spoke at length and in moderate terms in his own defence, and brought many accusations against Sosius and Antony."

For the consuls, this triumph of force could not be allowed to stand. "As they did not dare to reply to [Octavian] and could not bear to be silent," in Dio's sharp words, they secretly left Rome and set sail for the east. They were accompanied by between three and four hundred of Rome's one thousand senators—republicans or supporters of Antony.

On the limited evidence available it is hard to be sure whether or not this move was a defeat for Octavian. Unlike the former triumvir, the consuls could claim legitimate political authority and, although the senators who joined them were a minority of the total membership, they were a substantial number of the ruling elite. What is more, it was uncertain how many of those who stayed behind were fully signed-up supporters of Octavian. Seasoned observers of the political scene will have seen a comparison with the flight from Rome in 49 of Pompey the Great and most of the Senate when Julius Caesar invaded Italy and launched the first of the civil wars. Ahenobarbus and Sosius could argue that they were taking "Rome" with them.

It looks as if Octavian was taken aback when he learned what had happened. He needed to neutralize the rebuff; pretending it was what he had always had in mind, he claimed that he had sent the senators away voluntarily. Anyone else who wanted to leave had his full permission to do so.

The upheavals at Rome were concentrating minds wonderfully. It was now certain that there was to be another round of civil war. Throughout the Roman world, men of importance in the state were considering their position: with whom were they to side?

# XIV

# SHOWDOWN

ANTONY'S PREPARATIONS FOR WAR WERE NEARING COMPLE-tion; soon it would be time to move west from his base at Ephesus, to Greece. For the first time since Alexander the Great, one man controlled the entire seapower of the east. Antony also commanded an army of thirty legions with twelve thousand light-armed infantry and twelve thousand cavalry. Most of the soldiers were easterners, for Octavian had prevented him from recruiting in Italy. They were not necessarily inferior in quality to Roman legionaries, although in a crisis they might not be so loyal.

In early 32 B.C., it became obvious to everyone that Antony and Cleopa-tra had made an important and highly controversial decision. She was to accompany Antony on the campaign, in which she meant to play a full part. In no small measure as a result of Octavian's propaganda, the queen had become very unpopular among Romans, who disapproved of a for-eign potentate interfering in their affairs. Her emergence as the co-general, in effect, of a Roman army further alienated opinion.

When Ahenobarbus and the others arrived from Rome, they were irri-tated by what they found. The consul cordially disliked Cleopatra, refusing to address her as queen and calling her simply by her name. He strongly advised Antony to send her back to Egypt to await the outcome of the war. Herod the Great of Judea, a bitter enemy after years of merciless bullying by the queen, gave Antony some confidential and cruel advice: Cleopatra's continuing presence would damage his chances; the path to success was to put her to death and annex Egypt. At one point Antony did order her back home, but then relented, taking the line of least resistance, and let her stay. There were even reports that he was growing frightened of her.

In April 31 B.C., the multitudinous military machine set off on its slow journey to Greece.

. . .

Octavian's strategy was to sit and wait. It was obvious that Antony was heading for Greece, but, although it would have been in Octavian's tactical military interest to get there first, it was not in his political interest to do so. This was because he did not wish to be seen as what in truth he was: the aggressor, and the invader of his onetime partner's agreed territory. That would neither harmonize with his new emphasis on legality nor win a war-exhausted public to his side. Antony must be left free to move westward, so that he might receive the opprobrium for opening hostilities.

In the meantime, Octavian had to maintain and enlarge his army and fleet. There was no alternative but to raise additional taxes. An unprecedentedly severe income tax was levied (25 percent of an individual's annual earnings) and riots immediately broke out. Octavian became as unpopular as he had been ten years earlier, when the Triumvirate had been forced to raise money for the war against Brutus and Cassius.

In this climate of fear and rage, he took a bold step. At some point during 32 B.C., he held a kind of personal plebiscite, in which people were required to swear their loyalty to him. Later, he wrote proudly: "The whole of Italy [and the western provinces] voluntarily took an oath of allegiance to me and demanded me as its leader in the [forthcoming] war." He claimed that half a million citizens bound themselves to him. We do not need to accept this suspiciously round number when conceding that the exercise was a surprising success.

It was still less than fifty years since the War of the Allies, when the peoples of Italy rose up against Rome to claim their rights and were granted full Roman citizenship. Octavian was a provincial, as were many of those who managed his regime. Italians were now getting their own back after centuries of Roman dominance. They liked the new status quo and did not want Antony and his eastern queen to threaten it. Anger over the new taxes was cooling off; something more than simple self-interest guided a growing Italian self-consciousness, a new patriotism.

Then came an extraordinary stroke of luck.

Lucius Munatius Plancus had been one of Antony's closest advisers ever since defecting to him after Mutina in 43 B.C. He threw himself into the spirit of things at Alexandria. He flattered the queen shamelessly and, if an unfriendly commentator is telling the truth, was willing to humiliate himself to please. Sometime in the early summer of 32 B.C., however,

Plancus began to get very worried about the situation in which he found himself.

In May or June of that year, Antony finally divorced Octavia and told her to quit his house in Rome. Octavia seems to have been an affectionate and maternal woman, for when she left the family home she took with her all of Antony's children, except for his eldest son by Fulvia, the teenaged Antyllus. He left Rome to join his father in Greece, where he delivered the embarrassing news that Octavia had looked after him with great kindness.

The impact of the divorce on Roman opinion was serious for Antony. It was not simply that he had behaved cruelly to a loving wife, but that he had done so in favor of a foreign queen. The decision to send her away drew awkward attention to Cleopatra.

At this delicate juncture, Plancus came to a new judgment. This was that in the imminent contest Antony was more likely to lose than not. It was time to pack bags. Plancus slipped out of Athens, where Antony and Cleopatra were spending some time before taking the field, and made his way as inconspicuously as possible to Italy.

What was the basis of this change of heart? Octavia's dismissal was not enough in itself to power his defection, even if it supplied a pretext. Plancus noticed the corrosive effect Cleopatra's presence in the campaign was having on Antony's Roman supporters, and gauged that it would blunt the thrust of Antony's military strategy: it would hardly be feasible for a foreign queen to help to lead an invasion of Italy.

Having arrived in Rome, Plancus presented himself to Octavian and announced that he knew most of Antony's secrets. One of these was tempting to exploit: at some point in the past few years, Antony had lodged his will with the Vestal Virgins at the little round Temple of Vesta in the Forum.

Although Octavian was trying hard to present himself as a standard-bearer for traditional values, here was an opportunity too good to be missed. He sent a message to the Vestal Virgins asking them to hand over the document. They refused, saying that if he wanted it he would have to come himself and seize it, which he proceeded to do. Before making any public announcements, Octavian read through the document in private and marked the passages least to Antony's credit; these he read out to the Senate. He drew special attention to Antony's wish to be buried in Alexandria. Octavian's former brother-in-law also left legacies to his children by Cleopatra and reasserted that Caesarion was Julius Caesar's child.

These revelations had a dual effect. Many senators thought Octavian's action in taking the will was "extraordinary and intolerable." However, the document was cast-iron evidence that the great Roman general had somehow been transformed into an easterner. Such a bad impression was created that even Antony's supporters in the Senate voted to deprive him of the consulship that had been planned for him in the following year. Octavian felt he was now in a position formally to declare war.

But the opponent had to be Cleopatra. This was partly because Octavian needed to avoid an accusation of restarting the civil war he claimed to have ended; also, he did not want to make official enemies of Antony's Roman supporters, some of whom might wish to follow Plancus' example.

The Romans had an antique ceremony for declaring war. Octavian went to the Temple of Bellona, goddess of war, in the Campus Martius. On a strip of land in front of the temple that was officially denominated as foreign territory stood the small *columna bellica,* or column of war. Bellona's priests, called *fetiales,* threw spears, smeared with the blood of a sacrificed pig, into this ground.

Once the ritual was complete, Rome was officially at war with Egypt.

In its basic essentials the promontory of Actium on the coast of western Greece, and the inland Ambracian Gulf it guards, look today much as they did two thousand years ago. A low scrubby sandy tongue of land, lying only a few feet above sea level, Actium stretches northward toward a larger and hillier two-fingered peninsula. Between them, a half-mile-wide strait squeezes its way from the open sea into the gulf, twenty-five miles long and from four to ten miles wide.

It would be a dull, even slightly dreary place, but for the spectacular mountains that crowd the distant skylines; like the steep seating of an open-air Greek theater on a colossal scale they look down on the stage of Actium. Twenty miles to the west looms the towering rock of the island of Leucas, lying almost close enough to the mainland to touch it.

Today Actium bustles in the summer. Young tourists arrive at the small airport and crowd the sea with yachts. Actium boasts three marinas; one of these is the Cleopatra Marina, which occupies a position on the strait from which two thousand years ago an observer would have been able to watch the queen of Egypt in her splendid galley sail by into open waters and her destiny. There are boatyards, and numerous tavernas and bars line the waterfront. A tunnel is planned to join Actium to the northern promontory and the pleasant harbor town of Preveza.

In the first century B.C., things were quieter. Actium was a center for pearl fishing and a small village on the headland made a useful jumping-off point for travelers. Nearby, on the shore where the strait was narrowest, there stood an old temple and a grove of trees sacred to Apollo, founded five hundred years previously.

By the end of 32 B.C., the main body of Antony's fleet was based in the safety of the Ambracian Gulf. At the narrowest part of the strait leading to the sea, two towers were constructed (probably where today's Venetian towers stand), from which catapults could hurl missiles and fireballs at any passing galleys.

The ships had spent much of the summer and autumn ferrying the army to Greece and then establishing a defensive line down its Adriatic coast. A squadron guarded Leucas, the Actium roads, and the islands in the south. It protected the entry into the Corinthian Gulf and the port of Patrae (today's Patras), where Antony and Cleopatra had established their headquarters. A garrison guarded the Methone promontory. Another force was placed on the headland at Taenarum. In addition, there were Antonian troops on Crete, and four legions held the province of Cyrenaica next to Egypt.

During the winter of 32–31 B.C., Antony's army was distributed among these strongpoints on the western coast from Corcyra to Methone, with the largest part gathered at Actium.

At first sight Mark Antony's strategy is hard to fathom. On the two most recent occasions when Greece had been the theater of operations, the opposing generals had focused their attention on the north of the country and the Via Egnatia, that strategically important route to Byzantium and the east. That was where Pompey the Great had based himself in 49 and 48 B.C.; Brutus and Cassius had marched west along it to meet their doom at Philippi.

By contrast, Antony placed no defenses at all north of Corcyra, a hundred miles south of the great highway. Had Octavian wished to do so, he might have sailed from Brundisium to Epirus in the expectation of an easy landfall. Some have argued that Antony's purpose was to cover the route to Egypt. However, it is highly unlikely that Octavian would have risked his army and fleet on a long journey to invade Egypt, assuming that Antony remained in Greece. An Egyptian foray would have left Italy defenseless against invasion. The most that can be said is that Antony's deployment would protect an escape to Egypt if that was ever to become necessary.

A more convincing explanation can be hazarded. The safest, shortest, and most sensible crossing point from Greece to Italy was from northern ports, for instance Dyrrachium and Apollonia. By occupying southern Greece, Antony may have wished to make it clear to all that he had no intention of invading the Italian peninsula. Many people, including his own supporters, would have opposed such an enterprise so long as Cleopatra accompanied him. The thought of a foreign queen marching into Rome at the head of an army was universally and totally unacceptable.

Antony's plan can only have been to tempt, or at least allow, Octavian to transport his army into Greece. The fleet at Actium could then move north and mount a general blockade, preventing provisions and reinforcements from coming to Octavian's assistance. Once the trap was closed, the Roman empire's leading commander would delay offering a set-piece battle. With his safe supply route from Egypt, Antony would have all the time in the world, whereas Octavian, whom he knew already to be short of money, would soon also be short of food. Bottled up and desperate for an encounter, Octavian and his army would be easily finessed into a weak defensive position and routed.

On January 1, 31, Octavian, now aged thirty-two, resumed an official constitutional role when he entered on his third consulship. His colleague was a onetime republican, the talented Marcus Valerius Messalla Corvinus, in place of the excluded Antony. The consuls set off for Brundisium, accompanied by seven hundred senators and many *equites*.

Octavian had the smaller of the two armies, eighty thousand soldiers to the enemy's one hundred thousand. The difference was mainly accounted for by the number of Antony's auxiliary or light-armed troops. Octavian's legions were more experienced than Antony's mainly eastern levies, having been blooded in the Illyrian campaign.

Octavian made it clear that he expected senior personalities at Rome to accompany his army. The independent-minded Pollio, now more or less retired from politics, boldly refused, telling Octavian: "My services to Antony are too great and his kindnesses to me too well-known. So I will steer

clear of your quarrel, and will be a prize for whoever wins." Maecenas
stayed behind to watch the political situation at Rome.

Bitter experience had taught Octavian to respect his own limitations as
a commander. He appointed Agrippa to take direct charge of the fleet,
and of the design of the campaign as a whole. Once they had learned Antony's dispositions, the two men agreed on a plan that employed speed
and surprise to turn the tables on Antony and trap him.

The first blow was to be struck at the earliest possible date. Even before
the end of the stormy winter break, if at all feasible in early March,
Agrippa would sail south more than five hundred miles to the Peloponnese, the southern half of Greece. His objective was to attack and capture
the strongly defended fort of Methone. From this base he would then try
to pick off Antony's other garrisons along the Greek coast.

Two outcomes from this raid were envisaged. First, the supply line to
Egypt would be cut and Antony's soldiers and sailors would soon be short
of food. The time pressure would be reversed. Second, Antony would
have to send warships against Agrippa and in doing so would weaken his
naval garrisons.

The next step would be for Octavian to transport his forces from Brundisium to somewhere near the Via Egnatia in the north, then to march
south at once with all speed to corner Antony and prevent him from
moving his army out of the confined area of Actium into central Greece,
where he would be free to harass and perhaps outmaneuver Octavian.

This was a hugely daring plan, for it meant moving a fleet across open
seas (presumably, if it was not to be detected it could not hug the coast)
and risking the catastrophe of a Mediterranean storm. As it turned out,
the enterprise was crowned with total success, although we do not have
the details or the exact sequence of events. Methone fell and Octavian immediately, and without any kind of trouble from either the enemy or the
weather, transferred the main part of his army across the Adriatic Sea,
landing somewhere between the Via Egnatia and Corcyra—perhaps at
Panormus (today's Palermo in Albania).

The first news of these events to reach Antony and Cleopatra at their
headquarters was that the enemy held a small place some miles north of
Actium called Toryne, the Greek word for ladle. It was a sign of the ner-
vousness of the high command at Patrae that the queen cracked a seriously bad joke to mask the general consternation: "What is so terrible
about Caesar Octavian having got hold of a ladle?"

• • •

When Octavian arrived at Actium, he made camp on the northern promontory. He found an ideal spot, a hill today called Mikhalitzi about five
miles north of the channel into the Ambracian Gulf. Four hundred feet
high, it commanded good views all around. Immediately to the south lay
enough flat ground for a battle, should that be called for.

The site had two disadvantages. First, it had no weatherproof harbor,
only the nearby bay of Comaros, which was open to western gales even
after a protective breakwater was constructed (traces of which survive).
Walls were built down to the beach from the camp to guard against surprise attack by land. Second, water had to be brought in, either from the
river Louros, a mile and a quarter or so to the northeast, or from a couple
of springs on the southern plain.

Soon after his arrival, Octavian drew up his fleet in open water and offered battle, but the enemy, undermanned and performing poorly, wisely
declined to come out of safe anchorage. Antony was having trouble recruiting oarsmen and retaining them. Plutarch claims that he was so
short of men that his warship captains were "press-ganging travellers,
muledrivers, reapers, and boys not yet of military age from the exhausted
provinces of Greece."

Antony arrived from Patrae in a couple of days, together with Cleopatra,
who lived with him in the camp. He transported his army from Actium
to the northern peninsula—this may have been at the end of April—
and built a new camp facing Octavian's. He was ready and eager for battle.

But Octavian was no longer looking for a fight, for the indispensable
and indefatigable Agrippa had captured the island of Leucas, giving him a
safe harbor on Antony's doorstep and making it extremely difficult for
supply ships from Egypt—which would already have run the gauntlet up
the west coast of Greece—to gain entry to Actium.

This was a terrible blow. Provisions ran very short and Antony had to
break the stranglehold. The longer he waited, the stronger Octavian, with
safe logistical support from Italy, would become; by the same token, Antony's position could only deteriorate. He needed to deprive the enemy of
water. He took control of the springs in the plain beneath Mikhalitzi
without difficulty and sent a strong force of cavalry on the long trek
around the Ambracian Gulf to establish itself above the enemy camp and
thereby cut off access to the Louros. But Octavian's able general Titus Statilius Taurus launched a sudden, vigorous counterattack and drove off

Antony's horse. One of the eastern client kings took the opportunity to desert.

As time passed, the health of the soldiery at Actium began to deteriorate. The almost nonexistent tides of the Mediterranean failed to wash away the detritus of a large army and fleet occupying a crowded space with few facilities. During the long, hot summer months an epidemic ravaged Antony's camp—perhaps dysentery or malaria. Men died and morale fell.

After weeks of squabbling about what to do next, Antony led a determined attempt to break out by land, probably in early August. At the same time his fleet, commanded by Sosius, sailed under cover of a thick mist and routed the small enemy squadron that was blockading the exit from the straits of Actium. The plan was probably for Sosius to meet up with Antony and his land forces at some convenient point on the coast.

Unfortunately for Antony, by pure chance Agrippa arrived on the scene with the rest of the fleet and drove Sosius back into harbor. Antony then engineered another cavalry engagement (perhaps by attacking Octavian's water supply again), but was repulsed. This precipitated the defection of King Amyntas of Galatia with two thousand cavalry.

Loyalty everywhere decayed. Client kings and Roman senators alike followed in Amyntas' footsteps, slipping away to the camp on the hill at Mikhalitzi. The most wounding betrayal was that of Domitius Ahenobarbus. Suffering from a fever (doubtless he was infected by the sickness raging at Actium), he put out in a small boat and sailed the few miles north to the bay of Comaros. According to Plutarch, "Antony, although he was deeply grieved by his friend's desertion, sent not only his baggage but all his friends and servants after him, whereupon Domitius died almost immediately, as if he longed to repent as soon as his treachery and disloyalty became public knowledge."

Antony's magnanimity was short-lived, however; as usual when rattled, he grew cruel. He caught two distinguished deserters and, *pour encourager les autres,* awarded them unpleasant deaths. An Arabian client king was tortured before execution and a hapless senator was tied to horses and pulled apart.

Despite these displays of self-indulgence, Antony understood that something had to be done, and soon, if disaster was to be averted. He withdrew his troops from the northern promontory back to Actium and called a council of war.

• • •

Looking down from his camp, Octavian saw smoke billowing up from the anchorage where the Actium channel turned left and then right before entering the Ambracian Gulf. There Antony's fleet was based. Flames were consuming the smaller galleys and all the transports.

It was obvious what was happening. Antony was preparing for an engagement of some kind. He did not have enough oarsmen to man the entire fleet, and, so that they might not fall into the hands of the enemy, was destroying the ships he could not use. It looked as if the final encounter was approaching.

A deserter named Dellius (the man who had advised Cleopatra on how to attract Antony) gave Octavian a full account of the enemy's intentions: Antony meant to attempt a breakout by sea. This was not a stupid decision. Taking a demoralized army through the steep passes of the Pindos mountains would be no easy task, whereas it was a reasonable bet that a good part of the fleet would escape, manned with the pick of Antony's legionaries. They could join the eleven or twelve legions in Egypt and Cyrenaica, and live to fight another day. So it might be hoped.

The question facing Octavian—or, more precisely, Agrippa—was how to react. In a sense, the issue was largely moot. What was about to happen might look and sound like a battle, but in truth (they told themselves) the war's outcome had already been decided. Most people now knew this, and were acting accordingly; hence the avalanche of high-level desertions. Whether Antony and Cleopatra made their getaway mattered little; to catch and kill them on the spot would save time, that was all.

History does not record exactly what Octavian and Agrippa planned to do, but we can make a good guess from the facts of the situation and what we know actually took place. They lost no time deciding that if Antony offered battle at or near the mouth of the Actium strait, they would hold back. This was for the obvious reason that they would lose the advantage of numerical superiority if they fought in confined waters.

Octavian and Agrippa agreed not to let Antony's fleet through the blockade without opposition; it might be difficult to catch up with the fleet, and its escape scot-free would give Antony the initiative and have a damaging impact on opinion among the armed forces and in Italy. But if they waited in the open seas, sooner or later Antony would be forced to come out and meet them on waters of their choosing. When that happened, they would try to outflank him in the north (the obstacle of

Leucas prevented that maneuver in the south). They would then either surround his smaller fleet, or force him to elongate and thin his line of ships, which would make it easier for their galleys to surround individual enemy ships and pick them off.

The balance of forces at sea decidedly favored Octavian. Although Antony's fleet had numbered about five hundred when it mustered at Ephesus, it is unlikely that he now had enough rowing crews for more than 230 ships, and he may have been able to man far fewer; whereas Octavian disposed of more than four hundred ships. Antony's galleys were larger than Octavian's and had more oarsmen, but they were probably no less maneuverable; this, of course, was in his favor.

Antony was forced to delay whatever move he planned, for on August 29 the fine weather broke. Four days of storm followed, and inactivity. On September 2, the weather cleared and the morning came up blue and sunny. The fleets took to the water.

Agrippa, to whom Octavian had wisely delegated tactical command, loaded eight legions and five praetorian cohorts onto his ships (that is, about forty thousand men, approximately ninety per galley), which he deployed about one mile off the headlands Parginosuala and Scylla, which marked the entry into the Actium narrows. There Agrippa waited to see what the enemy would do.

Antony divided his fleet, which was carrying twenty thousand legionaries and some archers, into four squadrons. One of these was Cleopatra's, with sixty ships in total, including some merchantmen. The queen herself was on her flagship, the *Antonias,* together with vast quantities of gold and silver coin, ingots, and other valuables. The personal safety of the queen was important, of course, but it was absolutely essential that the war chest did not find its way to Octavian or to the bottom of the sea.

The remainder of the army, totaling about fifty thousand men, was under the command of Publius Canidius Crassus, a long-standing partisan of Antony who had campaigned with great success in Armenia. If the fleet managed to make a getaway, he was to march to Macedonia, if possible, and then the east.

Before setting off, Antony gave his ships' captains the unusual order to take their sails with them, claiming this would help to ensure that not a single enemy ship escaped capture. Sails were seldom if ever used in bat-

tle (they took up too much room when stowed and reduced maneuver-
ability when set); his men, seeing through Antony's flimsy rationale, realized with dismay that he was not confident of victory, indeed that he
anticipated flight.

Dellius had briefed Agrippa about Antony's arrangements, including
the decision to load the sails. Also, the men from the two armies who
were not with the fleets lined the shores to watch events at sea. Octavian's
soldiers were able to see exactly what Antony was doing in the strait and
may very well have kept their commanders informed, by small boat or
some form of signaling.

As anticipated, the ships emerged from the strait, rowing in file, and
deployed in two lines that stretched between the headlands. There they
halted. Cleopatra's squadron hung behind the lines, and did not look as if
it was going to play an active part in the battle.

Antony waited hopefully for the enemy to accept the bait, sail toward
the opening of the strait, and give battle. The ploy failed, for Agrippa sensibly refused to move. A very long pause followed that lasted all morning.
The two fleets, perhaps a mile apart, rested on their oars.

Agrippa waited for Antony to accept that his bluff had been called, move
his ships forward, and leave the comparative safety of the strait for the open
sea. This he eventually did, stationing himself with the squadron on the
right. The command of his left wing was given to the competent Sosius.

At this point our sources are blinded by the fog of battle and we have
only the broadest and vaguest view of what happened. Plutarch gives a
good general impression:

> The fighting took on much of the character of a land battle, or, to be more exact, of
> an attack on a fortified town. Three or four of Octavian's ships clustered around each
> one of Antony's and the fighting was carried on with wicker shields, spears, poles,
> and flaming missiles, while Antony's soldiers also shot with catapults from wooden
> towers.

Having a greater number of war galleys, Agrippa could draw up his
fleet in two lines, and probably did so, while Antony was restricted to one.
Fairly early in the engagement, Agrippa began to feel his way around the
enemy's northern flank. Antony's ships responded by edging northward

themselves, perhaps swinging around from a north/south to a west/east axis. This had the effect of weakening Antony's center, and to a lesser extent Agrippa's.

The battle had been going on for a couple of hours. Although Antony's ships were putting up a good fight, Agrippa must have been feeling well pleased. There was no way the enemy line would be able to break through.

Then an astonishing thing occurred. In the early afternoon, the wind shifted (as it regularly did every day) toward the north. Cleopatra's squadron, lurking in the background and taking no part in the fighting, suddenly hoisted sail and plunged through the weakened center, where there was a fair amount of empty sea between groups of embattled galleys. The queen's own ship was easy to distinguish because it had a purple sail.

The change in wind direction meant that once Cleopatra's squadron had rounded Leucas, it could speed south with a following breeze in its sails and make its escape, easily outrunning Octavian's sailless ships. Antony immediately extricated some vessels from his position in the north. His flagship being too heavily engaged to escape, he transferred to another and made after the queen with a small flotilla.

The ancient sources wrongly suppose that Cleopatra lost her nerve and fled out of cowardice, and that Antony followed her because he was besotted by love. Quite clearly, this was not the case. The stowing of the sails, the order of battle (with the queen's ships kept in the rear, fresh and clear of the fighting), and the timing of the breakout to catch the afternoon wind indicate that the couple were acting out, with complete success, a carefully laid plan. While Agrippa was aware (thanks to Dellius) that a general breakout was intended, he was not expecting Cleopatra to make a getaway while the rest of Antony's ships kept him occupied. He had played unknowingly into her hands by sailing north to outflank Antony's right and so thinning his line.

Antony presumably hoped that other ships of his would also be able to break away, but they were fully engaged trying to fend off Octavian's larger fleet. After about an hour, the wind strengthened. Some of Antony's ships began to give up the unequal struggle and surrendered. Others withdrew into the Actium strait.

It is often difficult at the height of a battle for generals or admirals to know what is going on around them. Had Octavian won, or had he lost? He suspected he was the victor, but could not be absolutely sure. The light was failing. There was a swell. It was not always easy to distinguish enemy ships from those of friends. If he received any reports from across a battlefront that was probably not less than four miles long, he could not rely on them. As he was somewhere in the center of his line, he would have witnessed the queen's departure under full sail, but could have had no idea that Antony had left the scene with her.

What Octavian did see was some sort of retreat by enemy ships. During the wars against Sextus Pompeius he had learned the hard way that admirals were often obliged to spend a sleepless night after a battle at sea. Now that he and Agrippa had probably succeeded in bottling up what remained of Antony's fleet, they wanted to avoid any risk of it slipping away under cover of darkness or at first light. So, uncomfortable and dangerous though it was, they kept their ships at sea in the Actium roads throughout the hours of darkness.

At daylight Octavian, now back on land, could assess the outcome. He saw now that he had won at least a partial victory. About thirty or forty enemy galleys had been sunk and about five thousand of Antony's troops killed. The commanders of the remaining one hundred thirty or one hundred forty ships briefly considered their position, realized it was hopeless, and surrendered. However, a sizable army of up to fifty thousand men was holding together under Canidius Crassus, who started leading it toward the Pindos mountains and the relative safety of Macedonia. Unless that force could be neutralized in some way, the battle of Actium would simply be a passing incident in the war, not its decisive encounter. So he marched after Antony's legions.

As things turned out, he did not need to worry. Until the day after the battle, the soldiers had no idea that their commander had abandoned them. The men longed to see him and were sure that he would soon turn up from somewhere or other. But the days passed with no sound or sight of him, and their confidence collapsed. The time had come for them to do a deal with the victor. In essence, the soldiers demanded to be treated as if they had been on the winning side. After a week of tough negotiations, Octavian agreed to keep the legions in being instead of disbanding them and, most important, he promised to give them the same rewards as the victorious army.

The deal done, Canidius and other senior officers wanted no part of it. One night they left camp secretly and made their sad way to Antony.

# XV

# A LONG FAREWELL

## 3 1—3 0 B.C.

IT TOOK A LITTLE WHILE FOR NEWS OF ANTONY AND CLEO-
patra's doings after Actium to filter back to Octavian. Following his escape, Antony soon caught up with the queen's squadron. They made for
the attractive and well-appointed port of Paraetonium, just inside Egypt's
western frontier and 180 miles from Alexandria.

Now the tourist resort of Mersa Matrouh, this small coastal town com-
mands a large and beautiful lagoon with miles of sandy beach. In this delightful spot (promoted today as a "corner of paradise"), Antony plunged
into the deepest gloom. He had hoped to make contact with four of his legions in Cyrene, but they declared for Octavian and refused to meet him.
He sent Cleopatra ahead to Alexandria, where her ships arrived garlanded
as if in victory. Before the truth came out, she had any potential opponents killed. In the meantime, her disconsolate paramour was able, in
Plutarch's dry words, "to enjoy all the solitude he could desire."

Octavian sent a victory dispatch to Rome, but, patient and methodical as
ever, was in no hurry to deal with Antony and Cleopatra. He decided to
spend the oncoming winter on the island of Samos.

Many more soldiers were under arms than were needed or could be afforded. Octavian sent Italian veterans above a certain age back to Italy for
formal discharge, but gave them neither land nor money because for the
moment he had none. There were soon disgruntled mutterings, and
Agrippa was sent back to deal with the problem.

There was other evidence that the regime was unpopular. Maecenas
uncovered a plot to assassinate Octavian on his return to Italy. It was in-
eptly masterminded by Marcus Aemilius Lepidus, son of the self-seeking
former triumvir and a nephew of Marcus Brutus. "A young man whose
good looks exceeded his prudence," he was put to death. Dio writes that

Antony and Cleopatra schemed to "actually kill [Octavian] by treachery." Were they, one wonders, ever in touch with young Lepidus?

It is a sign of Octavian's managerial good sense that while he was away from Rome, he was willing to delegate powers to Agrippa and Maecenas, men who had been at his side throughout the long adventure and whom he trusted completely. He allowed them to read in advance his dispatches to the Senate, and correct them if they so wished. He had a duplicate made of his seal ring—the image of a sphinx—so that they could seal his letters up again.

The Donations of Alexandria were swiftly canceled. While deposing many minor princelings, Octavian confirmed on their thrones most of the major client kings—Amyntas of Galatia, who had defected to him with his cavalry; Polemo of Pontus, who had stayed behind in his kingdom; and Archelaus of Cappadocia. These were capable rulers, who knew it would be in their interest to remain loyal to whoever was in charge of the Roman empire. His former colleague was a good judge of character and Octavian saw no reason to disturb the arrangements he had made. So far as directly governed provinces were concerned, trustworthy colleagues were appointed in due course as proconsuls; for example, Cicero's son, Marcus, frequently drunk but a safe pair of hands, was given Syria.

The newly formed province of Armenia was irretrievably lost, for its deposed king had seized the distraction of the Actium campaign to reclaim his realm. Octavian coolly ignored this insult to Roman power and interests. The question of what to do about the eastern frontier—the Armenians, the Medes, and behind them the fierce Parthians, who still held the lost standards of Crassus—would have to wait. He was too busy.

In January of 30 B.C., Agrippa wrote to Octavian on Samos that he was unable to handle the Italian veterans, who were now openly mutinous, and that his presence was urgently needed. This was the worst possible time of year to undertake a long sea journey, but there was nothing for it. When Octavian disembarked at Brundisium, he was met by the entire Senate (except for a couple of praetors and the tribunes), many *equites,* and large numbers of ordinary citizens. He received an enthusiastic welcome. It was usual for senators to meet a returning statesman outside the gates of Rome, but for them to travel three hundred miles was a unique honor. Official Rome recognized that it was now under the control of one unchallenged ruler.

Not willing to be left behind, the angry veterans marched down to

Brundisium as well. Octavian wasted little time in meeting their demands, although he did not have enough ready cash to pay them all off on the spot and was obliged to issue promises postdated to the expected fall of Alexandria. The veterans were reluctantly satisfied, and after a month on Italian soil Octavian returned to Samos, where he laid plans for the invasion of Egypt.

In theory, Antony and Cleopatra had no reason to despair, for they still ruled half the Roman empire, and all its financial and human resources should have been at their disposal. But since Actium, people of power in the eastern provinces were unwilling to supply yet more soldiers to bolster what they judged to be a lost cause.

When Antony eventually arrived in Alexandria from Paraetonium, he abandoned the palace and his friends, living by himself in a quayside house beside Alexandria's great lighthouse, more than three hundred feet high, on the island of Pharos. On January 14, 30 B.C., he entered his fifty-fourth year. The queen eventually tempted him from self-indulgent misery by throwing a spectacular birthday party for him. According to Plutarch,

> *Cleopatra and Antony now dissolved their celebrated Society of Inimitable Livers and instituted another, which was at least its equal in elegance, luxury and extravagance, and which they called the Order of the Inseparable in Death. Their friends joined it on the understanding that they would end their lives together, and they set themselves to charm away the days with a succession of exquisite supper parties.*

The couple knew that with the arrival of spring Octavian would march against them. They had no realistic prospect of escaping to some other part of the world, although they had briefly thought of Spain and Cleopatra had tried and failed to organize an expedition to Arabia. The star-crossed lovers were cornered. Their only recourse now was to negotiate and, assuming that failed, to prepare for a last, futile stand.

The queen had plenty of money and still commanded the loyalty of her people. An army and a fleet were assembled. To cheer up the Alexandrians, a great ceremony—almost as splendid as the Donations of Alexandria—was held, at which the sixteen-year-old king of kings, Ptolemy XV Caesar, alias Caesarion, and Antony's son by Fulvia, the fourteen-year-old Antyllus, officially came of age.

Octavian received a succession of envoys from Alexandria who laid various proposals before him. He listened, but conceded nothing. Although he declined to make his own position clear, his policy was in fact straightforward: he wanted to win the great prize of Egypt, that rich, self-contained, and exotic realm which had attracted the greedy gaze of eminent Romans for more than a century—and he wanted to win it for himself, not simply for Rome.

Octavian's plan of attack was yet another pincer movement. Four Antonian legions that had switched loyalties would invade from Cyrenaica, which lay west of Egypt; in a signal mark of favor, Octavian appointed to command them the thirty-year-old Gaius Cornelius Gallus, although he was only an *eques* and previously best known as a fine lyric poet.

Octavian marched through Syria at the head of a substantial army toward the Egyptian frontier. The campaign was unlikely to be problematic, so this time Agrippa's services were not required. Octavian judged himself capable of managing on his own.

At last Antony bestirred himself. Believing that there was a good chance of winning over his legions, he marched back, at the head of a strong force of infantry and a powerful fleet, to Paraetonium where Gallus had installed himself. But his attempt to win back the legionaries and take the town failed, and his ships were trapped in the harbor and either burned or sunk.

The rest of Antony and Cleopatra's forces were stationed at Pelusium, a port on the easternmost edge of the Nile delta. It straddled the coastal route that skirted the Sinai desert and, being the only means of entry by land into Egypt from the east, was strategically important. Pharaohs throughout the ages had always taken care to give it a strong garrison. However, Pelusium fell with little or no resistance, perhaps surrendered by Cleopatra or else quickly stormed. If the former, she was creating a distance between herself and Antony—as may well be, for her first loyalty was always to her kingdom and the preservation of her own power. This and other accounts of her behavior during this time may have been lifted from Octavian's propaganda, which often stressed the queen's eastern deviousness and Antony's humiliating status as a dupe. However, it is perfectly possible that Cleopatra saw no advantage in going down with Antony and tried to save herself.

Octavian seems to have encountered little or no resistance in his advance on Alexandria. He passed the fashionable suburb of Canopus and set up camp near the racecourse or hippodrome, just outside the city walls. When he received the news that Pelusium was lost, Antony rushed back to Alexandria and, on its outskirts, surprised and routed an advance guard of enemy cavalry. Elated by the victory, he returned to the palace and embraced Cleopatra while still in full armor. He then introduced to her a soldier who had displayed unusual valor in the engagement. As a reward, the queen gave him a golden helmet and breastplate. He took them, and that night deserted to Octavian.

With hopeless bravado Antony challenged his onetime colleague to single combat, as if they were a pair of Homeric heroes. He can hardly have anticipated an acceptance. Octavian responded dismissively: "There are many different ways by which Antony can die."

On July 31, Antony decided to launch an all-out attack by land and sea on the following day. At dinner he ate and drank particularly well, telling the people around him that he did not expect to survive the battle. That evening, or so the story goes,

> about the hour of midnight, when all was hushed and a mood of dejection and fear of its impending fate brooded over the whole city, suddenly a marvellous sound of music was heard . . . as if a troop of revellers were leaving the city, shouting and singing as they went. . . . Those who tried to discover a meaning for this prodigy concluded that the god Dionysus, with whom Antony claimed kinship and whom he had sought above all to imitate, was now abandoning him.

Gods were imagined to leave besieged cities before they fell—Troy, Athens, Jerusalem. If the story has a basis in fact, perhaps Alexandrians were hearing Octavian, supported by a soldiers' chorus, conducting an *evocatio*; in this ceremony, a Roman general used to call on the gods of an enemy city to change sides and migrate to Rome.

On August 1, as soon as it was light, Antony sent his fleet eastward to meet Octavian's ships, and he drew up his remaining land forces on rising ground between the city walls and the hippodrome. The upshot was an almost comic fiasco. The ships raised their oars and surrendered without a fight; the fleets immediately combined and set a new course for the city. The cavalry deserted and the foot soldiers ran away.

Antony made his way back inside the walls of Alexandria and fell into a rage. He is reported to have shouted out that Cleopatra had betrayed him to the very men whom he was fighting for her sake. Terrified, she had word sent that she was dead.

There was only one thing now to be done. Antony went to his room and took off his armor. He asked his body servant to run him through, but the man suddenly turned away and fell on his sword instead. Antony then stabbed himself in the stomach and fell on the bed. The wound not only failed to kill him but soon stopped bleeding. Racked with pain, he begged bystanders to put him out of his misery, but they ran from the room.

The queen heard what had happened and sent word for Antony to be brought to her. She was hiding in a large mausoleum she had commissioned, which stood half complete in the palace grounds near a temple of Isis. Fearful of being surprised, she refused to unseal the doors, and she and two woman servants laboriously pulled the dying man with ropes up to a high window. Plutarch writes of the queen "clinging with both hands to the rope and with the muscles of her face distorted by the strain." Cleopatra beat and scratched her breasts in the traditional manner of a grieving widow, and smeared her face with blood from Antony's wound. He did his best to calm her, and, true to character to the last, called for and drank a cup of wine before expiring.

One of Antony's bodyguards brought Octavian the dead man's bloodstained sword, and it is said he withdrew into his tent and wept. Usually he kept his feelings under control, and we hear of him breaking down in tears on only one other occasion: when he received an account of Julius Caesar's funeral. If he did weep now, it could have been the result of a snapping of tension after years of struggle rather than empathy. Octavian had never gotten on with Antony, and he is unlikely to have grieved for a man whom he had schemed to clear from his path for most of his public career. Alternatively, the incident was invented, and merely illustrated the victor's highly developed skill at news management.

Octavian may have been the ruler of the Roman world, but he had never seen a great Hellenistic megalopolis before. He was familiar with cities that, like Rome and Athens, had grown untidily and organically over many centuries—crowded, noisy, ugly conurbations devoid of wide avenues and splendid vistas. So Alexandria made a great impression on him.

Founded in 331 B.C. by Alexander the Great, the twenty-five-year-old Macedonian king who conquered the Persian empire, the city was built on a narrow bar of land with the Mediterranean on one side and a shallow lake, called Maraeotis (today's Lake Mariout, smaller and shallower than in ancient times), on the other. A little way offshore lay an island, Pharos, with its celebrated lighthouse, which was three miles long and gave protection from storms.

As in a modern American city, the street plan was based on a grid. A mile-long mole or dike was built between the shore and the island of Pharos, so creating two harbors, the Great harbor on the east side and the Eunostus (or Happy Return) harbor to the west. A canal from Lake Maraeotis in the south connected the city to the Nile and so to Egypt both as a production center and a market.

The city was a runaway success. In the first century B.C., the total population may have been about the same size as that of Rome, up to one million. With its grand overall look, Alexandria, rather like Haussmann's Paris in the nineteenth century, became a center for culture and fashion throughout the eastern Mediterranean. Strabo called it the "greatest emporium of the inhabited world."

Octavian was now free to enter the city, and on foot he led his men through the Gate of the Sun, not far from the hippodrome outside the walls, and along one of the city's main streets, the Canopic Way. Nervous crowds had gathered. Octavian made a point of being accompanied by Areius, an Alexandrian citizen and a well-known philosopher and rhetorician. This friendly gesture was presumably calculated to allay the fears of the people, for it was an accepted custom of war that a captured city could be given over to pillage by the victors.

Octavian and his party made their way to the Gymnasium, where the triumvir and the queen had probably held the ceremony of the Donations of Alexandria. The place was packed: when Octavian came in and mounted a speaker's dais, the audience was beside itself with fear and all present fell on their faces. He announced that he had no intention of holding the city at fault for the conduct of its rulers. At Areius' request, he granted a number of pardons.

· · ·

Octavian's next destination was the Royal Palace, which lay north of the Canopic Way; here he would find the queen. He sent ahead as his envoy an *eques* called Gaius Proculeius, a close friend of his whom, it so happened, Antony in his last moments had recommended to the queen. Proculeius was under instruction to do whatever was needed to capture her alive.

The "palace" took up an entire fifth of the city, along the quayside of the Great harbor. We can imagine a large park or campus dotted with mansions, temples, and pavilions of one kind or another. The complex has almost entirely disappeared under later buildings and there are no ruins to visit; however, some of it sank into the sea as a result of an earthquake and tidal wave in the fourth century A.D., and is now being explored.

The main palace building stood on Cape Lochias, a promontory at the harbor opening. A twentieth-century historian writes: "No Latin ruler, gasping for air in the hot Roman summer, had nearly so attractive a situation as these Greek rulers of the Egyptian people."

Somewhere in the vicinity, Cleopatra sat desolate in her mausoleum, awaiting her conqueror. She had gathered there all the most precious items of royal treasure—gold, silver, emeralds, pearls, ebony, ivory, and cinnamon (an extremely costly spice in those days and regarded as a fit present for royalty)—and also a great quantity of firewood and tinder. These preparations transmitted an implicit threat to Octavian: if he did not treat her well, she would set fire to the lot.

The ancient sources report that this consideration weighed heavily with him, although it cannot have been decisive: the queen can hardly have had personal possession of the kingdom's entire reserves of precious metals—and, even if she had, they would survive a fire. The loss of the jewelry and other precious items would be a pity, but was not a matter of high importance.

Proculeius soon arrived outside the mausoleum, to which he managed to gain entry by a trick. He noted that the upper window through which the dying Antony had been dragged was still open; while someone distracted the queen by engaging her in conversation through the door of the mausoleum, Proculeius leaned a ladder against the wall and climbed in through the window accompanied by two servants. He captured Cleopatra and placed her under guard. She was allowed to preside at Antony's funeral (not before Octavian had inspected the corpse), but her spirit was broken and she fell ill. She remained a prisoner inside the mausoleum.

(Possession of Egypt solved Octavian's financial problems once and for all. When in due course the kingdom's bullion reserves were transported to Rome, the standard rate of interest immediately dropped from 12 percent to 4 percent. There was plenty of money to settle his account with the veterans and to buy all the land they required [unsurprisingly, land values doubled]. Ample resources were also available for investing in public works, and the much-tried people of Rome received generous individual money grants.)

Not long after her arrest, Octavian called on the queen. He knew her (one assumes) from her stay at Rome as Julius Caesar's guest and lover nearly fifteen years previously, but her bedraggled appearance now must have made her nearly unrecognizable. According to Plutarch, "she had abandoned her luxurious style of living, and was lying on a pallet bed dressed only in a tunic, but, as he entered, she sprang up and threw herself at his feet. Her hair was unkempt and her expression wild, while her eyes were shrunken and her voice trembled uncontrollably."

Octavian asked her to lie down again and sat beside her. Cleopatra then tried to justify her part in the war, saying she had been forced to act as she did and had been in fear of Antony. Octavian demolished her excuses point by point, and she changed her manner, begging for pity as if desperate to save her life. Octavian was pleased by this, for it suggested that the queen did not intend to kill herself. He wanted her to live, the ancient sources claim, for she would make an admirable display in the triumph he intended to hold in Rome.

However, Publius Cornelius Dolabella, a young aristocrat on Octavian's staff who was "by no means insensible to Cleopatra's charms," warned her that Octavian was about to leave Egypt and that she and her children were to be sent away within three days. So far as she was concerned, this was the end. She arranged for an asp—the Egyptian cobra—to be smuggled in to her in a basket of figs. She dismissed all her attendants except for two faithful ladies-in-waiting, and closed the doors of the mausoleum.

"So here it is," she said, lifting away the figs to reveal the snake, and held out her arm to be bitten (another version has her provoking the snake with a golden spindle till it jumped out of a jar and bit her). She was thirty-nine. Plutarch reports that she was found "lying dead upon a golden couch dressed in her royal robes. Of her two women, Iras lay dying at her feet, while Charmion, already tottering and scarcely able to hold up her head, was adjusting the crown which encircled her mistress's brow."

How much of this romantically tragic ending is true? Mists of propaganda have clouded the historical record, and a degree of skepticism is in order. Octavian would surely have found the queen's survival more inconvenient than otherwise. Executing a woman was not the Roman way, and her appearance at his triumph in Rome might well have been counterproductive; he will have recalled how her half sister, Arsinoe, had won the crowd's sympathy when led in chains in one of Julius Caesar's triumphs. No, far better for the queen to be persuaded to do away with herself. It may be that, when she showed no signs of taking this step, Dolabella, probably half her age and far from being sincerely her *cavaliere servente,* was instructed to leak his employer's travel plans in the hope that the information would edge her over the precipice, as indeed it did.

As for the method of Cleopatra's death, it is safest to agree with Dio's judgment that "no one knows clearly in what way she perished." The story of the asp is problematic, for an individual one is typically about eight feet long, rather large for a basket of figs and inconvenient to handle. Also, a single bite by an asp is not necessarily fatal, and even when it is, as much as two hours may pass before life is extinguished.

It is possible that Octavian arranged for Cleopatra's murder and put about the fiction that she killed herself. However, there is no evidence for this. All that can be said is that the queen's removal was to his advantage, and that he showed no qualms in having the boys Caesarion and Antyllus caught and killed. Their coming-of-age ceremony was their death warrant, for it had qualified them as culpable adults. (The younger children, the twins Alexander Helios and Cleopatra Selene, and Ptolemy Philadelphus, were spared. After adorning Octavian's triumph, they joined the stable of youngsters being looked after by the kindly Octavia. When Cleopatra Selene grew up, she married the scholarly King Juba of Numidia, by whom she had a son and a daughter. She probably took her brothers with her to North Africa; nothing more is heard of them and we may guess that they led quiet lives, doing their best to avoid the world's dangerous attention.)

Octavian enjoyed being a tourist, but unlike many Romans abroad he was no looter of beautiful and costly objects; the only item he personally took away from the palace of the Ptolemies was a single agate cup. He visited some of the sights of Alexandria, dazzling in white limestone and marble.

The first and foremost of these was the tomb of Alexander the Great, which stood at the crossroads of the city's two main avenues. Alexander had died in 323 B.C. His embalmed body in its gold and crystal coffin was the new city's most sacred relic. Not a trace of the corpse or the building that housed it, the Soma, remains, although it probably stood on the site of today's Mosque of the Prophet Daniel.

At thirty-three, Octavian was the same age as Alexander when he died. A great admirer of the Macedonian, he wanted to see the mummy and honor it; so it was temporarily removed from its coffin and burial chamber and displayed in public.

The young Roman gazed at the body for a time, then paid his respects by crowning the head with a golden diadem and strewing flowers on the trunk. He was asked, "Would you now like to visit the Mausoleum of the Ptolemies?" To which he retorted, "I came to see a king, not a row of corpses."

The Alexandrians were doubtless impressed by Octavian's admiring curiosity, but the effect may have been lessened when he accidentally knocked off part of Alexander's nose.

Octavian's friend Areius may have introduced him to the Mouseion, or Place of the Muses. This was a group of buildings in the palace grounds, linked by colonnaded walks and facing the Soma. They included richly decorated lecture halls, laboratories, observatories, a park, and a zoo. Generously funded by the Ptolemies, the Mouseion was a center for scientific research and literary studies.

Its library was world renowned. Staffed by many famous Greek writers and literary critics, it contained a vast collection of books, perhaps about 500,000 in all, and was open to anyone who could read. (Julius Caesar was accused of having accidentally burned it down during his brief Alexandrian war of 48–47 B.C.; in fact, only a part of it was destroyed.)

All in all, Octavian's stay in Alexandria will have given him a clearer concept of what a capital city might be, both architecturally and culturally. Here the art of state persuasion, whether recorded in carved stone or on inked papyrus, was at its most refined. In particular, the Ptolemies had shown how intellectuals and artists could flourish in a form of tamed liberty, or free and de luxe bondage. Rome could not be rebuilt in a day, but Octavian returned from Egypt determined to create a city whose public symbols manifested an appropriate splendor.

. . .

Egypt now lost the independence it had enjoyed (with a few intervals) for thousands of years and would not regain until the twentieth century A.D. Octavian handed it over, as was proper, to the Senate and people of Rome, but in many ways it became his private fiefdom. As well as being "lord of the two lands" (that is, Lower and Upper Egypt), Octavian was recognized as king of kings, an ironic echo of the grandiose title that Antony had accorded Cleopatra. The Egyptians soon accepted their Italian pharaoh. Modern archaeologists have recently discovered a telling example of assimilation: an image of the Egyptian jackal-headed god, Anubis, guarding the entrance of a tomb, but dressed and armed as a Roman soldier.

Any ruler of the Roman empire had good reason to set Egypt apart from the run-of-the-mill province. As the Mediterranean's major producer of wheat, it was Rome's bread basket. This made it much too dangerous to allow a senator, a full-dress member of the ruling class, to govern the kingdom; Octavian appointed an *eques,* his friend the poet Gallus, to become its first prefect.

The new governor was energetic and effective, but his splendid status as deputy pharaoh seems to have gone to his head. He indulged in "indiscreet talk when drunk" about his imperial employer, set up statues of himself, and had a list of his achievements inscribed on the pyramids. A colleague informed on him, and in 27 B.C. Gallus was dismissed. Octavian merely denied him access to his house and the privilege of entering the provinces of which he was the proconsul. But the Senate exiled him and confiscated his estates. Octavian in tears thanked the Senate for supporting him in his painful severity.

"I am the only man in Rome," he said, "who cannot limit his displeasure with his friends. The matter must always be taken further."

Reportedly, Gallus felt so humiliated by his disgrace that he took his life (although another story was told that he died while having sexual intercourse). Like that of Salvidienus Rufus, his fate was an awful warning to others in leading circles.

The Mediterranean world had had plenty of time between Actium and the deaths of Antony and Cleopatra to consider the final conclusion of the civil wars and reckon with the unchallenged supremacy of Octavian. Honors cascaded on him from every quarter, including the right to use *Im-*

*perator,* the title with which soldiers acclaimed victorious generals, as his permanent first name. Other awards he declined with a well-judged display of modesty.

The senatorial decree that gave Octavian the greatest pleasure was the formal closing of the gates of the tiny Temple of Janus. This building stood in the Forum and had perhaps originally been a bridge over the stream that used to cross the square (long since covered over and turned into a drain). Janus was the god of gateways; he had two faces, one looking forward to the future, the other to the past. The temple had doors at either end, which were closed in times of peace and open in times of war. The Romans were a warlike people and the doors were almost always open.

That they were shut now was a great compliment to Octavian, and a symbol of the much heralded, much delayed arrival of peace throughout the empire.

# XVI

# ABDICATION

## 30–27 B.C.

OCTAVIAN DID NOT ARRIVE BACK IN ITALY UNTIL AUGUST 29, 30 B.C. He was consul again (he had been regularly holding the consulship since his triumviral powers ran out in 31). Like Julius Caesar, he knew he could not govern successfully alone, and he made it clear that reconciliation was the order of the day. In his official autobiography, he claimed: "Wars, both civil and foreign, I undertook throughout the world, on sea and land, and when victorious I spared all citizens who sued for pardon."

The claim of clemency should not be taken at face value. Many were forgiven, but some were not. Sosius was given employment, while Antony's loyal army commander, Canidius, who was unfairly criticized for abandoning his legions after Actium, was executed: despite having boasted that he did not fear dying, he is reported to have lost his nerve at the end.

Vengeance was also taken on the dead. Antony's memory was formally expunged. His name was obliterated from the Fasti, the state registers of official events. His statues were removed. It was to be as if he had never existed. The Senate, not unprompted surely, voted that no member of the Antonius clan should be named Marcus (a measure that was later repealed). His birthday was made a *dies nefastus,* an unlucky day, on which public business could not be conducted.

What had taken place, the meaning of the campaign that had been won and lost, needed to be attractively dramatized as an irreversible turning point in history. Actium, which had really been no more than a scrappy breakout from a blockade, was transformed into a great battle—a duel between Rome and anti-Rome, between good and evil.

The poets associated with Maecenas worked on an imaginative rewriting of history. Horace produced an ode that celebrated Octavian's achievement at Actium (in fact, as we have seen, the credit for the campaign goes to Agrippa) and blackened Cleopatra's name. He described her as

> *Plotting destruction to our Capitol*
>
> *And ruin to the Empire with her squalid*
> *Pack of diseased half-men—mad, wishful grandeur,*
>     *Tipsy with sweet good luck!*
> *But all her fleet burnt, scarcely one ship saved—*
> *That tamed her rage; and Caesar, when his galleys*
> *Chased her from Italy, soon brought her, dreaming*
>     *And drugged with native wine,*
> *Back to the hard realities of fear.*

In this vivid caricature, there is not a single accurate assertion. As we have seen, Cleopatra was not plotting the end of the Roman empire, all her fleet was not burned, Octavian did not chase her anywhere, certainly not from Italy, and there is no evidence that the queen was a drunk. However, it is fine poetry.

It was the leading poet of the age, Virgil, who drew the fullest picture of the battle in his great national epic about Rome's beginnings, the *Aeneid*. Prophetically engraved on the shield of Julius Caesar's ancestor Aeneas, Octavian is envisioned at the head of *tota Italia,* all Italy. The star or comet that blazed in the night sky for a week after Caesar's assassination shines above Octavian as he sets sail against the corrupt and cowardly east.

> *High up on the poop [he] is leading*
> *The Italians into battle, the Senate and People with him,*
> *His home gods and the great gods: two flames shoot up from his helmet*
> *In jubilant light, and his father's star dawns over its crest.*

Defining the past in glowing terms was only half of what needed to be done if the victorious regime was to establish itself firmly in the hearts and minds of the ruling class and of the people at large. It was also important to present Octavian as the natural ruler of Rome—to develop a personality cult and an iconography of power. This was to be achieved by two means.

First, Octavian made the little complex of houses on Rome's Palatine

Hill, where he and Livia lived, a symbol of his authority. Some of these buildings substantially survive (although at the time of writing they are closed to the public). A ramp connected them to an adjacent temple of Apollo, which was an integral part of the complex. Octavian had vowed to build it during the wars against Sextus Pompeius, but its construction only became a major project after Actium; the temple was dedicated in 28 B.C.

Almost nothing of it remains now, but it was as splendid an edifice as could be designed. Its walls were of solid bright-white marble (the walls of Roman temples were usually of brick and concrete with marble cladding). The doors were gilded and inlaid with ivory. On the roof stood a chariot of the sun. The temple was surrounded by, or connected to, a portico of *giallo antico,* a speckled yellow marble from quarries in Numidia.

The Sibylline Books were removed from their traditional home in the cellars of the Temple of Jupiter on the Capitol and stored under a colossal statue of Apollo that stood in front of the new temple. The books were a much-valued collection of oracular utterances in Greek hexameters, which were consulted in times of trouble, not to discover the future but to learn how to avert the anger of the gods. Their presence in the precincts of Octavian's house was a telling emblem of his unique role in the state.

The temple was not used simply for religious purposes. It became, in effect, a cultural center. Remembering Alexandria and taking up a plan of Julius Caesar's before his murder, Octavian located two public libraries there, one for books in Greek and the other for those in Latin. Medallion portraits of famous writers were affixed to the walls. Here authors delivered public readings and the chief librarian, a polymath called Gaius Julius Hyginus, taught classes.

Octavian also received a personality makeover. The object was to give him something of the sparkle of divinity, or at least of semidivine, heroic status. Stories began to circulate of his miraculous childhood and of prophecies that foreshadowed his current greatness. It is uncertain when these first emerged and whether they were invented by the regime or unofficially encouraged as spontaneous urban myths. But it is plausible that from this time new accounts of Octavian's childhood appeared that lent legitimacy to his political dominance.

Dio preserves an unconvincing tale that echoes one told of Alexander the Great's mother and was no doubt designed to encourage a direct comparison. When Julius Caesar decided to make Octavian his heir, he was influenced by "Atia's [his mother's] emphatic declaration that the youth had been engendered by Apollo; for while sleeping in his temple, she said, she thought she had intercourse with a serpent, and it was this that caused her at the end of her pregnancy to bear a son."

On the day of Octavian's birth, Atia dreamed that her intestines were raised up into the sky and spread out all over the earth, and during the same night her husband, Octavius, thought that the sun rose from her womb. The following day the elder Octavius came across a learned expert on divination, Publius Nigidius Figulus, and explained what had happened. Figulus replied: "You have begotten a master over us!"

An even grander (and even less likely) endorsement was devised: one night the elder statesman Cicero dreamed that Jupiter was going to appoint a senator's son as ruler of Rome. The boys all presented themselves at the Temple of Jupiter Optimus Maximus (Best and Greatest) on the Capitol. The statue of Jupiter stretched out its hand and said: "Romans, you shall have an end to civil wars, when this boy becomes your leader."

Another senior senator and leading traditionalist, Quintus Lutatius Catulus, had a similar experience: when the boy was walking in a procession to the same temple of Jupiter, Catulus saw the god throw what looked like a figurine of Rome in the form of a goddess into the lap of his toga.

There is ingenious method behind these stories. The three men cited were safely dead, so they could not be invited to confirm or deny their accuracy. In fact, Catulus died before Octavian's fourth birthday, rather early for the young hopeful to be taking part in a public ceremony.

More significantly, Nigidius, Cicero, and Catulus had all been distinguished republicans. They had opposed Julius Caesar, and the first two had sided with Pompey in the civil war. The point of the anecdotes is that they gave the young revolutionary, whose career had been founded on illegality and violence, a respectable, conservative pedigree.

In August of 29 B.C., Octavian celebrated three triumphs—over Dalmatia, where he had campaigned successfully in 35 and 34; over Cleopatra (meaning Actium); and over Egypt (meaning the capture of Alexandria). They were magnificent affairs, during which the spoils of Egypt were displayed on large carts. An effigy of the dead Cleopatra lying on a couch was a prize exhibit and her surviving children, Alexander Helios, Cleopatra Selene, and Ptolemy Philadelphus walked in the pageant.

After them rode Octavian, in the traditional chariot drawn by four horses, wearing a gold-embroidered toga and a flowered tunic. On his head was a laurel wreath signifying victory. Usually the general being honored by a triumph followed the holders of the offices of state and the Senate; but, on this occasion, Octavian went first, in a clear visual demonstration of his political predominance.

A few days later the Senate House, or Curia Hostilia, rebuilt after the mob burned it down on the day of Julius Caesar's funeral, opened for business with the new name of the Curia Julia; a new speakers' platform was constructed, decorated with *rostra,* ships' prows, from Actium, and the temple to the now deified dictator, erected on the spot in the Forum where he had been cremated on an impromptu pyre, was dedicated.

Octavian had once been proud to call himself *divi filius,* for it authorized his power in the eyes of his adoptive father's adoring soldiers and ordinary Roman citizens. But since the Sicilian War he had not used the title so frequently and now, from this high point of celebration, Octavian's propaganda begins to make even less of Julius Caesar than in the past: the dictator had been an extremist, who destroyed old Rome, and the new Rome wanted to associate itself with tradition rather than innovation.

Sharp-eyed observers were struck by the fact that Octavian was accompanied during his triumph by two teenagers, riding on the chariot's right and left trace horses. One was Gaius Claudius Marcellus, his sister Octavia's fourteen-year-old son, and the other was Tiberius Claudius Nero, his wife Livia's eldest son, thirteen.

Their arrival on the verge of adulthood promised to transform the dynamics of Octavian's inner circle. Octavia was about six years older than her devoted brother. She adored her son, an attractive and intelligent boy, "cheerful in mind and disposition," and, just as Julius Caesar had done in his own case, Octavian took a special interest in his development.

Tiberius was also a promising lad, but he was not of Octavian's blood and so took second place in his plans. The man who was now in sole command of the Roman empire was beginning to consider how to ensure his regime's long-term future. With his always uncertain health, it was not too soon to establish a dynastic succession; if his nephew fulfilled his promise, he would be an ideal heir.

There was another thing: Octavian liked and trusted youth. He and his "band of brothers," his two trusted former school friends, Agrippa and Maecenas, had set out together on their great enterprise to avenge Caesar's murder and win power when in their late teens. The challenges they faced called forth their talent; now Octavian was looking forward to promoting the new younger generation that was about to emerge. Perhaps as early as 29 B.C., he arranged for the minimum ages of officeholders to be reduced: in the case of a quaestor, from thirty years to twenty-five; of a consul, from forty-two to thirty-seven. Senators' sons were expected to familiarize themselves with administration; they were allowed to wear the purple-striped toga, which was the uniform of a senator, encouraged to attend Senate meetings, and given officer posts during their military service.

Sadly, Octavian and his beloved Livia were childless, although she suffered one miscarriage. It is curious that both had had children by their former spouses. Perhaps, as one classical source has it, this was a case of physical incompatibility, but more probably some illness led one or the other to become infertile.

As yet the boys were too young to help shoulder the burdens of government. That remained the task of Agrippa and Maecenas, although little love was lost between them. The former was "more a rustic at heart than a man of refined tastes," although he admired great art and argued that all paintings and sculptures should be nationalized rather than spirited away into private collections where they were never seen. He was a collector on a grand scale, spending an astonishing 1.2 million sesterces on two paintings—one of them depicting the Greek hero Ajax and the other Aphrodite—which he installed in the public baths he built.

By contrast, Maecenas could almost "outdo a woman in giving himself up to indolence and soft luxury." He delighted in silks and jewels; he was an epicure, who introduced to fashionable dining tables a new delicacy, the flesh of young donkeys; and he was reputed to have been the first person to build a heated swimming pool in the capital. He was married to the beautiful but arrogant Terentia. They were always quarreling, but her husband remained fond of her and invariably sought reconciliation. It was said of him that he married a thousand times, although he only had one wife.

Terentia attracted, and apparently won, Octavian's favors, but this seems not to have affected the two men's relationship. Although he was uxorious, Maecenas was not monogamous. He had many affairs, including one with a famous actor, Bathyllus, a freedman and friend of Octavian. Although sleeping with men was apparently not to his taste, Octavian had no objection to multifarious lifestyles among members of his circle.

Octavian used to poke fun at his friend's precious, overelaborate style of writing, by parodying it in personal letters to him. Macrobius, a writer of the fifth century A.D., quotes an example: "Goodbye, my ebony of Medullia, ivory from Etruria, silphium from Arretium, diamond of the Adriatic, pearl from the Tiber, Cilnian emerald, jasper of the Iguvians, Persenna's beryl, Italy's carbuncle—in short, you charmer of unfaithful wives."

Though his private life was colorful, Maecenas showed sleepless energy in times of crisis, and he gave excellent political advice. He did not seek public political office, preferring to operate informally, behind the scenes. As we have seen, he cultivated the finest poets of the age, ensuring that, so far as possible and without the application of censorship, geniuses such as Virgil and Horace stayed on message.

Agrippa could not stand Maecenas' exotic and effeminate manners. Straightforward, direct, and loyal, he was the finest general and admiral of the age. He made up for Octavian's lack of military skills, as had been tacitly acknowledged by the award of the *corona rostrata* for his services in the Naulochus campaign. The war against Sextus Pompeius would not have been won without him, and he had been discreetly invaluable in Illyricum. Now, as the mastermind of victory at Actium, he received the right to display an azure banner and (of more practical value) the freehold of country estates in Egypt.

Agrippa was completely loyal to Octavian and to the public service. In fact, he regarded them as one and the same, and it would be a bad day for the regime were he ever to see them as different. Completely trusted, he became (in effect) Octavian's deputy—nearly his equal, but always a step behind when on parade.

According to a near contemporary historian, Agrippa "was . . . well-disciplined to obedience, but to one man only, yet eager to command others; in whatever he did he never admitted the possibility of delay. With him, an idea was implemented as soon as it was thought of." Portrait busts show a man with hard and determined features, someone whose disapproval was to be feared—perhaps even by his friend and master? He held official posts, but was as uninterested in the trappings of authority as Maecenas, albeit for a completely different reason. While Maecenas could not really be bothered with power (being satisfied with influence), Agrippa cared for it passionately—but only for its reality.

Although no records survive of Agrippa's private opinions, we may surmise that he watched Octavian's growing affection for Marcellus with unease. As the young man grew up, Agrippa could well find an inexperienced heir interfering in his freedom of action, interposing himself between him and Octavian. That would not do.

The end of the civil wars brought a substantial peace dividend. A grand total of sixty legions under arms in 31 B.C. was reduced to the minimum necessary to guard the empire from external invasion. Octavian set the number at twenty-eight legions, or about 150,000 men, all of whom were Roman citizens. These were brigaded with about the same number of auxiliary troops, noncitizens recruited from the less Romanized and less militarily secure provinces (for example, Gaul and northern Africa). These auxiliaries often served near or in their homelands—a sensible policy, for it gave the provinces an active role in their own defense.

The army was permanently stationed where it was most needed: along the imperial frontiers in the east and northern Africa, Spain, northeast Gaul, and what we now call the Balkans. These dispositions were adequate, but there was no reserve to send to trouble spots in times of emergency. Intent on reducing public expenditure and seeing no great and imminent threat, Octavian was willing to take the risk of a lean military establishment.

He then turned his attention to civilian matters. According to Suetonius, he gave serious consideration after Actium to bringing back the Republic, but everything we know about Octavian—above all, his slow, undeviating pursuit of mastery—suggests that this must be a misunderstanding. What he did do was give very careful thought to the kind of polity that should now be installed. Dio imagined that a debate took place at this time in Octavian's presence, in which Agrippa put the case for a democratic or, in effect, republican constitution, and Maecenas argued the benefits of monarchy. Though such a discussion probably never took place, it is true that Octavian found a way forward that married these two opposing positions. As usual, he took his time, and a good three years passed before he came to a conclusion.

In 28 B.C., Octavian held his sixth consulship, this time alongside Agrippa. All the acts of the triumvirs were annulled, and assurances given that there would never be a return to the terrible past. The consuls assumed *censoria potestas,* the powers of censors. The censors were two senior officials elected every five years. They had three main tasks: first, to hold a *lustrum* or general ritual purification of the people; second, to conduct a census of Roman citizens; and third, to supervise the conduct of citizens, and more especially of members of the Senate.

The census held by Octavian and Agrippa revealed that there were 4,063,000 citizens (we do not know whether the number included women and children). A more ticklish job was to identify and weed out senatorial undesirables. The number of senators was reduced from one thousand to a somewhat more manageable eight hundred. As Suetonius records, this was a highly unpopular procedure. At the meeting when the outcome of the review of the Senate was announced, Octavian is said to have worn a sword and steel corselet beneath his tunic. Senators were allowed to approach only after their togas were searched.

The regime was not yet quite ready to chart a course for the long term, but an awkward incident took place which strongly suggested that a new political framework must be put in place sooner rather than later. People needed to know what the rules of the political game now were.

Marcus Licinius Crassus, the able grandson of Julius Caesar's onetime colleague, returned to Rome from a highly successful campaign on the Macedonian frontier. He claimed not only a triumph but also *spolia opima.* This high and rare honor was granted to a general who had killed the enemy commander with his own hands and stripped him of his armor— namely, the *spolia opima,* or splendid spoils. This was what Crassus had done. In the history of the state, only two men had achieved this feat previously.

Unchallenged control of the legions was crucial to Octavian's hold on power, and so he felt it important that no other independent personality should be allowed to win a military reputation. It was unthinkable for Crassus to dedicate the armor of his defeated opponent, according to the traditional ritual, in the tiny antique Temple of Jupiter Feretrius on the Capitol. So a technicality was cited to prevent him. Crassus was allowed his triumph, but nothing more is heard of him; we must suppose that excessive keenness brought his military career to a premature end.

. . .

At last in 27 B.C. Octavian, now thirty-six years old, was ready to unveil his constitutional blueprint. On January 1, he entered his seventh consulship with Agrippa again as his colleague. On the Ides (the thirteenth of the month) he made a most extraordinary speech to the Senate—perhaps the most important speech of his life. Dio gave him words that cannot have been very far from those he actually uttered:

> *I lay down my office in its entirety and return to you all authority absolutely—authority over the army, the laws and the provinces—not only those territories which you entrusted to me, but those which I later secured for you.*

For most of Octavian's listeners, the statement came as a shock. No one knew exactly how to react, and his cautious audience either believed him or pretended to. While he was speaking, senators broke in with shouts and interjections.

When he sat down, the protests continued. With a great show of reluctance, he allowed himself to be persuaded to accept an unusually large "province" for ten years, consisting of Spain, Gaul, and Syria, presumably with proconsular authority; he would be able to choose deputies, or legates, to rule them on his behalf while he remained consul at Rome. All other provinces would fall under direct senatorial management in the old way: that is, the Senate would appoint former consuls and praetors to govern them.

A grateful Senate voted Octavian new honors. The doorposts of his house on the Palatine were decorated with laurel and the lintel with oak leaves for having saved the lives of Roman citizens (as coins had it, *ob cives servatos*). A golden shield was set up in the Senate House, as he later proudly recalled, "in recognition of my valour, my clemency, my justice and my piety."

In a remarkable innovation, Octavian was given a new *cognomen,* by which he was to be known in future. There had been an idea of calling Rome's second founder, as the rhetoric had it, by the name of its original founder Romulus. But Romulus had made himself king and, according to one story, had been murdered by angry senators. A much better proposition was Augustus, meaning Revered One; and so it was agreed. Octavian's official name was now Imperator Caesar Augustus.

A modest title was adopted for everyday use: *princeps,* "first [or leading] citizen." It had respectable precedents: the leader of the Senate had always been called *princeps senatus,* an honor now accorded to Augustus, and men such as Pompey and Crassus had also been known as *principes.* A new name signified a new start. Octavian, the bloodstained triumvir, was now Augustus, the law-abiding *princeps.*

In making these arrangements, Augustus aimed primarily at persuading the Senate that he was not heading in the same direction as his adoptive father—toward, that is, an out-and-out autocracy, even toward something like a Hellenistic monarchy. If enough senators believed that he intended to follow in Julius Caesar's footsteps, Augustus ran a high risk of incurring his own Ides of March.

Also, there was no one on hand, apart from the Senate, to help Augustus in the laborious job of running the empire. He needed the collaboration of the ruling class, and this they would be unlikely to supply unless they were satisfied with the new order of things.

The Senate was not quite the body it had been. New men from the Italian countryside had filled the many gaps left by the old governing families that had been weakened in the civil wars or had lost their money and estates. Many came from regions that had received citizenship as little as fifty years before. Theirs was an Italian rather than a Roman identity. Even more controversially, leading men from southern Gaul and Spain, provinces that had long since adopted the Roman language and culture, were recruited as senators. All these arrivistes saw their fate as inextricably linked to the new regime. So did a good number of impoverished aristocrats, for the astute Augustus took good care to fund them generously and thereby constrain their freedom to oppose him. He bound other noble clans to him by arranging marriages with his relatives.

Nevertheless, members of the Senate still held a residual, deeply felt belief in Rome's constitution. They would not accept one-man rule; and they expected the state to remain a collective enterprise even if led by one man.

The presentation on January 13 of 27 B.C. was a piece of theater, of course. The Senate and the people remained, as they always had been, the sole sources of legal authority, but Augustus did not hand back any real power. In the last analysis he owed his dominant position to the army (and to a lesser extent to the people, who could be relied on to reelect him as consul for as many terms as he liked). It was no accident that his gover-

norship of Spain, Gaul, and Syria gave him the command of twenty legions. The legions had legitimate reason to be there: the northern of the
two Spanish provinces was still not entirely subdued; Gaul remained unruly; and Syria abutted the untrustworthy Parthians. But, by comparison,
the "senatorial" provinces, to be governed by proconsuls in the ordinary
way, were calm; only three of them required armies, and in total, they
commanded five or six legions. Thus, most of Rome's armies were under
the command of the *princeps;* as long as they and their commanders stayed
loyal, he was safe.

Another important source of Augustus' power was patronage. He had
inherited Julius Caesar's empire-wide *clientela,* and no doubt he had greatly
expanded it even before Actium won him Antony's *clientela* too. His authority across the empire was expressed through a web of personal connections and loyalties, to which no other Roman could remotely aspire. In
every community large or small, leading men were under an obligation to
him, and were usually rewarded with the gift of Roman citizenship.

Augustus was pleased to boast: "When I had put an end to the civil
wars, having acquired supreme power over the empire with universal
consent, I transferred the Republic from my control into that of the Senate and People of Rome." That was literally correct—the machinery of
constitutional government came creakily back into operation—but for
anyone with eyes to see, the truth of the matter was obvious. The *princeps*
admitted it himself, stating baldly: "After this time, I exceeded everybody
in authority."

This was acceptable because Augustus held no unconstitutional or
novel office. Broadly speaking, he was acting within precedent. Also, he
gave back to the political class its glittering prizes. Once more it became
worthwhile to compete for political office (even though the *princeps* tended
to select the candidates). The ambitious and the able could win glory on
the floor of the Senate or in the outposts of empire.

It would be wrong to suppose that Romans failed to understand what
was going on. They were not deceived. They could see that Augustus'
power ultimately rested on force. However, his constitutional settlement
gave him legitimacy and signaled a return to the rule of law. For this,
most people were sincerely grateful.

Augustus' "restored Republic" was a towering achievement, for it transformed a bankrupt and incompetent polity into a system of government

that delivered the rule of law, wide participation by the ruling class, and, at the same time, strong central control. It installed an autocracy with the consent of Rome's—and indeed of Italy's—independent-minded elites. Some Roman historians, among them Tacitus a century or so later, mourned the death of liberty, but at the time politicians, citizens, and subjects of the empire recognized that the new constitutional arrangements would bring stability and the promise of fair and effective public administration.

If Julius Caesar had lived he would probably have devised a far more radical scheme, imposing a brutally abrupt transition from a republican past to an imperial future. Augustus may have been less brilliant than his adoptive father, but he was wiser. He understood that if his new system was to last, it should be seen to grow out of what came before. Rather than insist on a chasm, he built a bridge.

# XVII

# WHOM THE GODS LOVE

## 27–23 B.C.

AUGUSTUS' POLITICAL SETTLEMENT WAS A GREAT COUP, and attracted wide support. The *princeps* took care not to overplay his hand. He tactfully absented himself from Rome for nearly three years to allow the new constitutional arrangements time to settle in. He continued to be elected consul, but left day-to-day administration to his annual colleagues, among them the indispensable Agrippa.

In the meantime, the huge *provincia* called for his attention. Augustus' first stop was Gaul, where rumor had it that he intended to complete the task Julius Caesar had left unfinished in 54 B.C.—an invasion of the remote island of Britannia, perched on the edge of the known world. But Augustus was too busy to waste his time on such a diversion.

During the civil wars, Gaul had fallen into turmoil; Augustus' presence reasserted Roman authority. After establishing order and conducting a census, he moved on to Spain, where a thornier problem awaited. The native tribes in the northern of the two Spanish provinces, especially the Astures (whence the modern Asturias) and the Cantabri (in the area of today's Santander and Bilbao), had never been fully subdued. Augustus led a campaign against them, but this time he was without Agrippa to help him. The tribes used guerrilla tactics, hiding in their mountain fastnesses and cleverly avoiding the full-scale battle for which the legion was designed and for which they themselves were poorly adapted. Whenever the Romans marched in a given direction, they found themselves facing enemy fighters on high ground in front of them. In valleys and woods they stumbled into ambushes.

The *princeps* was superstitious, and devoutly believed in premonitory signs. He always carried a piece of sealskin as an amulet against thunder and lightning, which he feared. During the Spanish campaign, the amulet worked its magic for him. On a night march during a thunderstorm, a flash of lightning scorched his litter and killed a slave who was walking ahead with a torch. In thanks for this narrow escape, he built the Temple of Jupiter Tonans (the Thunderer) on the edge of the Capitol overlooking the Forum. It was known for its magnificence and contained famous works of art. Augustus often visited it.

As so often when he faced a crisis (particularly a military one), Augustus fell ill—according to Dio, "from the fatigue and anxiety caused by these conditions." He took the waters in the Pyrenees and convalesced in Tarraco (today's Tarragona). His deputy swiftly brought the fighting to a successful conclusion, which was attributed (of course) to the genius of the *princeps*. The illness seems to have lasted at least for a year, although our sources tell us nothing of its nature. To pass the time Augustus wrote an autobiography, which he dedicated to Agrippa and Maecenas. Sadly, the book has not survived.

During the late Republic, the wives of senior Roman officials did not often travel abroad with their husbands. Augustus himself ruled that the legates he appointed to the provinces at his disposal should not spend time with their wives or, if they insisted on doing so, then only outside the campaigning season (generally March to October).

However, we have it on good authority that Livia accompanied her husband on his travels to west and east. She was probably with him in Gaul and Spain, although she will have stayed safely in the rear when Augustus was with the army, and tended him when he was ill.

Livia was an able businesswoman and over the years accumulated numerous properties and estates across the empire. Her tours around the Mediterranean as Rome's first lady allowed her to inspect her acquisitions and check that they were being well managed. In Gaul she owned land with a copper mine. Her property portfolio also included palm groves in Judea and estates in Egypt, including papyrus marshes, arable farms, vineyards, commercial vegetable gardens, granaries, and olive and wine presses.

It may have been Augustus' poor health that prompted him in 25 B.C. to take the first concrete step to arranging a dynastic succession: he married off his daughter and only child, Julia (by his second wife, Scribonia), who was now fourteen, to his nephew, the twenty-year-old Marcellus. Augustus being absent in Spain, Agrippa presided over the wedding; what he thought of the young man's promotion is unknown, for he kept his own counsel.

The Senate voted Marcellus special honors; he was given the senior ranking of a praetor for official occasions. So far as the honors race was concerned, he received permission to stand for the consulship ten years before the legal minimum age of thirty-seven, and was counted as a former quaestor, the most junior elective post. This meant that he would be able to serve as an aedile in 23 B.C. The post would give him a chance to make his mark with the average citizen in Rome, for he would be in charge of the city's public entertainments for the year. Spectacle at its most extravagant was what the public demanded, and they would show their appreciation at the ballot box. His uncle made sure that Marcellus had an unprecedented budget.

Rome had not seen its *princeps* for three years. At last, in the middle of 24 B.C., he struggled home, still weak and uncertain of his survival. If he hoped that his political settlement had been fully accepted and was working smoothly, he was to be disabused. In late 24 or early 23 B.C., Marcus Primus, the governor of Macedonia, one of the Senate's provinces, was taken to court for having gone to war without permission with a friendly Thracian tribe. It was a serious offense for a proconsul to take an army outside his province.

Among Primus' defenders was one of the consuls for 23 B.C., Aulus Terentius Varro Murena, a trusted and senior follower of the *princeps*. He was Maecenas' brother-in-law, and the poets Virgil and Horace were his friends (he had lent the party of poets his house at the resort of Formiae on their journey from Rome to Brundisium in 39 B.C.). He seems to have been a dashing, impatient sort of fellow, and Horace took it upon himself to offer an ode of advice.

> *The loftiest pines, when the wind blows,*
> *Are shaken hardest; tall towers drop*
> *With the worst crash. . . .*

Primus' defense was that he had been ordered to launch a campaign by both the *princeps* and Marcellus. This was most embarrassing, for in theory Augustus only held authority in his own *provincia*. Of his own accord he attended the court where the trial was being held. The praetor, or presiding judge, asked him if he had given the man orders to make war and he replied that he had not.

Murena made some disrespectful remarks about the *princeps,* and asked him to his face: "What are you doing here, and who asked you to come?"

"The public interest," Augustus drily replied.

It is no surprise that Primus was found guilty; he was very probably sent into exile. However, many observers at the time must have thought it unlikely that Primus would have claimed to have acted under orders unless he had actually done so. The affair revealed the *res publica restituta,* the "restored Republic," as something of a sham.

The Primus affair led to the formation of a little-understood conspiracy against Augustus. The leader was a young republican called Fannius Caepio. Apparently, the consul Murena was implicated, although Dio thought the charge might be false, "since he was notoriously rough-tongued and headstrong in his manner of address towards all alike." The plot was uncovered and the accused men condemned to death in absentia. In constitutional theory, the execution of a serving consul was a contradiction in terms, for the Republic's chief executive had supreme authority; if he broke the law, charges could only be brought against him after his term of office had expired. Once again, the libertarian pretensions of the regime were exposed.

What the aims of the plotters were and how they were revealed cannot now be recovered. Perhaps there was no conspiracy at all—or, rather, the *princeps* organized a setup. But why? We cannot tell. If it was a serious attempt to overthrow the new order, it was evidence the settlement of 27 B.C. was not working.

The story has a sad footnote. Maecenas confided the discovery of the Caepio conspiracy, a state secret, to his wife, Terentia. Murena was her brother, and she seems to have warned him that he was in trouble. Augustus found out what had happened, and from that moment his friendship with Maecenas cooled. They remained on reasonably good terms, but the Etruscan aesthete was no longer a full member of the inner circle.

The year 23 B.C. had not gotten off to a good start, but Marcellus in his role as aedile made a brilliant success of the games. Throughout the summer, a canopy sheltered the Forum, where a temporary wooden arena was erected for the gladiatorial displays. Novel, slightly scandalous acts included a woman of noble birth taking part in a stage performance and an *eques* dancing in a ballet.

However, the mood in Rome was darkened by the onset of a plague.

Epidemics were terrifying and not infrequent occurrences in a large crowded city such as Rome. What disease struck on this occasion is unknown; it may have been smallpox, bubonic plague, or typhoid fever. Scarlet fever and influenza have also been recorded by Greek and Roman medical writers.

Augustus fell ill again. Suetonius has it that he was suffering abscesses on the liver. According to Celsus, whose *On Medicine* was published in the first century A.D., the symptoms of liver disease were

> *severe pain in the right part under the praecordia [the region of the body about the heart], which spreads to the right side, to the clavicle and arm of that side; at times there is also pain in the right hand, there is hot shivering . . . [in bad cases] after a meal there is greater difficulty in breathing; then supervenes a sort of paralysis of the lower jaws.*

Recommended treatment included the application of hot water in winter and tepid water in the summer, but "all cold things must be especially avoided, for nothing is more harmful to the liver."

Augustus was in despair, for there seemed to be no hope of recovery; it appeared that the new regime was about to end. This would be a tragedy not just for him but for many others in public life. He had to take what steps he could to ensure a permanent legacy.

He gathered around his bedside the officers of state and leading senators and *equites*. He spoke to them on matters of public policy and handed his fellow consul, Gnaeus Calpurnius Piso, the *breviarium imperii*, a book that recorded the empire's financial and military resources.

Many were expecting the *princeps* to bequeath his authority to Marcellus, whom he had only too evidently been grooming. But this had been a long-term plan, and the boy was too young and inexperienced to hold supreme power now. Agrippa would have had little trouble deposing him once Augustus was dead. Bowing to this reality, the dying man handed Agrippa the symbol of his authority: his signet ring bearing the head of Alexander the Great.

Much to everyone's surprise, including his own, the *princeps* recovered. His doctor, Antonius Musa, turning medical orthodoxy on its head, decided to abandon the hot fomentations he had been using to no avail in favor of cold baths and cold potions. The shock treatment worked. (It has been suggested that Augustus was, in fact, suffering from typhoid fever, which could well have been the cause of the epidemic devastating Rome at the time; cold packs were a well-known treatment for the disease in the nineteenth and early twentieth centuries.)

The convalescent *princeps* showed that he was aware of the general unpopularity of his dynastic plans by bringing his will to a meeting of the Senate. He intended to read it out, as proof that he had no successor in mind, but in the event, to show their confidence in him, the senators would not permit it.

The settlement of 27 B.C. needed revision and it was time to make a fresh start. Augustus resigned as consul on July 1 and let it be known that he would no longer be a regular candidate. For him to continue holding the consulship year after year was stretching constitutional propriety very thin, for it made the post look like a permanent one, not so far from Julius Caesar's unpopular dictatorship for life. Too, the office entailed a good deal of routine business and time-consuming ceremonial, and as long as Augustus held it he was blocking off access to one of Rome's two top jobs every year, so irritating political aspirants.

But if he was to give up the consulship, the *princeps* would need some other source of *imperium*. With typical ingenuity, he came up with two devices. For some years he had been awarded *tribunicia sacrosanctitas,* or the immunity from physical attack given to a tribune of the people. Now he decided to assume *tribunicia potestas* in perpetuity: he would enjoy the power of a tribune without actually having to hold the post. That power was considerable. Tribunes attended Senate meetings and were entitled to present laws for approval by the people. They could also veto *any* officeholder's decisions, including those of other tribunes.

Augustus recognized that *tribunicia potestas,* together with his enormous *provincia,* gave him almost all the authority he needed to govern without hindrance. He dated his "reign" from when it was awarded, on July 1, 23 B.C., and added the *potestas* to his long list of titles. However, a couple of gaps needed to be filled. Proconsuls, or provincial governors, lost their *imperium* when they crossed the *pomerium*—the sacred boundary of Rome— and entered the city. That would mean that when he was in the city the *princeps* would only have the status of a private citizen. Thanks to his prestige, or *auctoritas,* his wishes would usually be obeyed, but on occasion there might be some awkwardness. So the Senate voted that Augustus' proconsular *imperium* should not lapse when he was inside the city walls.

The Marcus Primus affair had thrown an embarrassing light on Augustus' relations with the governors of senatorial provinces, in whose business he had no right to meddle—in theory. To correct this problem, he was granted a general and overriding proconsular authority (*imperium maius,* "greater power"), the right to intervene anywhere in the empire as and when he chose. It was a right he exercised very discreetly and with the utmost caution, for by tradition a Roman governor had a free hand during his term of office.

The reforms considerably strengthened Augustus' position, but the real winner from the crisis of 23 B.C. was Agrippa. He had been shown to be indispensable; now he, too, received *imperium proconsulare* (but not *imperium maius*). This probably gave him some kind of general authority in the eastern provinces, where Augustus dispatched him in the autumn. In effect, Agrippa was now the empire's co-regent.

Too much information has been lost for us to be sure, but it looks very much as if the *princeps* had had his wings clipped. Perhaps the governing faction—that is, all those men whose fortunes, livelihoods, even lives depended on the regime's continuance—made its leader acknowledge that the state was not his personal property and that an insurance policy (to wit, Agrippa) needed to be taken out against some future mortal illness.

It has even been speculated in modern times that what had taken place was a "secret *coup d'état*" in which Agrippa and Livia joined forces. There is hardly anything to back this up—except that Tiberius, Livia's eldest son, was betrothed, perhaps already married, to Agrippa's daughter, Vipsania. This could be interpreted as a sign that the two most important people in Augustus' life felt the need to jointly protect themselves against the dynastically domineering *princeps*. It also appears that Octavia and Livia did not get on, and that the latter was irritated by the former's promotion of Marcellus. Equally, though, Augustus and his canny wife could have seen the value of neutralizing the prickly Agrippa by making him a member of the family.

At the time, many observers interpreted Agrippa's departure as exile. According to Suetonius, he "had felt that Augustus was not behaving as warmly towards him as usual, and that Marcellus was being preferred to him; he resigned all his offices and went off to Mytilene." Some held that Agrippa did not want to oppose or seem to belittle the young man. In another view, on his recovery Augustus found out that Marcellus was not well disposed toward Agrippa because of the delivery to Agrippa of the seal, and so ordered Agrippa to the east. A writer in the following century wrote of the "scandalous sending away of Agrippa."

It is not necessary to see these two accounts—co-regency and "exile"— as mutually exclusive. Augustus and Agrippa were grown-up politicians. Both of them (and perhaps especially the latter) held a somber commitment to the public interest, not to mention the advantage of their governing party (which they saw as much the same thing). It is possible that they agreed not only about Agrippa's promotion, but also on the desirability of a tactful withdrawal to allow Marcellus to emerge onto the public stage without Agrippa's overshadowing presence.

When looking to the future, Agrippa and the sickly Augustus had to accommodate a number of possible outcomes. If the *princeps* were to die soon, Agrippa would presumably take over. His humble birth and rough tongue made him unpopular with the old nobility, and he did not have the huge advantage of being a member of the Caesarian, almost-royal family; but he was omnicompetent, and would do.

If both men lived for another fifteen or twenty years, a perfectly reasonable supposition, Marcellus would be an appropriate dynastic successor, assuming that meanwhile he showed sufficient ability at the business of government. To make assurance doubly sure, Livia's promising sons, Tiberius and the fifteen-year-old Drusus, would also be trained in public administration.

Whatever was or was not going on behind the scenes, the professional partnership between Augustus and Agrippa went on from strength to strength. When the two men's powers were renewed in 18 B.C., Agrippa was granted the same *tribunicia potestas* that the *princeps* held. His energy and effectiveness were undimmed.

Then the worst possible thing that Augustus could imagine took place. In the autumn of 23 B.C., before his games were over, Marcellus fell ill and died. He was only twenty-one years old. He was given the same medical treatment by Musa as his uncle, but this time it did not work. The *princeps* delivered a eulogy at his funeral and placed his body in the great circular family mausoleum he was in the process of building (Marcellus' gravestone and the later one of his mother survive). A new theater on the far side of the Capitoline Hill from the Forum, the foundations of which had been laid by Julius Caesar, was named the Theater of Marcellus in his honor. (Part of its exterior wall can still be seen.)

Octavia never recovered. She refused to have a portrait of her son or to permit anyone to mention his name in her presence. She came to hate all mothers and, more especially, Livia, whose Tiberius would now inherit the happiness *she* had been promised. She spent more and more of her time in darkness and paid little attention to her brother. Becoming something of a recluse, she stayed in mourning for the rest of her life.

She did attend a special reading by the poet Virgil of extracts from his new epic about the foundation of Rome, the *Aeneid*. Its hero is the Trojan prince, Aeneas; the poem tells the story of his escape from the sack of Troy and his arrival at Latium, where he rules over a kingdom that is the precursor of Rome. At one point in the narrative, Aeneas visits the underworld, where he meets not only the great dead but also the shades of the unborn. He notices a good-looking but downcast youth, and asks who he is.

The phantom of Aeneas' dead father tells him that it is the future Marcellus:

> *Fate shall allow the earth one glimpse of this young man—*
> *One glimpse, no more. . . .*
> *Alas, poor youth! If only you could escape your harsh fate!*
> *Marcellus you shall be. Give me armfuls of lilies*
> *That I may scatter their shining blooms and shower these gifts*
> *At least upon the dear soul, all to no purpose though*
> *Such kindness be.*

Virgil's style of recitation was "sweet and strangely seductive." When he reached the line "*Tu Marcellus eris,*" "Marcellus you shall be," Octavia is said to have fainted, and was revived only with some difficulty.

Almost certainly the young man was one of the many Romans who succumbed to the epidemic sweeping through the city, but soon rumors were put about of foul play. It was whispered that Livia had poisoned him because he had been preferred to her sons for the succession. If true this would have been an ill-judged move, for in the following year Augustus arranged for his daughter, Julia, Marcellus' widow, to marry Agrippa, a formidable alliance likely to produce dynastic progeny.

The main victim of this arrangement was Octavia's daughter, Marcella, who was divorced from her husband, Agrippa, to make room for her first cousin. In the regime's innermost circles, no room was left for sentiment, and the Julian family's women were disposed of according to the political imperative of the hour. Apparently the *princeps* took the decision on the advice of Maecenas, who told him, "You have made him [Agrippa] so powerful that he must either become your son-in-law, or be killed."

Livia's reputation for murderous scheming, once acquired, proved impossible to expunge. This was partly because in the ancient world (as in the magical world of the fairy tale) stepmothers were expected to behave badly. The great Greek tragedian Aeschylus described a reef in the sea as a "stepmother to ships." Women, living as they did in a male-dominated society, must have felt that they could only protect their futures by advancing their sons' interests. Enough of them lived up to the stereotype, persecuting the children of their husband's first marriage, that fathers sometimes had their children adopted and brought up in another family.

Although Augustus never formally adopted Marcellus, he had treated him as an honorary son, so Livia found herself cast as a stepmother, with all the ugly connotations that that status entailed. There is no evidence that she acted in any way improperly, although it is legitimate to assume that she would do her best for her own boys. Augustus and Octavia were kind to children to whom they were not related by blood—notably, Antony's offspring by Fulvia and Cleopatra; it is hard to imagine them failing to notice and correct any cruelty on Livia's part.

The accusations against Livia need to be set in the context of the Romans' exaggerated fear of death by poisoning. It was, for example, widely and probably inaccurately rumored that poison had been sprinkled on Pansa's wound after the fighting at Mutina in 43 B.C., and that this had either been arranged by the then Octavian, or at least been done in his interest. Cicero's speeches as a criminal lawyer reveal a high incidence of reported poisoning cases.

Surprising deaths were likely to have been from undiagnosed natural causes. Poison scares often coincided with plagues, and there are well-attested cases of food poisoning, especially from contaminated fish. The practice of boiling down wine in lead pans to create a cooking sauce will have led to many illnesses and premature deaths. Some years later a close friend of Augustus, Nonius Asprenas, gave a party after which 130 guests fell ill and died, presumably from food poisoning. Asprenas was taken to court for murder, but (after a show of support by the *princeps*) was acquitted.

There was little that Livia could do in the face of this anonymous gossip. A woman had no locus as a public figure and was obliged to suffer slander in silence.

## XVIII

# EXERCISING POWER

### 23–17 B.C.

ANYONE WHO RULED A LARGE EMPIRE IN THE ANCIENT WORLD
faced an almost insurmountable challenge: how was he to make a difference? Augustus might reign in Rome, but who would notice the fact in
northern Gaul or Syria?

Travel was slow and often dangerous; weeks might pass before the *princeps* learned of a serious development on the Parthian frontier, months
before any substantial reaction could be implemented. The pace of communications also slowed the analysis of complex problems. Important
branches of knowledge—geography, for example, and economics—were
in their infancy, so there were insufficient reliable and accessible data on
which to base policy decisions. From a modern perspective, events took
place in slow motion and in a fog.

Augustus and Agrippa took the business of empire seriously, realizing
that it would be difficult to achieve anything without being on the spot
themselves. Both men spent years away from Rome, traveling from province to province. Sometimes they exchanged places, one of them picking
up where the other left off.

For some years after the settlement after Actium, the eastern provinces
were largely left to their own devices. In 26 B.C., there was an unsuccessful
Roman expedition to Arabia Felix (the southwest corner of the Arabian
peninsula, today's Yemen), probably aimed at opening up a trade route; in
the following year, Galatia (in central Anatolia) was annexed as a province.

When the *princeps* sent Agrippa to the east in 23 B.C., we do not know exactly what his mission was. He made the island of Samos his headquarters
and it can be assumed that his presence was intended to be a reminder of
Roman power. It is possible that he also had an important unpublicized
task—to gain intelligence on the Parthians. It would be useful to settle the

unfinished business of the Roman defeat at Carrhae in 53 B.C., and, in particular, to negotiate the return of the army standards that the Parthians had captured (as well as those lost in 36 B.C. by Antony). The *princeps* was not interested in resuming hostilities and hoped for a long-term entente.

He intended either to join Agrippa or to take over from him, but was detained by trouble in Rome. The river Tiber overflowed its banks and flooded the city. The plague of the previous year continued throughout Italy and farmers stopped tilling the fields. Food shortages followed. The panic-stricken and angry mob did not trust old-style republican politicians to govern effectively and called for Augustus to be appointed dictator. It besieged the Senate House and threatened to burn it down with the senators inside it if they did not vote for the appointment.

The episode showed how fragile the *princeps'* underlying position was. The careful balance between autocracy and a restoration of the Senate's authority had been designed to reconcile the ruling class to the Augustan order. However, it irritated the people—that is, the hundreds of thousands of citizens who lived in or near Rome. They wanted to see Augustus seize absolute power openly and unambiguously.

Not only would it have been unwise to listen to such calls, it would have been illegal, for Mark Antony had abolished the dictatorship in 44, shortly after the Ides of March. Any attempt to restore the post would infuriate mainstream senatorial opinion. Augustus made it clear that he would do no such thing.

When facing disgrace a Roman would tear his clothes in public, and this was what the *princeps* did to dramatize his refusal to be moved. He went up to the crowd, bared his throat, and swore that he would rather be stabbed to death by its daggers than accept the appointment. Instead, he had himself made commissioner for the grain supply, rapidly put an end to the food shortages, and arranged for the annual appointment of two former praetors to supervise the distribution of grain in the future. Although, so far as we know, Augustus did not reform the system of production and distribution, he did his best to ensure that shortfalls were quickly made good and he used his own financial resources to alleviate famine.

At long last in the autumn of 22, Augustus, probably taking Livia with him, set out on a leisurely journey eastward. His first stop was Sicily. News came from Rome of more unrest among the people, who had elected only a single consul in the hope that Augustus would occupy the vacancy. This he refused to do, but recalled Agrippa to return from the east and restore order at Rome. It was now, in 21 B.C., that, in a further sign of his growing authority, Agrippa married the eighteen-year-old Julia despite her father's absence.

Agrippa then moved on to his next assignment in Gaul and Spain. He campaigned in Aquitania and elsewhere; he also encouraged the building of Roman-style cities and networks of roads. He then went to northern Spain, where he resumed Augustus' not entirely successful war of pacification. In 19 B.C., he finally subdued the unruly tribes whom the unmilitary *princeps* had found it so hard to defeat a few years before.

In the meantime, Augustus devoted time and attention to adjusting the boundaries and rulers of the smaller client kingdoms along the empire's eastern frontier; but his real aim was to do a deal with King Frahâta of Parthia. His tactic was to run a diplomatic campaign alongside the threat of a military one. A pretender to the Parthian throne had kidnapped one of Frahâta's sons and escaped with him to Rome. Augustus had sent the boy back to his father on condition that all the Roman standards and any surviving prisoners-of-war were returned. He now invited Frahâta to live up to his side of the bargain.

At the same time, a military expedition was organized against the strategically placed kingdom of Armenia. The aim was to depose its anti-Roman king, Ardashes, and replace him with a quisling. If Armenia was to fall within Rome's sphere of influence, the Parthians would be outflanked with a hostile northern frontier.

The general whom Augustus chose to lead his legions against the Armenians in 20 B.C. was his stepson Tiberius, who was now twenty-two years old and eligible for the jobs that would surely have gone to a living Marcellus.

He was strongly and heavily built and above average height; his shoulders and chest were broad and his body was well proportioned. He had a handsome, fresh-complexioned face, although his skin tended to break out in pimples. He had a large crown, tight lips like his mother's, and piercing eyes. He let his hair grow long at the back, a habit of the Claudian clan.

Tiberius was not at all religious, but he did believe in astrology and therefore saw the world as governed by fate. Like Augustus, he was terrified of thunder, and when the skies loured he would put a laurel wreath on his head, to lightning-proof himself. He was devoted to Greek and Latin literature. He especially loved ancient myths and legends. He enjoyed the company of professors of Greek literature, whom he delighted in asking abstruse and unanswerable questions: such as "Who was Hecuba Queen of Troy's mother?," "What song did the Sirens sing?" "By what name was Achilles called when he was disguised as a girl?" His speaking style was encumbered by so many affectations and pedantries that his extempore speeches were considered far better than those he prepared.

Augustus arranged for Tiberius to enter public life in his late teens; the young man undertook high-profile prosecutions and special commissions, among the latter, the crucial task of reorganizing Rome's grain supply. He acquitted himself well. The *princeps* was pleased, for he was keen for Tiberius and his brother, the eighteen-year-old Drusus, to share the burden of government. They were to be the packhorses of the regime, for the *princeps* had not given up his dynastic ambitions. In 20 B.C., Agrippa's union with Julia produced a boy, Gaius. If he survived the multiple potentially lethal ailments of infancy, he could become the heir to empire, and on this occasion Augustus' old school friend would be hardly likely to object.

But that was for the future. In the meantime, Tiberius led an army into Armenia. As it turned out, there was no fighting to be done, for the Armenians rose against their king and killed him before the Romans arrived. Tiberius crowned his successor, a pro-Roman exile, with his own hands.

Confronted with the Armenian takeover, Frahâta made the judgment call for which the Romans had been hoping. Although Augustus had no intention whatever of attacking Parthia, he was now in a strong tactical position if he wished to do so. The king handed over the standards and the prisoners.

Although the Roman public would have preferred a thoroughgoing military victory, this was a great diplomatic achievement, of which Augustus was extremely proud. Relations between the two empires moved from glacial to cautiously warm, where they remained for some time. In the official account of his life, the *princeps* allowed himself some exaggeration: "I compelled the Parthians to restore the spoils and the standards of three Roman legions to me and to ask as suppliants the friendship of the Roman People."

• • •

Disturbing news arrived from Rome. In the absence of both the *princeps* and Agrippa, the public mood had grown feverish. The people left one of the consulships for 19 B.C. unfilled and agitated for Augustus, once again, to assume the vacant post.

A certain Egnatius Rufus, who, according to an unfriendly critic, was "better qualified to be a gladiator than a Senator," volunteered to fill the gap himself. In 21, when he was serving as aedile, he had made himself very popular by creating Rome's first fire service (paying out of his own pocket for a troop of some six hundred slaves) and had been elected praetor in the following year. Strictly speaking this was illegal, for the rules called for an interval of some years between successive elective posts in the honors race.

Egnatius' candidature for the consulship was blocked, but this was not the end of the story, for he was soon arrested, tried, condemned, and executed for plotting to assassinate Augustus. Whether there was any truth in this is unknown, but it would not be surprising if the authorities decided to eliminate a great nuisance by inventing a capital charge. Augustus put an end to further agitation and speculation by nominating a second consul for the year.

The *princeps* had devoted much of the previous decade to the provinces. On his return to Rome in 19 B.C., he turned his mind to domestic affairs. In the first place, the constitutional settlement needed some further adjustment. He had to find some means of calming public opinion, which remained hostile to the Senate. Also, there were a couple of aspects of a consul's *imperium* that neither Augustus' *tribunicia potestas* nor his *imperium proconsulare* covered.

First, he held no *imperium* specific to Italy, and consequently had no authority to command troops on Italian soil. This was awkward, because after Julius Caesar's death both Antony and the then Octavian formed large bodyguards, the *cohortes praetoriae* that we know as Praetorian Guards. After Actium, Octavian retained his cohorts to act as a peacetime security force and stationed them in and around Rome. There were nine cohorts in all, amounting to a maximum of 5,400 men. It was time that the control of these soldiers was placed on a proper footing.

Second, Augustus did not have first place—at least, not officially—in the conduct of senatorial business. A consul had the right to be the first to propose legislation or to speak on a given topic, so the *princeps* was obliged to wait his turn. This was inconvenient, and might also be embarrassing, if senators did not receive a cue about Augustus' wishes at the beginning of a debate.

So in 19 B.C. some form of consular *imperium* was conferred on the *princeps* although he did not actually have to hold consular office (following the same principle as with *tribunicia potestas*). The ancient sources disagree on, and are unclear about, the precise nature of this authority or the term for which it was awarded. It may be that Augustus' proconsular *imperium*, granted for ten-year periods and renewed, was simply extended to include Rome and Italy. A certain vagueness at the time may have suited all sides. Whatever form it was couched in, though, this new power completed Augustus' political mastery of the state.

It is possible to guess at the shape of an unstated concordat from what actually happened in the coming years. A generation of *nobiles* had been drastically thinned out during the civil wars by death in battle or by proscription, but now their children had grown up; if, as they were told, the Republic had been restored, they expected to have the same access to the consulship (and other senior posts) that their fathers had had. It was, they knew, their birthright. For the next five years or so, the consular lists are crowded with old republican names—Cornelius Lentulus, Licinius Crassus, Calpurnius Piso, Livius Drusus.

During the triumvirate, a new custom had come into being whereby consuls served only for part of the year and were regularly replaced by one or more "suffect" consuls. Although this was a useful and cheap means of rewarding loyalty and producing proconsuls to help govern the empire, it also devalued both the splendor of the office and its executive effectiveness. Augustus more or less eliminated suffects; most consuls now served for an entire term, so regaining much of their prestige.

For a time, we do not hear of popular agitation and riots in the streets. This may be explained by the gaps in our inadequate surviving sources, but it does appear that the role of the people in political life declined from this point on. They still elected officeholders, but candidates were nominated or preapproved by the *princeps,* presumably after informal consultations with the interested parties.

All of this suggests an arrangement out of which everyone got something. His added consular authority completed Augustus' hold on power and convinced a suspicious Roman public that he was genuinely in charge of the state. By contrast the *nobiles* welcomed their return to the consulship, and were grateful to Augustus for his efforts to restore their ancient *dignitas*.

Augustus was a reformer who liked to move forward at a snail's pace. In many aspects of his administration, change and innovation proceeded step by step over many years.

Time and again, he did his best to improve the functioning of the Senate, which, together with the people, remained the legal source of authority in the state. Rather than appoint more censors, the *princeps* decided in 18 B.C. to use his new consular authority to act as a censor himself (as he and Agrippa had done in 28 B.C.) and review the membership of the Senate. He raised the minimum wealth of a senator from 400,000 to 1 million sesterces, a substantial sum of money. This set a significant distance between the senatorial and the equestrian orders, and helped to create a distinct senatorial class. Birth as well as property became a qualification. In the days of the Republic only senators could lay claim to senatorial status, but from now on sons of senators acquired the status as of right, while others were obliged to apply for it.

As the *princeps* had discovered ten years previously, cleansing the Senate of its reprobates was a tricky and unpopular exercise. His dream was to reduce it to three hundred members, which would make it a much more effective legislative body. He devised an ingenious scheme, which was intended to achieve his objective with the least possible blame attaching to him.

He selected thirty senators, each of whom was then to choose a further five. Each group of five would choose one of its number by lot, who would become a senator. This man would repeat the process, which was to continue until three hundred senators had been found. The scheme being too clever by half, various malpractices developed, the proceedings ground to a confused halt, and Augustus was obliged to take over the selection himself. He ended up by creating a Senate of six hundred members and seriously annoying a large number of people. In compensation, he gave various privileges to those who had been expelled. They were allowed to stand for election to the various offices of state; in due course most of them returned to the Senate.

The exercise had been an almost complete waste of time and energy. For all his *auctoritas,* his *dignitas,* and his *imperium,* the *princeps* knew that he touched the Senate, the heartland of the republican idea, at his peril. He also knew when to admit defeat. There was always time, and he could return to the subject in the future.

So the Senate remained a somewhat unsatisfactory institution. Augustus always treated it with great respect and took trouble to consult it. He encouraged freedom of expression and his speeches were often interrupted by remarks such as "I don't understand that!" or "I'd dispute that if I had the chance!" However, its members did not take their responsibilities as seriously as he would have wished. In 17 B.C., fines for nonattendance were increased and quorums were set for certain classes of business.

Sometime between 27 and 18 B.C., the *princeps* took a step aimed at expediting decision-making, which recognized the difficulty that any deliberative body has in agreeing on clear-cut actions. He set up a senatorial standing committee, which consisted of himself, one or both consuls, one each from the quaestors, aediles, and praetors, and fifteen other senators chosen by lot. Some members changed every six months and the whole committee once a year, except for the *princeps.* Its task was to prepare business for full sessions of the Senate.

A group of twenty-one is still rather too large to be efficiently executive, and the rapid turnover must have prevented it from building a collective esprit de corps or devising long-term policies. This was probably as the *princeps* intended, for he reserved strategic planning to himself and a small, informal group of advisers, the *amici Caesaris,* "Caesar's friends." The standing committee's job must mainly have been to receive and discuss already prepared positions, and to act as a sounding board of senatorial opinion. It probably worked by consensus and guided discussion in the full Senate.

The Senate's powers remained advisory in principle, and bills were still laid before popular assemblies for approval. However, its decrees or *senatusconsulta* were increasingly regarded as binding, especially when specifically supported or initiated by the *princeps.*

Both the Senate and the *princeps* acquired new legal powers. The old republican courts of law, the *iudicia publica,* remained in being, presided over by praetors. But cases of treason or otherwise high political importance could be brought to one of two new courts, the *princeps* in council or the consuls in the Senate, against which there was no appeal. The ever growing number of citizens made it impractical to remit all criminal prosecutions to Rome, so proconsuls were given the authority to carry out judicial functions.

Under the Republic, any citizen found guilty of an offense had the right to appeal to the people. However, Augustus was given the authority to overturn a sentence of death by the use of his *imperium*. So *provocatio ad populum* gave way to *appellatio ad Caesarem,* an appeal to Caesar.

Augustus sought to improve the honesty and efficiency of imperial administration. Without interfering excessively in local ways of doing things, he and Agrippa introduced orderly governance throughout the empire and, in the Gallic and Spanish provinces and Africa where they were missing, the benefits of urban living. Regular censuses were held to enable a fair assessment of the provincial tax burden, and tax collection was made fairer.

In Rome itself, the *princeps* borrowed Egnatius Rufus' idea of maintaining a troop of six hundred slave firefighters (in A.D. 6, this was expanded into seven cohorts of firemen, each cohort being responsible for two of the fourteen districts into which Augustus divided the city). Three *cohortes urbanae,* or urban cohorts, were established to police the city.

Augustus did not interfere in the local government of Italy. He left its four hundred or so towns and cities to manage their own affairs as they had always done, except in two respects. He divided the peninsula into eleven departments for the purpose of the census of citizens and of the registration of public land. And, more important, he recognized the need for speedy communications. He tried to persuade senators to invest some of the spoils of successful military campaigns in improving and extending the Italian road network. When that failed, he himself took over the *cura viarum,* the responsibility for roads, and made large donations from his own pocket for road construction.

Regular relay stations were established, where state couriers and government officials could change horses and chariots and spend the night at the station's hostel. Local authorities provided the chariots and horses, and officials using the service paid a fixed charge. As the system developed, an experienced military man was placed in charge of it as the *praefectus vehiculorum*. Eventually an infrastructure emerged that significantly improved communications with all parts of Italy and the provinces to the north.

In the days of the Republic, it had been expected of prominent men that they spend large sums on public works; outstanding examples were the imposing stone theater built by Pompey the Great and the new forum commissioned by Julius Caesar. As we have seen, Augustus and Agrippa followed in their footsteps and invested heavily in new public buildings and refurbishments in the city.

With the passage of time, various senatorial commissions were created—for example, the *curatores viarum,* who made sure that roads were kept in a good state of repair, and the *curatores locorum publicorum,* who were responsible for maintaining public buildings and temples. These groups were not themselves public construction agencies, but worked through local officials and contractors to effect repairs.

Augustus introduced greater order into the day-to-day management of the empire than had existed in the past. In the absence of a professional civil service, officeholders with *imperium* in the Republic, such as consuls and praetors, used to govern from their town houses in Rome and used slaves and servants, family and friends to expedite business. Augustus governed in the same way, but on a much larger scale. He employed a growing army of slaves and freedmen to undertake the routine tasks of administration.

However, it was not politically acceptable for such people to be the official face of the regime. The *princeps* thus established a governmental career structure for the upper classes. Young men of the senatorial order who showed promise could spend a lifetime as well-paid public administrators.

When they were in their late teens, after military service, they could seek minor posts as *vigintiviri* (literally, "twenty men"). They worked for a year in the mint, were in charge of the streets of Rome, managed prisons and executions, and judged legal cases involving questions of slavery or freedom. They then served either as tribunes of the people (except for patricians) or as aediles. They could stand for one of the twelve praetorships, after which they might command a legion or govern a minor province. The most successful could aspire to the consulship, followed by the governorship of a major province or one of the curatorships at Rome.

The Senate only produced senior administrators, and the *princeps* also looked for assistance in less important jobs from the *equites.* Whether they were senators or *equites,* able men became professional servants of the state, receiving a salary and living out long and interesting careers. The fact that Augustus twice enacted antibribery laws, in 18 B.C. and 8 B.C., not only illustrates his commitment to clean government, but also suggests that his efforts may have met some resistance. Inch by inch, though, prototypes of the institutions that we take for granted in a modern state were beginning to emerge. The amateurish and corrupt mechanisms of the Republic were gradually replaced by something resembling an honest state bureaucracy.

Rome's public treasury, the Aerarium, was based at the Temple of Saturn in the Roman Forum and was managed by two praetors. We have no exact information of the exchequer receipts from taxes, customs duties, and tribute payments from client rulers, but it is unlikely that large sums of money moved to and from Rome. Each province had its own treasury, from which the *princeps* would draw for local military and administrative purposes, and in many cases there would not have been a large surplus to send to Rome.

The main claim on the empire's resources was the army—namely, twenty-eight legions and an equivalent resource of auxiliary units. This was not a large force for so extensive an empire, but the financial burden was considerable. A soldier's basic pay was nine hundred sesterces a year, entailing an aggregate expenditure of 140 million sesterces. However, the real cost of maintaining the army was considerably higher, for the cavalry was better paid than ordinary infantrymen; and officers, from centurions to the legionary commanders, or legates, earned very large salaries. On top of this came expenditure on military equipment, the empire's fleets, and the elite Praetorians in Italy.

Augustus was enormously rich. His wealth came from his inheritance from Julius Caesar, from legacies (it was the done thing to remember the *princeps* with a generous bequest), the profits of the proscriptions and the civil war, and large estates in various parts of the empire. In his official memoir, he notes with satisfaction that he spent 600 million sesterces on land bought in Italy for his veterans and 260 million sesterces elsewhere. In lieu of farms, some demobilized soldiers received money grants, totaling 400 million sesterces.

In addition to these phenomenally large sums of money, the *princeps* often topped up the Aerarium from his own pocket when it ran low of funds. In practice, it was difficult to distinguish between the treasury and the privy purse.

In summary, Augustus' reforms of the way governmental power was exercised were not particularly controversial, nor were they widely understood to be revolutionary, when seen individually, but taken together they expressed four slow and irresistible trends. First, the *princeps* was accumulating more and more power to himself, whether by streamlining the legislative and decision-making process, speeding up governmental communications across the empire, or enhancing his judicial role.

Although it was increasingly clear who was in charge, the senatorial ruling class acquiesced in the autocracy because of the second trend of Augustus' reign: the enhancement of the Senate's workload and prestige. When Augustus developed a career structure for the imperial administration, he was not simply improving the quality of governance, but creating high-status, well-paid jobs.

Senators will also have been pleased to witness the declining importance of the people—the third trend, and one the citizens of Rome were themselves willing to countenance as they experienced the benefits of life under the principate. They had no wish at all to return to the inefficiencies of the Republic.

Fourth, Augustus introduced the beginnings of a public bureaucracy, with the increasing use of nonpolitician freedmen and slaves who handled day-to-day business.

Romans distinguished between *imperium,* power, and *auctoritas,* authority. It was evidence of the remarkable success of the Augustan system that the *princeps* was able to command obedience simply through his authority, and was very seldom obliged to draw on the brute power at his disposal.

# XIX

# THE CULT OF VIRTUE

## 20S B.C.—A.D. 9

ONE OF THE MOST REMARKABLE FEATURES OF THE AUGUS-tan regime was that speech remained free. No secret police knocked on the doors of dissident writers at four in the morning.

The *princeps* understood that independence of spirit was central to a Roman's idea of himself. His claim to have restored the Republic would not have been acquiesced to, nor his rule accepted, if he had attempted to muzzle opinion. In fact, he would have found it hard to do so, for he did not have a secret police at his disposal.

What was more, there was no need to restrict citizens' rights to self-expression, for there was little outright opposition. The whole point of his constitutional settlement was that it attracted a broad consent among the ruling class. What critics there were could be allowed their say without risking revolution.

This is not to say that rising men did not practice self-censorship, or that poets and historians failed to flatter. As we have seen, the *princeps* and his unofficial "minister of culture," Maecenas, well understood the power of literature to promote official values.

But there was another, more subtle and more compelling reason for the license Augustus allowed commentators—historians and poets. This concerned his core beliefs. Like many of his fellow Romans, he deeply disapproved of the decadent society around him, which had abandoned the severe Roman virtues of the past. He wanted writers like Titus Livius (in English, Livy) to speak their minds on this subject without fear or favor.

About the same age as the *princeps,* Livy was born in Patavium (today's Padua) in Cisalpine Gaul. He made no effort to follow a public career, instead devoting his long life to the writing of a monumental history of Rome, from the foundation to 9 B.C. He was one of Rome's first professional historians, for until then history had usually been a pastime for retired politicians.

Livy's worldview was moral and romantic, and most thinking people of his age shared it. In the preface to his magnum opus, he stated that writing history was a way of escaping the troubles of the modern world: "Of late years wealth has made us greedy, and self-indulgence has brought us, through every kind of sensual excess, to be, if I may so put it, in love with death both individual and collective."

The trouble was seen to have begun in the second century B.C., when, somewhat absentmindedly, the Senate acquired its empire in the east— first Greece and Macedonia, then Asia Minor and Syria. Leading Romans began to copy the extravagant lifestyle of Asiatic Greeks. The culminating metaphor for Roman decadence was the career of Mark Antony and his sexual subversion by Cleopatra.

This perceived moral decline was accompanied by political collapse at the hands of a succession of selfish dynasts. The greatest of them, Julius Caesar, broke the Republic, which for centuries had embodied in constitutional form the traditional Roman virtues, now lost. Although himself a dynast, Pompey the Great, who opposed Caesar in the civil war, gave his life for the republican cause, and came to be a symbol of it.

According to Tacitus, Livy "praised Pompey so warmly that Augustus [whom he knew personally] called him 'the Pompeian.'" The historian never called Brutus and Cassius bandits and parricides, their "fashionable designations today."

Livy was not alone in his overt republican sympathies. In the *Aeneid,* Augustus' poet laureate dared to rehabilitate that most die-hard of republicans, the pigheaded purist Marcus Porcius Cato, who led the optimates against Julius Caesar and died by his own hand after his defeat in Africa.

The victor of Actium was not the only great Roman to be depicted on the shield of Aeneas. In a vision of the underworld various historical figures are shown waiting for their lives to begin. Virgil points to where "the righteous are set apart, with Cato as their lawgiver." Elsewhere, the poet delivers Julius Caesar a veiled rebuke: "Turn not your country's hand against your country's heart!"

The *princeps* did not demur from this kind of talk. He transferred the statue of Pompey the Great from the hall where Caesar had been assassinated to a much more prominent position on an arch facing the grand door of Pompey's Theater. He remarked of Cato that "to seek to keep the constitution unchanged argues a good citizen and a good man."

Augustus knew and liked Virgil. Indeed, in 19 B.C., when returning to Rome after his Parthian success, the *princeps* met him in Greece shortly before the poet died at the age of fifty-two. Virgil was dissatisfied with his masterpiece, which he had finished but not corrected, and when his health began to fail he asked his friend the poet Lucius Varius Rufus to burn it in the event of his death. Varius refused to obey his orders and, acting under the authority of Augustus, published the epic.

The reason for Augustus' tolerance of these rehabilitations, and his cultivation of revisionists such as Livy and Virgil, was simple. The ideology of the regime was to restore the Republic. This could be advocated, in the first instance, by praising the ideal commonwealth of Rome's early centuries, but also, it necessarily followed, by championing its more recent standard-bearers, the men whom Julius Caesar had destroyed. It followed that Augustus was obliged to reject his revolutionary past (and by implication, his adoptive father) and show that he was a true republican.

To this end, freedom of speech was essential. The *princeps* had to let the regime's opponents celebrate their lost leaders, so that he could be seen to agree. It would have been too odd, too barefaced for him to bury Julius Caesar and exhume Cato and Pompey himself. He needed an opposition, so that he could quietly join it.

To revisit the heroic past was not just a retrieval, but a rebirth. Virgil drew an analogy between the original founding of Rome and its refoundation by Augustus, between his sober and devout Trojan hero, Aeneas, and the sober and devout *princeps*.

Rome's destiny, Virgil wrote, was to "rule an Italy fertile in leadership / And loud with war . . . and bring the whole world under a system of law." History culminates in the inaugurator of new *Saturnica regna*, the reign of Jupiter's father, Saturn, when men lived in virtuous simplicity:

> *And here, here is the man, the promised one you know of—*
> *Caesar Augustus, son of a god, destined to rule*
> *Where Saturn ruled of old in Latium,*
> > *and there*
> *Bring back the age of gold.*

The point was that Romans would not merit their imperial role unless they also tackled excessive consumption, sexual immorality, and the general failure of moral fiber. Once again the *princeps* recruited his constellation of great poets to assist him. Horace mostly celebrates a happily amoral sensuality outside the bonds of marriage, but in his *Odes,* the first three books of which were published in 23 B.C., he devoted a group of poems to the untypical theme of moral renaissance. He wrote of the "large inconvenience of wealth" and compared the citizens of Rome, to their disadvantage, with the barbarous Scythians, unexpectedly cast as noble savages.

> *Family pride*
> *Is their rich dower, chastity shy to glance aside,*
> *Faith in the marriage tie;*
> *Sin is abhorred; the price of scandal is to die.*

This censoriousness chimed with Augustus' thinking. For some years during the twenties B.C. he meditated on social legislation, designed to purify morals and encourage the family. Among respectable opinion, there was a consensus about the failings of Rome's ruling class: divorce was easy; young people were reluctant to marry; the birthrate appeared to be falling; sexual license was widespread; some rich men avoided a public career.

By contrast, traditional standards of behavior in provincial society in Italy were still upheld and the patterns of family life were little changed. This was the world in which Augustus had spent his childhood; his memories of Velitrae may have given a personal edge to his desire to restore Roman values.

Legislation concerning the family would be a distinct and probably unpopular innovation, and the *princeps* took his time before laying any proposals before the Senate. He may have sought to do so in or around 29 B.C., but stayed his hand. Now, probably in 18 B.C., he brought forward a body of laws designed to encourage marriage and procreation. His aim was not only to foster traditional values, but also to create new generations of imperial soldiers and administrators.

Augustus drew an explicit link with a more austere and fecund past when he read out to the Senate the entire text of an old speech on the need for larger families, made by a censor, Quintus Caecilius Metellus Macedonicus, in the middle of the second century B.C. The dry and unsentimental Metellus said:

> *If we could get on without a wife, Romans, we would all avoid that annoyance; but since nature has ordained that we can neither live very comfortably with them nor at all without them, we must take thought for our lasting well-being rather than for the pleasure of the moment.*

The *princeps* presented the so-called Julian laws (*leges Juliae,* after his clan name) in person to an assembly of the people. For the first time, the *lex Julia de adulteriis coercendis* transformed a woman's adultery from a private offense into a public crime. Since time immemorial, a rough-and-ready custom allowed a husband (in theory, at least) to kill his wife if taken in adultery, either on his own account or upon the judgment of a family council. His only alternative, and the one usually chosen, was divorce. The woman lost all or part of her dowry.

The *princeps* felt that this was unsatisfactory. According to his new law, an offended husband was obliged to divorce his wife immediately and then prosecute her for adultery in a special court. Penalties included banishment and confiscation of half the male lover's property (if the couple were caught in flagrante, the husband was allowed to kill him). The woman was forbidden to marry a freeborn citizen in the future.

The law was not quite so severe in practice as appears at first sight, for unless a husband divorced his wife, she could not be prosecuted. A husband who took no action could be charged with condoning the offense, but only if he had actually caught his wife with another man, or if he could be shown to have profited by her activity—say, by pimping for her.

These were both unlikely circumstances and, in a generally permissive climate, it is uncertain that many husbands took advantage of the new legislation. They may have reflected that they themselves might be caught by it if (as was not uncommon) they were conducting an affair with a married woman. According to Suetonius, this was a situation in which Augustus often found himself. Moral campaigns are most likely to succeed if led by someone who has nothing with which to reproach himself.

Unsurprisingly, the *princeps* faced skepticism and laughter at his philandering. Unfazed, he advised senators to "guide and command your wives as you see fit," he said. "That is what I do with mine."

The amused senators pressed the *princeps* to tell them exactly what guidance he gave Livia. He uttered a few unwilling words about a modest appearance and seemly behavior, but seemed quite untroubled by the inconsistency between his words and deeds.

On another occasion, when Augustus was sitting as judge, a young man was brought before him who had taken as wife a married woman with whom he had previously committed adultery. This was most embarrassing, for it was exactly how the *princeps* had behaved when he married Livia in 38 B.C. Uncomfortably aware of the coincidence, he recovered his composure only with difficulty. "Let us turn our minds to the future," he said, "so that nothing of this kind can happen again."

A *lex Julia de maritandis ordinibus* addressed the low birthrate in the upper classes (if Suetonius is to be believed, the general population was rising). It was revised in A.D. 9 as the *lex Papia Poppaea;* exactly what was in the original legislation cannot now be certainly known, but the general thrust was philoprogenitive.

The legislation set penalties for bachelors and childless couples, mainly limiting their right to inheritance under wills. After divorce or widowhood, women were expected to remarry within a fixed time. There were incentives, too: a father of one child was allowed to stand for public office one year earlier than the age stipulated in the regulations. The siring of three children (four in Italy outside of Rome; five in the provinces) exempted a man from certain legal duties.

How effective were his measures? No statistics survive; we have only anecdotes. The literary record gives the impression that, legislation or no legislation, many men of the ruling class did marry and have children. Perhaps some took their time before doing so, but a glance at the family trees of leading personalities shows that most of them produced two or three children who survived to adulthood, and some had larger families (Agrippa, for example, fathered five children).

On the other side of the account, piquantly, Marcus Papius Mutilus and Gaius Poppaeus Sabinus, the consuls who brought in the *lex Papia Poppaea,* were both unmarried, as unkind observers noted. Augustus and Livia were childless, albeit involuntarily, and for all his fine words Horace never married.

Over the years the legislation was repeatedly reviewed and amended, which rather suggests that those against whom it was aimed found their way around its prohibitions.

•  •  •

Roman society depended on millions of slaves from every corner of the empire—Gaul and Spain, northern Africa, Greece, the eastern provinces. To function properly, Rome required their passivity, if not their loyalty.

The continuing flow of wealth into Italy in the first century B.C. was accompanied by a huge increase in the number of slaves, and so of those who could be freed. Enfranchisement (and, with citizenship) was popular not only as a reward for long and loyal service; ex-slaves were also a source of votes at election time, and manumission freed an owner of the duty of supporting old or sick slaves. A freedman, or *libertus,* was still linked to his former owner, for he had to join his *clientela* and owed him a continuing duty of loyalty and support.

Much of the Roman public believed that there were too many *liberti:* they were swamping the citizen body, diluting its Italianness. This appears to have worried Augustus too, who expressed a wish in his will to "preserve a significant distinction between Roman citizens and the peoples of subject nations." It is reported that when Livia once asked him to make a Gallic dependent of hers from a tribute-paying province a citizen, he refused, offering exemption from tribute instead. He said: "I would rather forfeit whatever he may owe the Privy Purse than cheapen the value of Roman citizenship."

Remarks of this kind seem to have been aimed at assuaging public fears rather than representing his real opinion, however, for in practice the *princeps* encouraged freedmen who showed energy, enthusiasm, and talent.

The formal methods of enfranchisement all took time to bring into effect, so owners were allowed to free slaves informally, by a simple written or verbal declaration. However, this did not confer citizenship; probably in 17 B.C., a *lex Junia* gave these informal enfranchisees a form of "Latin rights," a second-class citizenship without voting rights.

In later years a *lex Fufia Caninia* limited the number of slaves whom an owner could free in his will, and a *lex Aelia Sentia* imposed some age limits: an owner had to be over twenty years old before he could give a slave freedom, and a slave over thirty before he could receive it. But these measures were designed to regulate manumission, not to prevent it.

Social reform was insufficient by itself to renew Rome. Writing before 28 B.C., Horace addressed his fellow citizens:

*You shall pay for each ancestral crime,*
*Until our mouldering temples are rebuilt*
*And the gods' statues cleansed of smoke and grime.*

*Only as servants of the gods in heaven*
*Can you rule earth.*

From a couple of years or so before Actium, Augustus recognized the importance of encouraging the state religion. In addition to the Temple of Apollo interconnecting with his house on the Palatine, and that of Jupiter Tonans on the Capitol, Augustus built or refurnished many temples, all of them associated with him, his family, and the regime.

One of the most splendid was the Temple of Mars Ultor (Avenging Mars) on the Capitol. Vowed at the battle of Philippi, it was the centerpiece of a huge new Forum of Augustus which was dedicated in 2 B.C. Like the Parthenon in Athens, the temple was large enough to have eight columns across the front. In its *cella,* or hall, stood images of Augustus' ancestors, and Rome's long ago recovered legionary standards were displayed. Here the *princeps* received foreign embassies; here the Senate debated questions of war, and young Roman boys celebrated their coming of age.

However, something more than marble buildings was required to bring about a religious renaissance. Some great event was called for, a sacred ceremony that would bring citizens together to celebrate the dawning of a new age. It was found in an unusual quarter.

A little to the north of the city in the Campus Martius was a volcanic cleft, at the bottom of which stood a subterranean altar known as the Tarentum or Terentum. Here a nocturnal festival was held in honor of Dis and Proserpina, the gloomy deities of the underworld. Called the Ludi Tarentini, the festival took place over three nights once every century (the interval was set so that no one would be able to attend more than once).

Augustus and his religious advisers decided to rebrand the festival, naming it the Ludi Saeculares, Centennial (or Secular) Games, in the summer of 17 B.C. (and decreasing the periodicity to 110 years).

The ceremonies themselves needed some cheering up. Torches, sulfur, and asphalt were distributed to the entire citizenry, to encourage mass participation in a fiery purification rite. Dis and Proserpina were dismissed, being replaced by the Fates, divine beings who watched over the fertility of nature and of humankind, by the goddess of childbirth, and by Mother Earth. Some daytime celebrations were added in honor of Jupiter, Juno, Apollo, and Apollo's sister Diana. In other words, the old melancholy emphasis on death and the passing of an era was transformed into a forward-looking invocation of the future.

The Ludi culminated in a splendid ritual in the Temple of Apollo on the Palatine. An inscription recorded the program for the day: "After a sacrifice was completed by those thereunto appointed, twenty-seven boys and twenty-seven girls who had lost neither father nor mother, sang a hymn, and so likewise on the Capitol. The hymn was written by Q. Horatius Flaccus."

The chubby little poet of the pleasures of private life kept a straight face for once and produced something as solemn and grand as the occasion warranted. He struck all the notes that his master and friend expected.

> Goddess [Diana], make strong our youth and bless the Senate's
> Decrees rewarding parenthood and marriage,
> That from the new laws Rome may reap a lavish
>     Harvest of boys and girls.

The main message was that the *princeps* had brought back old Rome and breathed new life into the *mos maiorum*. A procession of abstract personifications was conjured up in calm, high-flying verse:

> Now Faith and Peace and Honour and old-fashioned
> Conscience and unremembered Virtue venture
> To walk again, and with them blessed Plenty
>     Pouring her brimming horn.

Ten years had passed since the "restoration" of the Republic. Augustus, now aged forty-six, had established his power without getting himself assassinated. Once a faction leader who had expropriated the Republic, he had successfully recast himself as a new Romulus. The regime had laid claim to embodying the Roman state, and few of those who attended the Ludi Saeculares will have gainsaid it.

However, almost invisible cracks, beyond evidence but not beyond the scrutiny of suspicion, hint at strains in the heart of government. The execution of Murena, the estrangement from Maecenas, the impression of an alliance between Agrippa and Livia to put a brake on the *princeps'* dynastic plans, the brushes with death—these all stood in uneasy contrast with the public symbolism of order, stability, and permanence.

XX

# LIFE AT COURT

AUGUSTUS WANTED TO SHOW THE ROMAN WORLD THAT HE practiced what he preached. The simplicity of his personal life during his four decades of rule was to mirror his public policies.

His daily routine when he was *princeps* seems to have changed little over the years and was studiedly austere. His house on the Palatine, next to Livia's house, was modestly appointed. Its substantial remains confirm Suetonius' description of it as "remarkable neither for size nor for elegance; the courts being supported by squat columns of peperino stone, and the living-rooms innocent of marble or elaborately tessellated floors." The building had a private side with small living spaces and some larger public staterooms.

Suetonius also remarked on the *princeps'* study. "Whenever he wanted to be alone and free of interruptions, he could retreat to a study at the top of the house, which he nicknamed 'Syracuse' [perhaps alluding to the workroom of Archimedes, the great Syracusan mathematician and experimental scientist] or 'my little workshop.'"

This room has been discovered and reconstructed. The walls and ceiling are painted in red, yellow, and black on a white ground. Motifs include swans, calyxes, winged griffins, candelabra, and lotus flowers. All these images were derived from the art of Alexandria, which was popular in Rome in the first century B.C., and may have reflected the impression the city made on Octavian during his visit in 30 B.C.

The *princeps* used the same bedroom all the year round for more than forty years. He is said to have slept on a low bed with a very ordinary coverlet. A small windowless chamber, finely decorated with frescoes featuring the comic and tragic masks of theater, survives, which may have been Augustus' bedroom.

The couches and tables that furnished the house were preserved at least until Suetonius' day; many of them, he wrote after examining them, "would hardly be considered fit for a private citizen."

Like their aristocratic contemporaries, Augustus and Livia are likely to have slept apart. The *princeps* awoke with dawn to the sounds of a stirring household. A poor sleeper, he would often drop off during the day while he was being carried through the streets and when his litter was set down because of some delay.

Slaves bustled about cleaning the house, with buckets, ladders to reach the ceilings, poles with sponges on the ends, feather dusters, and brooms. In the days before electrification, every minute of natural daylight was precious, so Augustus did not lie in but got up at once. He wore a loincloth and undertunic in bed, so when he rose all he had to do was slip his feet into his shoes. He took care not to thrust his right foot into his left shoe, for he believed that would bring him bad luck. He probably cleaned his teeth with dentrifice, a powder made from bone, horn, or egg or shell-fish shells.

The *princeps* paid little attention to his hair, and when it was cut had several barbers working in a hurry at the same time. Sometimes he had his beard clipped and at other times was shaved. When at the hairdresser's, he used to read or write.

Unless he was due to preside over a public ceremony or attend a meeting of the Senate, Augustus wore house clothes woven and sewn for him (or so it was sedulously said) by Livia and his female relatives. He felt the cold badly, and in winter protected himself with four tunics and a heavy toga above an undershirt; below that he wore a chest protector, underpants, and woolen gaiters. His shoes had thick soles to make him look taller. A change of better clothes and shoes was always at hand in case he was unexpectedly called on to appear in an official capacity.

A Roman breakfast (*ientaculum*) was a quick and simple affair—some cheese and olives (possibly prepared as a paste to spread on the cheese), some bread dipped in water, honey, or diluted wine. The business of the day started with a *salutatio;* when the doors of the house were opened a crowd of clients or dependents arrived to pay their respects. Senators often attended and were greeted with a kiss. However, anyone was admitted and was allowed to present a request. Augustus behaved in a relaxed and friendly manner; once a petitioner was in such a state of anxiety that he laughed and said: "Anyone would think you were offering a penny to an elephant!"

Once the morning reception was over, Augustus was free to work by himself in his "Syracuse," and to hold meetings with his staff as well as with politicians.

Augustus' and Livia's houses witnessed a mix of personal and business life (the *domus* or home, and the *familia Caesaris* or Caesar's household). They were far too small for administrative needs, so other neighboring buildings on the Palatine were bought up, creating a government quarter. Because the new Temple of Apollo adjoined Augustus' house, its spaces—the *cella* and the Greek and Latin libraries—could be used to house official events or large meetings.

As is always the case with autocracies, a court developed—that is, not so much a place as a social group, which acted as an intermediary between the ruler and society at large. It accompanied Augustus on his travels away from Rome. Distinctions of power and influence were carefully graded and essentially expressed the degree of access a given person had to the ruler. Augustus went to a great deal of trouble to conceal the thoroughly unrepublican reality of his absolute authority, and took care to act much as any ordinary consul or other officeholder would. He was scrupulously polite to other members of the nobility, exchanging social visits with them and always attending their birthday celebrations.

A group of trusted intimates emerged, the *amici Caesaris,* or friends and political allies of Caesar. It was not a formal grouping, but if an *amicus* lost his status for any reason, this was a terrible thing. Once a consul-elect, Tedius Afer, learning that a spiteful comment of his had enraged Augustus, committed suicide by jumping from a height.

It was far more unusual for a family member to forfeit his or her place in the *princeps'* circle. Their relationship to Augustus gave them a more or less permanent position; a daughter or a nephew might misbehave but remain a daughter or a nephew. As in courts throughout history, important relatives probably came to represent different political points of view, and courtiers gathered behind them in cabals as they perceived their interests to dictate. Thus we detect in 23 B.C. what may have been shadowy groupings around Octavia and Marcellus on the one hand, and Agrippa and Livia on the other. Policy, love, and friendship were often hard to disentangle.

Running the empire entailed a huge amount of complicated administrative work, much of which was performed by freedmen. These had a number of important advantages over family members and social equals:

there was an inexhaustible supply of them, and, unlike aristocratic members of the ruling class, they obeyed direct orders. They had no political constituency and their fate was bound up with that of their employer. Crucially, they reported to nobody but the *princeps,* and so what they did was easily kept secret.

For this reason, little is known about how Augustus organized his staff. To judge by the officially designated separate departments established by later emperors, they may have been loosely arranged in groups that dealt with correspondence, with petitions, with foreign embassies and delegations, and with legal matters. There must have been an archiving function and an accounts department to manage Augustus' vast wealth.

A few freedmen—among them Licinus and Celadus—became close friends of the *princeps.* When he wanted to be completely incommunicado he hid himself away in a suburban villa owned by a freedman who had been a member of his bodyguard. However, bad behavior was strictly punished; when an imperial secretary was found to have leaked the contents of a confidential letter, Augustus had his legs broken.

Augustus cultivated a simple, easy style of speaking and writing and disliked what he called the "stink of far-fetched phrases." He conveyed his meaning as plainly and directly as possible; so, for example, he would repeat the same conjunction several times for clarity, even though the effect was awkward. Letters of his seen by Suetonius employed some rather odd expressions, perhaps deriving from his provincial childhood. For example, he liked to say "wooden-headed" ( *pulleiacus*) for "crazy" (*cerritus*), "feel flat" (*vapide se habere*) for "feel bad" (*male se habere*), and "be a beetroot" (*betizare*) for "be sluggish" (*languere*). Of a sudden or swift action, he would say it was "quicker than boiled asparagus." He often wrote "they will pay on the Greek Kalends," a proverbial expression meaning "never," for the Kalends, signifying the first day of a month, were a purely Roman term. Favorite Greek maxims included "More haste, less speed" and "Give me a safe commander, not a bold one"; he liked the Latin tag "Well done is quickly done."

Augustus wrote a number of prose works of various kinds, some of which he read aloud to close friends in the same way that professional authors used to do in lecture halls. They included an "Encouragement of Philosophy" and some volumes of autobiography (written during his illness in Spain in 24 B.C.). Augustus' attempts at verse were few and far between. He wrote a poem in hexameters, "Sicily," and a few epigrams, which he composed at bathtime.

People often wrote with a reed quill on sheets of papyrus, using sponges to erase text and clean the quill. When Augustus tried his hand at a tragedy about the Greek hero Ajax, who went mad and killed himself with his sword, he was dissatisfied with the result and destroyed it. When some friends asked: "What in the world has become of Ajax?" he replied: "Ajax has fallen on his sponge!"

Augustus seems to have been slightly dyslexic. Uninterested in correct spelling, as determined by grammarians, he preferred to write words as they were pronounced, and often transposed syllables and letters or omitted them. When he wrote in cipher he used the same very basic code that Julius Caesar did; he simply wrote "B" for "A," "C" for "B," and so on (using "AA" for the last letter of the alphabet).

The mornings of *fasti* (lucky) days were devoted to public business: meetings of the Senate (which, in theory at least, could last until sunset but no later), court cases, and religious ceremonies. So the *princeps* would often find himself out and about in central Rome.

Senior Roman officials not only commanded political authority, they also dispensed justice in the courts. Augustus attended assiduously to his legal work, often staying in court until nightfall. If he happened to be unwell, he had his litter carried to the open-air judicial tribunal in the Forum. As a judge, he was conscientious and lenient. He speeded up the legal process, striking off the lists lawsuits that were not promptly pursued. Once he tried a case of parricide, the punishment for which was being sewn up in a sack with a dog, a cockerel, a snake, and a monkey and thrown into a river or the sea. Anxious to save the guilty man from this terrible fate, he asked him: "I take it, of course, that you did not kill your father?"

When appearing in public Augustus liked to present himself as being no more important than any other leading senator. He did his best to avoid leaving or entering Rome in daylight hours because that would have compelled the authorities to give him a formal welcome or send-off. When he was serving as consul, it was inevitable that he was seen in public as he moved from Senate meeting to law court to temple ceremony and sacrifice. He usually walked from one engagement to another through the streets of Rome, although sometimes he was carried about in a closed litter.

Although Augustus was perfectly capable of speaking extempore in public, he was always afraid of saying too much, or too little. So he not only carefully drafted his speeches to the Senate and read them out from a manuscript, but he also wrote down in advance any important statement he planned to make to an individual, and even to Livia (it says something of her own clerical tidy-mindedness that she kept and filed all Augustus' written communications with her).

Most Romans had lunch, a snack much like breakfast, about midday, but Augustus seldom observed regular mealtimes, eating as and when he felt hungry. "I had some bread and dates while out for my drive today," he noted in a letter, and informed another correspondent: "On the way back in my litter from the Regia [the "Palace," a tiny and ancient building in the Forum, the official headquarters of the *pontifex maximus*], I munched an ounce of bread and a few hard-skinned grapes."

He was a light eater and preferred plain food to gourmet dishes. He especially liked coarse bread. This was made of crushed or ground wheat (if the latter, it often contained bits of grit from the stone mill, which could grind down the eater's teeth), and could be cooked without leaven or kneading. The resulting loaf was as hard as rock. Other favorite foods were small fishes, hand-pressed moist cheese (probably like today's Italian ricotta), and green figs.

Augustus drank little alcohol. His limit was a pint of wine-and-water (ancient wine was strong and rich and was almost always diluted); and if he went beyond that he made himself vomit it up. He seldom touched wine before the main meal of the day. Instead he would quench his thirst with a piece of bread dunked in water; or a slice of cucumber or a lettuce heart; or a sour apple, either fresh or dried.

In the afternoon the *princeps* could enjoy some leisure. He used to lie down for a while without taking his clothes or shoes off. He had a blanket spread over him, but left his feet uncovered.

Augustus had learned to pamper his health. He suffered from various minor conditions. Sometimes the forefinger of his right hand became so weak when it was numb and shrunken with the cold that he could hardly

THE ROMAN FORUM AS IT WAS TOWARD THE END OF AUGUSTUS' LIFE

A. Tabularium, or archive.

B. Temple of Concord.

C. Temple of Saturn, where the Treasury was based.

D. Basilica Julia, a shopping and conference center.

E. The Rostra, or speakers' platform.

F. Temple of Castor and Pollux.

G. Temple of the Deified Julius Caesar, built on the site of his cremation.

H. Temple of Vesta, where the Vestal Virgins tended an eternal flame. Here leading Romans could deposit their wills.

I. The Regia, headquarters of the Pontifex Maximus.

J. Basilica Aemilia, a shopping and conference center.

K. Curia Julia, the new Senate House commissioned by Julius Caesar.

L. Forum of Julius Caesar, completed in the dictator's lifetime.

M. Temple of Venus Genetrix (Venus, the Mother or Ancestress of the Julian clan; here Caesar placed a gold statue of Cleopatra).

N. Forum of Augustus, which the *princeps* dedicated together with the

O. Temple of Mars Ultor (Mars the Avenger) in 2 B.C.

The Palatine Hill today, where ruins mingle with trees, as seen from the Roman Forum. This was where the rich and the fashionable lived in the first century B.C. Augustus and Livia both had houses there and offices for their staff. Under the empire, the hill became a government quarter and the official residence of the emperors (from Palatine comes the word *palace*).

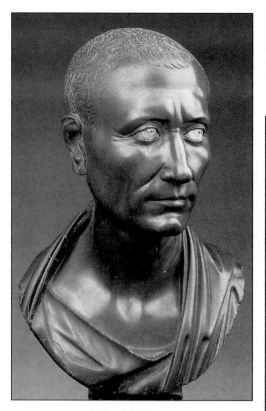

Julius Caesar's intelligence and quickness of mind are well conveyed in this green basanite bust with inlaid marble eyes, carved about fifty years after his assassination in 44 B.C.

A fine bust of Mark Antony in green basalt. Found at Canopus, a suburb of ancient Alexandria, it offers not the bluff, hard-drinking soldier, but a reflective and high-minded ruler—the kind of man that Cleopatra would perhaps have preferred him to be rather than the one he actually was.

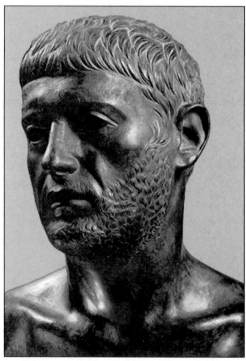

Sextus Pompeius, Pompey the Great's younger son, posed a serious threat to Octavian. His melancholy expression and his beard and mustache, which Romans only grew to mark some tragic event or personal misfortune, suggest that this portrait in bronze was completed after Sextus' defeat at Naulochus in 36 B.C. and subsequent death.

A Roman warship with soldiers on board. This marble relief dates from the 30s B.C., and the crocodile by the prow suggests a reference to the sea campaign against Cleopatra that culminated in Actium.

Alexandria as it appeared in ancient times. The view is of Canopic Way, one of the city's main avenues. In the foreground is the crossroads near which stood the tomb of Alexander the Great. In the distance the Heptastadion can be seen, the great causeway that led to the island of Pharos and created the city's two harbors.

Cleopatra, a portrait in marble probably made in Italy when she was a young woman. It conveys something of the charm of her personality, which captivated Julius Caesar.

Augustus' much-loved sister Octavia. A kindly woman, she brought up Mark Antony's children, including those he had by Cleopatra. She never recovered from the death of her twenty-year-old son, Marcellus, in 23 B.C. The marble bust dates from about 40 B.C.

Augustus' wife, Livia, in middle age. This study, made in her lifetime, evokes an efficient woman of affairs, discreet but decisive.

Augustus and Agrippa at the height of their powers. These marble busts were carved in the 20s B.C. They are realistic character studies that illustrate the two men's different personalities—the one astute and calculating and the other energetic and determined.

The tall man in the center of this relief has been identified as Agrippa. His head is veiled in his capacity as a priest attending a ritual sacrifice. In front of him walk two religious officials, the *flamines diales,* with their pointed hats, and a *lictor,* or ceremonial guard, carrying the *fasces,* an ax inside a bundle of rods. The little boy holding onto his toga may be either his son Gaius or Lucius. The boy is looking back toward his mother, Julia. The man walking behind her is probably Mark Antony's son Iullus Antonius, later to become Julia's lover. The stone carving comes from the *Ara Pacis Augustae,* or Altar of Augustan Peace. Inspired by the friezes on the Parthenon, it was dedicated in 9 B.C.

A contemporary portrait of Tiberius as a young man setting out on a distinguished career as soldier and public servant.

Young Gaius Caesar, Agrippa's son by Augustus' daughter Julia, whom the *princeps* adopted and groomed as his successor. The marble bust dates from about the time of his consulship in 1 B.C. or during his eastern mission.

Agrippa's last son, Agrippa Postumus, born after his father's premature death in 12 B.C. The contemporary sculptor has captured a sense of danger and intensity in his youthful subject.

This onyx cameo, the *Gemma Augustea*, is an example of mendacious art at its finest. Made in A.D. 10 the seventy-three-year-old *princeps* is presented as a half-naked youth. He is seated next to a personification of Rome, beside whom stands Augustus' grandson Germanicus. On the left Tiberius alights from a chariot. Beneath is a scene of defeated and humbled barbarians. The overall impression is of serenity and success. In fact, the mood at Rome was nervous and gloomy, for Augustus was just recovering from the greatest threat to his authority during his long reign, the loss of three legions destroyed in an ambush in Germany the previous year.

A fresco of an actor's mask from a room in Augustus' house on the Palatine Hill, which may have been his bedroom. The *princeps* enjoyed theater and, to judge by his last words, saw himself as a performer. He asked the people around his bedside: "Have I played my part in the farce of life well enough?"

This image of Augustus is a majestic statement in stone of his *imperium* and *auctoritas,* his power and authority. Probably made in A.D. 15, the year after his death, it shows him as a beautiful young man, whose ageless features combine aspects of his actual appearance and the classic lineaments of the god Apollo, Augustus' favorite in the Olympian pantheon. Found at his wife Livia's villa at Prima Porta outside Rome.

write, even when wearing a horn finger-brace. For some years he suffered from bladder pains, but these disappeared after he passed gravel in his urine. He could not tolerate sunlight even in winter; so he always wore a broad-brimmed hat when he was outdoors.

Some seasonal ailments recurred—an expanded diaphragm in early spring and when the sirocco blew, catarrh. He found it hard to endure extremes of heat and cold. He became rheumatic and took the waters at some sulfur springs between Rome and Tibur (today's Tivoli).

Medical practitioners could do little to cure most disorders, so sensible doctors concentrated their energy on preventive medicine. Celsus advised moderate exercise and cautioned against excess in eating, drinking, and sexual intercourse. Although the last activity may be counted as an exception, it would appear that Augustus adopted this kind of regimen.

"He who has been engaged during the day, whether in domestic or public affairs," wrote Celsus, "ought to keep some portion of the day for the care of the body." During the civil wars Augustus took exercise by riding and fencing on the Campus Martius. With the arrival of peace, he used to play catch with two companions, or handball with groups. He soon gave this up and confined himself to riding, or taking a walk at the end of which he would work up a sweat by wrapping himself in a cloak or blanket and sprinting or jumping. Sometimes he went fishing.

On other occasions, especially when the weather was bad, he played dice or marbles with *deliciae*. Augustus was always on the lookout for little boys with pretty faces and cheerful chatter, and he loathed people who were dwarfish or disabled, seeing them as freaks of nature and harbingers of misfortune.

Romans usually took a bath in the afternoon, after exercise and before the main meal of the day, either in their own bathhouse at home if they were rich enough to afford one, or at the public baths, such as Agrippa's splendid new Thermae. Once again, Augustus' watchword was moderation in everything. He did not have a full bath too often, and instead was given a rubdown with oil or took a sweat by the fire after which he was doused with water that had been either warmed or allowed to stand in the sun to remove its chill.

Livia awoke at about the same time as her husband and their respective days ran along broadly parallel lines, only intersecting from time to time. In bed she will have been wearing a loincloth, a brassiere or a corset, and a tunic reaching to a little below the knee. When she got up she stepped into some shoes and put on a finely made *stola* or long tunic. Above this she could drape a wrap or mantle (*amictus*).

Fashionable women preferred cotton from India (available since the Parthian entente with Rome) to linen or wool, or silk imported mysteriously from the distant undiscovered Orient. White and black were popular, as well as bright colors such as purple, yellow, and blue. Scarves could be worn, tied at the neck; a *mappa*, or kerchief, dangling from an arm could be used to wipe dust or perspiration from the face.

According to the poet Ovid, Livia was too busy to devote much attention to her appearance.

> *Don't suppose you'll ever catch her*
> *Completely at leisure; she's scarcely time for her own*
> *Toilet.*

However, as a great lady, she was expected to meet a certain standard. She employed numerous dressers (*ornatrices*) as well as staff to look after her wardrobe. One person was responsible for tending her ceremonial garments and accessories. A *calciator* made her shoes. A masseuse (*unctrix*) helped keep her physically in good shape.

Livia was in overall charge of the family's clothes, but that she personally spent much time at the loom or with the needle may be doubted. Otherwise how were members of staff designated as wool weighers (*lanipendi*) and sewing men and sewing women (*sarcinatores* and *sarcinatrices*) meant to be spending their time? The sculpted busts of Livia that survive show her wearing no jewelry and, despite the fact that she used the services of a *margaritarius*, a pearl setter, it may be that she dressed conservatively and liked to be, in Horace's famous phrase, "*simplex munditiis*" or "simple in her elegance."

Like her husband, Livia would not have washed first thing in the morning; however, her hair needed to be dressed. This could take some time and she will have made use of an *ornatrix*. The fashionable hairstyle of wealthy women of Livia's day had the hair drawn forward from the middle of the head, and then pulled back up into a topknot. On the sides, the hair was taken back in plaits to behind the head. Stray wisps of hair might fall over the forehead and down the nape of the neck.

Roman women used cosmetics, and we may suppose that Livia was no exception. Creams, perfumes, and unguents were widely sold. Makeup for the face consisted of a grease base, often lanolin from unwashed sheep's wool, mixed on small plates with various colored substances—ocher or dried wine lees for rouge; black from ash or powdered antimony for the eyebrows and around the eyes. Chalk and, dangerously, white lead were applied to the face and arms.

Livia had a robust constitution. Like her husband, she ate sensibly. Late in her life she attributed her good health to the wine she habitually drank; this was a highly select vintage from Pucinum, a rocky promontory in the Gulf of Trieste where a small *castellum* used to stand (and nowadays the Castle of Duino).

Drinking wine was not Livia's only prescription for longevity. She produced recipes for various ailments, some of which have survived. One of these was for inflammation of the throat and was a concoction of opium, anise, aromatic rush, red cassia, coriander, saffron, cinnamon, and other herbs mixed with Attic honey. Another promised to relieve nervous tensions and included fenugreek, Falernian wine, olive oil, marjoram, and rosemary. This was cooked and strained and mixed with half a pound of wax. It was to be rubbed gently into the body.

Livia's interest in homemade medicines, employed (it may be guessed) on reluctant relatives and members of her household, could well have contributed to the reputation as a poisoner that she acquired after Marcellus' death.

How exactly Livia passed her time received little attention from contemporary historians. Although a Roman upper-class woman was free to go out, attend public entertainments, visit temples, and play an active role in high society, she was not expected to have a public career; rather, she was to pursue a vocation of looking after her husband and children. She ran the household while her spouse entered politics, fought wars, and governed provinces. In his absence, she would make sure that all was well on his estates and with his finances. Even more important, she would tend the family's political connections and, when necessary, pull strings behind the scenes.

Provided she adhered to the rules, an intelligent Roman woman like Livia would have little difficulty in bending them to her purposes. She was well advised to take account of two models of feminine behavior, one to admire and the other to avoid. In the first category was Cornelia, mother of the Gracchi brothers, reformers who lost their lives in struggles with the Senate in the second century B.C. Once, when another woman who was a guest in her house showed off her jewelry, the finest in existence at that time, Cornelia kept her in talk until her children came home from school, and then said: "Here are *my* jewels." When the boys were grown, she helped them in their political careers, and she bore their loss "with a noble and undaunted spirit."

The alternative paradigm illustrated the grave danger a woman faced if she tried to play too active a part in a man's world. In the following century, a certain Sempronia, mother of Caesar's assassin Decimus Junius Brutus, associated herself with the radical politician Lucius Sergius Catilina.

> *Among their number [women who joined Catilina] was Sempronia, a woman who had committed many crimes that showed her to have the reckless daring of a man. Fortune had favored her abundantly, not only with birth and beauty, but with a good husband and children. Well educated in Greek and Roman literature, she had greater skill in lyre-playing and dancing than there is any need for a respectable woman to acquire, besides many accomplishments such as minister to dissipation. There was nothing that she set a smaller value on than seemliness and chastity, and she was as careless of her reputation as she was of her money.*

This is a nearly contemporary assessment of a woman as able and attractive (it would appear) as Cornelia. Lubricity does not sit easily with the roll call of her good qualities, and her sexual history, whatever it may really have been, was evidently a metaphor for political impropriety. Sempronia had stepped out of line and so her personal character had to be blackened.

Livia had no intention of making the same mistake. She kept a low profile, which won her much respect. She took care not to meddle in what her husband saw as his business and turned a blind eye to his sexual liaisons (not a word was ever whispered impugning her chastity). She was completely discreet and kept silent about all she knew. The *princeps,* for his part, respected her intelligence and often consulted her. It is a mark of his respect and affection, we can assume, that he did not divorce her and find another wife who might have borne him a son. Many of his contemporaries would have done precisely that.

Tacitus saw Livia as a feminine bully who controlled her husband, but she is said to have believed that she had no real power over Augustus and that she exerted influence only because she was always willing to give way to his wishes. A number of recorded occasions illustrate Augustus' readiness to refuse her requests, but he may have followed her recommendations at other times. It seems most likely that he treated her as he did other senior officials in whom he had confidence; like any chief executive of a large organization, he would expect his advisers to make sure that their advice was consistent with his overall policies and, if it was, he would be inclined to accept it.

Livia's morning was devoted to handling domestic matters and supervising her substantial business interests. After lunch she took a bath, and it was now that the greatest amount of time and attention will have been given to her toilette. If guests were coming to dinner, she would need to look her best.

The Roman year was punctuated by holidays during which lavish public entertainments were staged. Augustus was aware that these shows—especially the *munera*, the gladiatorial displays—were important for the ongoing popularity of the regime.

The *munera* were extraordinarily expensive even for the *princeps'* deep pockets and he usually limited funding to two regular seasons, lasting between six to ten days in December and up to four in March. Most of the year's numerous other feast days were devoted to the very popular chariot races at the Circus Maximus and to drama and dance spectaculars at various theaters in the city, including the one dedicated to the memory of Marcellus.

The Circus Maximus (which was used for gladiatorial displays as well as the races) was overlooked by the steep slope of the Palatine Hill. Augustus had a habit of watching shows from the upper rooms of houses on the Palatine that belonged to friends or his freedmen. Occasionally he sat in the *pulvinar,* a roofed platform at the Circus on which a couch carrying images of the gods was placed and which was used as a box by him and members of his family.

Augustus did not always arrive at the beginning of the games or even for the first day or so, but he always presented his excuses and appointed a substitute "president." He did not repeat Julius Caesar's mistake of reading papers and dictating replies during performances, a habit much disliked by the crowd. He watched intently "to enjoy the fun, as he frankly admitted to doing." Augustus' favorite sport was boxing; in the professional game he liked to pit Italians against Greeks, but he also had a taste for slogging matches between untrained roughs in narrow street alleys.

The *princeps* took a friendly interest in professional entertainers of all kinds and got to know some of them personally. However, there were limits of propriety on which he insisted; he banned gladiatorial contests *sine missione,* that is where a defeated fighter could not be reprieved and so had to be killed by his opponent. Augustus wanted to see bravery, but disliked pointless bloodshed. He also severely punished actors and other stage performers for licentious behavior. Women were not allowed to watch athletic contests (competitors did not wear clothes), and Augustus barred them from sitting alongside men at other entertainments; they were banished to the back rows.

The picture of virtue, industry, and economy does not tell the complete truth. Away from Rome and out of the public view, Augustus and his family lived in grand and extravagant style. Suetonius claims that his country houses were "modest enough"; he cannot have visited the rocky island of Pandateria (today's Ventotene) thirty miles or so west of Naples, where the *princeps* built a palace, now undergoing a major excavation.

The island's longer axis lies north–south and runs a little more than one and a half miles. All we know of Pandateria in antiquity is that it was plagued with field mice, which nibbled the sprawling grapes. It has no springs or rivers and large cisterns were built to collect rainwater. A small port was constructed, cut into the tufa, for landing building materials, food, wine, and other supplies. In the north, the island narrows and rises to a small plateau (where today's cemetery stands). Here lie the remains of a building with many rooms, which were probably reserved for servants, slaves, and guards. The ground then dips and narrows into a small valley, where fountains played and a colonnaded portico with seats created a pleasant spot for conversation. A steep stairway led down to a small quay, giving family members and their guests private access to the villa.

Finally, the main house was reached by walking up from the valley to where it perched on a rocky promontory overlooking steep cliffs. The building was shaped like a horseshoe with a garden in the middle; it contained dining rooms, a bathing complex, and other living spaces. At the tip of the promontory, a viewing platform offered an uninterrupted panorama of sky and sea.

Here was secret splendor, where the *princeps* could entertain his intimate circle in undisturbed privacy. This was as it needed to be, for some of his friends were disreputable, not the kind of people with whom he should be seen in public. His dear Maecenas was a sybarite, but a civilized and able man. The same could not be said of the son of a wealthy freeman, the unappetizing Publius Vedius Pollio, who apparently helped establish a taxation system in the province of Asia after Actium. On one occasion Vedius went too far, even for his august friend.

Vedius had tanks where he kept giant eels that had been trained to devour men, and he was in the habit of throwing to them slaves who had incurred his displeasure. Once, when he was entertaining Augustus at dinner, a waiter broke a valuable crystal goblet. Paying no attention to his guest, the infuriated Vedius ordered the slave to be thrown to the eels. The boy fell on his knees in front of the *princeps,* begging for protection. Augustus tried to persuade Vedius to change his mind. When Vedius paid no attention, he said: "Bring all your other drinking vessels like this one, or any others of value that you possess for me to use."

When they were brought, he ordered all of them to be smashed. Vedius could not punish a servant for an offense that Augustus had repeated, and the waiter was pardoned.

Despite his public endorsement of strict private morals, Augustus apparently led (as already noted) a various and vigorous sex life. It was common knowledge, according to Ovid, that his house

> *though refulgent with portraits*
> *of antique heroes, also contains, somewhere,*
> *a little picture depicting the various sexual positions*
> *and modes.*

Mark Antony once accused Augustus of dragging a former consul's wife from her husband's dining room into the bedroom—according to the startled Suetonius, "before his eyes, too!" Friends, among them a slave dealer called Toranius, used to arrange his pleasures for him, stripping women of their clothes so that they could be inspected as if they were slaves up for sale. Even as an elderly man Augustus is said "still to have harboured a passion for deflowering girls, who were collected for him from every quarter, even by his wife!"

The great attract gossip, and it is not mandatory to believe these saucy tales. However, it is worth noting that, according to the sexual mores of upper-class Romans, there was nothing especially out of the ordinary about the behavior attributed to the *princeps* (consider, at a lower social level, Horace's unabashed confessions). Antony launched his accusation only because he was on the defensive about Cleopatra. Augustus' sexual rapacity seems to have been a matter of common report throughout his life.

After exercising and bathing, Augustus and Livia approached the high point of the day, the *cena* or main meal. This started at about three in the afternoon and was an important means by which Romans socialized. It was not exclusively a family affair and guests were often invited. Clubs and societies of every kind held regular feasts, and leading aristocrats invited one another to an annual *cena*.

Dinner parties took place in the *triclinium*. This was a dining room furnished with three communal couches, which were covered by mattresses and arranged along three sides of the room with a table in the center (for larger gatherings the triple-couch layout was simply repeated). There were also tables for drinks. Up to three diners per couch reclined alongside one another, like sardines, with their heads nearest the table and their left elbows propped on cushions. Lying down to eat was a highly prized luxury; when Cato vowed to eat his meals upright as long as Julius Caesar's tyranny lasted, he was felt to be making a real sacrifice. Women sat on chairs, although it was becoming fashionable for them to recline with the men. If allowed to be present, children used stools in front of their fathers' places.

An advisory inscription on the wall of a house at Pompeii from the first century A.D. gives a good idea of how lively these social events could be:

> Do not cast lustful glances or make eyes at another man's wife.
> Do not be coarse in your conversation.
> Restrain yourself from getting angry or using offensive language. If you cannot do
>    so, then go home.

Augustus gave frequent dinner parties, but in his case there was no need for instructions of this kind. These were rather elaborate occasions and great attention was paid both to social precedence and to achieving a good balance of personalities on the guest list. Usually not greatly interested in eating, the *princeps* would often arrive late and leave early, letting his guests start and finish without him.

An usher (*nomenclator*) announced the diners as they entered. Their hands and feet were washed before they were shown to their places. They were provided with knives, spoons, and toothpicks, as well as napkins. Forks had not yet been invented as tools to eat with; guests helped themselves to food with their hands. Waiters brought in dishes and bowls and laid them on the table. Debris, such as shells and bones, was dropped onto the floor and swept up.

The meal opened with the *gustatio,* tasting, during which appetizers were served—various pulses, cabbage in vinegar, pickled fruit and vegetables, strongly spiced mashes of shrubs and weeds such as nettle, sorrel, and elder, and snails, clams, and small fish. A fashionable delicacy was stuffed and roast dormice. A wine-and-honey mixture accompanied the *gustatio*.

The main course consisted of a variety of meat dishes; favorites included wild boar, turbot, chicken, and sows' udders. Fifty ways of dressing pork were known. There were no side dishes, but bread rolls were available. A sauce called *garum* or *liquamen* was added to almost everything. *Garum* was made from slowly decomposed mackerel intestines; its closest (if distant) modern equivalents are Thai or Vietnamese fish sauce and Worcestershire sauce. Finally, dessert consisted of fruit, nuts, and cakes soaked in honey.

Wines were served with the food, but the serious drinking began only when the meal was over. Sometimes people drank at will, but the *commissatio,* a kind of ceremonial drinking match in which cups were drained at a single draught, was a more organized method of inebriation. A master of ceremonies, the *rex bibendi* (literally, "king of what is to be drunk"), would be appointed on the throw of a dice. The *rex bibendi* was in charge of mixing the wine and setting the number of toasts which everyone had to drink.

Conversation flowed, and Augustus was an excellent and welcoming host with a talent for drawing out shy guests. He often enlivened his *cenae* with performances by musicians and actors or circus artistes and storytellers. Sometimes he would auction tickets for prizes of unequal value or paintings with their faces turned to the wall. Guests were required to take pot luck and bid blindly.

Most Romans went to bed early, but the *princeps'* day was not yet done. After dinner was over, probably about sunset (some less reputable *cenae* went on deep into the night), he withdrew to a couch in his study. There he worked until he had attended to all the remaining business of the day, or most of it—reading dispatches, dictating correspondence to secretaries, and giving instructions.

Augustus was usually in bed by eleven and slept seven hours at the outside. A light sleeper, he woke up three or four times in the night. He often found it hard to drop off again and sent for readers or storytellers. He loathed lying awake in the dark without anyone sitting with him.

At last, the ruler of the known world drifted into sleep.

# XXI

# GROWING THE EMPIRE

WHEN AUGUSTUS RETURNED HOME PROUDLY FROM THE EAST
in 20 B.C. after his negotiations with King Frahâta, he brought with him
the captured legionary standards and peace with Parthia. He announced
that he had no intention of adding to Rome's provinces. In his judgment,
"the existing number was exactly sufficient," and he wrote in these terms
to the Senate.

As so often, it is as well to look below the surface of what the *princeps*
said to what he exactly did. At bottom, he was an aggressive imperialist.
Under his rule, Rome gained more new territory than in any comparable period in its previous history. His real position is set out in his official
autobiography, *Res Gestae,* where he boasts: "I enlarged the territory of all
provinces of the Roman People on whose borders were people who were
not yet subject to our *imperium.*"

Public opinion expected nothing less of Rome's ruler. Republican law
had forbidden the Senate to declare war without provocation, without a
casus belli, and indeed Rome (like Great Britain two millennia later) had
acquired much of its eastern empire without altogether intending to do
so. But now the idea that Rome had an imperial destiny was one of the
ways by which the regime justified itself in the public mind.

Virgil writes of a Caesar "whose empire / shall reach to the Ocean's
limits, whose fame shall end in the stars"; Horace begs the goddess of luck
to "guard our young swarm of warriors on the wing now / to spread the
fear of Rome / into Arabia and the Red Sea coasts."

The phrase "Ocean's limits" reminds us how small and fuzzy at the
edges was the Roman world. Accurate navigational equipment not having been invented, most explorers—usually they were traders—did not
travel very far from the Mediterranean.

The Romans believed that the world's landmass was a roughly circular disk consisting only of Europe and Asia, and that it was surrounded by a vast expanse of sea, Oceanus. They had no idea that the American and Australasian continents existed, nor that there was land beyond India. The landmass itself surrounded the Mediterranean Sea and Greece and Italy. The island of Britannia perched on its northwestern edge. The Roman empire took up a large part of the world as its inhabitants believed that world to be, and it was very tempting for its ambitious rulers to dream that they might one day conquer it all.

Maps were rare in the classical time; the first known world maps appeared in fifth-century Athens. Borrowing from Alexandrian models, the Romans, with their imperial responsibilities, recognized the practical importance of cartography. A world map was commissioned by Julius Caesar, probably as part of a triumphal monument he built on the Capitoline Hill, which showed him in a chariot with the world, in the form of a globe, at his feet.

Augustus commissioned his deputy, Agrippa, to work on a more detailed map, the *orbis terrarum* or "globe of the earth." This showed hundreds of cities linked by Rome's network of roads; it was based on reports sent in by Roman generals and governors, and by travelers. The result was a broadly recognizable picture, although distances and shapes became less and less accurate the farther places were from Rome.

The main purpose of the map was as an aid for imperial administrators, provincial governors, and military commanders; as a visual representation of the empire, it was also a powerful metaphor of Roman power. The map was painted or engraved on the wall of the Porticus Vipsania, a colonnade built by Agrippa's sister, and was on permanent public display. Copies on papyrus or parchment were made for travelers, or information copied down.

As we have seen, Augustus and Agrippa spent many years abroad in different corners of the empire. Between 27 and 24 B.C., the *princeps* was in Gaul and Spain; between 22 and 19 B.C. in Greece and Asia; and between 16 and 13 B.C. in Gaul. Meanwhile, Agrippa spent 23 to 21 B.C. in the east, 20 and 19 in Gaul and Spain, and 16 to 13 B.C. in the east again. They spent their time quelling revolts, reforming or reviewing local administrations, and, above all, superintending the consolidation and expansion of the empire.

It is hard to tell whether the two men reacted to circumstances as they arose or pursued a long-term strategy. The impression is given of an orderly progression in the years that followed Actium from one priority to another. As we have seen, the eastern provinces and client kingdoms were reorganized. The frontier of Egypt was pushed southward and contact was made with the Ethiopians. An attempt was made to conquer the Arabian Peninsula, which failed. The negotiations with the Parthians were brought to a successful conclusion. Gaul and Spain were pacified.

A glance at the *orbis terrarum* showed that three great interrelated challenges were yet to be answered. First, the Alps were in the hands of fierce tribes and it was impossible to reach the eastern provinces by land around the top of the Italian peninsula. Second, the frontier of Macedonia was vaguely defined and hard to defend. Third, although the river Rhine, the existing Gallic frontier, ran from the North Sea to the Alps, there was constant westward pressure on it from Germanic tribes.

The ideal solution would be, first, to win control of the Alps and then move north to establish a defensible frontier lined with legions along the river Danube. In this way, buffer provinces in the north would protect Italy and Macedonia from direct attack. If the Rhine and the Danube were to mark the empire's permanent boundary, a major strategic weakness would be likely to cause trouble in the future. This was that the heads of the two rivers formed a salient with its apex where the modern city of Basel stands today. The salient would allow hostile German tribes to operate on interior lines, giving them a huge military advantage.

So the final step would be to invade Germany and create a new frontier at the river Elbe. This would eliminate the salient and create a border roughly in a straight line between the North Sea and the Black Sea. Also, the territory thus gained would helpfully protect Gaul from eastern marauders.

This three-part plan of action may well have emerged through happenstance over the years, but its intellectual coherence and the fact that its constituent elements are interdependent strongly suggest that it was consciously conceived sometime after 19 B.C. and the final pacification of Spain. It would have been intended as a broad framework to guide future military activity, if not as a precisely worked-out blueprint.

If this was the case, it is not too fanciful to guess that the plan's inventor was the man who had won all of Augustus' wars for him: the indispensable Agrippa.

•   •   •

Important changes were taking place in the "divine family," with multiple consequences for its members and for Rome itself. The marriage in 21 B.C. between the daughter of the *princeps,* Julia, and Agrippa succeeded where Augustus and Livia had conspicuously failed: it produced two sons, "an heir and a spare." (Two daughters, Julia and Agrippina, quickly followed.) Gaius was born in 20 B.C. and Lucius in 17. With the arrival of the second boy, Augustus adopted them both and brought them up in his house. They were known thereafter as Gaius Caesar and Lucius Caesar. It was as if they were the offspring of two fathers, with Julia playing only a subordinate role as a human incubator.

The dynastic intention was patent, but this time instead of one "Marcellus" there were two, doubling the chances of survival. This development has been presented as leaving Livia and her sons, Tiberius and Drusus, out in the cold. Concerned as ever to maintain the continuity of the bloodline, the *princeps* certainly did not see them as successors. It was widely suspected at the time that Livia would do everything she could to promote their cause, but there is no evidence that she schemed to subvert her husband's settled intentions. Indeed, she would have been most unwise to allow any disharmony to appear between her and her husband. That Augustus is never recorded to have complained about her and that she remained in high favor throughout his life argue strongly for her loyalty and discretion.

In any case, Tiberius and Drusus had nothing whatever to complain about. Twenty-five and twenty-one years old, respectively, they had already shown signs of talent and ambition and been rewarded for it. The *princeps* was inventive at making the best use of the human material at hand, and as always was more than willing to nurture and promote youth. He arranged for both his stepsons to be granted a special dispensation to hold office before the permitted minimum age and he gave them various challenging jobs. Tiberius' marriage to Vipsania was a happy one. Relations with their stepfather were warm. Tiberius could be somewhat dour, but Drusus was universally popular.

Some undated letters of Augustus survive that speak of his affection for them both. On one occasion he describes to Tiberius how he and Drusus spent all day gambling during a public holiday, playing for high stakes (here, incidentally, he shows himself in an attractive light, for absolute rulers can be poor losers at games):

*Your brother Drusus made fearful complaints about his luck, yet in the long run was not much out of pocket. . . . I lost twenty thousand sesterces; but that was because, as usual, I behaved with excessive sportsmanship. If I had dunned every player who had forfeited his stakes to me, or not handed over my legitimate winnings when dunned myself, I would have been at least fifty thousand to the good.*

In another letter he replies to Tiberius' good wishes: "My state of health is of little importance compared with yours. I pray that the gods will always keep you safe and sound for us, if they have not taken an utter aversion to Rome."

Both young men showed an aptitude for the military life and generalship, qualities that the *princeps* had every intention of exploiting.

Events precipitated, or supplied the pretext for, initiation of the imperial grand strategy. In 17 B.C., Marcus Lollius, a venal, wealth-grabbing new man and a favorite of Augustus, suffered a defeat in Gaul at the hands of some Germanic tribes. The battle was of no real importance and the reverse was quickly avenged, but a legionary standard was lost.

The *princeps* decided to treat the setback as a grave emergency and traveled to Gaul to take matters in hand himself, bringing with him Tiberius (whom he seems to have appointed governor of Long-haired Gaul). Once arrived, he found there was nothing for him to do, for, learning that Lollius was preparing a punitive expedition and that Augustus himself was on his way, the tribal horde had vanished back into its own lands. Nevertheless, the *princeps* remained in Gaul for three years.

Why so long? The information that survives prevents a confident answer. Some unkind tongues at Rome supposed that he wanted to leave Rome so that he could pursue his affair with Maecenas' wife, Terentia. This is possible—if a little odd, for Livia likely accompanied her husband on this as on his other expeditions. It may have been on this occasion that Augustus turned down her request to grant citizenship to a Gaul, and one source dates a curious (if possibly fictional) incident to this time.

Apparently a plot against the *princeps* was discovered while he was in Gaul, implicating among others a grandson of Pompey the Great, a foolish young man called Gnaeus (or possibly Lucius) Cornelius Cinna. Augustus spent sleepless nights and anxious days wondering whether to execute him; according to Dio, Livia persuaded him that clemency would calm his critics and so was more likely than severity to deter future plots.

Augustus was probably laying the ground for a series of major military offensives. He reorganized the army, demobilizing a large number of time-expired soldiers who had joined up after Actium and settling them in Gaul and Spain. This was presumably accompanied by a recruiting drive. The length of a legionary's service was extended to sixteen years (and twelve for members of the Praetorian Guard). At about this time Lugdunum (today's Lyon) seems to have begun to operate as a major mint, coining gold and silver with which to pay legions on campaign in Gaul and Germany.

In 17 or 16 B.C., hostilities opened when the governor of Illyricum launched an attack on a couple of Alpine tribes, probably inhabitants of the region between Como and Lake Garda. Then in 15 B.C., to avenge some alleged atrocities on Roman citizens, Tiberius and Drusus headed a two-pronged attack into Raetia, an area covering today's Switzerland, Liechtenstein, and western Austria, and into the lands of the Vindelici, in southern Bavaria. It seems to have been an easy victory, for the young commanders achieved all their aims in a single summer campaign. In the following year, Roman forces conquered and annexed the Maritime Alps.

As a rule, Roman armies won their wars against "barbarian" tribes in Spain, Gaul, or Germany by a preponderance of force, but they found it very difficult to stamp out the last embers of resistance. Time and again the enemy recovered, regrouped, and returned to the offensive, often using guerrilla tactics. Tiberius and Drusus decided to prevent a future Alpine revolt by a simple but brutal means: mass deportations of men of military age. Enough people were left behind to keep the area inhabited, but too few to launch an uprising. The new province of Raetia came into being. The geographer Strabo visited the region a generation later and reported a continuing "state of tranquillity." If so, it was the tranquillity of desolation.

Not only had stage one of the military strategy been swiftly and brilliantly completed, but in the process stage two had been launched. This was because Raetia's northern border was the river Danube, and a little additional fighting led to the acquisition of the neighboring territory of Noricum to the east (roughly the rest of Austria). Noricum abutted Pannonia, whose tribesmen had been defeated in Octavian's Illyrian wars; although the Pannonians had been neither conquered nor occupied, for the time being they were quiet.

On Pannonia's eastern borders, Moesia had already been subdued, although it was not felt necessary to turn it into a formal province for a generation or so. Pannonia was a lurking problem that would sooner or later have to be solved, but for the first time in its history Rome faced no direct threat south of the Danube.

This was a real and permanent achievement, and Augustus was well pleased. He commissioned a huge celebratory monument, the Tropaeum Alpium (Trophy of the Alps). Fifty feet high, it was a great square stone edifice, which supported a wide circular tower surrounded by columns and topped with a great stepped roof, like a squat spire. On the apex there probably stood a statue of the *princeps*. The monument's still impressive remains can be seen at La Turbie, near Monaco.

In 13 B.C., the state's two leading men returned to Rome, the *princeps* from Gaul, Agrippa from the eastern provinces, where he had spent the last three years. Augustus apparently recognized that the burden of empire demanded two co-rulers; Tiberius and Drusus were emerging as effective deputies. When they grew up, little Gaius and Lucius, in whom the genes of Augustus and Agrippa were mingled, would be the final inheritors of the Roman state.

It was an ingenious and ruthless scheme. However, its success would depend on the survival of all the parties; also, on the willingness of Tiberius and Drusus, after years of power and fame, to step aside at the right moment, remaining forever in second place. It would be asking a lot of their generosity, but Augustus was always implacable where the interests of the state and the "divine family" were at stake.

The Theater of Marcellus was finally dedicated by Augustus; the associated festivities included a performance of the Troy Game, an elaborate cavalry display. Boys of good birth joined societies that offered training in horsemanship, and they showed off their prowess in a mock battle between two groups of teenaged riders.

In what was probably his introduction to public life, little Gaius, only seven years old, took part in the game (presumably nominally), and put in an appearance at a theatrical performance. When he entered the theater the audience leaped to its feet and cheered him to the echo, and so Tiberius, who was presiding, let the boy sit next to his grandfather instead of in his designated place. Augustus expressed his annoyance in no uncertain terms, for he did not want the children to be spoiled by public attention they had done nothing to deserve. Later he gave Tiberius a sharp tongue-lashing.

Power was for use, not for ornament. Augustus did not allow Tiberius and Drusus to celebrate even well-deserved triumphs, although they received triumphal insignia (that is, they had the honor of a triumph although none was actually held). In theory, the brothers did not qualify for the honor, for they were not army commanders themselves, but deputies or *legati* of their stepfather. But a more important principle was at stake. Only the *princeps* should be a *triumphator,* for no one else was allowed to rival him for military glory. The last senator to hold a triumph had done so in 19 B.C. Agrippa, the greatest general of the day, loyally held back, refusing to accept three triumphs when offered. However, Tiberius had no cause for resentment: this year he was consul for the first time, at the age of twenty-nine.

Splendid ceremonial aside, some important public business was put in hand. Augustus and Agrippa had their *imperium* renewed for another five years, and for the first time Agrippa was awarded *imperium maius,* the overriding authority that allowed him to give orders to provincial governors. This was a momentous event, for it placed him for the first time on completely equal terms with the *princeps.*

Despite the reforms of the past fifteen years, the Senate was still not working as well as it should. The adoption in 18 B.C. of a million sesterces as the new wealth minimum for membership had had the unintended consequence that qualified men who wished to avoid service were able to plead poverty (not always honestly) and so win exemption from senatorial status. Not enough suitable men were making themselves available for the *vigintiviri,* the junior administrative jobs that opened a political career.

During his absence from Rome, Augustus had arranged for a decree allowing him to open the *vigintiviri* to selected *equites.* Now that he was back in the city, he reviewed the entire membership of the Senate and compelled senatorial malingerers—that is, young men of the senatorial class who possessed the necessary property qualification but tried to conceal it—to take their proper places.

Fighting apathy in the ruling elite was an uphill struggle, and Augustus' adjustments made little real difference. The great offices of state and senior army appointments gave status to those who held them. But the fact that power was gathered into one man's hands, not widely distributed as it had been under the Republic, was the real reason that many young men were less interested in a public career than their forebears had been. There was nothing Augustus would or could do about that.

A long-overdue departure at last took place. Self-seeking, self-indulgent old Lepidus had spent a quiet quarter of a century in retirement. Augustus had dropped him as triumvir but left him with his private fortune and his position as *pontifex maximus*. In 13 B.C. he died, full of years if not of honor.

Now that Lepidus had gone, Augustus succeeded him as *pontifex maximus*. Finally, he had reached the commanding heights of the Roman religious establishment. He was in a stronger position than ever to accelerate his efforts to restore traditional religious values. Most educated Romans were skeptics and rationalists yet still harbored a belief that Rome's greatness was in some way due to its piety. If the *pax deorum,* the goodwill of the gods, were not maintained, then disaster could be just around the corner.

As we have seen, Augustus' temple building and restoration program was only one aspect of his policy; he also continued to revive lost religious practices, increasing the number of priests and enhancing their privileges. He revived old fellowships, such as the *fratres arvales,* or "land brothers," who handled spring ceremonials to promote the crops. Ordinary citizens were catered for with the revival of local cults in the city's neighborhoods: at ceremonies to propitiate the *lares compitales,* the spirits of the main crossroads in every ward in the city, their images were garlanded with wreaths of flowers twice a year. The *princeps* sealed his long-standing popularity with the people by associating these cults with that of his "genius," the spirit that protected him and his family.

This was as far as Italian opinion would let him go. Julius Caesar had been deified when safely dead, and Augustus knew better than to have himself declared a god in his lifetime. However, elsewhere throughout the empire he encouraged the dual cult of Rome as a goddess and of himself as a godlike being. This gave provincials the opportunity to stage loyalty ceremonies and encouraged an imperial esprit de corps.

It was time to complete stage two of the military strategy. The Alps had been won and two Danube provinces created. But the Pannonian tribes were becoming restive again, and a Roman general led an expedition against them in 14 B.C. Toward the end of the following year, Augustus decided it was time to impose a permanent solution and gave Agrippa overall direction of the war. Although winter had begun, Agrippa embarked on his campaign at once. We have no details, but the Pannonians seem to have quieted down, and Agrippa returned from the Balkans, crossing by sea to Brundisium.

The real reason for his return may have been his health, for in March of 12 B.C., when he arrived in Campania on his way north to the capital, he fell gravely ill. Although at fifty he was still comparatively young, no surviving source has revealed what he was suffering from. Perhaps nobody knew. A fierce Balkan winter may have had something to do with it, and it is reported that in his final years Agrippa suffered unendurable pain from gout. On medical advice, and without informing Augustus, Agrippa took an agonizing course of treatment, plunging his legs into hot vinegar when a paroxysm of the disease was at its worst.

Augustus learned of his colleague's illness while he was presenting some gladiatorial games in honor of Gaius and Lucius. He immediately set out from Rome, but Agrippa was dead when he arrived. The blow was devastating. The two men had been friends from boyhood, and had shared the astonishing adventure of their lives. Even when their relationship was severely tested, they had remained true to each other. Augustus knew that without Agrippa's military talent he would have been lucky to have reached his present eminence.

Many prodigies and portents were recorded, which served to underline the seriousness of Rome's loss. The one that will have made the greatest impression as far as Augustus was concerned was the burning down of the hut of Romulus, next to his house on the Palatine. This had happened before, thanks to careless priests, but the culprits this time were said to be crows. The birds dropped onto the hut flaming fragments of meat, which they had snatched from some sacrificial altar.

It was the custom for widows to remarry, and the *princeps* gave careful consideration to Julia's future. He flirted with the idea of giving her to some political nonentity, even an *eques*. The trouble was that Julia would remain a great lady and, being an independent-minded person, might be willing and able to exert political influence on her own account from the security of a separate household. Better by far to keep her inside the family circle. In that case the only two available candidates were Drusus and

Tiberius; but Drusus' wife, Antonia, was Octavia's daughter and thus able to produce children of Augustus' bloodline. She had already given birth to a son, called Germanicus after his father's victories, and more offspring might be anticipated.

Tiberius, now thirty-one years old, was the better choice, Augustus felt. His wife, Vipsania, was Agrippa's daughter by his first marriage and dynastically unimportant. Unfortunately, Tiberius loved Vipsania and was most unwilling to divorce her. What was more, he strongly disapproved of Julia, who (according to Suetonius) had made a pass at him during Agrippa's lifetime.

Such considerations did not trouble the *princeps,* for whom duty trumped personal preference. In 11 B.C., he required Tiberius to put Vipsania away and marry his daughter. This he did, but continued to miss his first wife. Once accidentally catching sight of her, he stared at her with tears in his eyes and an expression of intense unhappiness. This was noticed and precautions were taken against his ever seeing her again.

At first, Tiberius pulled himself together and made an effort; he and Julia lived affectionately enough as man and wife until a child that was born to them died in infancy. By then he had come to loathe her and renounced marital relations.

Livia is sometimes credited with promoting the match. Perhaps: she would hardly be human if she did not look out for her sons, and she won a reputation among her acquaintances for discreet scheming. A sharp-eyed great-grandson, who knew her in her extreme old age, nicknamed her after the Greek hero most famous for deviousness and sagacity. He called her *Ulixes stolatus,* Ulysses in a frock. However, no evidence survives of her intervention, and Augustus' choice of Tiberius was a logical one, which needed no special pleading.

For his father-in-law and (assuming her approval) his mother, Tiberius' feelings were irrelevant. But he was a private, silent, and introverted man, whose obedience masked obstinate emotion. He had given way on this occasion, but would the time come when he broke free from the heartless and demanding *princeps*?

Personal loss was not allowed to halt the progress of imperial expansion. Tiberius took over from Agrippa in Illyricum and Pannonia, and Drusus commanded the legions on the Rhine. In the spring or early summer of 12 B.C., the brothers launched simultaneous campaigns. To be in close touch with events as they unfolded, the *princeps* spent time in Aquileia and other towns in northern Italy.

The older brother fought the Pannonian tribes for four years, but faced few major difficulties because the enemy seemed unable to unite against a common threat. He deployed his usual ruthlessness, deporting most of the men and selling them into slavery. It appeared that the Pannonian problem had been solved once and for all, and that the last gap along the Danube frontier had been plugged.

Drusus had a more difficult time, although he won victory after victory. He also worked hard to encourage Gallic unity under the aegis of Rome. A great altar to Augustus was erected in a temple at Lugdunum at the confluence of the rivers Rhône and Saône. The altar carried an inscription with the names of all Gaul's sixty tribes, and each tribe contributed a symbolic image of itself.

Propaganda in Gaul was matched by warfare on the far side of the Rhine. Drusus launched a succession of annual incursions. In 12 B.C., he sent a fleet up to the river Weser, and then having won the seacoast marched deep into German lands as far as the mid-Weser. However, he was not such a safe pair of hands as Tiberius and could be foolhardy. He was obsessively ambitious to win the *spolia opima*—as mentioned earlier, this was Rome's greatest and rarest military prize, awarded to a commander in chief who personally killed an opposing general—and he used to chase German chieftains across the battlefield at great risk to himself.

The young general twice got into severe difficulties. Evidently failing to understand the vigor of non-Mediterranean tides, he once allowed his fleet to become stranded when the sea ebbed, and just managed to extricate himself from the resulting danger with help from a friendly local tribe. On another occasion Drusus was ambushed in a narrow pass and faced annihilation. Fortunately, his attackers were overconfident and lost formation when they came to close quarters. Only the cool professionalism of the Roman legionary saw off the enemy.

By the fourth year, Drusus reached what was probably his ultimate destination, the river Elbe. After stiff fighting, he defeated the Marcomanni, a tribe strategically placed between the heads of the Elbe and the Danube. These were fine achievements, which earned the popular general triumphal regalia.

The brothers' successes were impressive, but impermanent. Drusus raided rather than conquered; at the end of each year's campaigning, he left fortresses, but withdrew his army into Gaul. The relative incompetence of the Pannonians concealed bitter anti-Roman feeling. They did not accept the verdict of the war.

The year 9 B.C. began well for Augustus. On January 30 (Livia's birthday, and perhaps her fiftieth) a great Ara Pacis, Altar of Peace, commissioned four years previously, was completed in Rome. Entirely made of marble, it was a sizable square enclosure, with two doorways. Inside, some steps led up to a large three-sided altar; drains were built in to allow the blood from slaughtered sacrificial animals to be washed away. Reliefs around the outside of the walls, inspired by the Parthenon marbles, depicted a grave procession of Roman notables headed by Augustus and Agrippa, with Livia and various relatives, including Gaius and Lucius.

The altar completed a grouping of magnificent structures that asserted the greater glory of the *princeps* and the stability of the regime. The Mausoleum of Augustus was the largest example of its kind; erected in a prominent location between the Via Flaminia leading north from the city, and the Tiber, it was a circular building about 262 feet in diameter, on top of which was piled a mound of earth planted with cypress trees and surmounted by a statue of Augustus. Next door stood a square four-walled enclosure covered by a metal grating. This was the *ustrinum,* where the dead were cremated before their ashes were placed in the mausoleum. Oriented toward the Ara Pacis was the Horologium Augusti, a vast sundial whose pointer was an obelisk that the *princeps* had brought back from Egypt. Lines marking months, days, and hours were inlaid in bronze on the dial's face. At equinoxes, one of which was September 23, Augustus' birthday, the shadow on the dial fell on the entrance to the altar. (Unfortunately, after a while the sundial started telling the wrong time, probably because an earthquake disturbed the alignments.)

The ruins of the mausoleum survive, as does the Ara Pacis, which reopened to the public in 2005 after a long period of restoration. The *ustrinum* is gone; of the Horologium, only the obelisk remains (it now stands in front of the Italian parliament).

Fate intervened once again to lop off another member of the "divine family." In the late summer or autumn of 9 B.C., while he was at his summer headquarters, the twenty-nine-year-old Drusus had a riding accident and broke his leg. It was quickly apparent that he was not going to recover, although it is uncertain why. The Roman army employed experienced medical teams, and on campaign deployed well-equipped field hospitals. In the nature of military life, fractures were common; military surgeons had a good knowledge of how to deal with them, and the techniques of splinting and setting bones described in ancient medical texts are not greatly dissimilar to modern practice.

Some of the literary sources write of an illness rather than an accident, which may mean that it was not the broken leg that killed Drusus, but later complications. An inflammation and fever may have supervened. If there was an open wound, perhaps an infection took hold; without effective antibiotics, that could have led to gangrene and amputation.

Tiberius heard the news of Drusus' accident when he was at Ticinum (today's Pavia) in northern Italy reporting to Augustus about his Pannonian campaign. He rushed off in a panic to his brother. After crossing the Alps he covered two hundred miles at full stretch in a day and a night, changing his horses at intervals. The achievement was all the more remarkable in that he was traveling through unsettled territory that had only recently been conquered, with a Gallic guide as his sole companion.

As Tiberius approached his brother's camp, someone went ahead to announce his arrival. Almost at his last gasp, Drusus ordered his legions to march out to meet him and salute him as commander in chief. He died shortly afterward, and the anguished Tiberius accompanied his body back to Italy, walking in front all the way. For most of the journey, the coffin was carried by leading men from the towns and cities through which the procession passed. Augustus and Livia met the cortège at Ticinum and traveled with it to Rome.

Livia was shattered by the death of her son. As she followed his body she was moved by the pyres that were lit in the dead man's honor throughout the country and the crowds that came out to escort Drusus on his way.

She did not know how to comfort herself in her grief. Areius, the Alexandrian philosopher and family friend, counseled her not to bottle up her feelings, so she displayed pictures of Drusus in public places and in her private apartments and encouraged her friends and acquaintances to talk about him. However, unlike Octavia when Marcellus died, Livia maintained her dignity, and was widely respected for not overstating her grief.

Drusus' much-loved wife, Antonia, the daughter of Mark Antony and Octavia, and her children—two boys, Germanicus and Claudius, and a girl, Julia Livilla—moved in with Livia. The dual household on the Palatine was also home to Gaius and Lucius, Agrippa's boys whom Augustus had adopted, and the orderly bustle of officials was counterpointed by the unruly sounds of children's voices.

Drusus was given a splendid sendoff. His body lay in state in the Forum, where Tiberius delivered a eulogy. Augustus gave another in the Circus Flaminius. After cremation, his ashes were laid in the Mausoleum of Augustus.

Everybody liked Drusus, and it was clear that his family was shocked by his sudden death. However, it did not take long for conspiracy theorists to weave a curious tale. This was that Augustus suspected Drusus of being a revolutionary who wanted to bring back the "old Republican constitution." Tiberius was supposed to have treacherously shown the *princeps* a letter from Drusus suggesting they broach the subject with their stepfather. So Augustus recalled him from Germany and had him poisoned. Suetonius reports the allegation, only to dismiss it. Rightly so, for how could the arrest of Drusus have been concealed and the charade of a funeral procession stage-managed? Suetonius writes: "In point of fact Augustus felt so deep a love for Drusus while he lived that, as he admitted to the Senate on one occasion, he considered him no less an heir than were his sons," Gaius and Lucius.

Yet there may be some truth in the claim that the brothers held republican sympathies. They could well have discussed the kind of state they would like to see in the long term, with Tiberius agreeing to raise the matter with Augustus. In 9 B.C., the year of Drusus' consulship, Augustus took some measures to strengthen the Senate; these could have been concessions to Drusus' wishes. Two regular meetings were to be held every month on days freed from legal and other business. Fines for nonattendance by senators were increased, and strict attendance records were kept.

Two other men whom the *princeps* loved joined the roster of death in the following year: Maecenas and Horace. Together with Agrippa, Maecenas had been with Augustus from the beginning. Although their relations had cooled, and Maecenas' political influence declined, the two men were still friends. Maecenas remained loyal and always advised against despotic measures, recommending that nothing be done to limit freedom of speech and opposing the death penalty for political enemies.

Maecenas was something of a hypochondriac. In the last three years of his life he seems to have suffered from a perpetual fever; he found it hard to sleep, and arranged for music to play quietly in another room. But he put up with his infirmities, writing a little poem to his dear friend Horace:

> *Cripple my hand,*
> *my foot and my hip;*
> *shake out my loose teeth.*
> *So long as I'm alive,*
> *everything's all right.*

Maecenas feared death, and Horace reassured him with a touching ode, in which he promised not to outlive his patron

> *The same day shall heap earth*
>
> *over us both. I take the soldier's oath:*
> *you lead, and we shall go together, both*
> *ready to tread the road that ends*
> *all roads, inseparable friends.*

It was many years since Maecenas had talent-spotted Horace and introduced him to Augustus. The *princeps* had grown very fond of the tubby little poet. He used to call him "my purest of pricks" (*purissimum penem*) and "little charmer" (*homuncionem lepidissimum*). They shared a certain dry and cool realism about life.

Once Augustus asked Horace to work for him as a secretary to help him draft his correspondence. This was the last sort of job the poet would enjoy, and he declined. The *princeps* showed no resentment. He wrote to him good-humoredly: "Even if you were so arrogant as to spurn my friendship, I decline to return your scorn!"

Augustus greatly admired Horace's poetry and was always trying to persuade him to write on political or public themes. The "Secular Hymn" and the odes about Tiberius and Drusus were the result. When Augustus was piqued at finding that he made no appearance in Horace's satires and epistles, many of which took the form of conversations with friends, he protested: "I have to say I am most displeased with you, that in your copious writings of this sort you 'converse' with other people and not with me. Are you afraid that posterity will condemn you if you appear to have been my friend?"

When Horace's health was in decline, Augustus wrote again: "Do as you please in my house, as if you were living with me, for this is how I always wanted our relationship, if only your health permitted it."

In September of 8 B.C., Maecenas died. Two months later Horace fulfilled his promise, only a little late, and followed him. He was buried close to his friend's tomb.

The deaths of Agrippa and Drusus within four years of each other transformed Roman politics. The ages of the key players throw light on the realities of the situation. The *princeps* was fifty-four years old (a year younger than Julius Caesar had been when he died). Tiberius was thirty-three and in his prime. The young hopeful gentlemen, Gaius and Lucius Caesar, were eleven and eight respectively; it would be a good ten years before they were ready to play a full part in public life, by which time Augustus would be in his mid-sixties, a ripe old age for the period.

Two things must have been clear to Augustus. If his dynastic plans were to succeed, then, by hook or by crook, he needed to survive for another decade, for if he did not Tiberius would have to succeed him, just as Agrippa would have done rather than Marcellus in far-off 23 B.C. And Tiberius was the only senior and experienced adult on hand to help Augustus run the empire. His stepson was essential, for now.

Augustus was an autocrat who valued and acted on advice, but the persons on whom he depended emotionally and professionally were falling away. Agrippa; Octavia, who had died in 11 B.C.; Drusus; Maecenas—all gone. The astute Livia was on hand, of course, and the taciturn Tiberius, more experienced on the battlefield than at court. But from now on one senses a growing rigidity of mind in the *princeps*.

# XXII

# A FAMILY AT WAR

## 7 B.C.—A.D. 9

AUGUSTUS WAS NOT A MAN TO BE DAUNTED BY DEATH AND bereavement, and the business of government did not pause. A census was held and the Senate list revised, once again. A measure was taken to ensure that "Augustus" became a household word. Just as the month of Quintilis had been retitled July in honor of Julius Caesar, so Sextilis was translated into August.

In 7 B.C., Augustus' powers were renewed, this time for ten years. Tiberius held his second consulship, but, despite the fact that he was tacitly expected to assume Agrippa's role as deputy to the *princeps,* he received no official acknowledgment that he had become *collega imperii,* or sharer of power.

He had plenty of work to do, taking over Drusus' command and campaigning for two years on the German frontier. (Meanwhile Augustus went to Gaul to monitor events from close at hand, taking with him Gaius, now twelve years old.) As usual Tiberius, who was winning a considerable record as a commander, was victorious. Repeating his treatment of the Alpine tribes in 15 B.C., he deported forty thousand Germans to the Gallic side of the Rhine, where they could more easily be supervised and controlled.

At last he was allowed the distinction of celebrating a full triumph. However, the land between the Rhine and the Elbe remained contested territory. Rome could march about, win battles, and build forts, but it failed to extinguish resistance. Its armies continued to winter on the western bank of the Rhine.

The most notable and far-reaching development at this time was a process rather than a single happening: the boys were growing up. Their adoptive father devoted time and energy to their education. He gave them reading, swimming, and other simple lessons, and behaved as if he were their professional tutor. Whenever they dined in his company, he had them sit at his feet, and when they accompanied him on his travels they rode either in front of his carriage or on each side of it.

During their childhood, Augustus took care to keep Gaius and Lucius in the public eye, and they became darlings of the people. This was politically important, for Augustus could recall that when he entered public life in his late teens, he inherited Julius Caesar's popular support and from it drew much-needed *auctoritas*. The same protection would be invaluable if he, Augustus, were to die before the boys were old enough to have established themselves in power.

One result of this policy was that Gaius and Lucius began to behave badly—something the *princeps* had hoped to prevent. They showed little inclination to model themselves on Augustus. It is easy to imagine that his omnipresence in their lives became stifling and unbearable. A loving father is not necessarily a good teacher of his own children. Dio reports:

> *They not only lived in an excessively luxurious style, but also offended against decorum; for example, Lucius on one occasion entered the theatre unattended. Virtually the whole population of Rome joined in flattering the two . . . and in consequence the boys were becoming more and more spoiled.*

The Roman tradition was to keep the young on a tight leash, so, on the face of it, it is hardly credible that the *princeps* was unable to discipline two small boys, if he really wanted to. He may have feigned irritation to allow Gaius and Lucius to acquire public identities independent of his own in the popular mind.

Unfortunately, the people went one step too far. At the elections for 5 B.C., Augustus stood for consul so that he could preside over the fifteen-year-old Gaius' coming-of-age ceremony. He was of course voted in without trouble, but the people unexpectedly elected Gaius as his colleague in office. The *princeps* never nominated the boys for offices of state without adding the qualification "provided they deserve this honor." On this occasion, Gaius was obviously too young to be deserving, but while vetoing the election Augustus conceded that he could hold the consulship in A.D. 1, when he would be twenty. For now, he awarded Gaius a priesthood, and allowed him to attend Senate meetings and sit in the seats reserved for senators at public spectacles and banquets. A year later he appointed Gaius *princeps iuventutis* (literally "leader of youth"), or honorary president of the *equites*.

The publicity surrounding the boys unsettled Tiberius. He had come to detest Julia and his labors were only too clearly designed to benefit a couple of inexperienced and annoying teenagers.

Augustus chose this moment at last to promote him to Agrippa's position as *collega imperii* by awarding him tribunician status and *imperium maius*. Perhaps he recognized and wished to appease his stepson's discontents, perhaps he wanted to deliver a warning to the unruly Gaius and Lucius that they were not, after all, indispensable. More probably, being a supreme realist, the *princeps* saw it was time to recognize facts. He had no choice but to yoke himself to a man who, while he no longer seemed to be the enthusiastic collaborator of earlier years, was essential to good governance of the empire.

Augustus dispatched Tiberius, equipped with full powers, to settle unrest in Armenia. This client kingdom had been quiet since the successful negotiations between Rome and the Parthian empire in 20 B.C., but now Augustus' appointee as king, Dikran II, died. A struggle ensued between two pretenders to the vacant throne, one of them a Roman nominee and the other a nationalist.

Tiberius then did an extraordinary thing. Before setting off from Rome to take up his commission, he announced without warning his immediate retirement from public life. The official reason he gave was that "he was weary of office and needed a rest." Everyone was bemused. How was it that a thirty-six-year-old man, in excellent health, famous and successful, had decided to throw in his cards?

Tiberius' personality and motives are confusing and in many ways irrecoverable. A gloomy fatalist, he was more used to wielding power than ambitious to win it. If not a republican, he was a believer in senatorial government, and he seems to have been oppressed by the responsibilities he shouldered as Augustus' stepson. He took well to warfare and was more at ease among the simplicities of military life than the soiling compromises of politics.

A popular explanation at the time, and still the most plausible, was that he voluntarily resigned his place to make way for Gaius and Lucius, as Agrippa was supposed to have done for Marcellus. But was he acting from self-effacement, or frustrated anger? We do not know. The situation may not have been as simple as our inadequate sources imply. One fact to be borne clearly in mind is that Tiberius' abdication was partial and provisional. He resigned activity, not office. He retained the *imperium* and tribunician status he had just been awarded. He could have handed his powers back, and presumably Augustus could have arranged for their removal. Neither man did so.

It may be wise to consider the likely tensions at court. It would be very surprising if there were not factions on the Palatine Hill jockeying for position. Livia and her influential circle would support her two sons, now reduced to one; and Julia would wish to assure herself that Gaius' and Lucius' progress to supreme power was unimpeded. These groupings would surely have had action plans ready for immediate implementation in the event of Augustus' incapacity or death.

It may be that Tiberius' retirement was an acknowledgment of defeat in a sophisticated (and now irrecoverable) game. The Julian faction was in the ascendant and he could even have begun to worry about his personal safety in the long run (a good reason for retaining his powers). Alternatively, Tiberius may have felt that his services could not be dispensed with, and that a temporary absence would strengthen his position. He would have to be recalled. Did he even hope to arm-twist the *princeps* to rescind, tone down, or delay his plans to promote Gaius?

Augustus, of course, resisted any pressure to change his dynastic strategy, but he was too aware of the uncertainties of life to remove Tiberius from the board entirely. Circumstances could possibly arise in the future, unwelcome though they were to contemplate, that would call for his return to power.

Augustus did his best to persuade Tiberius to change his mind. So did Livia, but to no avail. Family quarrels often descend into childishness, and Tiberius went on hunger strike for four days to prove that he was serious. The *princeps* admitted defeat and announced the retirement to the Senate. He characterized it bitterly as an act of betrayal. It was a very long time since someone had said no to him.

Tiberius left Rome at once, hurrying down to the port of Ostia without saying a word to the troop of friends who had come to offer their farewells, and kissing only very few of them before he boarded his ship and sailed off. He traveled as a private citizen, accompanied by one little-known senator and a few *equites*. As he was coasting past Campania on his journey south, he received news that Augustus was ill. He cast anchor for a time, but soon guessed that the *princeps* was applying moral blackmail. He did not want to appear to be awaiting an opportunity to seize power. So he resumed his journey.

He decided he would live on Rhodes in the eastern Mediterranean, where he had had an enjoyable holiday many years before on his return from Armenia. The diamond-shaped island is nearly fifty miles long and in those days had between sixty thousand and eighty thousand inhabitants. Until the arrival of Rome, it had been a leading sea power; it was still a center of Greek culture. The land was fertile and figs, pears, pistachios, and olives were grown, as they are today.

Tiberius settled in a modest town house and acquired a villa not far away in the countryside. He behaved unassumingly, keeping his lictors (the guards who symbolized his authority) and his runners out of sight. He often strolled around the Gymnasium, where, Suetonius reports, "he greeted and chatted with simple Greeks as if they were his equals."

Tiberius wanted Augustus, and perhaps especially supporters of Gaius and Lucius, the "Julian faction," to believe that he was politically inactive, as indeed he was. It was awkward that distinguished Romans, traveling to eastern provinces on one commission or another, made a point of stopping off at Rhodes to pay their respects, but he could hardly refuse to receive them. Many governors had friendly connections with the self-made exile and, according to Velleius Paterculus, a military officer who served under Tiberius, lowered their *fasces* to him in acknowledgment that "his retirement was more worthy of respect than their official positions."

Nobody quite believed that the career of Tiberius was over.

Little is known of public affairs during the next few years. A regular system of suffect or replacement consuls, who took over from the original office-holders in mid-term, was reintroduced. The *princeps* reformed the procedures by which a provincial governor could be arraigned for extortion, and in 4 and 3 B.C. further settlements of military veterans were founded.

On the domestic front, a new generation was beginning to emerge. The dead Drusus had had several children by his much-loved wife, Antonia, three of whom survived. The eldest, Germanicus, was born in 15 B.C. and grew up into a courageous and good-natured boy. He was handsome, although his legs were somewhat spindly, a fault he tried to remedy by constant horseback riding after meals. He learned to become an excellent public speaker in Latin and Greek, enjoyed literature, and in adulthood wrote a number of comedies in Greek. Augustus became extremely fond of Germanicus.

Drusus' other son, Claudius, born in 10 B.C., was a problem. His childhood was marred by frequent illnesses. He was physically weak and he limped (perhaps the result of a polio attack); he developed a stutter and a nervous twitching of the head. His mother, Antonia, loathed him. She called him "a monster, not finished but merely begun by nature." Accusing anyone of stupidity, she would say: "He's as big a fool as my son Claudius." Livia also treated him with contempt and rarely spoke to him.

In fact, Claudius matured into an intelligent and studious youth. As a child, he set his sights on becoming a historian. Encouraged by the greatest historian of the age, Livy, he started work on a history of Rome. It opened with the murder of Julius Caesar, but skipped the civil wars that followed when Livia and Antonia warned him that he would not be allowed to publish an uncensored account of those years.

The third child was a girl, Livilla, whom Augustus regarded, as he did all his female relatives, as little more than dynastic marriage fodder. That no record of her early years survives is a reminder of the low value Romans placed on girls.

Like previous years of crisis, 2 B.C. opened well. The *princeps* held his thirteenth consulship, this time to mark the entry into the adult world of the fifteen-year-old Lucius, whom he designated consul for A.D. 4.

A popular campaign was launched to confer on him the title *pater patriae,* "father of his country." This would be a very great honor, seldom bestowed. It had been last awarded to Julius Caesar after the battle of Munda and before that in 63 B.C. to the orator Marcus Tullius Cicero, when he unmasked Catilina's conspiracy against the state.

Messalla was an honorable turncoat (by contrast, say, with the egregious Plancus) and continued to refer to Cassius, under whom he had fought, as "my general" even after he became one of the *princeps'* closest friends. He joined Mark Antony after the defeat at Philippi, and switched sides one final time, foreseeing the ruin that Antony's partnership with Cleopatra would bring about. He distinguished himself at Actium.

After that battle, the then Octavian joked: "You have fought for me as well as you did against me at Philippi."

Messalla cleverly replied: "I have always chosen the best and justest side!"

On February 5, at a meeting of the Senate, this distinguished man addressed his leader: "Caesar Augustus, the Senate agrees with the People of Rome in saluting you as Father of your Country." It was one of the proudest moments in Augustus' life, for the honor was clearly more than flattery: it reflected genuine respect.

With tears in his eyes, he replied: "Fathers of the Senate, I have at last achieved my highest ambition. What more can I ask of the immortal gods than that they may permit me to enjoy your approval until my dying day?"

After long years of construction, the Temple of Mars Ultor, or Avenging Mars, and the huge new Forum of Augustus of which the temple was the grand centerpiece, were opened to the public. To mark the occasion, Gaius and Lucius presided over horse races and their younger brother, Agrippa Postumus, aged ten (as his name suggests, he had been born after his father's death), took part in a staging of the Troy Game, with other teenaged riders from good families.

Entertainments included a gladiatorial contest and the slaughter of thirty-six crocodiles. The most ambitious event was a naval battle between "Persians" and "Athenians," for which a large artificial lake, eighteen hundred feet long and twelve hundred feet wide, was excavated beside the Tiber. This was spectacle on a scale that only Hollywood, two millennia later, would be able to imitate—with the difference that in Rome, real blood was spilled and real ships torched or sunk. Thirty triremes and biremes, equipped with rams, were set against one another, alongside many small vessels. Augustus proudly asserts that three thousand men, in addition to the rowers, fought in the engagement, although he does not record how many of them lost their lives. As at the original battle of Salamis in the fifth century B.C., the Athenians won the day.

Much to Augustus' dismay, his social legislation of 18 and 17 B.C. seemed not to have had the desired effect on Rome's ruling class. Young men-about-town behaved as badly as ever, spending most of their time chasing women instead of settling down and pursuing politics with due *gravitas*.

One of their trend-setters was the poet Publius Ovidius Naso (or, in English, Ovid). He was born into a well-to-do and ancient equestrian family in 43 B.C., and his dominating father did not want him to waste time writing poetry. But this was exactly what delighted young Ovid. Once when his father reprimanded him for scribbling verses instead of doing his homework, the boy cheekily replied by improvising a perfect pentameter, a line of verse with five feet: *"Parce mihi! Numquam versicabo, pater!"*—"Forgive me, Dad! I'll never write a verse."

Unlike Virgil and Horace, Ovid never entered Augustus' circle. This was hardly surprising, considering the subject matter of much of his poetry— namely, the obsessive pursuit of pretty girls. His *Amores,* "Love Affairs," first appeared in 16 B.C. and the *Ars Amatoria,* or "Art of Love," about 2 B.C.

Ovid did not believe in paying for sex and, although many of his poems may be about his wife, he enjoyed hunting down married women. He wrote a poem about trying to pick one up at a popular cruising ground, Augustus' Temple of Apollo on the Palatine. The only trouble is that she is guarded by a eunuch attendant. The poet begs him:

> *All we need is your consent to some quiet love-making—*
> *It's hard to imagine a more harmless request.*

Ovid was a well-known member of the smart set, whose first lady was Augustus' daughter, Julia, now thirty-eight years old and off the leash with Tiberius absent in Rhodes. She had been brought up strictly. Suetonius notes that she was under instruction "not to say or do anything, either publicly or in private, that could not decently figure in the imperial day-book." Among other things, this meant not consorting with young men, and any who were so bold as to make even the most innocuous advance risked being told off by the *princeps*. He wrote to Lucius Vinicius, for example, a young man of good position and conduct: "You have acted presumptuously in coming to Baiae to call on my daughter."

Despite or perhaps because of her upbringing, Julia grew into a free-spirited woman, with contradictory personality traits. She was well read and reportedly had a gentle and humane personality. However, anecdotes also survive of her sharp tongue and willfulness. Once she entered Augustus' presence wearing a revealing dress. On the following day she appeared in the most conservative of stolas. Her father expressed his delight and said: "This dress is much more becoming in the daughter of Augustus."

Julia replied: "Yes, today I am dressed to meet my father's eyes; yesterday it was for my husband's."

Augustus knew better than to shout at his daughter, but he repeatedly advised her to show more restraint. He believed she was just high-spirited, and once observed that he had two spoiled daughters to put up with—Rome and Julia.

Among friends, Julia acted and spoke without reserve; like Ovid, she saw nothing harmful in some quiet lovemaking. However, she took precautions. Contraception in ancient Rome was a hit-and-miss affair. Some women practiced coitus interruptus; others applied sticky substances, such as old olive oil, to the mouth of the uterus, or used vaginal suppositories. All these methods were unreliable, and Julia is said to have restricted full intercourse to times when she was pregnant. She once remarked: "Passengers are never allowed on board till the hold is full."

But she was very aware of her social position, and let no one forget it.

Very probably Julia's way of life differed little in kind from that of other fashionable women of her class, although it may have done so in degree. We are told that she took part in drinking parties in the Forum, walked the streets looking for excitement, and committed adultery with various leading Romans, among them Mark Antony's son by Fulvia, the forty-three-year-old Iullus Antonius. Despite these indiscretions, she and her friends took care for many years that no reports of sexual promiscuity reached her father's ears.

In 2 B.C., however, convincing evidence of her behavior was passed to the *princeps,* although the identity and motives of the informant are unknown. His reaction revealed a total loss of emotional control. He was so shocked and, it would seem, ashamed that he refused for a time to receive visitors. He wrote a letter informing the Senate of the case, but stayed at home and allowed a quaestor to read it out on his behalf. When he heard that a confidante of Julia, a freedwoman called Phoebe, had hanged herself, he cried out: "I should have preferred to be Phoebe's father!"

Iullus was either executed or forced to kill himself, and the other men in Julia's circle were banished to various parts of the empire. Nor was there much mercy toward Julia: Augustus sent her into exile; arranged Tiberius' divorce from her without consulting him; and gave orders that "should anything happen to her" after his death she should not be buried in the Mausoleum. He never forgave her and never saw her again.

The striking feature of these events is not so much Julia's immodesty, but her father's overreaction. Augustus' own private life could not stand scrutiny, but he had no qualms about applying a double standard. His anger leaps from the pages of the ancient sources, and was surely sincere. Julia's behavior defied the central beliefs of the regime. For a quarter of a century the *princeps* had promoted the old ways and the old days—tradition, sobriety, duty, womanly modesty, marriage. And now his own family, of whose virtues he had boasted, was shown to harbor rot in its core! He had expected his daughter to be a virtuous matron, on the model of Cornelia, but it turned out that she was a moral descendant of the vicious Sempronia, who had conspired with Catilina. Like her, Julia was witty, intelligent, and shameless.

Far exceeding the penalties specified by his own legislation, Augustus used the "solemn names of sacrilege and treason for the common offence of misconduct between the sexes." The men involved were probably tried in a treason court, although if the official version of what happened is the whole story, Julia's offense was personal and not really a crime against the state.

However, it is likely that Julia's disgrace had a political dimension. It would not have been the first time that a Roman woman making a political intervention was smeared with charges of sexual license (that is probably what happened to Sempronia). Interestingly, three of the men with whom Julia was supposed to have committed adultery were members of Rome's oldest families: Cornelius Scipio, Appius Claudius Pulcher, and Titus Sempronius Gracchus. These were once names to conjure with and evoked some of the most famous pages in the history of the Republic. Another of the men had been consul a few years earlier—Quinctius Crispinus Sulpicianus, to whom Velleius attributes "unique depravity disguised by forbidding eyebrows."

Tacitus has a telling paragraph about Gracchus:

> *This shrewd, misguidedly eloquent aristocrat had seduced Julia while she was Marcus Agrippa's wife. Nor was that the end of the affair, for when she transferred to Tiberius this persistent adulterer made her defiant and unfriendly to her new husband. A letter abusing Tiberius, which Julia wrote to her father Augustus, was believed to have been Gracchus' work.*

Here is evidence, admittedly obscure and partial, of infighting between two factions—one centered on Julia and her sons, and the other on Tiberius and, we may suppose, Livia. It is not known when Julia delivered her letter about Tiberius; perhaps she was defending herself against allegations he may have made against her, or alternatively she could have been taking advantage of his withdrawal to Rhodes. Even if the essence of the matter was a difference of personality, the conflicting dynastic interests of the parties meant that Julia's intervention must have had political implications.

One of the accusations leveled against Julia sounds innocuous, but it especially infuriated the *princeps*. In the Forum there was a small pool, called the Lacus Curtius, near which stood an enclosure containing a fig tree, an olive tree, and a vine (now replanted for today's tourists) alongside a statue of Marsyas with a wineskin over his shoulder. Marsyas was a satyr, a companion of the god Dionysus. He was skilled with the flute and challenged the god Apollo, who played the lyre, to a musical competition; he lost and the god punished him by skinning him alive.

The Marsyas story bore two meanings. First, it symbolized the eternal struggle between the Apollonian and Dionysian aspects of human nature. Second, the satyr came to be regarded as an emblem of liberty. That is why his statue in the Forum wore a *pileus* or Phrygian cap, such as slaves were given when they were freed.

Julia placed a wreath on Marsyas' head, presumably during one of her late-night sessions in the Forum. Decorating a statue in this way without official permission was not allowed, but, on the face of it, hardly qualifies as a serious offense.

Why did Julia honor Marsyas? According to one report, she prostituted herself in the privacy of the enclosure, so the wreath could simply have been discarded party gear. However, it is conceivable that she was making an antigovernment demonstration, calling for a return to Rome's lost freedoms. Bearing in mind her father's expropriation of Apollo as his tutelary favorite among the Olympians, and Marsyas' association with Dionysus, she could also have been signaling her disapproval of the *princeps*—even evoking the memory of the "New Dionysus," her lover's father, Mark Antony.

It may be no coincidence that in this year the people are reported to have pressed for some (unspecified) reforms. They sent the tribunes to talk with Augustus, who attended an assembly of the people and discussed their demands in person with them. Perhaps the agitation had something to do with his decision to restrict the number of citizens who could receive free grain (Rome's only concession to state-funded social welfare); and he distributed a possibly conciliatory grant of 240 sesterces to each citizen.

All this is speculation. However, Pliny, writing about Augustus in the middle of the following century, remarks (in passing, as of a fact which everyone knows) on "his daughter's adultery and the revelation of her plots against her father's life." This implies a common opinion that there was more to Julia's downfall than sexual promiscuity.

If there was an assassination plot, it is difficult to see what Julia and her supporters were hoping to achieve. We can reasonably assume that she loved her sons; killing Augustus at this time would have damaged rather than advanced their interests. Gaius and Lucius were much too young to succeed the *princeps,* and Tiberius, well liked by the legions, could be counted on to fill the power gap.

There is only one explanation that is psychologically and politically plausible. This is that Julia believed her sons' position would be weak in the event of her father's death in the coming five years or so, before they were mature enough to assert their rights and defend themselves. She would have found it useful to attract the support of an experienced male political figure. If she could marry her lover, Iullus Antonius, she would not only be satisfying her appetites, but Gaius and Lucius would have a high-profile protector during an awkward and dangerous interregnum. It is possible that the letter she sent to her father complaining about Tiberius was part of a campaign to engineer a divorce, for which she would need Augustus' permission. In a word, a conspiracy to control events after the *princeps* was dead has been misinterpreted as a conspiracy to see the *princeps* dead.

This line of thought suggests a fairly benign scheme, with whose aims Augustus would have had some sympathy. He would have been irritated by Julia's interference in his dynastic business, but surely not furious as we know him to have been. It follows that at least some of the tales about his daughter's rackety private life must have been true, or at least that he believed them.

Here, then, to summarize, is a best guess at the real story behind Julia's downfall. She headed a political faction, dedicated to promoting her sons' interests as eventual successors to Augustus. The boys, encouraged by him, were very popular with the people, and Julia as their mother spoke up for the concerns and grievances of Rome's citizenry. Her role was that of a loyal opposition within the regime. Her father found this a useful safety device for the release of political pressure, but she risked overstepping the line of acceptable lobbying.

When the scandal broke, a number of factors came together at the same time. With Tiberius' withdrawal to Rhodes, Julia was pursuing an innocuous plot to get permission to divorce him and marry Iullus Antonius, her purpose being to strengthen her position and her sons' in the event of the *princeps'* early death; she was associating herself (Marsyas) with growing popular discontent in Rome; and she and her private life discredited her father's conservative social policies.

Augustus was irritated by the first issue, alarmed by the second, outraged only by the third. He was accustomed to obedience within the family circle, and, assuming Julia's promiscuity to be public knowledge, he could hardly bear the ridicule and disgrace it would bring on him; it was this that powered his vengeful reaction. Throughout his life, Augustus was a master of self-control, but every now and again we can detect an overflow of deep and powerful feeling. He dearly loved his closest relatives—his wife, Livia; his sister Octavia; his grandsons Gaius and Lucius; and, it would seem, Julia. Perhaps his rage expressed an unspoken, unadmitted bitterness at the truth that he had bought his high place in the world by subduing the claims of affection to the imperatives of power.

No hint has come down to posterity about how Gaius and Lucius reacted to their mother's disgrace. Brought up in their grandfather's house, they may not have seen all that much of her. But if they were hurt or upset, they knew better than to cross a paterfamilias who expected everyone around him to fall in with his wishes, loyally and with no questions asked.

When Tiberius, far away on Rhodes, learned what had happened and that Augustus had used his name in the bill of divorce, he was privately delighted, but felt obliged to send a stream of letters urging a reconciliation between father and daughter. The motive for his kindliness was probably to avoid giving needless offense to Gaius and Lucius and their supporters, and to demonstrate to any doubters that his wife's fall from grace had nothing to do with him. Livia also seems to have acted generously toward Julia: an inscription suggests that she seconded a couple of slaves to her service.

The chosen place of exile was as comfortable as could be expected. It was the palace on the island of Pandateria. Oddly, it is reported that Augustus had one of Julia's country houses pulled down, because it had been built on too lavish a scale: perhaps the fault lay in the villa being on mainland Italy and visible to all, rather than hidden discreetly away.

Julia was forbidden to drink wine or enjoy any other luxury. Her aging mother, Scribonia, nobly volunteered to come and stay with her, but Julia was forbidden any male company, whether free or slave, except by Augustus' special permission, and then only after he had been given full particulars of the applicant's age, height, complexion, and any distinguishing marks on his body. The guards must have been male, but will not have strayed beyond the service block into the villa itself.

The public felt sorry for Julia, and pressure built for her pardon. "Fire will sooner mix with water than that she shall be allowed to return," said the unforgiving *princeps*. In response, agitators, showing a nice sense of humor, threw lit torches into the river. When a people's assembly called for her reprieve, he stormed: "If you ever bring up this matter again, may the gods afflict you with similar daughters or wives!"

After five years, Augustus relented to the extent that his daughter was moved to Rhegium, a Greek city on the toe of Italy where he had settled some veterans; they would be able to keep an eye on her. She was not allowed outside the city walls.

## XXIII

# THE UNHAPPY RETURN

### 2 B.C.—A.D. 9

AUGUSTUS STILL FELT BITTER ABOUT TIBERIUS' WITHDRAWAL, and the exile of Julia broke the last link, apart from the discreet Livia, between the two men. In 1 B.C., Tiberius' tribunician power and *imperium maius* expired. He no longer had any official position in the state. So far as the *princeps* was concerned that was the end of the relationship.

He received a letter from his stepson asking leave to return to Italy, now that he was a private citizen, and visit his family whom he greatly missed. Tiberius claimed that the real reason for his departure had been to avoid the suspicion of rivalry with Gaius and Lucius; now that they were grown up and generally acknowledged as Augustus' political heirs, his reason for staying away from Rome was no longer valid.

The plea was rejected, with a brutality that reveals pain. The *princeps* had not forgiven Tiberius for turning his back on him, and what he saw as his stepson's duty. He wrote: "You should abandon all hope of visiting your family, whom you were so eager to desert."

Augustus now faced a tricky problem in the east, where in 2 B.C. the already complicated situation in Armenia (which Tiberius had been expected to deal with before his resignation) had been complicated by the death, perhaps murder, of the Parthian monarch Frahâta. His son and successor, Frahâtak, took the opportunity to meddle in the buffer kingdom's affairs. Unless some action was taken, Augustus saw a danger that Armenia would move out of the Roman and into the Parthian sphere of influence.

The *princeps* decided to dispatch a military expedition to Armenia, but, of course, the obvious candidate to lead it was no longer available. He hesitated for a time, uncertain what to do, but there was no alternative to overpromoting Gaius, now aged nineteen, and giving him the *imperium* Tiberius had forfeited.

Of course, Augustus had no intention whatever of launching a war under the generalship of an inexperienced boy, however dear to him, against a wily opponent. What he was looking for was a diplomatic solution. He attached Marcus Lollius to Gaius as *comes et rector,* "companion and guide"—two potentially incompatible roles. Lollius had suffered a minor military defeat in Gaul at the hands of German marauders, but retained the confidence of the *princeps.* His main weakness was greed; he had made himself a very rich man by despoiling any province to which he was assigned. That aside, he was a safe pair of hands.

Gaius made his base on the island of Samos. Tiberius, anxious to demonstrate his loyalty, visited to pay him a courtesy call; this stiff and proud man humbled himself by throwing himself at his stepson's feet. Gaius gave him a chilly welcome, apparently on Lollius' advice (presumably briefed by the *princeps*).

Augustus' unease about his disgraced stepson was reinforced when he learned that some centurions of Tiberius' appointment had been circulating mysterious messages to various people, which appeared to be incitements to revolution. He fired off a letter of complaint to Rhodes. Thoroughly alarmed, Tiberius answered with repeated demands that someone, of whatever rank, be appointed to stay with him on Rhodes and watch everything he said or did. To avoid any distinguished visitors, he spent all his time at his country place and took to wearing Greek clothes (a cloak and slippers) rather than a Roman toga.

Meanwhile, Gaius spent time traveling in leisurely fashion through the region and showing the flag. He seems to have acted partly as a general and partly as a tourist. According to Pliny, his imagination was "fired by the fame of Arabia"; in A.D. I, the young commander, serving his consulship in absentia, marched south to look around and conducted some sort of campaign against the Nabataean Arabs.

The display of force had its intended effect on the Parthians, although Frahâtak began by blustering. He sent a delegation to Rome to give his version of events in Armenia and, as a condition of peace being restored in the kingdom, demanded the return of his brothers who were being brought up at Rome. The *princeps* replied with a sharp note addressed merely to Frahâtak, without using the title of king. The Parthian wrote back, tit for tat, referring to himself as King of Kings and to Augustus by his ordinary *cognomen* of Caesar.

The impasse was broken by the death of Rome's nominee for the Armenian throne. Presumably with Parthian approval, his rival, Dikran (one of the numerous members of the royal family called by this name, and not the same person as the aforementioned Dikran II), wrote to Augustus, not applying to himself the title of king and asking for the right to the kingdom. The *princeps* accepted Dikran's gifts, confirmed him as monarch, and advised him to visit his son in Syria, where he was cordially received.

In A.D. 2, Gaius and Frahâtak, also a young man, accompanied by equal retinues, held a carefully orchestrated conference on an island in the Euphrates (did Augustus advise on this arrangement, recalling the long-ago discussions among the triumvirs on the river island at Bononia?). They exchanged pledges and banquets. The Parthian recognized Armenia as within the Roman sphere of influence and dropped his request for the return of his brothers.

For his part, Augustus renewed *amicitia* between the two empires, silently agreeing to leave Parthia alone and accepting the Euphrates as marking the furthest extent of Rome's legitimate concerns. He had reason to be pleased; with the Parthian princes still under his control at Rome, he had won the game on points, with not a drop of blood spilled. All was well, and it would not be too long before the victorious commander returned home.

"*Dis aliter visum,*" as Virgil wrote in the *Aeneid*. The gods had different ideas.

A fond, anxious, and proud *princeps* kept a distant but sharp eye on his adopted son's progress. On September 23, A.D. 1, his sixty-third birthday, he wrote a letter to Gaius that gives a flavor of his love for the young man:

> *Greetings, my Gaius. My darling little donkey, whom Heaven knows I miss when you are away . . . I beg the gods that I may spend however much time is left to me, with you safe and well, the country in a flourishing condition—and you and Lucius playing your part like true men and taking over guard duty from me.*

Augustus will have been worried by a surprising development. At their island meeting, Frahâtak revealed to Gaius that Lollius had been taking bribes from kings throughout the east and, according to Velleius Paterculus, who was a military tribune on the expedition, had "traitorous designs." Gaius dismissed Lollius from his *amicitia,* his list of official friends, and the disgraced man drank poison to avoid the confiscation of his estate.

One day at a dinner party attended by Gaius, Tiberius' name came up in the conversation. A toadying guest promised that, if his general were only to say the word, he would sail straight to Rhodes and "fetch back the exile's head." Gaius declined the offer, but someone reported the incident to Tiberius, who, realizing that his position had become perilous, wrote again to Rome pleading to be allowed to come back. Livia backed him up with passion, and at last the *princeps* yielded, on the strict condition that Tiberius should take no part, and renounce all interest, in politics.

However, Augustus insisted that the final decision be left to Gaius. Had Lollius still been in place, he would have opposed the concession, but his replacement as adviser was well disposed toward Tiberius, who was allowed at last to leave an island that had once been a refuge but had become a prison. He slunk back into the city, sold his grand town house, and bought a discreet residence in a less fashionable district, where he lived in strict retirement.

The good news from the east was more than balanced by terrible news from the west. The nineteen-year-old Lucius had been sent to Spain, probably to gain military experience. On August 20, A.D. 2, he succumbed to a sudden illness at Massilia en route to taking up his commission. To show family solidarity, Tiberius wrote an elegy to his stepson. We do not know the cause of death, nor the impact it had on the divine family. It will have been only too bitterly clear, though, that Augustus' dynastic plans now hung by the thread of a single life.

The Parthian settlement was disturbed by the unexpected death of the Armenian king Dikran. Rome nominated a successor, but he, too, died, and his son ascended the throne. Once again, Armenian insurgents broke out into revolt, and Gaius saw some real fighting. While laying siege to a small town, he rashly approached the walls for a parley with the governor, who said he wished to change sides. He handed Gaius a document, then, while the Roman was looking at it, suddenly struck him with his drawn sword. The ploy was for naught: the governor was quickly overcome and killed, and the town captured.

The wounded man seemed to recover, but the injury took time to heal. According to Dio, Gaius did not enjoy strong health in the first place, and now he fell into a depression. A most surprising turn of events followed. In A.D. 4, Gaius wrote to Augustus announcing that he wanted to retire into private life; his intention was to settle somewhere in Syria. No explanation has come down to us, but it seems that he had lost confidence in himself, and in his ability or desire to fulfill the destiny his adoptive father had laid down for him.

Gaius' letter struck like lightning from a blue sky, and Augustus was dismayed. He informed the Senate of the young man's wishes, and wrote back begging his adopted son to return to Italy, and then do as he chose. Gaius' response was to resign all his duties with immediate effect and set off for home. He made his way south to the Mediterranean coast, where he caught a cargo ship. He disembarked at Limyra, a town in Lycia (today's southern Turkey), where he died on February 21. Presumably his wound had never healed. He was twenty-three years old.

For the *princeps,* nothing worse could now happen. He expended his fury on Gaius' tutor and attendants. During their employer's illness and final days, they were said to have behaved with arrogance and greed; worse, according to Velleius Paterculus, they encouraged "defects" in Gaius' personality "as a result of which he wished to spend his life in a remote and distant corner of the world rather than return to Rome." Augustus had them thrown into a river with weights tied around their necks.

The news of Gaius' death will have reached Rome not later than the end of March. Augustus was sixty-six years old and, according to Dio, exhausted "through old age and sickness." The ancient sources say nothing directly about his personal reaction to the deaths of Gaius and Lucius. The boys had spent much of their short lives in his company, for (as we have seen) he had acted as both father and schoolmaster. In his will, he referred to the "*atrox fortuna,*" malign fate, that had snatched them away. We can only imagine his grief at their loss.

Yet the *princeps* somehow found the energy to reconstruct the divine family. He had no choice but to beg Tiberius to rejoin him as his *collega imperii.* He paused for a time over the name of Germanicus, Drusus' delightful son, inheritor of his father's popularity; but Germanicus was only about seventeen years old and had had no experience to speak of in the art of government. Livia lent her voice to her son's cause in what Tacitus calls her "secret diplomacy." In fact, a whispering campaign accused her of having taken more tangible steps to advance Tiberius' return to the limelight.

Her stepmotherly treachery had supposedly delivered the deaths of

Lucius and then Gaius. It is certainly true that their disappearance undid the massive blunder of Tiberius' withdrawal to Rhodes, and his mother can hardly be blamed for speaking up for her son. It is implausible in the extreme that she could have suborned the governor of an Armenian town, but it is conceivable that the boys' doctors were in her pay; poisoned medicine could have hastened them to Hades. However, the odds on failure were surely far too high, and the consequences of discovery too dire, for an astute political operator to countenance accepting the risk.

It is a sign of the strength of Tiberius' position that at first he resisted the recall to office, if we can believe Velleius, and declined the offer of tribunician status, arguing against it both privately and in the Senate. This reservation was unlikely, of course, to have been sincere, for it was clear where both his duty and his interest lay, but it reflected a desire to extract the best possible deal. Tiberius felt he had been shabbily treated by Augustus. The *princeps* had a way of following his own agenda and taking no account of other people's wishes or feelings. If Tiberius was to return to power, it would have to be on his own terms. He insisted that Augustus wholeheartedly accept him as his successor, and do nothing whatever to subvert his position.

It took Augustus until June 26, nearly three months, before he was ready to announce his new dynastic arrangements. The situation facing him was rather like a change in the balance of a multiparty government. The grouping of senior political personalities who had supported Gaius and Lucius, the "Julian faction," was in retreat, and the bruised clique around Livia and Tiberius, the "Claudian faction," was in the ascendant. The final agreement, which must have been awkward to negotiate, established a coalition in which both factions were catered to. Tiberius received tribunician status for ten years and *imperium* to lead a military campaign in Germany. Augustus adopted him as his son, saying that he was acting *reipublicae causa,* "for reasons of state" (a remark that suggests the acceptance of bitter necessity rather than enthusiasm).

To satisfy the Julian faction, the *princeps* also adopted Agrippa Postumus, Agrippa's last living son. This was less politically significant than it might seem, for Postumus was an exceptionally difficult teenager. He was well-built and had an "animal-like confidence in his physical strength." Although he had committed no crime and been involved in no scandal, his personality was ill adapted to the pressures and constraints of public life. That he was not granted adult status until the following year, A.D. 5, at the late age of seventeen, and that he failed to win the privileges Gaius and Lucius had enjoyed, suggests that something was wrong. However, Augustus may have hoped that Agrippa would grow more responsible with the passage of time. In any case, he wanted to have another iron, however unsatisfactory, in the fire.

Also as part of the agreement, Tiberius was obliged to adopt his nephew Germanicus. Now nineteen years old, Germanicus was Augustus' great-nephew and so a member of the bloodline. In the following year the *princeps* married Germanicus to his granddaughter Agrippina (daughter of Julia and Agrippa); their offspring would double the genetic link back to him. If for once the gods were kind, imperial authority would eventually revert, after a Claudian diversion, to the Julian clan.

However, nothing could conceal the fact that the new concordat distinctly favored the Claudians. Tiberius was the winner. As might have been expected, his supporters were promoted and his enemies purged: this was probably one of the purposes behind yet another review of Senate membership that Augustus conducted later in the year. Having redetermined the succession and reorganized his government, the *princeps* sent Tiberius to campaign on the German frontier. Imperial expansion was close to his heart, as it had always been, but also it would conveniently remove his *collega imperii* from domestic politics and eliminate the need for the uneasy pair to work together on a daily basis.

But it could not eliminate the need entirely. The new son did not altogether trust the new father, and visited Rome as often as his military duties permitted—in Dio's words, "because he was afraid that Augustus might take advantage of his absence to show preference to somebody else." In his absence, the Julian faction might regain lost ground.

The family disputes were not yet over, although the ancient sources are scanty and cryptic. We hear distant detonations but do not witness the battle. The focus of a crisis that unrolled over three years or so were the remaining children of Marcus Agrippa and Julia—Postumus and his sister, the younger Julia, who must have been in her late teens or early twenties.

Postumus continued to do badly. Augustus was worried about letting him out of his sight, although he had no qualms about sending Germanicus to serve in the army. This was a pity, because military experience might have calmed Postumus down. No courtier, the young man spent much of his time fishing, and called himself Neptune after the god of the sea. He had bouts of rage and spoke angrily about Livia. He blamed his new paterfamilias for withholding his paternal inheritance from him. He also probably felt that he lacked advancement.

Matters grew so difficult that Augustus formally severed Postumus' ties with the Julian family and packed him off to Surrentum (today's Sorrento), probably in A.D. 6. The popular resort was not far from Cape Misenum, the naval base for one of Rome's fleets that his father had founded, and if Postumus was misbehaving politically as well as personally he could have been tampering with the loyalty of the sailors (the nickname of Neptune is suggestive). In any event, Suetonius records that "because [his] conduct, so far from improving, grew daily more irresponsible, he was transferred to an island, and held under military surveillance."

This took place in A.D. 7, and the island was low-lying Planasia, south of Elba (today's Pianosa; until recently, it housed an Italian army prison). It had been owned in the first century B.C. by a leading Roman family, and on it stood a villa, some baths, and a tiny open-air theater; it may have been another of Augustus' luxury bolt-holes like Pandateria, and exile there will not have been too incommodious.

In the following year, a mysterious scandal engulfed the younger Julia. She was banished to the tiny limestone island of Trimerus, off the Apulian coast (today's San Nicola in the Tremiti Islands). With a surface area of less than thirty-five acres, this was an isolated and confined spot, far from Rome. No grand villa has been discovered. Julia's living costs were paid by Livia.

The *princeps'* granddaughter's offense, like that of the elder Julia, was sexual promiscuity. The charge is likely to have had a basis in fact, for she gave birth to a child on the island, whom Augustus refused to acknowledge or have reared. Her lover was Decius Junius Silanus; Augustus revoked his *amicitia* and the young nobleman left Rome.

These misdemeanors may have concealed a more serious matter. The younger Julia's husband was Lucius Aemilius Paullus. It appears that he was accused of plotting against the life of the *princeps* and was executed. If his wife was accused of adultery, he must have been alive at the time of her banishment (one late commentator says she was once recalled, only to be exiled again) and his conspiracy probably took place in A.D. 8; so the banishment and the conspiracy may have been linked.

Whatever the politics of his troubles, Augustus' emotions were fully engaged. In future years, when anyone mentioned Agrippa or the two Julias in conversation, he would sigh deeply and sometimes quote a line from the *Iliad*:

*Ah, never to have married, and childless to have died!*

He referred to Agrippa and the Julias as "my three boils" and "my three running sores."

In A.D. 9, Augustus exiled Ovid to the semibarbarous outpost of Tomis (modern Constanta) on the Black Sea. His offense was made a state secret, although the poet dropped numerous hints in two sequences of poems, *Tristia* ("Sad Things") and *Epistulae ex Ponto* ("Letters from Pontus"), with which he bombarded his friends in Rome, begging for forgiveness and describing the miseries of life in distant Thrace.

The mystery has exercised and amused scholars for centuries. In summary, Ovid committed an *error*—a mistake—not a crime; he took no action himself, but witnessed others doing something that he should have reported to Augustus but did not. He caused the *princeps* deep pain. Ovid compares himself to the guiltless huntsman who inadvertently stumbled on the goddess Diana bathing in a spring; she turned him into a stag and set his dogs on him.

> *Why did I see what I saw? Why render my eyes guilty?*
> *Why unwittingly take cognizance of a crime?*
> *Actaeon never intended to see Diana naked,*
> *but still was torn to bits by his own hounds.*

His poem *Ars Amatoria*, especially the didactic pose he struck as a "tutor in love-making," was not the cause of his dismissal, but it did not help his case.

It is hard to make sense of this sequence of enigmatic events, but two factors may throw light on them. First, the years A.D. 6 and 7 were extremely testing for the regime. Military campaigns were under way abroad, but as yet victories had not been won. In Rome there was a severe famine, and emergency security measures had to be taken. Gladiators were banned, and to prevent the dumping of hungry mouths any slaves who were up for sale were banished to a hundred miles from the city.

Augustus and senior officials dismissed most of their staff, and senators were encouraged to leave Rome. Grain and bread were rationed, except for the poorest section of the population, whose grain dole was doubled. There was trouble, too, abroad. Pirates harassed shipping in some parts of the Mediterranean, and rebellions occurred in a number of provinces. King Juba of Mauretania required help from a Roman army to put down a serious revolt in northern Africa. Worse followed, for a great fire destroyed much of the city.

In Rome, the masses became restive and people talked openly of revolution. Dissident posters were distributed at night. An investigation was launched, only adding to the general commotion and apparently not coming to any conclusion. Do we have here telltale signs of the Julian faction at work, currying favor with the people as the elder Julia may have done when she garlanded the statue of Marsyas in the Forum?

As for the sad fate of Ovid, learned men have imagined that the poet accidentally saw Livia having a bath, or caught the *princeps* in an act of pedophilia, or came upon Julia and Postumus engaging in incestuous sex. The poet's own statements point to a political blunder. If he overheard or witnessed some act or conversation preparatory to a coup, the need for official secrecy is perfectly understandable. His reputation for celebrating sexual indecency provided a convincing cover story that distracted from Julia's real offense.

Ovid may have hinted at what this was. When he wrote what he did not do, he may have been pointing to what others *did*.

> *I never sought to procure universal ruin by threatening*
>    *Caesar's head, the head of the world;*
> *I said nothing, my tongue never shaped words of violence,*
>    *no seditious impieties escaped me in my cups.*

Careless talk at a drunken party is what seems to have done for Julia and implicated her poetical fellow guest in her ruin. Ovid with foolish tact "forgot" what he had heard or pretended not to have heard it. But presumably someone else present quietly informed the *princeps* of the conversation and who else had been within earshot.

. . .

It was not Augustus' fault that fate kept unpicking his arrangements for the succession, but his ruthless rearrangement of the lives of his close relatives led to one after another refusing to serve and perhaps even conspiring against him—Agrippa perhaps, Tiberius, Gaius, the two Julias, Agrippa Postumus. The consequence was the almost complete destruction of the divine family as an effective, mutually loyal group. The only survivors were the patient wife and her suspicious son.

Over the years, the *princeps* had allowed his household to be corrupted into a court where a family's ordinary loves and tiffs gradually mutated into political struggle. Maybe this was an inevitable development, but it was Augustus who set the inhumane tone. His insensitivity to the feelings of others (one thinks of Tiberius' thwarted love for Vipsania), his treatment of his relatives as pawns, created a deadly environment. It would not be surprising if, in time, blood relations came to bloody conclusions.

# XXIV

# THE BITTER END

## A.D. 4–14

DURING HIS STEPSON'S ABSENCE ON RHODES, AUGUSTUS HAD not been idle. The basic military dispositions of the empire were maintained—the fleet on the Rhine and a series of operational base camps along the river, which prevented incursions into Gaul by Germanic tribes and provided launch points for Roman expeditions into the eastern lands. Some forward camps were also built east of the Rhine.

Competent generals had asserted Roman dominion. One of them marched an army north from the Danube up to the river Elbe, on the far side of which he erected an altar dedicated to Augustus as a symbol of imperial power; he took care, however, to winter his troops on the Rhine. But while the lands between the Rhine and the Elbe were increasingly dependent on Rome, what the Romans called Germania was by no means entirely pacified.

Tiberius had last commanded an army in 8 B.C., the year after Drusus' death. In A.D. 4, when he was forty-six, he picked up where the two young brothers had left off all those years ago. His aim was to complete the imperial strategy. A powerful and hostile tribe, the Marcomanni, occupied land near the heads of the Elbe and the Danube (in modern Bohemia). It was essential to defeat them and take control of their territory. Then at last Rome would have a secure frontier running without interruption from the North Sea to the Black Sea. A synchronized pincer movement was devised for the culminating campaign of A.D. 6. The army of the Rhine was to advance from the river Main to Nuremberg and the army of Illyricum would move north under Tiberius' personal command.

Brilliantly conceived and brilliantly executed, the plan saw the two armies within a few days of converging on the Marcomanni, when news came of a great revolt in Dalmatia and Pannonia. Tiberius immediately

came to terms with the king of the Marcomanni and rushed off to Pannonia, where he was to spend the next three years fighting the rebels.

He was replaced in Germania by his fellow consul of 13 B.C., a competent but lackluster administrator named Publius Quinctilius Varus. The
new proconsul believed that Tiberius' victories had silenced all opposition; he saw his task as the transformation of a defeated territory into a
Roman province.

Back at Rome, the elderly *princeps* went on governing. In A.D. 4, he conducted a census, to register citizens and their property. The purpose was
to revise taxation indebtedness, doubtless upward. However, in light of
the uneasy public mood he applied the findings of the census only to
those who owned property in Italy worth more than 200,000 sesterces.

The terms of military service were reformed: new recruits were now
required to serve twenty years rather than the former sixteen; the cash
gratuity at the end of a soldier's service was set at twelve thousand sesterces, the equivalent of fourteen years' pay. Centurions were rewarded at a
much higher rate and could become wealthy men. The cost of these gratuities was becoming hard to bear and in A.D. 6 Augustus established an
*aerarium militare,* or military exchequer, which arranged for the payment of
gratuities (the state treasury continued to maintain the standing legions).
It was financed, unpopularly, by a death duty and a tax on the proceeds of
public auctions. Providing in this way for retired soldiers was a wise move,
for it cut the personal link between a general and his men, who in the
days of the Republic expected him to guarantee their future.

In A.D. 9 the *princeps* responded to agitation to repeal the law concerning
unmarried and childless individuals by consolidating his moral legislation
with the *lex Papia Poppaea.** The previous laws were confirmed, but some
concessions were made. Married people without children were no longer
treated as unmarried in the matter of inheritance. Childless widows and
divorced women were given a longer period of grace—two years and
eighteen months, respectively—before they were required to remarry.
Men debarred from receiving legacies because they were unmarried were
granted some time after being named in a will to marry.

· · ·

* See p. 240.

The news of the Pannonian revolt, which had brought Tiberius' German campaign to an untimely halt, deeply shocked Augustus and the Roman establishment. It was reported (perhaps with a touch of exaggeration) that the Pannonians had more than two hundred thousand infantry and nine thousand cavalry in arms. Velleius points out that the Pannonians were well-trained soldiers: "The Pannonians possessed not only a knowledge of Roman discipline but also of the Roman tongue, many also had some measure of literary culture, and the exercise of the intellect was not uncommon among them."

The rebel forces overwhelmed Macedonia with fire and the sword. Roman traders were massacred. The *princeps* reported to the Senate that Italy was at risk of invasion. He moved for a time to Ariminum (today's Rimini), to be closer to the theater of war and able to advise on developments.

Fresh from Germania, Tiberius did not have enough troops to quell the Pannonians decisively, but was able to make a stand with five legions. More legions were urgently summoned from the eastern provinces, but it would take them some time to reach the scene. The citizenry of Italy, in these uneasy times, refused to flock to the legionary standards, and Augustus raised levies from among the slaves of the wealthy, who were given their freedom when they enlisted. This was a bitter expedient, for throughout Rome's history, the recruitment of slaves had been a last, shameful resort.

Eventually the reinforcements from the east arrived, and Tiberius now mustered an army of a hundred thousand men. In A.D. 7 he launched a tough, brutal two-year campaign. He avoided pitched battles, preferring to divide his forces into separate columns and occupying all points of importance. Everywhere the legions devastated the countryside, while maintaining their own supply lines, and subdued the enemy by starving it.

Augustus wrote to his *collega imperii* in flattering terms: "Your summer campaigns, dear Tiberius, deserve my heartiest praise; I am sure that no other man alive could have conducted them more capably than yourself in the face of so many difficulties and the war-weariness of the troops." These generous words, however, concealed anxiety. The public mood was discontented, and Dio claims that the *princeps* believed Tiberius was marking time in order to remain under arms for as long as possible. His suspicion was that Tiberius wanted to strengthen his political position by building the army's personal loyalty to him.

If Augustus did believe this, he was surely mistaken; Tiberius had his hands full in what was widely held to be Rome's most dangerous war since that against Hannibal and the Carthaginians two centuries before. Whatever his reason (one senses a loss of nerve), the *princeps* sent the twenty-two-year-old Germanicus, quaestor in A.D. 7, with the levies of liberated slaves to join an irritated Tiberius, who said he had plenty of soldiers now, and sent some of the newcomers back.

By A.D. 8 the Pannonians had been vanquished; now that they had come to terms, the following year was devoted to dealing with the less problematic Dalmatians. The fighting was bitter and scrappy. Eventually the rebels accepted defeat and surrendered.

There is no doubt that Tiberius was a general of a very high order. He was a good strategist, a most efficient organizer, and well-liked by his troops; the empire was lucky to have him. He traveled back to Rome for victory celebrations, but the promised triumphs were never held, for within a few days, dispatches arrived from Germany, bearing disastrous tidings.

It was September and rain was falling. The territory west of the river Weser through which the Romans marched was a mix of wetlands, woods, and fields. Oak mingled with birch, beech, and alder. In the forest's densest parts there was little direct light and the pathways were narrow. In other places the soldiers passed cultivated fields and meadows with the occasional farmhouse or barn.

A Roman army on the march was an impressive sight. On this occasion the XVIIth, XVIIIth, and XIXth legions (about fifteen thousand men) were advancing through the countryside in column of route. In addition, there were archers, light-armed scouts, and cavalry, as well as artillery and baggage trains. At the head of this magnificent force was the proconsul Publius Quinctilius Varus.

His policy was to transform vanquished Germania into a Roman province as expeditiously as he could. That meant building roads and towns, encouraging trade, and introducing the tribespeople to Roman law. It appears that the Romans also levied taxes. Many of the legionaries were distributed in small detachments to local German communities that had asked for protection against outlaws and guards for supply columns. As Varus saw it, the army was there on a policing rather than a military mission.

In fact, the Romans were regarded as unwanted occupiers and a plot was formed to entrap and destroy the legions. The ringleader was a young Germanic chieftain, known to us only by his Romanized name of Arminius. In his late twenties, he understood the Romans and their war methods well, for he had served in the Roman army, probably in Pannonia. He had obviously made a good impression, for he received Roman citizenship and was appointed an *eques*. He was on Varus' staff and was constantly in his company.

Arminius' idea was not to rise in open rebellion, for he knew that a German horde would be unlikely to defeat the Romans in open battle. Instead, he intended to lure Varus away from the Rhine by sending him false reports of an uprising. Arminius would then lay an ambush for the Romans in what was supposed to be friendly country.

The plot was betrayed, but Varus could not bring himself to distrust his friendly Germans. Believing in Arminius' honesty, he took the bait, gathered his scattered forces, and marched off to put down the supposed rebellion. The conspirators, purporting to be loyalists, rode with the legions for a time, but then one by one made their excuses and slipped away.

Arminius had chosen the location for the ambush with great care. Archaeologists have discovered the site (at Kalkriese in Lower Saxony) and have unearthed the detritus of a battle. A level pathway led through woods, running between a steep hill and a great bog. Along the hillside the Germans built a camouflaged turf rampart at least seven hundred yards long, where the ambushers could lie in wait for the enemy, out of sight and out of mind. When the Roman column arrived, Arminius' men launched volleys of spears from behind the turf rampart and then charged. They achieved total surprise.

What happened next is uncertain, but, despite many casualties, a good number of legionaries and most of the officer corps survived and pushed on, under constant attack, passing through open country and then plunging into woods again.

On the third day after the ambush, the situation became hopeless and Varus and his staff realized that there was no escape. Even if it meant leaving their remaining soldiers leaderless, they agreed that there was only one honorable course of action. They nerved their courage for the "dreaded but unavoidable act" and committed suicide, running themselves through with their swords.

It was now every man for himself. Some soldiers followed Varus' example; others simply lost heart, dropped their weapons, and allowed themselves to be slaughtered by the enemy.

Of the three legions' fifteen thousand men, few survived to tell the tale. The Germans took about fifteen hundred prisoners, of whom two thirds were sold into slavery; a number of them eventually won their freedom and made their way back to Italy. The remainder were sacrificed as religious offerings. They were put to death in different ways; some had their throats cut, while others were hanged from trees, crucified, or buried alive. The German gods appreciated variety. Victims' heads were nailed to trees in the forest as a warning to any intending invasion in the future. Once they had exacted their punishments and removed their dead, the Germans left the scenes of battle as they were, for time and nature slowly to restore and conceal.

News that something terrible had happened percolated through the region, and all but one of the Roman fortresses on the eastern side of the Rhine were hastily evacuated. The "province" of Germania was lost.

Augustus was in his early seventies. He had been working at full stretch for fifty years and the last decade had been crammed with personal disappointment and political trouble. He no longer dealt with individual petitions, although with the help of assistants he still investigated legal suits and passed judgment, seated on a tribunal at his headquarters on the Palatine Hill. He gave up attending Senate meetings or people's assemblies, and entrusted the reception of foreign delegations to a trio of former consuls.

Like the outbreak of the Pannonian rebellion, the Varus disaster (in Latin, *Variana clades*) seemed to make the *princeps* briefly panic. He tore his clothes, as was the Roman custom when a man was facing shame and catastrophe, and did not shave for months. He was so upset that he would beat his head against a door, crying out: "Quinctilius Varus, give me back my legions!" He kept the anniversary as a day of deep mourning.

A record survives of an aged diva being brought back to the stage in A.D. 9 during celebrations to congratulate the *princeps* on "his recovery"; this reveals that he had been ill, although we know nothing about the nature of his condition or its gravity. It could have been a reaction to the loss of his legions.

Augustus sent Tiberius to take over the Rhine command, to counter any German invasion of Gaul or even Italy, and to demonstrate that Rome's military power was undiminished. At home he feared a popular uprising and sent military patrols around the city at night. Not trusting the Germans in his bodyguard, he sent them to various islands; he also deported the large Gallic and German community from the city. The terms of service of provincial governors were extended so that experienced men were in place to cope with any trouble.

The emergency exposed a serious potential weakness of Augustus' military strategy. Ever since his victory over Antony and Cleopatra, he had set the empire's military strength at twenty-eight legions, but this was only just sufficient to man the frontiers. There were no soldiers left over to form a mobile field army that could move quickly to a crisis point.

But the emergency soon passed. Arminius did not invade Gaul; Rome and the provinces remained tranquil. The indispensable Tiberius did what was required on the northeastern frontier, where he campaigned for three more years. However, he made no attempt to recover Germania as a Roman province, and the empire was never again to reach beyond the Rhine.

Had the regime really been at risk? Augustus' alarm reflected an innate caution. But also, for all the sonorous rhetoric about the restored Republic, his power essentially depended not on constitutional legality but on the support of the army and the people. If that was withdrawn, his day would soon be done. And imperial success was essential to the regime's popularity; indeed, the only event likely to shake the loyalty of either constituency was a major military defeat.

So it was reasonable to predict that the loss of three legions would entail serious political consequences. That it did not do so may owe something to the security measures that the *princeps* took, but is better seen as evidence that Augustus' constitutional settlement was firmly established. No oppositional grouping existed that was ready and able to exploit the situation.

For all that, the *Variana clades* was a real and substantial setback, which provoked a strategic review behind closed doors on the Palatine. The aggressive plan to settle Germania up to the Elbe, which we may guess Agrippa and Augustus to have devised twenty years previously, was revoked. From now on the Rhine was to be the permanent boundary between Romanized Gaul and the barbarians of central Europe.

The change was rational, based on close observation of the realities in both Rome and Germany. Arminius' failure to exploit his victory suggested that the Germans no longer presented a serious threat to the stability of Gaul, if they ever really had. As always, they were unable to combine in an alliance for any length of time. It simply was not worth going to the trouble and expense of reinstalling the province of Germania. Reconnoitering and occasional punitive expeditions would be enough to ward off any risk of attack.

In A.D. 12, the twenty-seven-year-old Germanicus held the consulship, but if there were expectations of a return to optimism they were disappointed. Although he was busy in the law courts, he achieved nothing of importance.

Augustus wrote a letter commending Germanicus to the Senate, and the Senate to Tiberius. His physical energy was waning and he did not read it out himself, for he could not make himself heard, but instead handed the document to Germanicus to read. Taking the war in Germany (now drawing to a close) as his excuse, he asked senators to forgo attending the morning *salutatio* at his house on the Palatine Hill, and not to feel offended if he no longer attended public banquets.

Natural disaster struck again: the Tiber burst its banks and the Circus Maximus was flooded. For the first time we hear of seditious literature being burned and the authors punished. Probably in this year, a well-known advocate in the courts, Cassius Severus, was banished to Crete for having "blackened the characters of men and women of the highest status by licentious writings." The *princeps* had not been the target, but, also for the first time, this kind of offense was dealt with under the treason law. Also, the Senate burned the "republicanist" writings of a historian, who committed suicide.

These reactionary moves strike a new, disturbing note, for one of the regime's more attractive traits in earlier years had been its acceptance, if not its endorsement, of free speech. An easy self-confidence had given way to anxiety. Perhaps this reflects the growing influence of Tiberius, who, despite his possible republican sympathies, had long been of an authoritarian cast of mind. Years before, Augustus had written to him: "You must not . . . take it to heart if anyone speaks ill of me: let us be satisfied if we can make people stop short at unkind words."

In the following year, A.D. 13, Augustus' *imperium* was optimistically extended for a further ten years, and (yet another first) Tiberius, now fifty-six, received equal powers. Even if old age was slowing him down, the *princeps* remained hardworking, busy, and clever. The 5 percent death duty introduced in A.D. 6 proved extremely unpopular among the upper classes. The Senate indicated that it would accept any impost except for the death duty, so Augustus set in motion plans for a land tax instead. He was well aware that that would present an even more alarming prospect; and indeed the Senate decided it would be best to stick to the devil they knew. The old manipulator had lost none of his skill.

Thoughts of death can never have been far from Augustus' mind throughout his long life: his health was poor in the first half of his career; until Actium, he regularly ran the risk of being killed in battle; and in Rome he was sharply aware that the Ides of March set a baleful precedent. He was only in his mid-thirties when he commissioned his splendid mausoleum.

Now certainty replaced possibility. In April of A.D. 13, Augustus assembled a number of documents, describing the achievements of his reign and leaving various instructions; it may be that a deterioration in his health prompted him to take this step. The documents were mostly written in his own hand, although his office staff will have done the research. In one sealed roll, he gave directions for his funeral. In another, he set out his record, which he wished to have engraved on two bronze columns at the entrance to his mausoleum. The *princeps* did not write the text all at once, but in his orderly way had begun it years previously and added to it from time to time; he only finally signed it off on May 13, A.D. 14.

Written in plain, dignified Latin, this second document became known as the Acts of the Deified Augustus, or *Res Gestae Divi Augusti;* copies were posted in different cities in the empire (translated into Greek where appropriate).

The *Res Gestae* is an astute piece of writing, of which a modern manager of public opinion could be proud; for while he tells no outright lies, Augustus casts the most favorable possible light on his activities. He never once mentions Mark Antony by name, whether as fellow triumvir or military enemy; nor does he go into any detail about his revolutionary past—it is as if the proscription never happened.

The third document Augustus prepared at this time, the *breviarium imperii,* was a statement of the number of serving troops in different parts of the empire, the reserves in the public exchequer and in the privy purse, and the tax revenues due for collection; he also supplied the names of the freedmen and slave secretaries who would be able to furnish further particulars under each heading, on demand.

Augustus also composed a homily directed at both Tiberius and the people, in which he advised them, among other things, to stay within the empire's current boundaries. This injunction partly reflected the success of his policy of imperial expansion along the Danube and partly the new chastened acceptance of the Rhine as the appropriate barrier between Gaul and the Germanic tribes.

Finally, the *princeps* wrote (or revised) his will, complex and surprising; it took up two notebooks and was penned partly in his hand and partly by two freedmen. He arranged for its deposit at the Temple of the Vestal Virgins; unlike the hapless Mark Antony, he was confident there would be no latter-day Octavian so bold as to open it before he was dead and buried.

Sometime during A.D. 13, Augustus strengthened the standing committee that he had created to expedite senatorial business. The consuls remained members, but all the other nominated officeholders were replaced by consuls designated for future years. Tiberius, Tiberius' son Drusus, and Germanicus also joined the committee. It looks very much as if the aim was to create a body strong enough to cope with the strains of transition from one reign to another.

Augustus' final months are surrounded by mystery. As in a detective novel, the reader is given too few facts with which to explain events and identify culprits. Much depends on intelligent guesswork and the interpretation of cryptic clues. The trouble is that this was real life, with no author to write a final chapter in which all is made clear.

In the late spring or early summer of A.D. 14, Augustus came to feel regret for Agrippa Postumus' exile. Taking a very few people into his confidence, he sailed to the island of Planasia, accompanied only by a court intimate, Paullus Fabius Maximus. Fabius was a distinguished figure, who had served as consul and governor in Spain. He was also a patron of the arts and had been a close friend of Horace and (a little surprisingly) Ovid. Tacitus reports on the encounter: "There [on Planasia] tears and signs of affection on both sides had been plentiful enough to raise a hope that the young man might yet be restored to the house of his grandfather."

Soon after their return, Fabius died, but not before having told his wife, Marcia, of the secret adventure, and she incautiously passed on the news to Livia. At her husband's funeral, Marcia was heard to sob bitterly that she had been the cause of his destruction. The implication was that, learning of this breach of confidence, an angry Augustus had withdrawn his *amicitia* from Fabius, who as a result felt obliged to commit suicide.

Augustus' last days are described at some length by Suetonius. In August A.D. 14, he and Tiberius prepared to leave Rome. They had recently conducted a census, which was held once every *lustrum,* or five years, and the *princeps,* despite his fading health, was well enough to preside over a purification of the Roman people that marked the end of the *lustrum.* The ceremony took place in a crowded Campus Martius.

All kinds of portent were recorded about this time—the usual melange of nonsense with, on this occasion, an actual event inflected by superstition. During the ritual, an eagle circled overhead several times and flew to the nearby Pantheon, where it perched above the first "A" of Agrippa's name in the dedication over the entrance. The *princeps,* seeing this, immediately took it to signify his imminent demise. So he told Tiberius to read out in his place the vows he was due to take as part of the ritual, for although he had composed them and had had them inscribed on a tablet, he did not want to make himself responsible for promises that could only be discharged after his death.

Tiberius was to travel to Illyricum and reorganize the recently vanquished province; Augustus, as a mark of signal favor, agreed to accompany him down the Via Appia as far as the town of Beneventum, about 130 miles south of Rome. Livia was in the party. Before arriving at the mosquito-ridden Pomptine Marshes, through which Horace and Maecenas had journeyed on their way to Tarentum for negotiations with Mark Antony, the *princeps* decided to transfer to a ship, but became indisposed and decided to detour to the island of Capri for a few days' rest and relaxation.

The party then crossed back to Italy and resumed its journey south. As planned, Augustus turned back at Beneventum to make his way to Rome but, feeling worse, instead stopped off at a family villa at Nola on the slopes of Mount Vesuvius, where his father, Gaius Octavius, had died during his praetorship in 58 B.C.

At this point Livia reappears in her role as poisoner. Tacitus reports: "Augustus' illness began to take a turn for the worse, and some suspected foul play on the part of his wife," who was worried about her husband's reconciliation with Agrippa Postumus. Dio goes further, albeit without committing himself:

> *Livia was afraid, some people allege, that Augustus might bring [Agrippa] back to make him emperor, and so she smeared with poison some figs which were still ripening on trees from which Augustus was in the habit of picking the fruit with his own hands. She then ate those which had not been smeared, and offered the poisoned fruit to him. At any rate, he fell sick from this or some other cause.*

Tiberius was recalled and rushed to Nola. According to Dio, Augustus died before his return and Livia concealed the news until her son had reached her side, fearing that in his absence there "might be some uprising." Guards were posted in the street around the villa and optimistic bulletins were issued from time to time. But Suetonius claims that Tiberius arrived in time to see Augustus alive. The dying man had a long talk with him in private, after which he attended to no further important business.

When visitors arrived from Rome, Augustus wanted to hear the latest news of Drusus' daughter, Livilla, who was ill. Finally, he kissed his wife, saying "Goodbye, Livia. Never forget our marriage." Just before he died, his wits seemed to wander, for he suddenly cried out in terror: "Forty young men are carrying me off!" (This was later interpreted as a prophecy, for the same number of Praetorians would form the guard of honor that conveyed him to his lying in state.)

Augustus had always hoped for a quick and painless death, and the gods granted his wish. The date was August 19, a little more than a month before his seventy-seventh birthday. He had been ruler of the Roman empire for almost forty-four years.

Immediately, a *codicillus,* an order, was sent to Planasia to execute Agrippa Postumus. The tribune in command of Agrippa's guard told a centurion to see to the matter. The young man was strong and large and put up a fight, despite the fact that he had no weapons. He was eventually dispatched, with some difficulty. The deed was done only in the nick of time, for a slave of his called Clemens, having heard of Augustus' death, immediately took a cargo ship to Planasia to rescue Agrippa, either by force or trickery. Unfortunately for Agrippa, the boat sailed slowly and Clemens arrived too late.

Meanwhile, the commander of the island guard set sail for Rome, where he presented himself to Tiberius and reported that the execution had been carried out. Tiberius vehemently denied having had anything to do with the matter, and insisted that the officer give an account of himself to the Senate.

According to Tacitus, the author of the *codicillus* was Gaius Sallustius Crispus, who, like Maecenas, did not trouble to hold public office, but operated behind the scenes. The grand-nephew of the historian Sallust, he became a "repository of imperial secrets."

Alarmed by Tiberius' decision to open Agrippa's death to public debate, Sallustius warned Livia that "palace secrets, and the advice of friends, and services performed by the army, were best undivulged. . . . The whole point of autocracy is that the accounts will not come right unless the ruler is the only auditor."

Tiberius was persuaded to remain silent. The matter was closed.

How should we best interpret the events surrounding the death of Augustus? The regime realized that the transition from one *princeps* to another, from the dominance of one man to the establishment of a dynasty, would be a time of great danger. All concerned took great pains to make everything run as smoothly as possible. The most likely threats would stem from civil dissidence in Italy and mutiny among the legions on the imperial frontiers. The focus for any trouble would be Agrippa Postumus, the last male representative of the Julian line.

The imagined account with which this book opens is an attempt to tell a coherent and feasible story of what occurred while rejecting as little as possible of the surviving ancient narratives. It incorporates most, but not quite all, that the sources report. It plausibly assumes that all the leading players—Augustus, Tiberius, and Livia, together with their advisers—devised a transition plan and were determined ruthlessly to implement it, whatever their personal feelings.

The most important charges that I have rejected are that Augustus changed his mind about who should succeed him and wanted to replace Tiberius with Agrippa, and that Livia acted to defeat him. Both are highly unlikely. Once the *princeps* had committed himself to Tiberius, whatever his reservations, he did everything within his power to promote his new co-ruler's interests. Even the minor decision to accompany him to Beneventum was a clear and public statement of support. In the absence of concrete knowledge, Roman historians filled in the gap by reference to the traditional image of the wicked stepmother, ever eager to supplant a true heir with her own child.

This does not mean that we have to reject the trip to Planasia. Modern scholars argue that Augustus was far too frail to undertake such an arduous journey, but this is unconvincing if we recall that in the days immediately before his death he was willing to travel by road to the Pomptine Marshes, sail to Capri and back to Italy, and then resume his journey to Beneventum, before retracing his steps.

Augustus' motive for the journey may have been purely sentimental; but the record of the way he treated his close relatives suggests a ruthlessness that precluded emotion. More probably, as I suggested, he wanted to assess whether Agrippa was in an insurrectionary frame of mind, and to reduce the chance that he would join an anti-Tiberius plot by feeding him delusive hopes of a return to favor at Rome.

If that was how things stood, there was no particular need to keep Livia in the dark. But whether or not she knew of what was afoot, Augustus was annoyed with Fabius Maximus because, by confiding in his wife, he had breached the total secrecy that was meant to cover the operation—in much the same way that Maecenas' gossiping to Terentia about her brother's conspiracy had led to his loss of influence with the *princeps*. A high value was placed on confidentiality at the court of Augustus. (However, Marcia's grief at her husband's funeral did not necessarily mean he had committed suicide; disgrace could have triggered an illness, such as a heart attack.)

In the introductory chapter, I proposed that Augustus' health unexpectedly improved, but that recovery came too late. According to this hypothesis, all the arrangements for the handover of power to Tiberius had been made and could not conveniently be revoked. It was necessary for him to die if the transition was not to falter. So, half in collusion with her victim, his loving wife, Livia, administered the poisoned figs. (Incidentally, we do know that the *princeps* liked the fruit, and that Livia cultivated a type of fig that was named after her; if there was a fig tree at Nola, perhaps she had had it planted.) Such a speculative explanation would account for her reported action, and accords with the gloomy sense of duty that characterized the political culture of the time. Roman history contains many examples of suicide for political reasons, and of assisted suicide.

Alternatively, and no less speculatively, it is possible that the story of the figs was a farrago invented and disseminated by people like Clemens and other populist agitators, to suggest mendaciously that Augustus did mean to designate Postumus as his true heir. Once again, the easy slander of Livia as the wicked stepmother dispensing poisoned fruit was too tempting to resist. It is puzzling, though, that a tale from so tainted and unrespectable a source should have had sufficient currency to enter the historical record. The truth of Augustus' death will never be known.

Finally, we must consider who originated the order to kill Postumus. Suetonius sums up the options: "Some doubt remains whether this order was left by Augustus to be acted on when he died; or whether Livia wrote it in his name; or whether, if so, Tiberius knew anything about it."

Sallustius can be acquitted, for even if he penned the *codicillus,* he will hardly have done so unprompted. Although Tiberius was the beneficiary, it is doubtful that he was involved, or had even been told about it. His angry insistence that Agrippa's death be debated by the Senate argues innocence of both the deed and the knowledge.

Livia seems never to have directly intervened in politics or initiated political action, but she was known to wield influence. For Sallustius to ask her to use her good offices with Tiberius was a sensible idea, not necessarily sinister. That the commander reported to Tiberius rather than her also tends to exonerate her. It is conceivable that she forged a letter from the *princeps,* but from what we know of her this would have been out of character.

By far the most probable culprit was Augustus himself. It is true, as Tacitus points out, that he had never before had any of his blood relations executed, but we know that he could act unforgivingly against those of them who threatened him. He killed Caesarion, Julius Caesar's illegitimate son, without a qualm, and treated the two Julias harshly. The visit to Planasia does suggest that he found the decision to kill his grandson difficult to make.

Augustus' signet ring was removed from his finger. His eyes were closed. Tiberius, being his closest relative, called him by name and said, *"Vale,"* "Farewell." Slaves belonging to undertakers washed and perfumed the corpse. A coin was placed in its mouth, to pay the ferryman to carry Augustus' spirit across the river Styx to the underworld.

The body was carried to Rome on the shoulders of senators from the neighboring municipalities and colonies of veterans. The August heat was insupportable and the journey was conducted by night. In the daytime the dead man lay in state in the town hall or principal temple of each halting place.

At Rome, Augustus' will was read out. The preamble ran: "Since fate has cruelly carried off my sons Gaius and Lucius, Tiberius shall inherit two thirds of my property"—a less than ringing endorsement of his chief heir. Tiberius received one hundred million sesterces, and Livia fifty million. Ninety million sesterces was set aside for small individual bequests to the soldiery and the people.

All of this was as might be expected. However, the *princeps,* so cautious and patient in his lifetime, sprang an astonishing surprise from beyond the grave: he adopted his wife. Just as Tiberius received the name of Augustus, so Livia received that of Augusta. As Augustus' daughter, she became a member of the Julian clan, and from now on was known as Julia Augusta.

What did Augustus intend by this extraordinary promotion? It was the only important political decision he ever made that was completely without precedent, and he left no explanation for it. However, in the first instance, we may readily conclude that it signaled Livia's contribution to the governance of the state during his reign. Everyone supposed she had been an important adviser behind the scenes, and the adoption was an official recognition of the fact. Augustus may also have wished to strengthen his wife's position after his death, so that she could exert some control or at least influence over Tiberius; her political skills could complement his largely military experience. Perhaps, even, he wanted to show the world how deeply he loved his wife.

Now that Livia had become Julia Augusta, she had an official constitutional position in the state for the first time in her life. Although technically without *imperium* or anything approaching it, she seemed to contemporaries almost to be co-ruler with her son. During the Senate debates about decrees passed in Augustus' honor, Dio reports that "she took a share in the proceedings, as if she possessed full powers." It is said that for a time Tiberius' correspondence carried her name as well as his, and letters were addressed to them both.

However, Tiberius held traditional views and disapproved of women openly intervening in public affairs. When the Senate voted her the honorific title of *parens patriae,* or parent of the fatherland, Tiberius rejected the offer on her behalf. It soon became clear that power lay with him alone, although, despite his annoyance at her elevation, he continued to seek his mother's advice in private.

The funeral of a leading Roman was an event that combined terror, splendor, and solemnity, and although we do not have the details of the order of service for Augustus, it will have broadly followed the regular procedure. As was always the case, the ceremony took place at night.

A procession formed to convey the body from the house on the Palatine to its last resting place. Almost the entire population of Rome turned out onto the streets, and troops lined the route to ensure public order. The procession was managed by a *dominus funeris,* or master of the funeral, attended by lictors dressed in black. It was headed by trumpeters playing mournful music, and girls and boys of the nobility sang a dirge in praise of the dead man.

Farce and laughter can be a means of purging grief, or at least alleviating it. A troupe of clowns and mimes was sometimes hired at funerals; the performers would follow the musicians and singers, led by an archimimus, who imitated the speech and gestures of the dead man.

Like most wealthy Romans, Augustus will have liberated some of his slaves in his will. They came next in the procession, wearing the special cap of liberty that was given to freedmen.

The bier then appeared. This was a couch made of ivory and gold and spread with a purple and gold pall. Beneath the covering, Augustus' body was hidden in a coffin; above it, a wax effigy in triumphal costume was displayed. The bier was accompanied by a statue of the *princeps* in gold and another of him riding a triumphal chariot. Statues of his ancestors were also carried, as well as personified images of the nations he had added to the empire, and of leading Romans of the past. Interestingly, Pompey the Great was among the company, but Julius Caesar was excluded on the grounds of his divinity.

The family, dressed in mourning, walked behind, among them Julia Augusta. The entire Senate were in attendance, as were many *equites,* and the Praetorian Guard. Anybody who was anybody was present.

The cortège stopped in the Forum, where Tiberius and his son Drusus, both dressed in gray, delivered eulogies. It then wended its way through the Porta Triumphalis, the gate through which triumphal processions entered the city, and arrived at Augustus' mausoleum in the Campus Martius. The awe-inspiring climax of the ceremony approached.

In the early Republic, Romans were usually buried, but by the end of the first century B.C. almost everyone was cremated. Augustus' body was laid on a pyre in the *ustrinum,* or crematorium, next to the mausoleum. Once the bier was in place, all Rome's priests marched around it, followed by the *equites.* Then the Praetorian Guard circled it at a run and threw on the pyre all the triumphal decorations (often valuable silver or gold plaques) any of them had received from the *princeps* in recognition of acts of valor.

Centurions lit the pyre, and as the flames rose an eagle was released and flew up into the sky, as if bearing Augustus' spirit into the heavens. A former praetor, presumably a man with an eye for the main chance, solemnly swore that he saw the spirit of the *princeps* on its journey upward. Julia Augusta rewarded his sharpness of sight with the huge sum of one million sesterces.

Perfume was thrown onto the fire, as well as things that the dead man would have enjoyed—cups of oil, clothes, and dishes of food. The ghosts of the dead, the *manes,* liked to drink blood, which reinvigorated them; this may have been supplied by gladiators, who were often hired to fight at funerals, their duels lit up by the flames.

When the fire had burned out, wine was poured over the embers. A priest purified those present from the taint of death by sprinkling water over them with a laurel or olive branch. The mourners were then dismissed, each of them saying "*Vale*" as he or she left the scene.

Eventually, only one person was left beside the ashes—Julia Augusta, widow and now daughter of the dead *princeps.* The old lady remained where she was for five days. Then, attended by leading *equites,* who were barefoot and wore unbelted tunics, she collected the bones and lodged them in the mausoleum.

# INTO THE FUTURE

THE FEARS OF THOSE PLANNING THE TRANSITION BETWEEN
Augustus and Tiberius regarding the frontier legions and the late Agrippa
Postumus were not groundless. On the news of the death of the *princeps*,
mutinies broke out on the Rhine and in the Balkans, which Germanicus
and Drusus put down with some difficulty. The mysterious slave, Clemens, stole Agrippa's ashes and then impersonated him, spreading the
rumor that Augustus' grandson was still alive. He was soon captured and
secretly executed. This strange tale only makes sense if we suppose that
the Julian faction, even at this late stage, remained popular among ordinary citizens. But it was the last throw of the dice. The tragedy of the children of Julia and Agrippa was complete.

Making a show of reluctance before the Senate, Tiberius assumed full
powers and authority. Broadly, the new emperor maintained Augustus'
policies. However, the divine family became increasingly dysfunctional.
Livia, or Julia Augusta as she now was, got on badly with her son once he
became emperor. Although he admired her sagacity, he was irritated by
the fact that she was credited with having made him emperor. In A.D. 26,
Tiberius abandoned Rome for Capri off the Bay of Naples, where he spent
the rest of his reign; his mother was probably one of the reasons for his
second and final self-exile.

Germanicus was given a commission in the east, but died in A.D. 19 at the
age of thirty-four, perhaps from poisoning (as usual, Livia was blamed). In
A.D. 23 his contemporary, Tiberius' son Drusus, also died; he may have been
a victim of the emperor's scheming favorite, Lucius Aelius Sejanus, but
more probably of an epidemic raging in Rome that year.

The elder Julia did not long outlive her unforgiving father, dying in
A.D. 14 at Rhegium. Postumus' death removed her last hope of recall. Ac-

cording to Tacitus, Tiberius pitilessly "let her waste away to death, exiled and disgraced, by slow starvation. He calculated that she had been banished for so long that her death would pass unnoticed."

The younger Julia never left her little island in the sun, and died some twenty years after her enraged grandfather had sent her there. Her lover, Silanus, was more fortunate. He was allowed to return to Rome in A.D. 20; Tiberius remarked quizzically that he was gratified that Silanus should return from his "pilgrimage to far lands."

As for Ovid, Tiberius and Livia turned a deaf ear to his pleas for a reprieve. He cultivated the young Germanicus, but to no avail. In A.D. 17 he died among his barbarians at Tomis. He asked that he be buried near his beloved city, Rome, and one can hope, but without much confidence, that this last wish was granted.

Livia died in A.D. 29 at the considerable age of eighty-six. Tiberius outlasted her only by eight years, and expired old and lonely in his island retreat in A.D. 37. He was alleged to have spent his last years engaged in elaborate pedophiliac pursuits.

Germanicus' son Gaius, nicknamed Little Boots, Caligula, by the troops when he was a small child, succeeded to the purple. Although intelligent, Caligula made poor decisions and almost certainly suffered from severe mental illness. Unkind gossip had it that he wanted to make his favorite horse a consul. He played practical jokes on his guards, who eventually lost their sense of humor and assassinated him, in A.D. 41.

For many years Drusus' lame son, Claudius, continued to be ignored. He lived quietly and lazily, moving between a suburban mansion and a villa in the country. Augustus left him the insulting sum of four thousand sesterces in his will, and Tiberius declined to employ him. He divided his time between drinking and gambling with low-life acquaintances, and writing copiously. He published an autobiography, a defense of Cicero, and an authoritative history of the Etruscans.

Claudius was more or less forgotten until brought to court by the emperor Caligula, who treated him as an unpaid clown. When Caligula was assassinated, Praetorian Guardsmen found Claudius hiding behind a curtain in the palace, took him to their camp, and hailed him as emperor. A nervous Senate agreed.

To general surprise, Claudius turned out to be rather a good emperor. He annexed the remote island of Britannia to the Roman empire. Despite the fact that the long dead Livia had made his early life a misery, he generously arranged for her deification.

Claudius had bad luck with his wives. The beautiful and wayward Messalina shared the elder Julia's taste for lively parties in the Forum where she mixed sex with politics. Her cuckolded husband reluctantly put her to death.

Messalina was followed by Germanicus' strong-minded daughter Agrippina, who persuaded Claudius to adopt her son Nero, and in A.D. 54 killed the gourmand emperor with a dish of delicious but poisoned (or perhaps poisonous) mushrooms.

In A.D. 15, Germanicus led an army across the Rhine and visited the battle sites where Varus lost his legions and his life. Tacitus gave an unforgettable description of the eerie scene:

> *On the open ground were whitening bones, scattered where men had fled, heaped up where they had stood and fought back. Fragments of spears and of horses' limbs lay there—also human heads, fastened to tree-trunks. In groves nearby were the outlandish altars at which the Germans had massacred the Roman colonels and senior company-commanders.*

The Romans never again attempted to expand their territory beyond the Rhine, and excitable historians in the nineteenth and twentieth centuries have argued that we owe to the *Variana clades* the millennia-long division of Europe into two parts—one touched by Rome, the other not: Britain and the Romance countries, and the Teutonic peoples of central and northern Europe. If Augustus had had his way and brought the frontier of his empire to the Elbe, there would have been "no Charlemagne, no Louis XIV, no Napoleon, no Kaiser Wilhelm II, and no Hitler."

This binary approach to European history oversimplifies a complicated story. The distance between the Rhine and the Elbe is not so great as to have brought about such dizzying consequences. Also, we must not forget that Roman culture spread its influence far beyond the imperial lands themselves. Rome's true inheritor, the Roman Catholic Church, was able to create a unified Europe that stretched from the Atlantic to the Urals, the culture of Christendom.

That said, the massacre at Kalkriese did mark a turning point in the history of Rome. With a few exceptions, such as the ephemeral conquests of the emperor Trajan in the second century A.D., the empire had more or less reached its natural extent by the death of Augustus. Rome's military and administrative capacity did not allow it to govern a larger territory.

There was much discussion at Rome about the late Augustus' virtues and vices. It was elegantly summarized by Tacitus:

> *Intelligent people praised or criticized him in varying terms. One opinion was as follows. Filial duty and a national emergency, in which there was no place for law-abiding conduct, had driven him to civil war—and this can be neither initiated nor maintained by decent methods. He had made many concessions to Antony and to Lepidus for the sake of vengeance on his father's murderers. When Lepidus grew old and lazy, and Antony's self-indulgence got the better of him, the only possible cure for the distracted country had been government by one man. However, Augustus had put the state in order not by making himself king or dictator, but by creating the Principate. The empire's frontiers were on the ocean, or distant rivers. Armies, provinces, fleets, the whole system was interrelated. Roman citizens were protected by the law. Provincials were decently treated. Rome itself had been lavishly beautified. Force had been sparingly used—merely to preserve peace for the majority.*

According to a second and opposing opinion, "filial duty and national crisis had been merely pretexts. In actual fact, the motive of Octavian, the future Augustus, was lust for power. . . . There had certainly been peace, but it was a blood-stained peace of disasters and assassinations."

Down the centuries, judgments have oscillated between these poles. But opposites do not have to be mutually exclusive, and we are not obliged to choose one or the other. The story of his career shows that Augustus was indeed ruthless, cruel, and ambitious for himself. This was only in part a personal trait, for upper-class Romans were educated to compete with one another and to excel. However, he combined an overriding concern for his personal interests with a deep-seated patriotism, based on a nostalgic idea of Rome's antique virtues. In his capacity as *princeps,* selfishness and selflessness were elided in his mind.

While fighting for dominance, he paid little attention to legality or to the normal civilities of political life. He was devious, untrustworthy, and bloodthirsty. But once he had established his authority, he governed efficiently and justly, generally allowed freedom of speech, and promoted the rule of law. He was immensely hardworking and tried as hard as any democratic parliamentarian to treat his senatorial colleagues with respect and sensitivity. He suffered from no delusions of grandeur.

Augustus lacked the flair of his adoptive father, Julius Caesar, but he possessed one valuable quality to which Caesar could not lay claim: patience. He had the practical common sense of an Italian country gentleman, for it was from that stock that he grew. He made haste slowly, seeking permanent solutions rather than easy answers. He did not revel in power; he sought to understand it. Plutarch has an anecdote that sums up Augustus' approach to his responsibilities. Hearing that Alexander the Great had been at a loss about what to do next after his vast conquests, the *princeps* remarked: "I am surprised the king did not realize that a far harder task than winning an empire is putting it into order once you have won it."

Perhaps the most instructive aspect of Augustus' approach to politics was his twin recognition that in the long run power was unsustainable without consent, and that consent could best be won by associating radical constitutional change with a traditional and moralizing ideology.

And what of the man himself? His public persona, the imperturbably calm young man of the statues, is unrevealing—to borrow Tennyson's phrase, "faultily faultless, icily regular, splendidly null." But luckily some of the ancient literary sources—above all, Suetonius—reveal the *princeps* in undress. Here is someone who loved his sister and spent fifty years happily married to his childless wife. In his personal life, he was not greatly interested in appearances, was a good friend, and had a self-deprecating sense of humor and sound judgment. It is impossible not to warm to the old man who adored his "little donkey" Gaius, and to sense the depth of his tragedy when, in their various ways, his closest relatives turned their backs on him—all except Livia.

The contrast between the splendor of state ceremonial and Rome's restored monumental center, on the one hand, and Augustus' austere lifestyle on the other, was, of course, a conscious policy, which magnified Rome while seeking to counter individual decadence. It would appear, though, that his simple habits had a basis in modest personal tastes.

Of course, there were two sides to Augustus' personality, which looked Janus-like in opposing directions: the affectionate family man was also the ancient lecher; the plain-living Roman built a secret holiday palazzo; loyal to his intimates, he was blind to their excesses and sometimes criminal failings; the loving parent with high expectations sometimes behaved like a demanding bully who insisted on having his own way; the cultivated patron of the arts could be a heartless killer when crossed in politics.

One senses, above all, that the suppression of ordinary human emotions which his public duties demanded of the *princeps* pulled against deep and powerful currents of feeling for those closest to him. This internal struggle may have fueled the fury with which he reacted to betrayals of trust.

But for all his flaws, the balance sheet ends in credit. For the most part, the private man lived decently according to the standards of the time, and the public man did terrible things, but usually for the public good.

It is argued that Augustus was merely the last in a line of unruly, Republic-busting dynasts who came and went throughout the first century B.C. Like a surfer, he rode a wave of change that was already rolling.

There is something in this. If the Actium campaign had had a different outcome, the trend toward autocracy might well have continued unabated. But would the careless and unfocused Antony have been able to build such an enduring edifice? One doubts it.

Augustus once wrote in an edict: "May I achieve the reward to which I aspire . . . of carrying with me, when I die, the hope that these foundations I have established for the state will abide secure." His hope was fulfilled. Of all Rome's emperors, he reigned the longest; and his work lasted, with modifications, for many generations. His successors all called themselves Augustus and cited his example (however differently they in fact behaved). State institutions continued to evolve in ways he did not predict, but in the main along the lines he set down.

Augustus devoted his long reign to perfecting and implementing two core policies—constitutional reform, and imperial expansion under one-man rule. But no less important was his management of the provinces. Working with his friend and partner, Agrippa, he spent many years touring the empire. He disciplined, if he did not entirely eliminate, the rapacity of imperial proconsuls; he encouraged urbanization and the Roman way of life; and he extended Roman citizenship to many thousands of provincials throughout the empire.

This had a hugely important consequence. It generated loyalty and gratitude to Rome. It made people feel that they were not victims of the empire, but its stakeholders. They were members of an imperial commonwealth. It was this shared consciousness that helped to bind Europe and the lands of the Mediterranean basin together for half a millennium and more.

How many statesmen in human history can lay claim to such a record of enduring achievement?

# ACKNOWLEDGMENTS

I AM GREATLY INDEBTED TO MY WISE AND INDEFATIGABLE editors, Will Murphy of Random House and, for the United Kingdom edition, Ed Faulkner of John Murray (publisher). As ever, I have enjoyed the unstinting support of my literary agent, Christopher Sinclair-Stevenson. Professor Robert W. Cape, Jr., of Austin College, Texas, was kind enough to comment most helpfully on a draft. But for all the guidance and advice I have received, I alone am responsible for any errors.

A generous grant from the Authors' Foundation enabled me to visit places associated with Augustus' career. I am most grateful to Dr. Irene Jacopi, director of the Palatine Hill and the Roman Forum, and architect Giovanna Tedone, both of the Soprintendenza per i beni archeologici di Roma, for taking the trouble to show me around the houses of Augustus and Livia (closed to the public for restoration).

The London Library, its helpful staff and its wide collection, greatly assisted my researches.

I am grateful to the following copyright-holders for reproduction permissions: Roman Forum reconstruction by John Connolly, akg-images; Palatine Hill, Photo Scala, Florence; Julius Caesar, Staatliche Museen zu Berlin; Mark Antony at Kingston Lacy, Bankes Collection, the National Trust; Sextus Pompeius, Hermitage Museum, Saint Petersburg; a Roman warship at the Gregorio Profano Museum, the Vatican Museums; watercolor of Alexandria by J-P Golvin, George Braziller, Inc.; Cleopatra, Staatliche Museen zu Berlin; Octavia, Museo Nazionale Romano, Roma; Livia, Musei Capitolini, Roma, author's photograph; Augustus, trustees of the British Museum; Agrippa, Musée du Louvre; Ara Pacis at Rome, Alinari; Tiberius at the museum of Ventotene, author's photograph; Gaius Caesar, trustees of the British Museum; Agrippa Postumus, Musei Capitolini, author's photograph; Gemma Augustea, Kunsthistorisches

Museum, Wien oder KHM, Vienna; Room of the Masks, Photo Scala, Florence; Augustus of Prima Porta, Alinari.

When quoting from Roman poets, I have used the following translations: James Michie's *Odes* of Horace (Penguin Books, 1964: copyright David Higham Associates); Niall Rudd's *Satires and Epistles* of Horace (Penguin Books, 1979); Peter Green's versions of Ovid, *Erotic Poems* (Penguin Books, 1964) and *Poems of Exile* (Penguin Books, 1994: copyright David Higham Associates); Cecil Day Lewis's *Aeneid* by Virgil (Oxford University Press, 1952); and E. V. Rieu's *Eclogues* by Virgil (Penguin Books, 1949). I have used John Carter's translations of Appian, *The Civil Wars*, and Cassius Dio, *The Age of Augustus* (Penguin Books, 1996 and 1987); D. R. Shackleton Bailey's translation of Cicero's letters (Penguin Books, 1978); Aubrey de Sélincourt's *Livy: The Early History of Rome*; Propertius' *The Poems*, translated by W. G. Shepherd (Penguin Books, 1985: copyright University of Oklahoma Press); Ian Scott-Kilvert's selection from Plutarch, *Makers of Rome* (Penguin Books, 1965); Rex Warner's selection from Plutarch, *Fall of the Roman Republic* (Penguin Books, 1958); Robert Graves's version of Suetonius, revised by Michael Grant, *The Twelve Caesars* (Penguin Books, 1979); and Michael Grant's translation of Tacitus' Annals, *On Imperial Rome* (Penguin Books, 1956). On occasion and for other prose authors I have either depended on the Loeb Classical Library or translated passages myself. The quotation from "Alexandrian Kings" can be found in C. P. Cavafy's *Collected Poems*, translated by Edmund Keeley and Philip Sherrard (The Hogarth Press, 1975).

The battle maps follow Johannes Kromayer and Georg Veith, *Heerwesen und Kriegführung der Griechen und Römer*, Munich, 1928.

# NOTES

## ABBREVIATIONS

Full publication data for modern works appears in the Sources section.

| | |
|---|---|
| Aesch Prom | Aeschylus, *Prometheus Unbound* |
| App | Appian, *Civil Wars* |
| Res Gest | Augustus, *Res Gestae* |
| Barrett | Anthony A. Barrett, *Livia* |
| Aul Gell | Aulus Gellius, *Noctes Atticae* |
| Caes Gall | Julius Caesar, *Commentaries on the Gallic War* |
| Carcopino | Jérôme Carcopino, *Daily Life in Ancient Rome* |
| Carter | J. M. Carter, *The Battle of Actium* |
| CAH | *Cambridge Ancient History, vol. 10* |
| Old CAH | *Cambridge Ancient History* (1923–1939), *vol. 10* |
| Castle | E. B. Castle, *Ancient Education and Today* |
| Dio | Cassius Dio, *Roman History* |
| Celsus | Celsus, *De Medicina* |
| Cic Att | Cicero, *Letters to Atticus* |
| Cic Brut | Cicero, *Letters to Brutus* |
| Cic De Or | Cicero, *De Oratore* |
| Cic Fam | Cicero, *Letters to His Friends* [*ad Familiares*] |
| Cic Phil | Cicero, *Philippics* |
| Connolly and Dodge | Peter Connolly and Hazel Dodge, *The Ancient City, Life in Classical Athens and Rome* |
| CIL | *Corpus Inscriptionum Latinarum* |
| Dupont | Florence Dupont, *Daily Life in Ancient Rome* |
| Florus | Florus, *Epitome of Roman History* |
| Fuller | J.F.C. Fuller, *The Decisive Battles of the Ancient World and Their Influence on History* |
| Grant Cleo | Michael Grant, *Cleopatra* |

| | |
|---|---|
| Grant Glad | Michael Grant, *Gladiators: The Bloody Truth* |
| Green | Peter Green, *From Alexander to Actium* |
| Green Erot | Peter Green (trans.), Ovid, *The Erotic Poems* |
| Hom Il | Homer, *Iliad* |
| Hom Od | Homer, *Odyssey* |
| van Hoof | Anton van Hoof, *Autothanasia to Suicide: Self-killing in Classical Antiquity* |
| Hor Cent | Horace, *Centennial Hymn* |
| Hor Ep | Horace, *Epistles* |
| Hor Odes | Horace, *Odes* |
| Hor Sat | Horace, *Satires* |
| ILS | *Inscriptiones Latinae Selectae*, ed. H. Dessau |
| Jackson | Ralph Jackson, *Doctors and Diseases in the Roman Empire* |
| Jos Ant | Josephus, *Antiquities* |
| Levick | Barbara Levick, *Tiberius the Politician* |
| Livy Per | Livy, *Periochae* |
| Livy | Livy, *Preface* |
| Macr | Macrobius, *Saturnalia* |
| Mart | Martial, *Epigrams* |
| Meijer | Fik Meijer, *The Gladiators* |
| Men Double | Menander, *The Double Deceiver* |
| Nic | Nicolaus, *Life of Augustus* |
| Ovid Am | Ovid, *Amores* |
| Ovid Ars Am | Ovid, *Ars Amatoria* |
| Ovid Pont | Ovid, *Epistulae ex Ponto* |
| Ovid Trist | Ovid, *Tristia* |
| Pliny | Pliny, *Naturalis Historia* |
| Plut Apo reg et imp | Plutarch, *Moralia, Apophthegmata regum et imperatorum* |
| Plut Aem Pau | Plutarch, *Aemilius Paullus* |
| Plut Ant Comp | Plutarch, *Antony and Demetrius Comparison* |
| Plut Brut | Plutarch, *Brutus* |
| Plut Cat Maj | Plutarch, *Cato the Elder* [Cato Major] |
| Plut Cat Min | Plutarch, *Cato the Younger* [Cato Minor] |
| Plut Cic | Plutarch, *Cicero* |
| Plut Ant | Plutarch, *Mark Antony* |
| Plut T & C Grac | Plutarch, *Tiberius and Caius Gracchus* |
| Plut Pomp | Plutarch, *Pompey the Great* |
| Powell/Welch | A. Powell and K. Welch, eds., *Sextus Pompeius* |
| Prop | Propertius, *Carmina* |

| | |
|---|---|
| Quint Inst Or | Quintilian, *Institutio Oratoria* |
| Sall Bell Cat | Sallust, *Bellum Catilinae* |
| Sen Contr 10 Praef | Seneca the Elder, *Controversiae 10 Praefatio* |
| Sen Suas | Seneca the Elder, *Suasoriae* |
| Sen Ep | Seneca the Younger, *Epistles* |
| Sen Clem | Seneca the Younger, *De Clementia* |
| Serv Ad Aen | Servius, *Ad Aeneidem* |
| Stambaugh | John E. Stambaugh, *The Ancient Roman City* |
| Strabo | Strabo, *Geography* |
| Suet Aug | Suetonius, *Life of Augustus* |
| Suet Clau | ————, *Life of Claudius* |
| Suet De Vir Ill | ————, *On Famous Men* |
| Suet Gaius | ————, *Life of Gaius* |
| Suet Galb | ————, *Life of Galba* |
| Suet Caes | ————, *Life of Julius Caesar* |
| Suet Nero | ————, *Life of Nero* |
| Suet Tib | ————, *Life of Tiberius* |
| Syme AA | Ronald Syme, *The Augustan Aristocracy* |
| Syme RR | Ronald Syme, *The Roman Revolution* |
| Tac Ann | Tacitus, *Annals* |
| Tac Dial | Tacitus, *Dialogus de Oratoribus* |
| Val Max | Valerius Maximus, *Memorable Doings and Sayings* |
| Varro | Varro, *Res Rusticae* |
| Vell Pat | Velleius Paterculus, *History of Rome* |
| Virg Aen | Virgil, *Aeneid* |
| Virg Ecl | Virgil, *Eclogues* |
| Virg Geo | Virgil, *Georgics* |

## PREFACE

xii  *"most events began"* Dio 53 19 3.

## INTRODUCTION

The introduction is an imagined narration of Augustus' death. I take as my premise the proposition that the sometimes extraordinary stories told by the ancient sources are broadly correct, and attempt as satisfactory an explanation as possible. My central assumption is that the regime was, overwhelmingly and rightly, determined to effect as painless a transition as possible from Augustus to his successor. I note that the regime's obsession with maintaining its power was accompanied by an undeviating patriotism and a willingness to sacrifice personal interests. Although there are problems and implausibilities with the stories, the explanation I offer is, just about, credible. This is how it might have happened. I use Suetonius' *Life of Augustus,* especially chapters 97 to 100; Tacitus 1 5, 6; Dio 56 29–30; Velleius 2 102, 123.

xxxiv  *"Poor Rome"*  Suet Tib 21 2.

## I. SCENES FROM A PROVINCIAL CHILDHOOD

The main ancient sources for this chapter are Suetonius and Nicolaus. The stories classical writers tell of the childhood of famous men are unreliable. That of Augustus is no exception. Children were of little intrinsic interest to Roman adults and their doings were seldom recorded, so historians devised fictional beginnings appropriate to their subjects' later lives and propaganda needs. I have tried to weed out obviously legendary material (to which I return when dealing with the period when it was probably invented). Nicolaus knew Augustus, who may have been the source of the more day-to-day events of his early life.

4   *"coin-stained hands"*  Suet Aug 4 2.
5   *"came from a rich old equestrian family"*  Ibid., 2 3.
9   *bad prognosis*  This story, told with circumstantial detail in Dio 45 1, may be a later invention by historians and biographers wishing to create an appropriately interesting childhood for Augustus.
9   *"a small room"*  Suet Aug 6.
9   *"a dignified person"*  Vell Pat 2 59 2.
10   *"a talking instrument"*  Varro 1 17.
11   *"I can prove"*  Suet Aug 7 1.
11   *"justly and courageously"*  Ibid., 3 2.
11   *many health hazards*  This paragraph draws on Jackson, especially pp. 37, 42–43, 46.
12   *by his maternal grandmother*  Nic 3.
13   *Atia won a reputation*  Ibid.
14   *"We must apply to our fellow-countrymen"*  Cic De Or 3 137.
14   *"There was not a great difference"*  Castle, p. 129.
14   *"a good man skilled in speech"*  Quint Inst Or 12 1.

14   *"humble origin"* Suet Gaius 23 1.

14   *He may have come from Venetia* Syme AA p. 44.

15   *According to Aulus Gellius* Aul Gell 16 16 1–4.

15   *born in this perilous manner* Pliny 7 45.

## II. THE GREAT-UNCLE

Most of the personal characteristics I ascribe to Julius Caesar, Pompey, Crassus, Cato, and Mark Antony are drawn from the accounts given in Plutarch and Suetonius. Again Nicolaus is useful. Caesar's own history of the civil war is accurate but self-serving. Appian is valuable.

18   *"From now onward"* Vell Pat 2 3 3.

19   *optimates* I use the English form, for the Latin word can only be used in the plural.

20   *"His dress was"* Suet Caes 45 3.

21   *"It was really very difficult"* Plut Cat Min 1 2.

21   *"That cannot be true"* Ibid., 19 4.

21   *"Caesar was the only sober man"* Suet Caes 53.

25   *"in common with Antony's"* Plut Ant 2 5.

25   *"provoked by the sight of her"* App 5 8.

25   *"for he often helped others"* Plut Ant 4 3.

26   *they quietly sent Gaius* Nic 4.

26   *"Let the dice fly high!"* Plut Pomp 60 2.

26   *"the new style of conquest"* Cic Att 174c (9 7c).

28   *"He does not know"* Suet Caes 36.

## III. A POLITICAL MASTER CLASS

Nicolaus remains a source for anecdotes about Gaius. Plutarch's and Suetonius' lives of Caesar throw light on Caesar's activities, as do Appian and the commentaries on the Alexandrian war and the African war, written by Caesarian supporters. Plutarch's life of Cato recounts his suicide. Here and elsewhere I am indebted to Michael Grant's *Cleopatra*.

29   *"I shall have the whole Senatorial"* Dio 45 2 5–6.

31   *"with body and limbs"* Suet Aug 79 2.

32   *"He attracted many women"* Nic 4.

32   *"he was of age"* Ibid.

32   *"The year/Drags for orphan boys"* Hor Ep 1 1 21–22.

32   *Alexander the Great's Macedonian commanders* For more on Alexander, see Green, Peter, *Alexander of Macedon* (London: Penguin, 1974), and on his successors the same author's *Alexander to Actium* (London: Thames and Hudson, 1990).

33   *"this little trick"* Plut Caes 49 2.

34   *"As far as they say"* Plut Ant 27 2–3.

34   *"Many rulers of Egypt"* Plut Ant 27 3–4.

35   *"enjoyed himself"* App 2 90. Some modern historians discount the historicity of this jaunt, largely on the grounds that Caesar would not be so irresponsible. However, one of the features of his character was an arrogant carelessness. Also, Appian says that he provides more detail (now sadly lost) of this adventure in his Egyptian history, from which it is reasonable to assume that the journey was well attested.

36   *"for a sight of the boy"* Nic 4.

36   *"he might bring on illness"* Ibid., 6.

37   *attitude toward suicide* This section is indebted to van Hoof.

37   *"had hard work to withstand"* Caes Gall 6 1.

38   *"take any cruel action"* Dio 43 15 2.

38   *"The Republic is nothing"* Suet Caes 77.

# IV. UNFINISHED BUSINESS

Appian and Dio provide the basic historical narrative, Nicolaus, Plutarch, and Suetonius color and anecdote.

40   *On the day of the triumph* Some generic details are taken from Plutarch's description of Aemilius Paullus' triumph (Plut Aem Pau 32–35).

41   *The most popular attraction* This section is indebted to Carcopino, Grant Glad, and Meijer.

43   *"He took care"* Nic 8.

45   *"according to my uncle's instructions"* Ibid., 10.

46   *"I have often fought"* Plut Caes 56 3.

47   *"He made a point"* Nic 11.

48   *"nothing womanly about her"* Vell Pat 2 74 2.

49   *It is probable that Octavius* When Nicolaus reports that he asked for, and received, permission to go home and see his mother, he does

not make it clear where Octavius was at the time of the request. It would make more sense if he was at Labici than en route to Italy (otherwise, why would he have asked leave to go to his journey's obvious destination?).

49 *"sexual gratification"* Nic 15.

49 *"should sail"* Celsus 1 1 1. It is worth noting that in later life, Octavius lived abstemiously, a habit that may well have been developed in his youth.

## V. A BOY WITH A NAME

Nicolaus gives most information about Octavian's stay at Apollonia and his return to Italy. He, Plutarch, and Suetonius give accounts of the Ides of March.

51 *"great and important city"* Cic Phil 11 26.

52 *"You must show yourself"* Nic 16.

53 *another letter from Atia* The implication when App 3 9–10 and Nic 16 are compared suggests that Atia wrote with the immediate news and then followed up with a second letter from her and Philippus; but the references could be to the same letter.

55 *knew that the assassination* Plut Ant 13 1.

55 *"Why, this is violence!"* Suet Caes 82 1.

55 *like a wild animal* App 2 117.

57 *"already had his eyes"* Nic 18.

59 *"followers call him Caesar"* Cic Att 366 (14 12).

60 *major eruption* R. Stothers, 2002: "Cloudy and Clear Stratospheres Before A.D. 1000 Inferred from Written Sources," *J. Geophysical Research,* Vol. 107, No. D23.

60 *"wars that grow in the dark"* Virg Geo 464–68.

60 *stars could be seen* Pliny 2 27 98.

60 *"everything to his name"* Cic Phil 13 11 25.

61 *"Heap as many insults"* App 3 28.

62 *"Could anything be"* Cic Att 388 15 10.

62 *"Octavian . . . does not lack"* Ibid., 390 15 12.

62 *"On the very day"* Pliny 2 23 93–94. Octavian wrote his autobiography, now lost, in 25 B.C. The discussion of the games is indebted to J. Ramsey and A. Lewis Licht, *The Comet of 44 B.C. and Caesar's Funeral Games* (Atlanta: Scholars Press, 1997), pp. 236f.

63  *"Mad with anger"* This paragraph and the following, including the quotations, are drawn from App 3 39.

## VI. FROM VICTORY, DEFEAT

Appian's and Cicero's speeches against Antony, the Philippics, are the best sources. Dio also covers the subject.

65  *"You will learn"* App 3 43.

66  *"He is very much a boy"* Cic Att 420 (16 11).

66  *"a blowout"* Cic Phil 3 8 20.

67  *"If your are successful"* Macr 23 12.

67  *"The Ides of March was a fine deed"* Cic Att 366 (14 12).

68  *"Gaius Caesar is a young man"* Cic Phil, 3 2 3.

68  *"this heaven-sent youth"* Ibid., 5 16 43.

68  *"I promise, I undertake"* Ibid., 18 51.

69  *"praised, honoured—and raised up"* Cic Fam 401 11 20.

71  *"He reflected on the way"* App 3 64.

71  *In the first week or so of April* My description seeks to reconcile differences among the sources—App 3 66–72, Cic Fam 378 10 30, and Dio 37–38.

72  *"they put the survivors"* App 3 70.

72  *"He did not reappear"* Suet Aug 10 4.

73  *"Though bleeding and wounded"* Ibid., 10 4.

73  *"It is quite incredible"* Cic Brut 12 2 (1 6 2).

74  *"Nature forbids me"* App 3 73.

74  *"I have given plenty of hints"* Ibid., 3 80.

74  *"this abominable war"* Cic Fam 384 10 14.

76  *"spineless readiness to serve"* App 3 92.

76  *twelve vultures* It can be argued that this story is a fiction put about by Octavian's propagandists. It seems unlikely, though, that such a public event was invented when thousands of Romans could give it the lie.

## VII. KILLING FIELDS

Appian provides a detailed narrative, and Dio also covers this period. Plutarch and Suetonius evoke the impact of Philippi on individuals. The discussion of Sextus Pompeius is indebted to *Sextus Pompeius,* Anton Powell and Kathryn Welch, eds.

79  *"he carried it out more ruthlessly"* Suet Aug 27 1.

80  *he let his own uncle* Plut Ant Comp 5 1.

80  *"Many people were murdered"* App 4 13.

81  *One tragic tale* Ibid., 4 30.

81  *A funerary inscription* Laudatio Turiae, ILS.

81  *"You provided abundantly"* Ibid., 2a.

81  *A year later* That is, after the battle of Philippi.

82  *"That matter was soon"* Laudatio Turiae II, ILS.

82  *"I did not take my father's line"* Suet Aug 70 2.

83  *still a very young man* App 5 133. For Sextus' age, see Powell/Welch, pp. 105–6.

83  *"Whoever makes his journey"* Quoted, from an unidentified play, by App 2 85.

84  *"With his greater mobility"* Ibid., 4 83.

85  *"His small boats"* Ibid., 4 36.

86  *"for the sake of ensuring harmony"* Vell Pat 2 62 3.

88  *According to Agrippa and Maecenas* Pliny 7 45.

89  *"[Octavian] heard of the situation"* Dio 47 37.

90  *"fog of war"* The phrase originated in the Napoleonic Wars and referred to the clouds of smoke produced by black gunpowder. The Prussian military thinker Karl von Clausewitz used the term to refer to the difficulty of getting reliable information, even of the most basic sort, during a war.

90  *"returned looking more like porters"* App 4 112.

91  *"Tell him I wish him"* Ibid.

91  *"gave orders"* Val Max 1 7 1.

91  *spent three days skulking* Pliny 7 148.

92  *"Some committed suicide"* App 4 115–16. Perhaps a generic description.

92  *"like women, inactive and afraid"* Ibid., 4 123.

93  *"as though they were tipping over"* Ibid., 4 128.

93  *"O wretched valour"* Dio 47 49 2.

93  *"Yes, that's right, but with our hands"* Plut Brut 52 3.

94  *"a singularly gentle nature"* Ibid., 29 3.

94  *"That's a matter for the carrion birds"* Suet Aug 13 2.

96  *Gnaeus Domitius Ahenobarbus* He is the Enobarbus of Shakespeare's *Antony and Cleopatra.*

96  *"We two once beat a swift retreat"* Hor Odes 2 7. Some have argued that leaving one's shield on a battlefield was a familiar literary device.

Maybe, but it must often have happened in real life. There is no reason to disbelieve the often autobiographical poet.


## VIII. DIVIDED WORLD

Appian and Dio are the main sources. Plutarch's life of Mark Antony is important, especially his famous account of Antony and Cleopatra's meeting at Tarsus.

98   *"People came in groups"* App 5 12.

98   *"From what other source"* Dio 48 8.

99   *"He learned from actual experience"* Ibid.

99   *"They came very near to killing"* Ibid., 48 9.

99   *"The civilian population"* App 5 18.

100   *"entirely clearing pirates"* Plut Pomp 26 4.

101   *"To most people"* Plut Ant 24 4.

101   *"circus-rider of the civil wars"* Sen Suas 1 7.

101   *"[She] was in a barge"* Plut Ant 26 1–2.

102   *"for the happiness of Asia"* Ibid., 26 3.

102   *"the soldier rather than the courtier"* Ibid., 27 1.

103   *"had earnestly devoted himself"* Dio 48 27 2.

103   *"And why should anyone"* Ibid., 48 10 4.

104   *surprised by a sudden sortie* Suet Aug 14.

104   *"I seek Fulvia's clitoris"* For these messages, see CIL 11 2.1 1901.

104   *"[Octavian] took vengeance"* Suet Aug 15.

105   *"our fatherland's Perusian graves"* Prop 1 22 3–4.

107   *"Because Antony fucks Glaphyra"* Mart 11 20.

107   *Octavian was accused of loose living* For the anecdotes that follow, see Suet Aug 68–70.

108   *"Look how the queen's finger beats the drum!"* Ibid., 68.

109   *"aggravated her illness deliberately"* App 5 59.

112   *"deeply attached to his sister"* Plut Ant 31 1.

112   *"in military and Roman fashion"* Dio 48 30 1.

113   *"Antony did not win general approval"* App 5 65.


## IX. GOLDEN AGE

Appian and Dio are the main sources, with material from Suetonius. Plutarch's life of Antony describes the encounter at Misenum in some detail.

Two of Virgil's eclogues and passages in the *Georgics* cast light on the political scene.

114  *"He was tall"* Suet De Vir Ill, Life of Virgil 8–11.

115  *"The Firstborn"* Virg Ecl 4 7–10.

115  *about to leave politics* It is possible that the poem was written a year earlier, in 41 B.C., before Pollio's consulship in 40 B.C.

115  *"For my part"* Macr 2 4 21.

116  *As soon as the crowd* For this account, see App 5 68.

118  *"My only ancestral home"* Plut Ant 32 3.

119  *"Shall I cut the cables"* Ibid., 32 4–5.

119  *gravis femina* Sen Ep 8 70.

120  *"I couldn't bear the way"* Suet Aug 62 2.

120  *"friendship gone mad"* Sen Ep 1 9.

121  *the sex of her child* Suet Tib 14 2, Pliny 10 75 154–5.

121  *Livia and the baby* Suet Tib 6 2.

123  *"What are you doing"* Dio 48 44 3.

123  *"How fortunate"* Suet Clau 1 1.

123  *The Roman marriage ceremony* I am indebted to Carcopino, pp. 87–88, and to Smith, p. 252, for my account of Livia's wedding.

124  *an eagle flew by* Suet Galb 1.

125  *White Poultry* Ad Gallinas Albas was rediscovered at Prima Porta outside Rome in the nineteenth century. Extensive ruins of the villa remain, although they are not open to the public. See *La villa di Livia a Prima Porta* (Rome, 1984), published by Messineo with co-author Carmelo Calci in the series *Lavori e studi di archeologia, pubblicati dalla soprintendenza archeologica di Roma.*

## X. FIGHTING NEPTUNE

This chapter depends mainly on Appian's militarily astute account of the Sicilian war in Book 5 of his *Civil Wars*, with some support from Dio and anecdotes from Suetonius.

128  *"At daybreak, as he looked out"* App 5 88.

130  *According to Homer* Hom Od 12 86ff.

130  *"as broad as a wagon road"* Strabo 5 4 5.

131  *"If the worst"* Plut Ant 35.

132  *"Come and see me"* Hor Ep 1 4 15–16.

132  *"Of small build"* Ibid., 1 20.

132    *"If I don't love you"*  Suet De Vir Ill (Life of Horace).

132    *a lighthearted poem*  The section that follows is based on Hor Sat 1 5.

132    *"second Rome"*  Cic Phil 12 3 7.

132    *"for ball-games"*  Hor Sat 1 5 49.

133    *"Here, like an utter fool"*  Ibid., 1 5 82–85.

135    *"I will win this war"*  Suet Aug 16 2.

135    *"He took a beating"*  Ibid., 70 2.

136    *"to steal over"*  App 5 109.

138    *believing he was about to be captured*  Pliny 7 147–49.

138    *"terribly distressed"*  Dio 49 5 4.

139    *"On the eve of the battle"*  Suet Aug 16 2.

140    *"bringing with him"*  Vell Pat 2 80 3.

140    *"was hit on the breastplate"*  App 5 125.

141    *"You will when you're dead"*  Ibid.

142    *. . . Antony's approval*  Ibid., 5 144.


## XI. PARTHIAN SHOTS

Appian and Dio are complemented by Plutarch, who in his life of Mark
Antony covers the Parthian expedition in detail.

144    *tribunicia sacrosanctitas*  There is confusion in the sources. Appian
wrongly says Octavian became tribune for life, whereas Dio asserts
simply *sacrosanctitas*. Dio gives two separate dates when Octavian was
given full tribunician power or *potestas,* 30 and 23; he may not have
accepted the offer on the first occasion, or perhaps only certain
powers. He first used *potestas* in 23.

147    *"jealous of [Ventidius]"*  Dio 49 21 1.

148    *nobody saw anything especially scandalous*  When Plut Ant 36 2 speaks of
"deep resentment among the Romans," this almost certainly reflects later propaganda about Cleopatra's evil influence over Antony.

149    *expelled a man from the Senate*  Plut Cat 17 7.

149    *"When your organ is stiff"*  Hor Sat 1 2 116ff.

149    *Horace had his bedroom:*  Suet De Vir Ill (Life of Horace).

149    *"every woman's man"*  Suet Caes 52 3.

151    *he prepared for suicide*  Florus 2 20 10.

151    *"greeted him"*  Plut Ant 43 1.

153    *"truly noble devotion"*  Ibid., 54 2.

## XII. EAST IS EAST AND WEST IS WEST

Dio's and Appian's histories of the Illyrian wars cover Augustus' campaigning. Dio's and Plutarch's lives of Mark Antony describe the Donations of Alexandria. Strabo provides topographical information.

154   *"considered to be the bravest"*  Dio 49 36 3.

156   *one leg and both arms*  Suet Aug 20.

156   *"beauty of person"*  Florus 2 23; Florus (c. A.D. 70 to c. A.D. 140) wrote a history of Rome based on Livy.

157   *Armenia was turned into a Roman province*  Within a couple of years the political situation went into reverse, and both Armenia and Media returned to the Parthian fold.

158   *"He had no complaint"*  Dio 49 36 1.

160   *Antony issued a coin*  See Grant, Cleo, p. 169.

161   *"give judgement on the Capitol"*  Dio 50 5 4.

162   *"And the Alexandrians thronged"*  C. P. Cavafy, "Alexandrian Kings." In Edmund Keeley and Philip Sherrard, trans., *Collected Poems* (London: The Hogarth Press, 1975).

## XIII. THE PHONY WAR

For the city of Rome, see Stambaugh, Dupont, and Connolly & Dodge. Dio, and Plutarch's life of Mark Antony, with support from Suetonius, are the main narrative sources.

164   *Near it stood a hut*  The bases together with post holes of three huts were recorded during excavations of this part of the Palatine in 1907. They can be dated to the eighth century B.C., about the time of the legendary foundation of the city.

166   *Agrippa took up the post of aedile*  For his activities, see Dio 49 42.

167   *"failed to conduct himself"*  Suet Aug 17 1.

167   *The Triumvirate's second term*  There is some dispute about the timing of triumviral terms. Appian says that the Triumvirate was due to expire at the end of 32 B.C. However, some argue that that would imply an unevidenced break at the end of 37 B.C. for one year. Augustus claims in *Res Gestae* an unbroken ten years as triumvir. On balance, the end of 33 B.C. seems the most likely date.

168   *"a madman"*  Suet Aug 86 3.

168   *"What's come over you?"*  Ibid., 69 2. I follow Michael Grant's opinion that

"*uxor mea est*" is the question "Is she my wife?," not the statement "She is my wife." See Grant Cleo, pp. 185–86. Some scholars believe that in 37 or perhaps 33 Antony agreed to become Cleopatra's prince consort. As I write (pp. 156–57), this is unlikely.

169  *"Your soldiers have no claim"*  Plut Ant 55 2.

170  *"Domitius and Sosius"*  Dio 49 41 4.

171  *"himself with a bodyguard"*  Ibid., 50 5–6.

171  *"As they did not dare"*  Ibid., 50 2 5–6.

# XIV. SHOWDOWN

Dio's and Plutarch's lives of Antony are the main sources. Carter gives the authoritative modern account of Actium.

172  *the path to success*  Jos Ant 15 [6, 6] 191.

173  *a kind of personal plebiscite*  The chronology is uncertain. I follow Syme RR, pp. 284ff.

173  *"The whole of Italy"*  Res Gest 25.

174  *lodged his will with the Vestal Virgins*  Some argue (for example, Grant Cleo, p. 193) that Antony would not be so stupid as to do this and that the document was a forgery. I disagree. Was Julius Caesar being stupid when he did the same thing before his planned departure for the east? There was a general assumption that people would play by the rules and avoid sacrilege.

174  *Octavian read through the document in private*  If the will was forged, or at least those parts of it that Octavian made public, why are there no reports of a rebuttal by Antony or his supporters?

175  *"extraordinary and intolerable"*  Plut Ant 58 4.

175  *the promontory of Actium*  My treatment of the battle of Actium, which follows, is indebted to John M. Carter's *The Battle of Actium,* an authoritative account. The ancient writers often describe accurately enough what took place, but without understanding why, and leaving out important incidents that have to be inferred. Nevertheless the broad outline of the battle is clear enough.

177  *"My services to Antony"*  Vell Pat 2 86 4.

178  *"What is so terrible"*  Plut Ant 62 3.

179  *"press-ganging travellers"*  Ibid., 62 1.

180  *"Antony, although he was deeply grieved"*  Ibid., 63 2–3.

183  *"The fighting took on"*  Ibid., 66 2.

## XV. A LONG FAREWELL

Plutarch's life of Antony is the main source for Antony's and Cleopatra's last days, supported by Dio. Peter Green's *From Alexander to Actium* gives background on Hellenistic culture and Ptolemaic Egypt.

186    *"all the solitude he could desire"*  Plut Ant 69 1.

186    *"A young man"*  Vell Pat 2 88 1.

187    *"actually kill"*  Dio 51 6.

187    *his seal ring*  This ring was later replaced by one with the head of Alexander the Great. His last seal ring showed Augustus' head and was used by his successors.

188    *his fifty-fourth year*  Three years have been proposed for the date of Antony's birth: 86, 83, and 81. I assume 83, the most popular date among modern scholars.

188    *"Cleopatra and Antony now dissolved"*  Plut Ant 71 3.

190    *"There are many different ways"*  Ibid., 75 1.

190    *"about the hour of midnight"*  Ibid., 75 3–4.

191    *"clinging with both hands"*  Ibid., 77 3.

192    *"greatest emporium"*  Strabo 17 1 13.

193    *"No Latin ruler"*  Ernle Bradford, *Cleopatra* (London: Hodder & Stoughton, 1971), p. 49.

194    *"she had abandoned"*  Plut Ant 83 1.

194    *"by no means insensible"*  Ibid., 84 1.

194    *"So here it is":*  Ibid., 86 1.

194    *"lying dead upon a golden couch"*  Ibid., 85 3–4.

195    *"no one knows clearly"*  Dio 51 14 1. For a helpful discussion of asp bites, see *Sunday Times* of London article, "Cleopatra and the Asp" by Richard Girling. November 28, 2004. www.timesonline.co.uk/article/0,,2099-1362193,00.html.

195    *It is possible*  For this theory, see W. R. Johnson, *Arion* (Boston: Boston University Press, 1967), p. 393 n. 16.

195    *he was no looter*  Suet Aug 71 1.

196    *"Would you now like"*  Ibid., 18 2.

196    *Julius Caesar was accused*  Green, p. 667 n. 151.

197    *"indiscreet talk when drunk"*  Ovid Trist 2 446.

197    *"I am the only man in Rome"*  Suet Aug 66 2.

197    *having sexual intercourse*  Pliny 7 184.

198    *a bridge over the stream*  See L. A. Holland, *Janus and the Bridge,* Papers and Monographs, American Academy in Rome. 21, 1961.

## XVI. ABDICATION

The quality of the ancient literary sources now declines sharply, and many episodes are only known about in general and partial terms. Sometimes years pass without explicit incident. This chapter draws on Suetonius, Velleius Paterculus, and (above all) Dio Cassius. The archaeological record is of considerable but occasional assistance. The description of the Palatine is indebted to the official guidebook, *The Palatine* (Milan: Ministero per i Beni e le Attività Culturali, Soprintendenza Archeologica di Roma, pub. Electa, 1998).

199  *"Wars, both civil and foreign"*  Res Gest 1 3.

200  *"Plotting destruction to"*  Hor Odes 1 37 6–12.

200  *"High up on the poop"*  Virgil Aen 8 678–81.

202  *"Atia's [his mother's] emphatic declaration"*  Dio 45 1 2–5; also the source for other episodes in this section.

202  *"Romans, you shall have an end"*  Plut Cic 44 3.

203  *"cheerful in mind and disposition"*  Vell Pat 2 93 2.

204  *minimum ages of officeholders*  See Syme RR, p. 369.

204  *physical incompatibility*  Pliny 7 57.

204  *"more a rustic at heart"*  Ibid., 35 26.

204  *a collector on a grand scale*  Ibid., 35 26 and 34 62.

204  *"outdo a woman"*  Vell Pat 2 88 2.

204  *heated swimming pool*  Dio 55 7 6.

205  *"Goodbye, my ebony of Medullia"*  Macr 2 4.

205  *"was . . . well-disciplined"*  Vell Pat 2 79 1.

207  *is said to have worn a sword*  Suet Aug 35 1–2.

208  *"I lay down my office"*  Dio 53 4 3–4.

208  *presumably with proconsular authority*  There has been much scholarly debate about the nature of Octavian's powers. Some say that they were proconsular (cf. Pompey's governorship of Spain in the fifties B.C.), others that his *imperium* as consul was sufficient. The difficulty with the latter explanation is that a consul's *imperium* lasted only one year. Even though Octavian had developed the habit of assuming the consulship annually, that could not guarantee authority over his *provincia* for a decade.

208  *"in recognition of my valour"*  Res Gest 34.

210  *"When I had put an end"*  Ibid.

210  *"After this time"*  Ibid.

## XVII. WHOM THE GODS LOVE

Dio is the main narrative source, with contributions from Suetonius and Virgil.

212    *Whom the Gods Love [die young]* Men Double, Fragment 4.

212    *The princeps was superstitious* Suet Aug 92 1.

212    *On a night march* Ibid., 29 3.

213    *"from the fatigue and anxiety"* Dio 53 25 7.

213    *Livia accompanied her husband* Tac Ann 3 34. Livia's grandson Drusus made this claim in A.D. 21.

213    *Livia was an able businesswoman* For Livia's business interests, see Barrett, chapter 9.

214    *Marcus Primus, the governor of Macedonia* Dio dates this episode and the Caepio plot to 22 B.C.; but Augustus' presence is required and in that year he was abroad. Also by that time he had *imperium maius* and was entitled to interfere where he wished.

214    *"The loftiest pines"* Hor Odes 2 10 4–8, 21–22. It is possible that the poem was written after Murena's fall, but presented as prophetic.

214    *The praetor, or presiding judge* Dio 54 3 3.

215    *"since he was notoriously rough-tongued"* Ibid., 3 4.

216    *abscesses on the liver* Suet Aug 81 1.

216    *"severe pain in the right part"* Celsus 4 15.

216    *"all cold things"* Ibid.

216    *It has been suggested* See John Buchan, *Augustus* (London: Hodder & Stoughton, 1937), p. 161.

218    *a general and overriding proconsular authority* There is a dispute whether this was *maius imperium proconsulare,* "greater proconsular authority," allowing him to override or give orders to governors of the senatorial provinces, or *aequum imperium proconsulare,* "equal proconsular authority," which would allow him to raise matters with governors but not to command them. The former is perhaps more probable (because of the discovery of five edicts from Cyrene that show Augustus intervening directly in provincial business: Ehrenberg and Jones *Documents* n 311, translated in Lewis and Rheinhold, *Roman Civilization* 2 36ff); if the latter, Augustus would have had to get his way by deploying his prestige, or *auctoritas*.

218    *"secret* coup d'état*"* Syme RR, p. 345.

218    *"had felt that Augustus"* Suet Aug 66 3.

218    *Marcellus was not well disposed* Dio 53 32 1.

219    *"scandalous sending away of Agrippa"* Pliny 7 149.

220    *"Fate shall allow the earth"* Virg Aen 6 869–70, 882–86.

220    *"sweet and strangely seductive"* Suet Virg 32.

220    *It was whispered that Livia* Dio 53 33 4.

221    *"You have made him"* Ibid., 54 6 5.

221    *"stepmother to ships"* Aesch Prom 727.

221    *poison had been sprinkled* Tac Ann 1 10.

221    *Nonius Asprenas* Suet Aug 56 3.

## XVIII. EXERCISING POWER

Dio is the main source, with Suetonius (his life of Augustus now being supplemented by that of Tiberius).

225    *He was strongly and heavily built* This description of Tiberius' appearance and personality is drawn from Suet Tib 68. Contemporary statues and busts of him have also been used.

226    *abstruse and unanswerable questions* Suet Tib 70 3.

226    *"I compelled the Parthians"* Res Gest 29.

227    *"better qualified to be a gladiator"* Vell Pat 2 91 3.

229    *an ingenious scheme* Dio 54 13.

230    *"I don't understand that!"* Suet Aug 54.

233    *In his official memoir* For these expenses see Res Gest 16.

## XIX. THE CULT OF VIRTUE

Dio provides the basic information. Virgil and Horace embody the Augustan regime's aspirations in verse.

236    *"Of late years"* Livy.

236    *"praised Pompey so warmly"* Tac Ann 4 34.

236    *"fashionable designations"* Ibid.

236    *"the righteous are set apart"* Virg Aen 8 670.

236    *"Turn not your country's hand"* Ibid., 6 833.

237    *"to seek to keep the constitution"* Macr 2 4 18.

237    *"rule an Italy"* Virg Aen 4 228–30.

237    *"And here, here"* Ibid., 6 791–94.

238    *"large inconvenience of wealth"* Hor Odes 3 1 48.

238    *"Family pride"* Ibid., 3 24 19–22.

239  *"If we could get on without a wife"* Aul Gell 1 6.

239  *According to Suetonius* Suet Aug 71 1.

239  *"guide and command"* Dio 54 16 4.

240  *"Let us turn our minds"* Ibid., 16 6.

240  *the general population was rising* Suet Aug 29 1, 46 1.

241  *"preserve a significant distinction"* Dio 56 33 3.

241  *In later years* The *lex Fufia Caninia* was passed in 2 B.C. and the *lex Aelia Sentia* in A.D. 4.

242  *"You shall pay"* Hor Odes 3 6 1–5.

243  *"After a sacrifice was completed"* Old CAH, p. 477.

243  *"Goddess [Diana], make strong our youth"* Hor Cent 17–20.

243  *"Now Faith and Peace"* Ibid., 57–60.


## XX. LIFE AT COURT

Most of the material in this chapter derives from anecdotes in Suetonius (with additional material about Livia from Barrett, and general information on daily life in ancient Rome from Carcopino, Dupont, and Smith). Suetonius seems usually reliable or at least plausible, for he had access to the imperial archives and quoted from documents, as well as to contemporary (but now lost) memoirs. Many of the anecdotes are undated and doubtless refer to different times in Augustus' reign.

245  *"remarkable neither for size"* Suet Aug 72 1.

245  *"Whenever he wanted"* Ibid., 72 2.

245  *"would hardly be considered fit"* Ibid., 73 1.

246  *"Anyone would think"* Ibid., 53 3.

247  *a court developed* This section is indebted to Andrew Wallace-Hadrill, "The Imperial Court," CAH, pp. 283–308.

248  *they may have been loosely arranged* This judgment is based on the departments known to have been established by later emperors.

248  *"stink of far-fetched phrases"* Suet Aug 86 1.

248  *Letters of his seen by Suetonius* Ibid., 87 1.

249  *"What in the world has become of Ajax?"* Ibid., 86 5.

249  *the last letter* "X" was the last letter for Latin words. "Y" was employed for foreign words; "Z" appeared in the earliest Roman alphabet, but ceased to be written. From the first century B.C. it returned into use when transliterating the letter ζ in a Greek word.

249  *"I take it, of course"* Ibid., 33 1.

249   *When appearing in public*   Ibid., 53 1–2.

250   *"I had some bread"*   Ibid., 76 1.

250   *"On the way back"*   Ibid., 76 2.

251   *"He who has been engaged"*   Celsus 1 2 5–7.

252   *"Don't suppose you'll ever catch her"*   Ovid Pont 3 1 142.

252   *a certain standard*   See Barrett, pp. 105–6. Livia's personal servants are recorded late in her life, but there is little reason to suppose that her household was much different at an earlier date.

252   *"simplex munditiis"*   Hor Odes 1 5 5.

253   *the wine she habitually drank*   Pliny 14 60.

253   *recipes for various ailments*   Barrett, pp. 110–12.

254   *"noble and undaunted spirit"*   Plut T & C Grac 19 1.

254   *"Among their number"*   Sall Bell Cat 23 3.

255   *a feminine bully*   Tac Ann 1 4.

256   *"to enjoy the fun"*   Suet Aug 45 1.

256   *"modest enough"*   Ibid., 72 3.

257   *the unappetizing Publius Vedius Pollio*   Dio 54 23.

257   *"though refulgent with portraits"*   Ovid Trist 2 521–24.

257   *dragging a former consul's wife*   For this paragraph, see Suet Aug 69 1–2, 71 1.

258   *"still to have harboured a passion"*   Ibid., 71 1.

258   *when Cato vowed*   Plut Cat Min 56 4.

258   *advisory inscription*   The inscription is at the "House of the Moralist."

## XXI. GROWING THE EMPIRE

Dio and Suetonius are the main sources, albeit somewhat thin.

261   *"the existing number"*   Dio 54 9 1.

261   *"I enlarged the territory"*   Res Gest 26.

261   *"whose empire"*   Virg Aen 1 86–89.

261   *"guard our young swarm"*   Hor Odes 1 35 29–32.

263   *This three-part plan of action*   This strategic analysis is indebted to J.F.C. Fuller's classic study, *The Decisive Battles of the Western World*. See vol. 1 of the abridged edition (1970), pp. 167ff. For a more ad hoc–ist interpretation, see Erich S. Gruen, "The Expansion of the Empire Under Augustus," CAH, pp. 147–97.

265   *"Your brother Drusus"*   Suet Aug 71 3.

265   *"My state of health"*   Suet Tib 21 6.

265   *a plot against the* princeps   This is one of those tiresome incidents that

bedevil the literary sources for the second part of Augustus' life. It is reported twice, in Sen Clem 1 9 and in Dio 55 14–22 (where Livia delivers a long curtain-lecture). Cinna's first names are given differently; Seneca probably dates the episode to 16–13 B.C. and Dio to A.D. 4. The whole affair sounds as if it could simply be a rhetorical exercise mistaken for a historical event. The truth? We shall never know.

266   *The length of a legionary's service*   Decided in 13 B.C. on Augustus' return to Rome.

266   *"state of tranquillity"*   Strabo 4 6 9.

270   *unendurable pain from gout*   Pliny 23 27.

271   *he strongly disapproved of Julia*   Suet Tib 7 2–3.

271   *A sharp-eyed great-grandson*   This was Gaius, nicknamed Caligula, Drusus' youngest son, and later emperor (A.D. 37–41).

272   *A great altar to Augustus*   Strabo 4 3 2.

272   *he used to chase German chieftains*   Suet Clau 1 4.

273   *Drusus had a riding accident*   Livy Per 142.

274   *Tiberius heard the news*   Val Max 5 5 3 and Pliny 7 84.

275   *"old Republican constitution"*   Suet Clau 1 4.

275   *"In point of fact"*   Ibid., 1 5.

275   *some truth in the claim*   See Levick, pp. 32–35.

276   *"Cripple my hand"*   Sen Ep 101 10ff.

276   *"The same day"*   Hor Odes 2 17 8–12.

276   *"my purest of pricks"*   All the anecdotes in this section about Augustus and Horace come from the life of Horace in Suet De Vir Ill.

## XXII. A FAMILY AT WAR

The often mysterious events of these years are inadequately covered by Dio, some of whose text is missing; Suetonius (in the lives of both Augustus and Tiberius) makes a contribution. Tacitus offers a few barbed insights.

278   *Their adoptive father devoted time and energy*   Suet Aug 64 3.

279   *"They not only lived"*   Dio 55 9 1–2.

279   *"provided they deserve"*   Suet Aug 56 2.

280   *imperium maius*   This is not explicitly stated in the sources; I follow Levick, pp. 35–36 and endnote 24, p. 237.

280   *a warning to the unruly Gaius and Lucius*   Dio 55 9 4.

280   *"he was weary"*   Suet Tib 10 2.

282   *"he greeted and chatted"*   Ibid., 11 1.

282   *Many governors had friendly connections*  See Levick, pp. 42–44.

282   *"his retirement was more worthy"*  Vell Pat 2 99 4.

283   *The eldest, Germanicus*  For this account of Germanicus, see Suet Gaius 3 1–1.

283   *"a monster, not finished"*  Suet Clau 3 2.

283   *"He's as big a fool"*  Ibid.

284   *"I have always chosen"*  Plut Brut 53 3.

284   *"Caesar Augustus, the Senate agrees"*  Suet Aug 58 2.

284   *"Fathers of the Senate"*  Ibid.

284   *a naval battle*  Dio 55 10 7–8 and Res Gest 4 23.

285   *Once when his father*  See Green, Erot, p. 19.

285   *"All we need is your consent"*  Ovid Am 2 2 65–66.

285   *"not to say or do anything"*  Suet Aug 64 2.

285   *"You have acted presumptuously"*  Ibid.

285   *"This dress"*  Macr 2 5 5. Macrobius is a late source, but there is no reason to distrust his stories about Julia.

286   *"Passengers are never allowed"*  Ibid., 2 5 9.

286   *"I should have preferred"*  Suet Aug 65 2.

287   *"should anything happen to her"*  Ibid., 101 3.

287   *"solemn names"*  Tac Ann 3 24.

287   *"unique depravity disguised"*  Vell Pat 2 100 5.

287   *"This shrewd"*  Tac Ann 1 53.

288   *an emblem of liberty*  Serv Ad Aen 3 20.

288   *It may be no coincidence*  Dio 55 9 10, and 10 1.

289   *"his daughter's adultery"*  Pliny 7 149.

290   *Livia also seems*  See Barrett, p. 51.

291   *"Fire will sooner"*  Dio 55 13 1.

291   *"If you ever"*  Suet Aug 65 3.

## XXIII. THE UNHAPPPY RETURN

Information on important events is scanty. Dio's and Suetonius' lives of Augustus and Tiberius are the main sources. The poet Ovid casts enigmatic light on the exile of the younger Julia and his own banishment.

292   *He received a letter from his stepson*  For this paragraph and the next, see Suet Tib 11 and 12.

293   *"companion and guide"*  Ibid., 12 2.

293   *"fired by the fame of Arabia"*  Pliny 12 31.

294   "Dis aliter visum"  Virgil Aen 2 58.

294  *"Greetings, my Gaius"* Aul Gell 15 7 3.

294  *Lollius had been taking bribes* Vell Pat 2 102 1, Pliny 9 58.

295  *"fetch back the exile's head"* Suet Tib 13 1.

295  *While laying siege* Florus 2 32 44–45.

296  *"defects"* Vell Pat 2 102 3.

296  *"through old age and sickness"* Dio 55 13 1a.

296  "atrox fortuna" Suet Tib 23.

296  *"secret diplomacy"* Tac Ann 1 3.

297  *"for reasons of state"* Suet Tib 21 3.

297  *"animal-like confidence"* Tac Ann 1 3.

298  *"because he was afraid"* Dio 55 27 5.

299  *"because [his] conduct"* Suet Aug 65 4.

299  *accused of plotting* Ibid., 19 1, and Scholiast on Juvenal 6 158; see Green, Erot, p. 57.

300  *"Ah, never to have married"* Hom Il 3 40. Hector is speaking to Paris.

300  *"my three boils"* Suet Aug 65 4.

300  *Augustus exiled Ovid* See Green, Erot, pp. 44–58, for an excellent and full account, which I follow.

300  *"Why did I see what I saw?"* Ovid Trist 2 103–6.

300  *In Rome there was a severe famine* For this section about discontent at Rome, see Dio 55 27.

301  *"I never sought to procure"* Ovid Trist 3 5 45–48.


## XXIV. THE BITTER END

For the last part of Augustus' life, we depend on Dio (despite lacunae), on the overenthusiastic Velleius, and on Suetonius' lives of Augustus and Tiberius. The site of the main ambush of Varus' legions has been discovered at Kalkriese in Germany (see *The Quest for the Lost Roman Legions: Discovering the Varus Battlefield,* by Tony Clunn [New York and Spellmount, Staplehurst, UK: Savas Beatie, 2005]).

305  *"The Pannonians possessed"* Vell Pat 2 110 5.

305  *"Your summer campaigns"* Suet Tib 21 5.

307  *his Romanized name of Arminius* It was wrongly thought by Martin Luther and others that the German for "Arminius" is Hermann. It may have been Armin.

307  *location for the ambush* The site was identified in the 1990s near the modern German town of Bramsche between the Ems and Weser rivers.

307   *"dreaded but unavoidable act"* Dio 56 21 5.

308   *"Quinctilius Varus, give me back my legions!"* Suet Aug 23 2.

308   *A record survives* Pliny 7 48.

310   *"blackened the characters"* Tac Ann 1 72.

310   *"republicanist"* Sen Contr 10 Praef 4–8.

310   *"You must not"* Suet Aug 51 3.

312   *stay within the empire's current boundaries* Tacitus (Ann 1 11) places this advice in the *breviarium*.

312   *In the late spring* Augustus' remorse over Agrippa Postumus is told with varying levels of detail by Pliny 7 150, Plutarch in his essay on talkativeness (although referring to a Fulvius rather than a Fabius), Dio 56 30, and Tac Ann 1 5.

312   *"There [on Planasia]"* Tac Ann 1 5.

313   *Augustus' last days* Suet Aug 97–100.

313   *During the ritual* Suetonius says only "the nearby temple"; the main temple built and dedicated by Agrippa was the Pantheon, to which the historian was very probably referring.

313   *"Augustus' illness"* Tac Ann 1 5.

314   *"Livia was afraid"* Dio 56 30 2.

314   *According to Dio* Ibid., 56 30 5.

314   *But Suetonius claims* Suet Aug 98 5.

315   *commander of the island guard* According to Suetonius (Tib 22 1), Tiberius did not announce Augustus' death until he received the news of Postumus' execution. This seems unlikely, for it would have entailed four or five days' silence. It would also be unnecessary, for no uprising could have been organized in such a short space of time.

315   *"repository of imperial secrets"* Tac Ann 3 30.

315   *"palace secrets"* Ibid., 1 6.

316   *recovery came too late* When rulers or heads of state die in office, *raison d'état* has been known to stimulate ruthless behavior: one recalls that the death of England's King George V in 1935 was hastened by his doctor so that it met the deadline for the London *Times* newspaper of the following morning!

317   *"Some doubt remains"* Suet Tib 22.

317   *Augustus' signet ring* These were routine actions when a Roman died: see Smith, see under *funus*.

318   *"Since fate has cruelly carried off"* Suet Tib 23.

318   *he adopted his wife* For a full discussion of Livia's adoption, see Barrett, Chapter 8 passim.

318  *"she took a share"*  Dio 56 47 1.

319  *The funeral of a leading Roman*  For this description of Augustus' funeral
     I have added generic data about Roman funerals from Smith, *funus,*
     to the accounts of Dio and Suetonius.

## INTO THE FUTURE

322  *"let her waste away"*  Tac Ann 1 53.

322  *"pilgrimage to far lands"*  Ibid., 3 24.

323  *"On the open ground"*  Ibid., 1 61.

323  *"no Charlemagne"*  Fuller, p. 181.

324  *"Intelligent people praised"*  Tac Ann 1 9.

324  *"filial duty"*  Ibid., 1 10.

325  *"I am surprised"*  Plut Apo reg et imp 207D.

325  *"faultily faultless"*  Tennyson, Alfred Lord  *Maul* 2 6.

326  *"May I achieve"*  Suet Aug 28 2.

# SOURCES

## ANCIENT SOURCES

The ancient literary sources for the life and times of Augustus are numerous, but all in their different ways flawed or limited. In general, much more information about the civil wars up to the deaths of Mark Antony and Cleopatra has survived. As noted in the preface, many important histories and memoirs have been lost.

Appian, a Greek from Alexandria who flourished about A.D. 160, wrote a detailed and usually dependable account of the civil wars, but he breaks off with the death of Sextus Pompeius. Cassius Dio, a leading politician who lived between about A.D. 150 and 235, was the author of a history of Rome in eighty books; only twenty-six survive, but fortunately these cover the period from 68 B.C. to A.D. 54, barring some lacunae. He is a diligent and careful writer, but anachronistically applies the political system of his day to the Augustan age.

Tacitus (c. A.D. 55–c. A.D. 117) was one of the greatest Roman historians, but his masterpiece, the *Annals,* discusses the reign of Augustus only summarily, for he is primarily concerned with the period from the accession of Tiberius to the death of Nero. His objectivity was affected by a strong animus against the imperial system.

Velleius Paterculus (c. 19 B.C.–after A.D. 31) served under Tiberius, whom he uncritically admired. His brief history of Rome is of uneven quality, but contains some valuable character sketches.

Toward the end of his life Augustus prepared an official record of his career, the *Res Gestae*. He tells no lies, but sometimes fails to tell the truth.

Plutarch, a Greek who lived between c. A.D. 46 and c. A.D. 120, wrote a series of *Parallel Lives* in which he recounts the life stories of eminent Greek politicians or generals and compares them with those of leading Romans, with whom he finds points of resemblance. He aims to bring out the moral character of his subjects rather than to narrate political events, and does so largely through anecdotes. His biographies of Brutus and Mark Antony are fine pieces of work, and throw much light on the period. However, he probably passes on propaganda against Antony without due skepticism, and sees Antony and Cleopatra's relationship in overly romantic terms.

Suetonius, who lived from c. A.D. 70 to c. 160, was one of Trajan's and Hadrian's secretaries, and had access to the imperial archives. His lives of the Caesars run from Julius Caesar to Domitian. His biographies of Augustus and Tiberius are of particular importance. His work is anecdotal and thematic, rather than narrative, but, while reflecting the interests and attitudes of his time, contains valuable information.

Cicero's letters and his great series of speeches against Mark Antony, the *Philippics,* are useful (if handled with caution) for the period up to his death in 43 B.C.

Nicolaus was a Greek historian who flourished at the end of the first century B.C.; a courtier of Herod the Great, he met Augustus and won his friendship. His fragmentary life of Augustus gives a detailed account of the conspiracy against Julius Caesar and his assassination, and includes plausible stories about Augustus' childhood (perhaps told him by his subject).

Strabo, who lived from c. 64 B.C. to A.D. 19, was a near contemporary of Augustus. He came from Pontus and traveled widely. He wrote a geographical study of the known world which contains useful economic information as well as descriptions of places.

Pliny the Elder (A.D. 23 or 24–A.D. 79) was an industrious writer, whose *Natural History* was an attempt to sum up all human knowledge. It contains much fascinating (sometimes nonsensical and bizarre) information about the arts, sciences, and beliefs of the day (including material about Augustus and his contemporaries).

Relevant and usually plausible anecdotes can be found in *Attic Nights* by the Latin author Aulus Gellius (probably born early in the second century A.D.); in *Saturnalia,* a fictional dialogue in which a wide range of different subjects are discussed, by Macrobius, a Roman philosopher who flourished about A.D. 400; and in *Memorable Facts and Sayings* by Valerius Maximus, who lived about the time of Tiberius.

Poets such as Virgil and Horace commented on political issues and events in their work and celebrated the Augustan regime. Ovid fell foul of the authorities in a major political and sexual scandal that implicated Augustus' granddaughter, and much of his later poetry took the form of appeals against his banishment.

The literary sources are complemented by an abundance of inscriptions, including *Fasti* (chronological lists of consuls and *triumphatores*) and Calendars, which cataloged festivals and other events by the days of the year. Octavian, Antony, and other leading personalities minted coins whose imagery conveyed important political messages. Octavian and Agrippa used architecture as a means of managing public opinion and asserting their political vision.

Translations of Appian's *The Civil Wars,* Dio Cassius' *The Reign of Augustus,* Horace's *Odes, Epistles, Epodes,* and *Satires,* Livy's *History of Rome,* Ovid's *Erotic Poems* (*Amores* and *Ars Amatoria*), *Poems of Exile* (*Tristia* and *Epistulae ex Ponto*), Pliny the Elder's *Natural History,* selected lives by Plutarch, Suetonius' *Lives of the Caesars,* Tacitus' *Annals,* and Virgil's *Eclogues, Georgics,* and *Aeneid,* have been published by Penguin Books, and editions of all the authors listed above, except for Macrobius and Nicolaus, are available in the original languages with facing-page English translations by the Loeb Classical Library of Harvard University Press. English translations of some texts can be found on the Lacus Curtius website (see below). Macrobius' *Saturnalia* has been translated by D. P. Vaughan (New York: Columbia University Press, 1969), and Nicolaus' *Life of Augustus* by Jane Bellemore (Bristol, Eng.: Bristol Classical Press, 1984).

## FURTHER READING

For a succinct overview of the period, I commend H. H. Scullard, *From the Gracchi to Nero: A History of Rome from 133 B.C. to A.D. 68,* fifth edition (London: Methuen, 1982). The *Cambridge Illustrated History: Roman World* (Cambridge, Eng.: Cambridge University Press, 2002) is an excellent survey for the general reader. Werner Eck's *The Age of Augustus* (Oxford, Eng.: Blackwell, 2003) (originally published in 1998 in German as *Augustus und seine Zeit*) is a compact, insightful study. *The Ancient City: Life in Classical Athens and Rome* (Oxford, Eng.: Oxford University Press, 1998) is a readable introduction to daily life in ancient Greece and Rome by Peter Connolly and Hazel Dodge, notable for the elegant illustrations that evoke the two cities as they were in their heydays. Gilles Chaillet's extraordinary *Dans la Rome des Césars* (Grenoble, Fr.: Editions Glénat, 2004) reconstructs the entire city as it would have looked at the beginning of the fourth century A.D.; it shows (sometimes speculatively) the appearance of Augustan buildings and Rome's general layout.

My researches into Augustus' life and times were guided, in the first instance, by Ronald Syme's *The Roman Revolution,* first published in 1939 by the Oxford University Press (OUP paperback, 1960), a classic that remains essential reading, both for its analysis of the politics of the Augustan regime and for its study of the Roman ruling class; and his *The Augustan Aristocracy* (Oxford, Eng.: Oxford University Press, 1986) further explores the history of, and interconnections between, leading Roman families in the late first century B.C. and the first century A.D.

The massive *Cambridge Ancient History,* volume X: *The Augustan Empire, 43 B.C. to A.D. 69,* is comprehensive and authoritative, and includes a full bibliography. The old *Cambridge Ancient History,* published between 1923 and 1939 by Cambridge University Press, is still worth consulting.

Other modern works I found variously helpful include

Barrett, Anthony A. *Livia: First Lady of Imperial Rome* (New Haven: Yale University Press, 2002)

Carcopino, Jérôme. *Daily Life in Ancient Rome* (London: Penguin, 1956 [originally pub. 1941])

Carter, John M. *The Battle of Actium* (London: Hamish Hamilton, 1970)

Castle, E. B. *Ancient Education and Today* (London: Penguin, 1961)

Dilke, O.A.W. *Greek and Roman Maps* (London: Thames & Hudson, 1985)

Dupont, Florence. *Daily Life in Ancient Rome* (Oxford, Eng.: Blackwell, 1993)

Fuller, J.F.C. *The Decisive Battles of the Ancient World and Their Influence on History,* vol. 1, abridged edition (London: Paladin, 1970)

Goldsworthy, Adrian Keith. *The Roman Army at War, 100 B.C.–A.D. 200* (Oxford, Eng.: Oxford University Press, 1996)

Grant, Michael. *Cleopatra* (London: Weidenfeld & Nicolson, 1972)

———. *Gladiators: The Bloody Truth* (London: Penguin, 1971)

Green, Peter. *From Alexander to Actium* (London: Thames & Hudson, 1990)

Jackson, Ralph. *Doctors and Diseases in the Roman Empire* (London: British Museum Press, 2000)

Keppie, Lawrence. *The Making of the Roman Army from Republic to Empire* (reprint, London: Routledge, 1998)

Levick, Barbara. *Tiberius the Politician* (London and New York: Routledge, 1999)

Meijer, Fik. *The Gladiators: History's Most Deadly Sport* (London: Souvenir Press, 2004)

Powell, Anthony, and Kathryn Welch, eds. *Sextus Pompeius* (London: Classical Press of Wales and Duckworth, 2002)

Southern, Pat. *Augustus* (London and New York: Routledge, 1998)

Stambaugh, John E. *The Ancient Roman City* (Baltimore: Johns Hopkins University Press, 1988)

Van Hoof, Anton J. L. *From Autothanasia to Suicide: Self-Killing in Classical Antiquity* (London: Routledge, 1990)

Walker, Susan, and Peter Higgs. *Cleopatra of Egypt: From History to Myth* (London: British Museum Press, 2001)

Wildfang, Robin Lorsch, and Jacob Isager. *Divination and Portents in the Roman World* (Odense, Denmark: Odense University Press, 2000)

Williams, Craig A. *Roman Homosexuality: Ideologies of Masculinity in Classical Antiquity* (London: Oxford University Press, 1999)

Some monuments of Victorian and early-twentieth-century scholarship retain their value, if consulted with care, as reservoirs of interesting but often obscure information. They include William Smith's splendid *Dictionary of Greek and Roman Antiquities* (1870), and Samuel Ball Platner's *A Topographical Dictionary of Ancient Rome,* revised by Thomas Ashby in 1929 (now challenged by L. Richardson's *A New Topographical Dictionary of Ancient Rome* [Baltimore: Johns Hopkins University Press, 1992]). Smith, Platner, and other compendiums can be found gratis on one or other of two excellent websites: Ancient Library, www.ancientlibrary.com, and Lacus Curtius http://penelope.uchicago.edu/Thayer/E/Roman/home.html.

# INDEX

## ABOUT THE AUTHOR

ANTHONY EVERITT's fascination with ancient Rome began when he studied classics in school and has persisted ever since. He read English literature at Cambridge University and served four years as secretary general of the Arts Council for Great Britain. A visiting professor of arts and cultural policy at Nottingham Trent University and City University, Everitt has written extensively on European culture and development, and has contributed to *The Guardian* and *Financial Times* since 1994. *Cicero,* his first biography, was chosen by both Allan Massie and Andrew Roberts as the best book of the year in the United Kingdom and was a national bestseller in the United States. Anthony Everitt lives near Colchester, England's first recorded town, founded by the Romans, and is working on histories of ancient Rome and Greece for teenagers.